ISLAM AND POPULAR CULTURE

ISLAM AND POPULAR CULTURE

EDITED BY KARIN VAN NIEUWKERK,
MARK LEVINE, AND MARTIN STOKES

UNIVERSITY OF TEXAS PRESS *Austin*

Requests for permission to reproduce material from this work should be sent to:
Permissions
University of Texas Press
P.O. Box 7819
Austin, TX 78713-7819
http://utpress.utexas.edu/index.php/rp-form

♾ The paper used in this book meets the minimum requirements of
ANSI/NISO Z39.48-1992 (R1997) (Permanence of Paper).

LIBRARY OF CONGRESS CATALOGING-IN-PUBLICATION DATA

Islam and popular culture / edited by Karin van Nieuwkerk, Mark LeVine, and
Martin Stokes. — First edition.
        pages   cm
    Includes bibliographical references and index.
    ISBN 978-1-4773-0887-5 (cloth : alk. paper)
    ISBN 978-1-4773-0904-9 (pbk. : alk. paper)
    ISBN 978-1-4773-0888-2 (library e-book)
    ISBN 978-1-4773-0889-9 (non-library e-book)
1. Islam and culture—Islamic countries—20th century.   2. Islam and culture—
Islamic countries—21st century.   3. Islam in mass media.   4. Popular culture—
Islamic countries.   I. Nieuwkerk, Karin van, 1960– editor.   II. LeVine, Mark,
editor.   III. Stokes, Martin, editor.
    BP161.3.I727   2016
    297.2'7—dc23   2015033637

doi:10.7560/308875

CONTENTS

ISLAM AND POPULAR CULTURE

INTRODUCTION: ISLAM AND POPULAR CULTURE

KARIN VAN NIEUWKERK, MARK LEVINE, MARTIN STOKES

ISLAM AND POPULAR CULTURE are topics of constant concern in the academic world as well as in the broader public sphere.[1] Yet studies of the history and contemporary dynamics of popular culture in Muslim societies remain relatively modest in number and scope (e.g., LeVine 2008, Van Nieuwkerk 2011). This can be explained at least in part by a frozen view of Islamic belief as being in an adverse relationship with popular culture: Islam is at best perceived as indifferent or even hostile. Although present in the broad corpus of Muslim belief, law, and practice, these two positions—indifference and hostility—are by no means the only or even dominant views, whether historically or today. Focusing exclusively on them precludes a view of the many possible relationships, which extend back over fourteen centuries. They constitute, in our view, an outstandingly suitable prism through which to study contemporary developments in the Muslim world.

This book brings a fresh understanding of these relations in the hope of providing a foundation for greater attention by scholars, as well as students, to the study of popular culture in Muslim societies. The Arab uprisings of the last four years have been eye opening in terms of the clear imbrication of aesthetics, politics, and religion that have been on display. This vibrant politics of popular culture has been visible in the form of revolutionary street theater, graffiti, caricatures, slogans, popular songs, poetry, satirical broadsides, television shows, and jokes. All of these have worked to create senses of community among protestors, particularly in live performance. But they have also become means of political communication and sites of debate about the revolutionary process. Moreover, most of these cultural practices have included the participation of (whether passively as consumers or observers, or actively as producers and disseminators) religiously grounded Muslims.

Before allowing the last four years of revolutionary "artivism" to skew a broader analysis of popular culture toward its most expressive and politicized

2 ISLAM AND POPULAR CULTURE

forms, we need to realize that such highly politicized forms of cultural expres-sion are not as common as the focus on them might suggest. First, with regard to the politics of the artistic community, it must be remembered that art is not inherently revolutionary, even if it does have the potential to encourage signifi-cant change. We must not neglect those artists who were absent from the pro-tests or even closely connected to the old regime, or the process of co-optation of several art forms by regimes. Popular culture can work in various ways: to criticize and resist or to sustain and enforce the regimes in power. Second, popular culture not only works against or with power structures, but power works through and within popular art itself. Third, the example of the recent Arab world uprisings encourages us to reflect on the intersection of Islam and popular culture. The initial outcome of the uprisings points in the direction of a stronger Islamist political presence. Some observers—including (devout) artists—fear the possibility of a ban on various art practices when Islamists are in power. Yet, as we demonstrate throughout this volume, Islamists them-selves have also turned to art for political and mobilizational purposes. Islam articulates various positions vis-à-vis popular culture, just as popular culture articulates a variety of political uses. This book demonstrates the variety, and the importance, of the contemporary processes in the Middle East, the larger Muslim world, and Muslim diaspora communities, which can be studied from the vantage point of Islam and popular culture.

ISLAM

The static view of Islam as contrary to popular culture rests on two points. One is the view of Islam as a unitary cultural, political, and theological field. The other, springing from it, is that Islam has a general problem with art. It is im-portant to be clear at the outset why both of these positions are problematic.

Regarding the first, it may be helpful to recall Talal Asad's classic essay, "The Idea of an Anthropology of Islam" (Asad 1986), in which he defines Islam as a discursive tradition. "[O]ne should begin, as Muslims do," he argues, "from the concept of a discursive tradition that includes and relates itself to the founding texts of the Qur'an and the Hadith" (1986: 14). The "discursive tradi-tion" includes dominant orthodox viewpoints. But, as Asad explains, "ortho-doxy is not a mere body of opinion but a distinctive relationship—a relation-ship of power. Wherever Muslims have the power to regulate, uphold, require, or adjust *correct* practices, and to condemn, exclude, undermine, or replace *incorrect* ones, there is the domain of orthodoxy" (1986: 15).

Asad reminds us that we need to understand "the historical conditions that enable the production and maintenance of specific discursive traditions, or their transformation . . ." (Asad 1986: 17). This will, indeed, be a consistent preoccupation in this volume. Asad's formulation emphasizes that the discursive tradition is not historically inert or immobile but constantly in motion, even as it claims to stand outside of time and history. The discursive tradition will always be preoccupied with current issues, always be trying to give shape and direction to an as-yet inchoate future. And it will be marked by the struggles of the past, of struggles against nonbelievers, of struggles against imperial rivals, of struggles against "heterodoxy," variously conceived, and of struggles against "secularism." The discursive tradition, then, is something, Asad insists, that we have to see in social, cultural, political, and historical context.

Over the last three or four decades, both anthropologists and historians have developed a more plural and heterogeneous conception of Islam. In part, this has been a reaction to orientalism. Said's well-known critique (Said 1976) painted a rather monolithic picture, one reluctant to recognize the variety and diversity of intellectual traditions prevailing in the West concerning Islam from the seventeenth century to the present day (Irwin 2007). But orientalists did see Islam at its most authentic in the Arab heartlands, roughly from the time of the Prophet to the Mongol invasions of the thirteenth century. And they encountered it primarily in texts, written in Arabic. As Said repeatedly pointed out, this conception of Islamic authenticity was one that suited colonial power, which could, among other things, present itself to colonized Muslims as a respectful guardian of tradition. But in focusing on a single historical moment of authenticity, the large part of Islam's history, its movement into Central, South, East, and Southeast Asia, Europe, and sub-Saharan Africa was condemned to secondary historical status. Marshall Hodgson's important survey of "Islamicate" society, which gave equal prominence to the medieval Islamization of Persia, Anatolia, the Balkans, and Central Asia, unsettled such orientalist habits of thought, and remains influential (Hodgson 1974).

Anthropologists also gravitated to the margins. Geertz's classic comparison of Moroccan and Indonesian Islam (Geertz 1971)—two locations considered, then, to be highly "marginal"—leads almost inescapably to the conclusion that these two kinds of Islam have little, perhaps even nothing, in common. The one is festive, saint-oriented, located in a mobile world of bargaining and negotiation. The other is courtly, contemplative, located in a rather stately world of order and hierarchy. Gellner's important discussion of the oscillation between urban and rural Islam in North Africa, between scriptural and saintly models of authority (Gellner 1980), also belongs to this moment. Michael Gilsenan's *Recognizing Islam* (Gilsenan 1982), a study that owes something to the Manchester School's emphasis on urban and postcolonial contexts, explores Islam in the transformations of everyday life in the slums of Cairo, in the colonial new towns of Morocco, and among the Lebanese feudal aristocracy. By the early 1980s, at least, the study of the Muslim world was no longer limited by terms of inquiry that prioritized early Arabian cultural and historical experience, and that failed to recognize difference and diversity.

But there are still problems. In stressing difference and diversity, one can fail to recognize what *produced* this difference and diversity, particularly colonialism. Colonizers in the Muslim world, as elsewhere, had an interest in appearing as guardians of tradition, in relieving themselves of tedious but relatively inconsequential areas of colonial governance, in "divide and rule" policies of one kind or another (see Asad 1973, Rosen 1989, Rabinow 1977, Mitchell 1991). The critique is, by now, long-standing. A consequence has been that relations between "centers" and "peripheries" in the Islamic world, spaces that have been repeatedly transformed by conquest and occupation, and routinely traversed by pilgrims and travelers (Eickelman and Piscatori 1990), were for a long time understood in rather static and ahistorical ways. This dichotomization of center and periphery, the one traditionally the province of historians and literary scholars, the other the province of anthropologists and social scientists, has been unhelpful (Lindholm 1996).

This volume, then, holds to the by-now conventional, if qualified, academic view of Islam as a world of diversity and difference. Its key interpretative and explanatory strategies are, necessarily, ones of "localization," of specifying place, time, community, political circumstance. But it also attempts to acknowledge the problems of such strategies. Colonial and postcolonial histories, Islam's "discursive tradition," new media systems, new global deployments of military power (viz. the "war on terror"), struggles for regional hegemony, the contemporary contours of Shiʿa-Sunni rivalry, and new ideologies of culture all forge region-wide, even global connections, as well as local scenes and senses of identity. These must be taken into account. The challenge continues to be one of connecting—historically and politically—local frameworks and broader contexts of understanding. It is one to which all of the case studies in this volume respond.

"ISLAMIC ART" AND AESTHETICS

Our second problem is that Islam is deemed to have a particularly thorny relationship with art and aesthetics. This contributes significantly to the problem of thinking about Islam and popular aesthetics. But why is this? First, proscriptions on art and music in the Qurʾan and the hadith, vague though they are, have meant that the West has mainly understood "Islamic aesthetics" in terms of geometrical ornament—abstraction, repetition, antihumanism. This under-standing arose at a moment when the West was turning to the non-Western world to reinvigorate its arts and crafts, sparking, among other things, a fascination with "Islamic" geometric patterning that persists to this day. Colonial era museums and galleries in the western world—such as the Trocadero "Art Musulmane" exhibition in Paris in 1878, began to display exhibitions of Islamic art, objects—miniatures, calligraphy, ceramics—lifted from local sites or cut out of manuscripts, presenting them to western publics in ways that radically decontextualized them. Art objects here were to be looked "at," not "through." They were not intended to aid an understanding of specific cultural moments or formations (Seljuq, Mamluk, Ottoman, Qajar, and so forth). They were to be appreciated as freestanding objects of beauty. "Islamic aesthetics" thus came to be understood in terms dictated by these museums and exhibitions, as decontextualized art objects, selected to lend support to western aesthetic preoccupations. They also neatly supported the more general orientalist proposition that the world of Islam was to be understood in terms of its lacks and its prohibitions. Islam was believed (incorrectly) to ban all visual representation, and to take a dim view of music, unlike the West. "Islamic aesthetics" were, in fact, a kind of antiaesthetic, a world of inert tradition and "ornament" tied to function, primarily serving to demonstrate why the world of Islam could never progress, why it would remain trapped in a beautiful but ascetic and motionless past.

Oleg Grabar was one of the first to debunk this myth in the field of art history (Grabar 1995). Grabar showed how "ornament" is an extremely diverse and complex art historical category and one that by no means prohibited visual representation. He also showed that it was just as much a preoccupation of the medieval Christian world as the Islamic. Victoria Gonzalez' work on the Alhambra and Gülrü Necipoğlu's study of the Topkapı Scrolls followed hot on its heels (Gonzalez 2001, Necipoğlu 1995). These scholars came to conclusions highly relevant to our popular cultural project, and are worth sketching in a little detail here.

First, they showed that Islamic visual aesthetics were highly developed, not impoverished or merely a compensation for the supposed blanket ban on all visual representation. The early Islamic philosophers attempted to reconcile both Platonic and Aristotelian conceptions of beauty with the demands of monotheism. In the Platonic case, worldly beauty was to be understood as an emanation of God's beauty, prompting a contemplative turn in his direction, away from this-worldly things. In the Aristotelian case, beauty was a quality of man-made objects, whose capacity to inspire love, awe, or amazement, for instance, might also inspire the pursuit of goodness and truth. Early encounters with the early Islamic world's neighbors (particularly the Sassanians and the Byzantines) provoked views that representative art and music were illegitimate, whether specifically as forms of idolatry or more general signs of decadence. A certain amount of hadithic commentary, dating from this period, articulated this growing distaste. But in medieval Andalusia, where such anxieties were less pronounced and where Aristotelian rather than Platonic philosophy was ascendant, visual representation was theorized in the broader field of optics (viz. the writings of Ibn Haytham in the late tenth and early eleventh centuries CE). These kinds of theories, about proportion, order, and position, extended across various other cultural domains—poetry, calligraphy, music, and miniature painting, for instance. This is "aesthetic" thinking in a rather modern sense (viz. Rancière 2004); certainly not a rejection or negation of aesthetics.

Second, they showed that practices of geometrical ornamentation needed to be interpreted in rather specific historical and political contexts and not simply assumed to be a timeless property of "Islamic art." Necipoğlu focuses on the Topkapı Scrolls, an Ottoman pattern book of geometrical ornament (*girih*) dating from the end of the fifteenth century. The geometrical aesthetic elaborated in these scrolls was, Necipoğlu shows, intricately connected with Sunni revivalism, with its roots in the tenth century CE (see also Tabbaa 2001). Aesthetic debates came to play a role in the emerging split between Sunni and Shiʿa worlds, which were to reach a peak in the fierce rivalry between (Sunni) Ottomans and (Shiʿa) Safavids in the sixteenth century. For the Sunnis, Qurʾanic revelation was a singular and decisive historical event, and not a continuous emanation of divine logic, as Shiʿa philosophers and theologians averred. Geometrical ornament was, then, pressed into the service of a rather specific, and rather specifically *Ottoman* political project. It emphasized the completed nature of Qurʾanic revelation, and thus signified Ottoman imperium and Sunni ascendancy. If geometrical ornamentation came to assume some kind of aesthetic dominance in at least some parts of the Islamic world, then it did so at a very specific moment and for a very specific reason.

The issue played out in rather similar ways in the field of music study. As is the case with visual representation, the Qurʾan is sometimes understood to "ban music." But nowhere in the Qurʾan is the term "music" used. The sections cited to support antimusic positions are thus vague in the extreme, referring to whistling, clapping, speaking in loud voices, and so forth. A later period of anxiety, again, absorbed by the need to distinguish the nascent Muslim community from the pomp and decadence of the Sassanian and Byzantine courts, and by the encounter with Greek philosophy, produced positions and rulings on this new subject, "music." The hadithic literature is, consequently, divided between condemnation and justification. The justifications, inevitably, became defensive and qualified. By the time of al-Ghazzali's *Ihya Ulum al-Din* (probably written sometime in the eleventh century), music was permitted in spiritual pursuits, at least in the eyes of some, as long as, in his famous formulation, it was regulated by *"zaman, makan wa ikhwan"* (time, place, and community), all of which imposed stringent conditions.

Western scholarship, turning to the music of the Muslim world much later than the study of Islamic art, absorbed these critiques and anxious justifications and heard in them the familiar refrains of "Islamic" censoriousness and prohibition. Music in the spiritual quest ("Sufism") was granted exceptional status in this scholarship, explained, like Sufi visual aesthetics, in terms of divine geometry (see Bakhtiar 1976). And it was understood to flourish only in "exceptional" situations of tolerance and liberalism, as in medieval Andalusia. More nuanced positions began to appear in the ethnomusicology of the 1980s, attempting to explain music in Muslim community life in ways that took account of local social structures, political transformations, ritual and communal traditions, and conflicting principles of cultural authority (Schuyler 1985, Qureshi 1986, Baily 1988). The "discursive tradition" and its complex and contradictory pronouncements on the subject of music were, here, just one element of a highly complex scene requiring a more local frame of analysis—Moroccan, North Indian, Afghan. So the study of expressive cultural systems, chiefly art and music, but others too, has been burdened with an orientalist insistence that we start with Islam's assumed censoriousness vis-à-vis aesthetics, and work from there. Art historians and ethnomusicologists have responded with alternative visions, but the problems are still deeply entrenched.

These problems appear even more deeply entrenched when one shifts the focus from demonstrably "high" or "traditional" culture to popular culture. The problem is one Roxanne Varzi aptly describes as the *"Reading Lolita in Teheran* syndrome" (Varzi 2008). The huge popularity of Azar Nafisi's book, particularly in the United States, shows how popular culture tends to surface in western understandings of the Middle East as a sign of resistance to and defiance of religious authority. But, as Varzi suggests, it involves a number of basic errors, alongside the perpetuation of old orientalist stereotypes. It assumes that the basis of cultural authoritarianism in Middle Eastern societies is "Islamic." It assumes that popular culture is, by definition, "western" and thus "secular." And it assumes that religious authoritarianism will always be hostile to expressions, and technologies, of popular pleasure. None of these assumptions hold water (see also Sreberny-Mohammadi and Mohammadi 1994). Each and every contribution to this volume suggests an alternative.

But before introducing them, it will be helpful to think further about what we mean by "popular culture."

POPULAR CULTURE

The other key concept of the volume's title, popular culture, is no less ambiguous than Islam. Its many possible meanings owe in good measure to the reality that its component terms themselves possess multiple and often contradictory connotations. And it is precisely the ambiguities and multiplicities inherent in the idea of popular culture that enables it to open up new ways of understanding the societies we explore here.

Raymond Williams famously pointed out that culture is "one of the two or three most complicated words in the English language," a claim that holds equally for most other languages and cultures too (Williams 1983: 87). In the modern era culture has been tied to the idea of "civilization," a meaning that is still favored by conservative scholars such as Samuel Huntington and Bernard Lewis (the latter of whom coined the term "clash of civilizations" popularized by the former in a famous *Foreign Policy* essay and then book [Huntington 1996]). Huntington explains that "the fundamental source of conflict in this new world will not be primarily ideological or primarily economic. The great divisions among humankind and the dominating source of conflict will be cultural." (Huntington 1996: 22) He then goes on to divide the world's culture into seven "civilizations," and clearly imagines culture in civilizational terms — that is, as a collection of customs, traditions, laws, books and "high" art produced by a society that by definition makes culture rigid and slow to change.

This problematic understanding of culture facilitates the simplistic demonization of Islam as a monolithic entity that is essentially hostile to something called "Western" civilization and even modernity as a whole. Although Islam and Muslim cultures have played crucial roles—through diffusion and cooperation as much as through conflict—in the shaping of the "West," the idea of culture as something static, as a collection of ideas or things that a person or group can possess (and lose) is analytically and historically problematic. A far more accurate way to understand culture is that it exists in its "performance" by the people who define themselves as part of it; that is, people "acting out" — living really—with the knowledge that others are watching and judging their "performance" (LeVine 2005a).

Culture, then, only exists as it is expressed by ordinary people (since most people in a society are ordinary) in their everyday lives. It is not a static identity but rather a site for the invention, intervention, and performance of many different and often conflicting identities that, depending on the situation, can be used to reinforce, or resist, larger nationalist or globalizing projects. This understanding of culture is important because regarded thus it constitutes the one space where citizens of the Muslim world, and everywhere else for that matter, can become active producers, and not just passive consumers of its innumerable experiences and products.

Thus on the one hand we can understand culture as including the ideas, customs, beliefs, and practices of a grouping of people that share a common history and language, which are important enough to sustaining that grouping to be transmitted across generations. But these ideas and beliefs are only understood in their expressions through public action, which is why culture also must be understood as referring to all the mundane practices of life that directly contribute to people's ongoing "life-narratives"—the stories by which we, chronically, interpret our existence. These stories are not static and fixed but are constantly performed and (re)invented through multiple identities that can either/both co-opt, adapt to, and resist hegemonic and totalizing projects.

If we can attest to a broad understanding of the meaning of "culture," how does this impact our understanding of the "popular" in "popular culture"? Popular culture is far more than just mass-produced entertainment. Indeed, commodified cultural production, circulation, and consumption have never been the only or even the dominant form of popular cultural experience. Various forms of cultural expression, from religious experience to sub- and countercultural "DIY" (do-it-yourself) musical cultures (punk, heavy metal, local traditional arts), all have long created and sustained popular cultures that are either largely outside the commodity chains or part of alternative systems of exchange that are not wholly determined by a purely capitalist ideology and logic.

What then constitutes the arena and boundaries of "popular" culture? John Storey is probably the most prolific writer on the history of the concept of popular culture and its boundaries (e.g., Storey 2001, 2003). Popular culture remains elusive as a concept because it implies otherness, that is, "popular culture is always defined, implicitly or explicitly, in contrast to other conceptual categories: folk culture, mass culture, dominant culture, working-class culture etc." (2001: 1). Popular culture can be defined as originating from the people, that is "folk culture," or as mass culture, imbuing it with additional meanings as commercial and as imposed or impoverished culture. Several approaches toward popular culture delineate popular culture as low class, separating it from elite high culture, attaching notions of inferiority to it.

The word popular in the sense of "well liked by many people" strengthens an understanding that creates a contrast between elites and the masses. In addition to the question as to how far this western distinction between low and high culture is applicable to the non-Western world, the shifting demarcation lines between what counts as high or as low points out that these evaluations are subject to the power to articulate and define boundaries. The "popular" and "elite" binary is problematic, also given the long history of popular "translations" of elite works of art and literature, and the reverse. Indeed, local cultures or sub-cultures are often established in opposition to the official/hegemonic culture. And while popular culture is often defined as mass (or majority) culture, it is still a place of continuous change, adaptation, and subversion.

We define popular culture as the expressive practices of everyday life, which include mass media products such as television shows and video games, individualized forms of expression like food and holidays, and of course, religion. The ambiguous nature of popular culture has the advantage of allowing those writing about it to offer the definition that best fits their particular analyses or research agenda and needs.

In our research, we look at the many different ways people use, interpret, and adapt even the most conventional mass-produced items in the course of daily life. We also study the more spectacular practices of groups of people who develop new cultural forms as well as maintain traditional ones. We are especially interested in the ways the expressive practices of popular culture convey, challenge, and influence social values, norms of behavior, and sense of identity. We study the exchanges and transformations of popular culture in global and historical contexts as well as among diverse groups within contemporary Muslim societies. While popular culture may at first appear to be a trivial matter, it turns out to be the site where many of the most important and controversial issues are explored and debated.

THE POWER OF POPULAR CULTURE

This brings us back to issues of politics and power as immanently part of popular culture, starting from defining what it is and, more important, analyzing how popular culture operates and works with and through power. Marx and his heirs have long focused on the "superstructural" role of cultural production in support of hegemonic ideologies and political economic systems. The Marxian analysis of culture became more sophisticated in the interwar period, as thinkers such as Gramsci and the members of the Frankfurt School developed theories of culture that profoundly changed the way scholars analyze it today. First, they saw cultural production not merely as a tool of economic domination but as a central arena for struggles for hegemony between contending social and political forces.

It thus serves as an area in which state and capitalist forces would invest large sums to ensure the power of culture reinforced rather than challenged their preeminent positions in society. In Gramsci's terminology, they went to great pains to ensure that the "common sense" (*senso commune*) of ordinary people, which always contains at least a kernel of critique of the dominant structures of their societies, could not develop into the politically sophisticated and transformative "good sense" (*buon senso*), out of which revolutionary thought and praxis could develop (cf. LeVine and Salvatore 2005).

Seminal Frankfurt School theorists such as Theodor Adorno (1944) and Walter Benjamin (1936) focused on the role of the technological transformation in popular culture and on its power in twentieth-century capitalist societies. They saw something particularly powerful about the production, distribution, and consumption of mass culture in the "mechanical" or "technological" age that made it an even more central location for social and political—and through them, economic—struggles between contending classes. While Benjamin argued that mass-produced culture had a potentially liberating effect on the working class, Adorno developed a far less sanguine view of the positive potential of mass or popular culture, feeling that its unique power would most naturally and effectively be used to deepen the power of the bourgeois class and state rather than challenge it. Specifically, popular culture would serve as a means to maintain existing structures and forms of authority, deceiving the masses and keeping them depoliticized through a focus on a highly ritualized "aura of style" that stunts people's imagination through the production of sameness and hampers autonomous thinking and acting.

It is hard to argue with Adorno's pessimistic view of mass culture given the innumerable uses to which its commodified exemplars have been put to use, from fascist pageantry to neoliberal revolutionary cultures. Indeed, the field of cultural studies as it developed out of the Birmingham School in the 1970s did pioneering work utilizing both Gramsci and the Frankfurt School precisely by showing how seemingly subversive cultural production diverted young peoples' energy away from direct political engagement toward "resistance through rituals" of style and consumption, a theme that has remained central to the field ever since (During 2007).

Indeed, as much as it can be a handmaiden of capitalist concerns, equally often popular culture can serve as a site of revolt, resistance, and at least potentially as a form of counterculture. And as James Scott has shown, cultural practice can do both at the same time, with subaltern groups who are forced to "adopt a strategic pose" in front of the more powerful, in fact using the same cultural practices and even vocabulary to resist them behind the scenes (Scott

1990). It is thus clear that both analytical approaches to the roles and power of popular culture within societies at large can provide examples of cultural production and experience to demonstrate their case.

Popular culture can thus take on both the form of resistance and of co-optation by states or movements to further their cause, producing a level of affective contradiction that has yet to be theorized adequately. At the very least, scholars must devote more attention to articulating the differences between mainstream popular culture (so-called "mass culture"), subcultures that express identities outside established norms, countercultures that directly challenge hegemonic or dominant cultural forms, norms, and ideologies, and revolutionary cultures that seek to replace one cultural, political, and/or economic system with another, quite different one (see LeVine, 2005a and b, 2008).

In this regard, a nuanced approach that brings popular culture in the domain of power while having an eye for both its potential to resist and to be co-opted is gained from the work of Gramsci. Of particular importance is his concept of hegemony, which Gramsci defines as "consent backed by the armour of coercion" (1971)—that is, how power elites win the consent of the majority of the people whom they govern while arrogating the right to use coercion and violence against those who oppose them. Without hegemony the exercise of power does not seem natural or legitimate; governments cannot rule and powerful social forces cannot control people for long periods by domination alone. Crucially, Gramsci argues that hegemony is never either fully realized or unchallenged.

Although not directly inspired by Gramsci, Foucault developed a similar argument that power is permanently contested and that even as the discourses and technologies through which power elites (both within states and surrounding governing institutions and apparatuses) govern—what Foucault describes as pastoral, sovereign, and disciplinary power—become more powerful, intrusive, and "productive" of the political subjectivities of their citizens, hegemony is rarely won decisively or permanently (see Foucault 1995 [1975], 2003 [1997], 2009 [2004]). Indeed, the struggles for hegemony inevitably produce oppositional discourses that have the potential to challenge and ultimately even overturn the forces presently ruling and/or governing society.

Is an approach that focuses on hegemony and regimes of power, or that simply regards popular culture as a pawn in power struggles or struggle for hegemony satisfactory? Or does popular culture have a space of its own? Is there something in popular culture and art that provides a space for creativity, for reflection on and distance from power structures? As Bayat (2007) holds, popular culture also contains elements of joyfulness, play, creativity, and fun. Fun presupposes a powerful paradigm about self and society that competes with and undermines the doctrinal power of the rigid, narrow, and exclusive regimes of power. It offers a different value system that conflicts with the paradigm maintained by those in power. It is a rival to exclusivist authority monopoly of truth and single discourses; it clashes and subverts one-dimensional discourses of doctrinal authority. Popular culture thus tends to work against exclusivist notions of power.

This closely corresponds with Johannes Fabian's observation regarding the power of popular culture. In *Moments of Freedom*, Fabian analyzes popular culture as spaces of freedom and creativity (Fabian 1998). Popular culture can create sites for individual or collective freedom but is not in itself liberating. With regard to freedom Fabian mentions: "If freedom is conceived not just as free will plus the absence of domination and constraints, but as the potential to transform one's thoughts, emotions, and experiences into creations that can be communicated and shared . . . then it follows that there can never be freedom as a state of grace, permanent and continuous . . . Freedom . . . comes in moments" (1998: 20–21). With regard to the moments of freedom created in popular culture Fabian mentions: "The issue of power and resistance in studies of popular culture . . . cannot be reduced to determining whether or not, or when and where, expressions of popular culture qualify as acts of resistance; what we need to understand is how popular culture creates power to resist power" (1998: 69). Power is constantly established, negated, and reestablished. "It is not its being power free that distinguishes popular culture . . . but its working against the accumulation and concentration of power, which, when institutionalized, cannot do without victims" (Fabian 1998: 133).

Popular culture is an extremely inspiring field to study regimes of power, including politics of repression and resistance through culture. It provides an alternative vision of self and society that works against one-dimensional regimes of power and defies concentration of power. It provides space to resist accumulation of power. Popular culture has accordingly the ability to continuously (re)create new moments of freedom. This ability of popular culture to unsettle established regimes of power and to work against exclusivist regimes of power makes it an important tool for studying sociopolitical transformation processes.

POPULAR CULTURE IN THE MUSLIM WORLD

What then is the added value of bringing Islam and popular culture together? Why do we think it provides a particularly valuable way to study contemporary developments in the Muslim world? Three key propositions follow from what we have been discussing thus far. First, popular culture helps us understand major processes of transformation in the Muslim world. Second, popular culture in the Muslim world does not equal "westernization," "secularisation," or "cultural grey-out"; rather, we must consider it under the broader and more flexible rubric of globalization. Third, popular culture in the Muslim world can no longer simply be viewed—and dismissed—merely as a decoration of, or distraction from, "real politics."

First, the field of popular culture is a rich field for understanding and analyzing social transformation processes in the Muslim world. It is part of everyday life for all people; it shapes imaginations and is a key site through which contestations for meaning occur. Popular culture and art not only reflect social change but also foreshadow transformations and help to bring them about. Two areas of transformation, common across the entire region, concern us in this volume. One is what Bayat, Kepel, and others describe as "post-Islamism," referring to the broad shifts in attitudes and strategies of diverse Islamist movements in various Muslim countries and among Muslim minorities in Europe (Bayat 2005, 2007; Kepel 2000; Roy 2004). The term is possibly a problematic one since we would like to avoid a rigid and monolithic definition of "Islamism." Yet, as many contributors to this volume stress, increasingly accommodating and populist attitudes toward popular culture on the part of Islamist authorities and movements have been a part of this turn (Otterbeck, Alagha, Stokes, Nooshin, and others, this volume). Popular culture has inescapably brought performing—and thus gendered and sexualized—bodies into the discursive frame of "post-Islamism" (Silverstein, Meftahi, this volume). So this "opening up" among some Islamist movements can be productively traced through a study of changing attitudes toward women and music, as a key figure of the Egyptian pious artist community observed (Van Nieuwkerk 2013, and this volume).

Another space of transformation is constituted by the contemporary uprisings in the Arab world. At the time of writing, it is very unclear where these will lead, and the picture is far from hopeful. But it is also clear to us that popular culture is a key to understanding the moment. Revolutions have always been accompanied by outbursts of cultural production from below, which reflects the energy released when hardened political and sociocultural systems suddenly are pried or explode open, releasing incredible amounts of cultural production—poetry, music, art, literature, and prose. These become important vehicles for conveying political messages, motivating people, and creating the solidarities necessary to take on state power and the violence it usually unleashes when faced with a serious threat. Beyond affective cultural production within various artistic or intellectual fields, there is also what LeVine and Reynolds describe in this volume as "theater of immediacy," a kind of performance activism whereby intensely powerful emotive public acts (such as the self-immolation of Tunisian fruit-seller Muhammad Bouazizi, which sparked the Arab uprisings) are also a part of popular culture, even though they are not in themselves normally considered artistic products (see also Becker, Schielke, and ter Laan, this volume).

Second, Roxanne Varzi's *"Reading Lolita in Teheran* syndrome" pushes many to assume, lazily, that mass-mediated popular culture in the Muslim world is synonymous with "secularism" and "westernization." This is assumed to make them the target of religious conservatives, who are always and everywhere presumed to be in mortal fear of the erosion of traditional cultural values and of the vitality and sexual energy of youth. And many assume the struggle to be futile—providing yet more evidence that a censorious Islam is completely out of step with history, and a world shaped, irreversibly, by global capitalism, by Coca-Cola, McDonald's, Marlboro, western rock and pop.

But this way of looking at things is highly problematic. Asad reminds us (2003) that secularism is not simply today's social world with religion successfully "subtracted," or neatly contained within the private sphere. This represents the stated goals of a project, not an existing historical or cultural state of affairs. Secularism has roots in western religious experience and social transformations. Elsewhere, as in Turkey or India, it has been associated with very particular, and still highly contested political projects—the one to create a political space free from (all) religion, the other to create a space where (all) religions can meet on neutral ground. Religious and secular lobbies are engaged in bitter struggles, in situations of growing mutual incomprehension, anxiety, and distrust. It can be hard for the outsider in these situations to see exactly where "religion" ends and "secularism" begins, or which things belong where. Popular culture is, in fact, where many of these struggles take place, with religious authorities in the Muslim world increasingly pragmatic in their bid to win hearts and minds, and secularists no longer able to monopolize its core meanings (love, freedom, the pleasures of consumption, cosmopolitanism, and so forth). The contributions to this volume all explore various kinds of struggle taking place today *within* the popular cultural domain over signs and symbols of religiosity and secularism (Kapchan, Winegar, ter Laan, Salamandra, this volume). The struggle remains a highly unsettled one. But it is clear that popular culture can never be assumed to be intrinsically *secularizing*.

Popular culture may, globally, be dependent upon media infrastructures introduced by the West: films, sound recordings, newspapers, the Internet, but, likewise, this has never simply meant *westernization*. From the outset, the new media industries sought local content for local markets. With each successive shift in production methods, local media industries broke away from western dominance; some were nationalized. In the 1950s Egyptian film and music—and, later, television—became important tools of state formation (Abu-Lughod 2005, Armbrust 1996) and regional influence, provoking reactions and imitations elsewhere. "Western" popular culture is, itself, multifaceted, a complex amalgam, in the field of music alone, of European folk, African American, Latin, and Caribbean elements. Muslim world societies have positioned themselves, both historically and geographically, in these shifting mediascapes and technoscapes (Appadurai 1996) for well over a century. They have reacted, or appropriated, or contributed their own voices to the global mix. Bollywood is today as much a part of whatever "global culture" might be as rap and hip-hop. In global popular cultural space, cosmopolitanism and eclecticism is the norm (Zubeida 2010; see also Salois, Rasmussen, Frishkopf, Hodgson, Stokes this volume).

Third, and finally, this volume attests to recent changes in the very notion of "culture," in the Muslim world as elsewhere. Neoliberal restructuring—the shrinking of the state, the marketization of the public sphere, the creation of the consumer citizen—has promoted an instrumental idea of culture. Culture is, increasingly, conceptualized as a kind of resource, a powerful way of attracting investment, business, and skilled labor to "global cities" and regional hubs (such as the European "capitals of culture") (see Yudice 2003, Sassen 2011, Keyder 1999). Where claims to cultural abundance might be harder to sustain in locations remote from the cosmopolitan global metropoles, "culture" may still be articulated as a resource for local tourism, or export (Cohen 2007, Guilbault 1993). And where the possibilities of even this are limited, "culture" may still serve as a means of channeling aid, for example in programs designed to alleviate youth unemployment or fostering peace and reconciliation. In all such cases, "culture" has come to be understood as a kind of tool, to be funded and deployed as a means to an end—"development," "peace," "growth," and so forth (al-Ghadhban and Strohm 2013, Winegar 2006).

These conceptualizations attach a new importance to culture as an economic resource and as an instrumental means of promoting the social goals of the neoliberal state—that is to say, of producing pliant, peaceful citizens who enjoy shopping. The importance attached to culture by the managers of the neoliberal state seldom extends to any real consideration of sustainability, social justice, and creativity in these cultural domains. It is, at best, a space of cynicism, or, as Yúdice puts it, more gently, "expediency" (Yúdice 2003). This "expedient" attitude toward popular culture can be felt in many of the contributions to this volume. In most of the case studies presented here, Islamist parties are either running neoliberal states or absorbing neoliberal language in opposition, because this is the language of power and electoral success.

This constitutes yet another reason for changing and more accommodating attitudes toward popular culture in the Muslim world. "Culture," here, too, is being thought of as a tool, as a resource, something that might be exploited for other goals, exchanged for other social goods, productive of "growth" and "development": in short, and following a point made long ago by Pierre Bourdieu, as capital (1984).

The critical consequences of this are considerable. Popular culture grounds new processes of social production and reproduction in the Muslim world, as elsewhere. It can no longer simply be considered "superstructural," to use the old Marxian language. On the contrary, as we have argued, it constitutes an infrastructure (see also Hirschkind 2009). And as such, it is a site of struggle, in the Islamic spaces discussed in this book, as in all modern societies. Neoliberal nation-states, religious authorities, and new media conglomerates all have a stake in this struggle. So, too, as we have argued, do the people, attempting to muddle through difficult and complicated lives in the slums of Cairo or Rabat, zones of conflict or emergency in Syria and Tunisia, the suburbs of Istanbul or Teheran, migrant neighborhoods in Bradford or Paris, or remote towns in northern Ghana. Forms of mass-mediated popular culture in the Muslim world are increasingly being recognized, and cultivated, as spaces of moral instruction and ethical self-fashioning. But these popular cultural forms will—for the foreseeable future—remain indissolubly linked with other forms of mass-mediated popular culture, forms that will continue to provoke laughter, dance, new fashion and hairstyles, song, empathy, tears, jokes, stories, dreams. In its multisensory embrace, in its repetitiousness and ubiquity, in its enlivening of bodies, it mobilizes conceptions of the human being that exceed the narrowly prescribed roles of citizen, consumer, believer, employer, laborer, housewife, unemployed youth. Popular culture in the Muslim world will continue to shape people's sense of participation, community, and political possibility, and ensure that they have a stake in the struggle.

NOTES

1. This book project is the result of the International Conference "Islam and Popular Culture" held in Amsterdam from the 8th until the 10th of March, 2013. This conference was also the conclusion of the research project "Islam and Performing Arts" (2007–2013) supervised by Karin van Nieuwkerk. Both the research project and the final conference were financed by NWO (The Netherlands Organisation for Scientific Research).

REFERENCES

Abu-Lughod, Lila. 2005. *Dramas of Nationhood: The Politics of Television in Egypt*. Chicago: University of Chicago Press.

Adorno, Theodor. 1944. *The Culture Industry: Enlightenment as Mass Deception.* http://www
.marxists.org/reference/archive/adorno/1944/culture-industry.htm. Accessed 4 March
2014.

Al-Ghadhban and Kiven Strohm. 2013. Ghosts of Resistance: Dispatches from Palestinian
Art and Music. In *Palestinian Music and Song: Expression and Resistance since 1900,* edited
by Muslih Kanaaneh, Stig-Magnus Thorsen, Heather Bursheh, and David McDonald.
Bloomington. Indiana University Press.

Appadurai, Arjun. 1996. *Modernity at Large: Cultural Dimensions of Globalization.* Minneapolis: University of Minnesota Press.

Armbrust, Walter. 1996. *Mass Culture and Modernism in Egypt.* Cambridge: Cambridge University Press.

Asad, Talal. 1973. *Anthropology and the Colonial Encounter.* London: Ithica Press.

———. 1986. *The Idea of an Anthropology of Islam.* Occasional Papers Series. Washington,
DC: Center for Contemporary Arab Studies.

———. 2003. *Formations of the Secular: Christianity, Islam, Modernity.* Palo Alto: Stanford
University Press.

Baily, John. 1988. *Music of Afghanistan: Professional Musicians in the City of Herat.* Cambridge: Cambridge University Press.

Bakhtiar, Lale. 1976. *Sufi: Expressions of the Mystic Quest.* London: Thames and Hudson.

Bayat, Asef. 2005. "What is Post-Islamism?" *ISIM Review* 16: 5.

———. 2007. "Islamism and the Politics of Fun." *Public Culture* 19, no. 3: 433–460.

Benjamin, Walter. 1936. *The Work of Art in the Age of Mechanical Reproduction.* https://www
.marxists.org/reference/subject/philosophy/works/ge/benjamin.htm. Accessed 4 March
2014.

Bourdieu, Pierre. 1984. *Distinction: A Social Critique of the Judgment of Taste.* Cambridge,
MA: Harvard University Press.

Cohen, Sara. 2007. *Decline, Renewal and the City in Popular Music Culture: Beyond the
Beatles.* Farnham, Surrey: Ashgate.

During, Simon, ed. 2007. *The Cultural Studies Reader.* 3rd ed. New York: Routledge.

Eickelman, Dale, and James Piscatori. 1990. *Muslim Travellers: Pilgrimage, Migration and the
Religious Imagination.* London: Routledge.

Eickelman, Dale, and Jon Anderson. 2003. *New Media and the Muslim World: The Emerging
Public Sphere.* Bloomington: Indiana University Press.

Fabian, Johannes. 1998. *Moments of Freedom: Anthropology and Popular Culture.* Charlottes-
ville: University Press of Virginia.

Foucault, Michel. 1995 (1975). *Discipline and Punish: The Birth of the Prison.* 2nd ed. Translated by Alain Sheridan. New York: Vintage Books.

———. 2003 (1997). *Society Must Be Defended. Lectures at the Collège de France, 1975–1976.*
Translated by David Macey. New York: Picador.

———. 2009 (2004). *Security, Territory, Population.* In *Lectures at the Collège de France,
1977–1978,* edited by Michel Senellart. Translated by Graham Burchell. New York:
Picador.

Geertz, Clifford. 1971. *Islam Observed: Religious Development in Morocco and Indonesia.* Chicago: University of Chicago Press.

Gellner, Ernest. 1981. *Muslim Society.* Cambridge: Cambridge University Press.

Gilsenan, Michael. 1982. *Recognizing Islam: An Anthropologist's Introduction.* London:
Croom Helm.

Gonzalez, Virginia. 2002. *Beauty and Islam: Aesthetics in Islamic Art and Architecture.* London: IB Tauris.

Grabar, Oleg. 1992. *The Mediation of Ornament.* Princeton: Princeton University Press.

Gramsci, Antonio. 1971. *Selections from the Prison Notebooks.* New York: International Publishers.

Guilbault, Jocelyne. 1993. *Zouk: World Music in the West Indies.* Chicago: University of Chicago Press.

Hirschkind, Charles. 2009. *The Ethical Soundscape: Cassette Sermons and Islamic Counterpublics.* New York: Columbia University Press.

Hodgson, Marshall. 1974. *The Venture of Islam: Conscience and History in a World Civilization.* Chicago: University of Chicago Press.

Huntington, Samuel. 1996. *The Clash of Civilizations and the Remaking of World Order.* New York: Simon and Schuster.

Irwin, Robert. 2007. *Lust for Knowing: The Orientalists and Their Enemies.* Harmondsworth: Penguin.

Kepel, G. 2000. "Islamism Reconsidered." *Harvard International Review* 22, no. 2: 22.

Keyder, Caglar, ed. 1999. *Between the Global and the Local.* Lanham, MD: Rowman and Littlefield, Global Istanbul.

LeVine, Mark. 2005a. *Why They Don't Hate Us: Lifting the Veil on the Axis of Evil.* Oxford: Oneworld Publications.

———. 2005b. "The Palestinian Press in Mandatory Jaffa: Advertizing, Nationalism and the Public Sphere." In *Palestine, Israel and the Politics of Popular Culture,* edited by Ted Swedenburg and Rebecca L. Stein, 51–76. Raleigh, NC: Duke University Press.

———. 2008. *Heavy Metal Islam: Rock, Resistance, and the Struggle for the Soul of Islam.* New York: Random House.

LeVine, Mark, and Armando Salvatore, eds. 2005. *Religion, Social Practice, and Contested Hegemonies: Reconstructing the Public Sphere in Muslim Majority Societies.* New York: Palgrave Macmillan.

Lindholm, Charles. 1996. *The Islamic Middle East: An Historical Anthropology.* Oxford: Blackwell.

Mitchell, Timothy. 1991. *Colonising Egypt.* Cambridge: Cambridge University Press.

Necipoğlu, Gülrü. 1995. *The Topkapı Scroll: Geometry and Ornament in Islamic Architecture.* Santa Monica, CA: The Getty Center for the History of Art and the Humanities.

Qureshi, Regula Burkhardt. 2006. *Sufi Music of India and Pakistan: Sound, Context, and Meaning.* Oxford: Oxford University Press.

Rabinow, Paul. 1977. *Reflections on Fieldwork in Morocco.* Berkeley: University of California Press.

Rancière, Jacques. 2004. *The Politics of Aesthetics.* London: Continuum.

Rosen, Laurence. 1989. *The Anthropology of Justice: Law as Culture in Islamic Society.* Cambridge: Cambridge University Press.

Roy, O. 2004. *Globalized Islam.* London: Hurst and Company.

Said, Edward. 1978. *Orientalism.* New York: Pantheon Books.

Sassen, Saskia. 2011. *Cities in a World Economy.* London: Sage.

Schuyler, Philip. 1985 "The Rwais and the Zawia: Professional Musicians and the Rural Religious Elite in Southwestern Morocco." *Asian Music* 17: 14–31

Scott, James C. 1990. *Domination and the Arts of Resistance: Hidden Transcripts.* New Haven: Yale University Press.

Sreberny-Mohammadi, Annabelle, and Ali Mohammadi. 1994. *Small Media, Big Revolution: Communication, Culture, and the Iranian Revolution*. Minneapolis: University of Minnesota Press.

Storey, J. 2001. *Cultural Theory and Popular Culture*. Upper Saddle River, NJ: Prentice Hall.

———. 2003. *Inventing Popular Culture*. Oxford: Blackwell Publishing.

Tabbaa, Yasser. 2001. *The Transformation of Islamic Art during the Sunni Revival*. Seattle: University of Washington Press.

Van Nieuwkerk, K. 2011. *Muslim Rap, Halal Soaps, and Revolutionary Theater*. Austin: University of Texas Press.

———. 2013. *Performing Piety: Singers and Actors in Egypt's Islamic Revival*. Austin: University of Texas Press.

Varzi, Roxanne. 2008. "Miniskirt Democracy: Muslim Women's Memoires." *London Review of Books* 30, no. 15 (July 31): 25–26.

Williams, Raymond. 1983. *Keywords: A Vocabulary of Culture and Society*. London: Croom Helm.

Winegar, Jessica. 2006. *Creative Reckonings: The Politics of Art and Culture in Contemporary Egypt*. Palo Alto: Stanford University Press.

Yúdice, George. 2003. *The Expediency of Culture: Uses of Culture in the Global Era*. Durham, NC: Duke University Press.

Zubeida, Sami. 2010. Cosmopolitan Citizenship in the Middle East. *Open Democracy*, 20 July 2010. http://www.opendemocracy.net/sami-zubaida/cosmopolitan-citizenship-in-middle-east. Accessed 7 March 2014.

PART I

POPULAR CULTURE: AESTHETICS, SOUND, AND THEATRICAL PERFORMANCE IN THE MUSLIM WORLD

THIS SECTION WILL INTRODUCE some key concepts and issues regarding the study of popular culture in the Muslim world: the importance of aesthetics, the power of sound, and the imaginative capacity of performance to move beyond merely reflecting the realities toward shaping and actualizing (utopian) futures.

Deborah Kapchan's chapter theorizes the power of sound for constituting pious subjectivities and provides insight in the practice of learning to listen to aesthetic sound, the "literacy of listening." It foremost shows how sound and practices of listening can become vehicles for Sufis to create a sacred place in a secular country such as France. Sufism embraces an aesthetic system in which listening plays a dominant role. Listening is not a passive act. These are learned performances in which the practitioners become transmitters not just of sound but of knowledge as well. In this chapter Kapchan analyzes the "sound knowledge" of one Sufi Muslim order in France in order to elucidate how learned auditory practices transport a once local and ecstatic religion outside its point of origin and also how listening restructures space and subjectivity. The performance of these aesthetic sensibilities in the public sphere creates a discrepancy in the larger secular culture of France—that is, it forms a rupture with and challenge to the prevailing divisions between secular and sacred aesthetics.

Martin Stokes's chapter also demonstrates that listening is at the heart of ethical and political projects in Turkey. The chapter discusses the connections between the rise of Islamist power in Turkey, the aesthetic domain, and contemporary mass media. By focusing on the art of popular religious vocalists, the chapter explores the quest for beauty among religious communities. The aesthetic domain, in this case study listening to religious pop music, is an ethical community-forging project. This project however has changed as the Turkish Islamist movement has transformed over the last twenty years. Stokes investigates what this means for the genre of religious pop. Religious pop in Turkey played a part in consolidating the Islamist hegemony, while in recent years it has become a routine and less remarkable aspect of it. Religious pop in Turkey is no longer a provocation of secularists, or in need of justification. It is simply one form of outreach and consciousness-raising among many. This shows that the aesthetic quest is not simply a "soundtrack to a political and economic transformation. It is part of that very transformation by forging communities and senses of participation." Accordingly, the aesthetic is productive and has a contributory role in creating communities of listeners, albeit in a highly complex and volatile way.

Mark LeVine and Bryan Reynolds develop a new theoretical approach to understand the different types of cultural performance that has come to define the Arab uprisings. To comprehend these modes of performance activism, they introduce the concept "theater of immediacy," defined as cultural performances that are not merely emergent—that is, in the process of formation— but also "emurgent." Combining the sense of emergence and urgency, this concept points at the rapidly developing and intense sociopolitical struggles that characterized the revolutionary moments of the Arab uprisings. Acts of extreme performance activism such as the public suicide of Muhammad Bouazizi are among the most powerful types of theater of immediacy. Yet, many engaged artists have long possessed a similar power to inspire and mobilize fellow citizens. Using several examples, LeVine and Reynolds illustrate how in times of intense sociopolitical conflict artists can function as sociopolitical conductors, creating networks for revolutionary activity that states find it very difficult to contain.

This section thus highlights the transformative power of popular culture through performance, sound, and aesthetics, while moving beyond an approach in which aesthetics is reduced to mere political tools of governance.

LISTENING ACTS, SECULAR AND SACRED: SOUND KNOWLEDGE AMONG SUFI MUSLIMS IN SECULAR FRANCE

DEBORAH KAPCHAN

WE ARE IN MONTPELLIER, France, April 2009. As the ceremony begins, Rquiyya lifts her prayer beads in the air, the sign for those gathered to begin to chant—first the *fatiha*, the "opening" prayer in the Qur'an. Then the Yassin *sura*. Then follow the names of God, *al-latif*, the subtle one; *al-qawi*, the powerful; *al-ʿaziz*, the dear. We chant for ninety minutes, and then the songs begin, some based on eighteenth- and nineteenth-century mystical poems or *qasaʾid*. Some have new lyrics praising the living shaykh, Shaykh al-Hamza. The French speakers enunciate in a beautifully inflected Arabic, though they don't know the meaning of the words they are pronouncing. Even the North Africans present at the ceremony were brought up speaking French. This is less important to them than the power the sounds contain. Most important, there is a regnant and articulate discourse about the power of listening.

In the last decade, much research and social theory has emerged about the rise of forms of religious behavior and the complexity of different forms of secularism (Asad 2003, Bowen 2009, Casanova 1994, De Vries and Sullivan 2006, Dressler and Mardain 2011, Jakobson and Pellegrini 2008, Mahmood 2005, Taylor 2003, 2007). Weberian ideas about the eventual disappearance of religion due to an increase of rationalism no longer hold sway (Weber 2002). Rather we find ourselves before a tidal wave of rising religious emotions, from Christian fundamentalism in the United States to Muslim conservatism in the Arab East, to say nothing of a proliferation of different forms of spirituality related and unrelated to organized religion, such as yoga schools and African dance classes. We are in a moment of heightened sacred affect.

With the rise of religious fervor, however, we are increasingly aware that secularism is not the neutral political baseline that ensures religious freedom for all (as has been thought in the United States and in France, for example), but is itself an ideology that demands belief and defense. While it is clear, following Talal Asad (2003), that every incarnation of secularism has its own particular history and must be evaluated accordingly, in France many see it as under attack, and consequently secularism has become an ideology that is just as strident as any fundamentalism. Indeed French historian Esther Benbassa (2012) refers to the current situation in France as *laïcité intergriste*, or secular fundamentalism.

In our current post–Cold War moment, when late capitalism and its consumption practices permeate the globe, and hallowed democracy does not fulfill its promise, the terms for political debate have changed. In order to live in a "post-secular"[1] world—that is, in a Euro-American context in which secularism is no longer mythologized as a neutral baseline that protects the rights of religious freedom, but rather understood as a political ideology[2]—it is necessary to recognize that the terms of the West (what scholars call the "global North"), are not universal. Indeed, it is essential to consider what Santos calls "epistemologies of the south"—ways of knowing that do not emerge from the occident. These ways of knowing often imply different hierarchies of the senses (Howes 2003). Rancière would say that there is a different "distribution of the sensible" at play, another way to embody cultural knowledge (Rancière 2010). What's more, it is important to understand that the global North and the global South are less geographic places than they are symbolic placeholders. The global South—its epistemologies and ontologies—exist in the northern hemisphere, just as the global North may be found in the southern hemisphere (Santos 2011).

It is clear that the Sufis in France described above practice in a climate that is less than hospitable to forms of Muslim religiosity. However, this neither prevents the spread of Sufism in France nor abates Muslim conversion among French citizens, a phenomenon that has been rising steadily.[3] How do Sufis create a sense of belonging in a country that is increasingly Islamophobic? I assert that sound, and more important, practices of listening, become main vehicles for this minority to create a sacred place in a secular land.

"Thinking with sound and music may offer the opportunity for thinking through issues of inclusion, coexistence and what a multicultural landscape might sound like in the age of information and global interdependency" (Bull and Back 2003: 15).

WHAT DOES SCHOLARLY attention to practices of listening facilitate? How can listening help us apprehend and thus understand other ways of being and knowing? And how can these questions help us reconceive modes of knowledge transmission?

In this chapter I examine what I refer to as "listening acts," conscious performances of (in this case, sacred) listening. Listening acts are not passive; indeed, I argue that they are learned performances in which the practitioners become transducers not just of sound but of knowledge as well, sound knowledge. In particular I analyze the sound knowledge of one Sufi (or mystical) Muslim order in France in order to elucidate how learned auditory practices transport a once local and ecstatic religion (based on one charismatic shaykh in northern Morocco) outside its point of origin, and also how listening restructures space and subjectivity, creating a form of sound knowledge. This takes place through what I have called the "literacy of listening" (Kapchan 2009a)—that is, the acquired ability to learn other cultures (specifically religious cultures, though not exclusively these) through auditory participation in its sound-worlds. French converts to Islam as well as lapsed Muslims returning to the faith via Sufism embrace an aesthetic system in which listening plays a more dominant role than it previously had. This redistribution of aesthetic sensibilities, accompanied by its performance in the public sphere, certainly creates a dissensus in the larger secular culture of France—that is, a rupture with and challenge to the prevailing equations between secular and sacred aesthetics. Yet it does so not ideologically but aesthetically. Contributing to a growing literature on how Muslims create ethical selves in bodily practices of devotion[4]—in prayer, discussion groups, sartorial practices and through the Sufi concept of deep[5] listening, or *sama'*—I analyze North African Sufism in diaspora,[6] where emotions related to secularism (*laïcité*) and Islam are often perceived to be in conflict (Asad 1993, 2003; Balibar 2004; Bowen 2004, 2009; Ewing 1997, 2003, 2005a; Frishkopf 2012; Hirshkind 2006; Kapchan 2010; Mahmood 2005; Werbner 2002, 2003).

SUFISM FROM MOROCCO TO FRANCE

And, therefore, did al-Khadir, when he was asked in the dream concerning Hearing say, "It is pure slipperiness, there stand not fast upon it save the feet of the learned."
AL-GHAZZALI 1907: 711–712

The Boutshishiyya Qadiriyya order is arguably the largest order in Morocco and is certainly the most politically important. The head of this order, Shaykh al-Hamza, lives in northern Morocco and is over eighty-five years of age. In the last decades this order has exceeded the bounds of Morocco and has spread to France, Belgium, the United Kingdom, Canada, and the United States. Its adoption, by French and North American citizens of North African descent as well as converts to Islam, involves a re-training of the body through disciplines related to listening. My work is based on research with a branch of this order begun in 1994–1995 during fourteen months of continuous residence in Rabat, Morocco, then continued in the south of France over an additional fourteen months in 2008–2009, and every summer since then.

My research began in Morocco in 1994 when I was in Rabat on a Fulbright research grant. Originally my entrée into the Sufi world was a personal one— my "official" research had to do with Gnawa trance ceremonies—musical rituals aimed to propitiate the spirits of those afflicted and possessed by spirits (Kapchan 2007). While perusing the shelves of Kalila wa Dimna bookstore in Rabat one day, I bought a book entitled *The Sufi Path (La Voie Soufie)*. The book jacket said that the author, Faouzi Skali, held a doctorate in anthropology from the Sorbonne. I was intrigued. Having always been attracted to esoteric worlds, I was curious to understand Moroccan Sufism experientially. I went to see Faouzi Skali in his home in Fes. He and his wife Katherine welcomed me warmly. Although we discussed anthropology, I told them I was interested in participating in Sufi ceremonies, not as a researcher but as a seeker. This was to transform over the years and in fact my position is always a liminal one in the order. (I continue to practice with the Sufis in France and Morocco when I am there, and have also given a lecture at the World Conference of World Sufism during the *mawlid* celebrations, the celebrations of the Prophet's birthday, in Madagh, Morocco). Faouzi sent me to a *muqaddema*, or overseer, in Casablanca, who held the ceremonies in her home. Although I was living in Rabat, I took the commuter train to Casablanca once a week for nine months to attend Sufi ceremonies. There I learned the vocabulary of Sufism as well as its aesthetic dispositions.

My initiation into this research was literally through my ears. I listened intently to the liturgy (the *wadhifa*), immersing myself in the prosodies of the Qur'anic verses recited, the names of God chanted, and the songs sung. The melodies took up residence in my body and accompanied me into other aspects of my life. However, it was only when I spent a year in France during my sabbatical (2008–2009) that I truly understood the aesthetic waters in which I was swimming. I settled in a small village outside of Nîmes and lived there for fourteen months. I knew there was a Boutshishiyya group in the vicinity of Orange, about one-and-a-half hours away. I had a car, and so I saw myself making that commute weekly in order to conduct what had by now become official research. But when I went to the Sunday market in my village for the first time, I noticed a Moroccan couple selling Moroccan leather goods. I struck up a conversation.

Salam alay-kum, I said.

Alay-kum salam, the woman answered me.

In the south of France, there are several North African vendors in the market-places that travel from town to town on different days. In the department of the Gard, a less affluent and more diverse region, there are many French who were either born in North Africa or were sons and daughters of the Pieds-Noirs. Consequently, many French shoppers stop and converse in rudimentary Arabic with the North Africans, who humor them by throwing back a few sentences. I was attempting to use Arabic phrases in the marketplace to ease tensions wrought by colonialism and build symbolic bridges across ethnic divides. But our conversation continued.

Where are you from? I asked her.

It is unlikely that someone who has not spent a lot of time in North Africa would ask this question right off the bat. It is a question that North Africans ask all the time of each other, since regional alliances speak legions, but only to those who are familiar with the associations between place and character regnant in Morocco or Algeria.

"I'm from the north," she answered, "outside Nador."

"Oh," I responded. "That's where Sidi Hamza is from." Sidi Hamza is the name of the living shaykh of the Boutshishiyya order.

"You know Sidi Hamza?" she asked.

"Yes, I have been practicing with the Boutshishiyya Sufis since 1994," I answered.

"But we are in the order!" she exclaimed. "We are having a meeting this afternoon. You have to come!"

And so my research began. It found me before I found it, in the very town where I was living in the south of France. This is what Moroccans would call *al-maktub*, destiny (literally, what is "written").

In retrospect it is easy to understand why I became aware of the different aesthetic system at work in this order only once I was in France. In Morocco, I was the only nonnative speaker of Arabic at the ceremonies. Thus, I imagined that my experiences with listening and sound took on a particular definition because of the heightened attention that I, as a nonnative speaker, brought to the experience. Many of the women in the order had been attendees for quite a while; but I was a newcomer to the liturgical context and its spiritual experience. There was not a meta-discourse in place to guide me. Although in 1994 the liturgy had been transliterated into the Latin alphabet, almost everyone followed along with the Arabic texts. In Morocco, I frequented women for whom this practice was second nature.[7]

When the order expanded to France, however, the liturgy and its accompanying chants and songs had to be transliterated. The texts were not translated, as Arabic remained the language of utterance and performance, yet there were necessary shifts, including the development of a discourse in French, not about the referential meaning of the liturgy (that remains untranslated even today), but about the ideas embodied in the practice.

The spread of Sufi Islam requires a translation of its key terms and metaphors: thus *sama'*, spiritual audition; *tawajjuh*, orientation (or spiritual transmission); *dhikr*, remembrance of God through recitation; *sirr*, secret. Such translation relies initially on the figure of the *tarjuman*—the translator or interpreter in Arabic, the bilingual and often bicultural figure that explains the worldviews, practices, the aesthetics and ethos, of one culture to another. Certainly Faouzi Skali is one such figure for the Boutshishiyyas. As the representative of the Boutshishiyya order for French converts in France (the shaykh's nephew Sidi Mounir is the representative for a more North African branch in France) and as a trained anthropologist who has authored many books on Sufism in French, Faouzi has been doing the work of intercultural translation for much of his career. In addition to receiving a United Nations' peace prize, he founded the Fes Festival of World Sacred Music, a festival that created the template for the Dalai Lama's sacred music festivals in Los Angeles and Geneva. This festival has also spawned innumerable other sacred music festivals around the globe, including Skali's second festival, the Festival of Sufi Culture (Kapchan 2008). Skali is not alone in his efforts at intercultural translation. Indeed, we may say that the spread of religion, as well as the spread of aesthetic systems, across linguistic and cultural boundaries, relies on liminal figures such as Faouzi Skali.

The practice of conscious listening (that is, spiritual audition or *sama'*) transmits a kind of "sound knowledge"—a nondiscursive form of affective transmission resulting from acts of listening (Kapchan 2015)—difficult to recognize, being an epistemology without a name in the West and in many other parts of the world.[8]

What part does listening play in Islamic devotion for Sufi Muslims in Morocco and abroad? How do ways of listening create a Sufi? How do new converts to Islam learn to listen deeply? And how is the popularity of the sacred genre of *sama'* moving Islam across the globe? In order to answer these questions, I am going to tell you a short story about listening, *sama*ʿ, in three acts. My work is ethnographically based. Like many Sufis, ethnographers believe that experience provides the basis for knowledge.

LISTENING ACT I: TO LISTEN AS A SUFI

*If Sama*ʿ *or "spiritual audition" or "Sufi chant" or yet again*
"Qasaîd" [poetry] is a wine that quenches the thirst of the spirit,
the ears are also cups serving this divine intoxication.[9]

In the quote above, praise poetry is the wine of divine intoxication. It would follow that the singer—the producer of the sound—would be the vehicle, the medium of this flow. However, this is not the case. It is the ears that are singled out as being the medium of this inspirational flow. The ears are portrayed as actively serving up the activity of listening. This makes sense of course. Listening is an activity. In Sufism, this is explicitly so. How do we listen to ourselves listening? We can feel ourselves moving, and we can hear ourselves talking or singing, but can we listen to ourselves listening? The genre of *sama*ʿ asks us to do that. *Sama*ʿ is a genre of sung chant, but it is also the process of listening to that chant. It is a technique of the ear. In order to produce *sama*ʿ— indeed, even in order to appreciate it—Sufis must learn to listen in another way—an extra-ordinary and conscious way. *Sama*ʿ is a technique that can be learned, and it functions as a pedagogy of personal and spiritual transformation. Like the voice, which can speak about itself, like writing, which can represent inscription, *sama*ʿ is listening as well as what is listened to—that is, it is both a practice and the thing produced. The person listening as well as the singer is called a *sami*ʿ*a* (*musami*ʿ*a* in classical Arabic).

Sufis in Morocco and France congregate in people's homes. The meetings often float; there is a schedule, and each week a different host. Sometimes the liturgies are held in apartments in subsidized housing complexes on the outskirts of cities, towns, and villages. Sometimes they are held in extremely comfortable single-family homes. The class orientation varies across the order, but whether in an apartment or a villa, ceremonies take place with the supplicants sitting on quilted mats and pillows on the floor, usually in a room without furniture. Thus, rooms in private residences are transformed into sacred places of worship.

There are several forms of worship that are practiced. In one form, the liturgy begins in silence, the leader holding up her prayer beads to signal that prayer should begin. At that time, there is an interiorized sound: *la ilaha ila allah*, there is no god but God, ten thousand times. The words roll over and over in the mind as the fingers roll over the polished wooden prayer beads. But there is a bodily accompaniment as well, as the tongue moves quickly across the upper palette and then descends — *a ilaha ila allah*. It is important to "utter" the phrases, even if quietly (*khas-ak t-ntuq*). This creates an intersensory experience, a rhythm between silent word, moving tongue, and rosary fingers that in turn becomes a bodily memory, in which, as phenomenologist Edward Casey notes, "the past is co-immanent with the present" (1987). What's more, there are occasional emergences of sound, as if the utterances bubbled up and turned to sonority when hitting the air, refusing to be confined to the body, the sound body exceeding its flesh. The women begin by listening to the resonance of their own barely audible whispers. This resonance is first experienced as the echo of one's own voice reverberating in the cavities of the head, but then ripples outward and inward, with incoming whispers, and the clicks of strings of beads rising and falling like a waterfall.

Sometimes the women begin with the spoken liturgy (*wadhifa*), that is with a recitation of several Qur'anic verses (*surat al-yassin, surat al-waqi'a, al-fatiha*), before the remembrance section (*dhikr*) in which the women chant some of the ninety-nine names of God aloud — *allah, al-latif, al-'aziz*. The Yassin Sura is complex. It is long. The women who have been in the order for more than a year usually know it by heart. Nonetheless, many of the women read the transcript in Latin letters. It is marked with asterisks that note the phrases — one asterisk for a fall in intonation, the second for the completion of the phrase and a breath. In fact, the lessons in listening begin here, as the majority of these women are not Arabic speakers. They come to the ceremonies, and they learn to listen.

When I began the France-based research in 2007, most of the women were in their twenties and thirties. In a group of fifteen, twelve women were second generation French North Africans, and three were French converts to Islam. In France the population of people of North African descent is estimated to be between 5 and 9 percent of the total population.[10] After the withdrawal of the French protectorate from Morocco in 1956, as well as the horrific Algerian War of Independence from France (1954–1962), North African immigration to France surged. The changing demographics in France over the last several decades has given rise to a multiculturalism that challenges the hegemony of French cultural practices and also puts into question the adequacy of political systems based on *laïcité*, secularism, as a defining governmental practice. As French courts delay trials because of Ramadan[11] and annul marriages based on false claims of virginity,[12] and as massive advertising campaigns are launched on billboards and television to sell special foods during Ramadan,[13] the French secular public is more and more aware that historical notions of *laïcité* are not shared.

LISTENING ACT II: LEARNING TO LISTEN

How is it that non-Arabic speakers in France become competent performers of Sufi songs and prayers in Arabic? Of course, there are many places in the Muslim world where non-Arabic speakers learn to recite the Qur'an beautifully (Nelson 2001; Rasmussen 2010). But unlike pedagogies in Qur'anic schools, where phrases are taught slowly and over years, the Sufi initiates in France undergo a complete immersion into the ritual all at once. No one gives them individual lessons. They come to the ceremony, and they learn to listen. When I asked Soumaya, who knows the entire liturgy by heart, how she learned it, she humbly said, "just by assiduity"—that is, concentration and absorption. When I asked her how long it took, she replied, "only a few months." I asked another young woman, "But you, Halima, you understand Arabic, don't you?" "Just a little," she admitted. "Then how is it you speak so beautifully," I said. A force d'écouter, she answered, "just by listening." Il faut écouter avec le coeur, "you have to listen with your heart." Second generation French North Africans and French converts become Sufi initiates by learning to listen in new ways. This is because there is already an extant methodology for spiritual audition in Islamic mysticism called sama'.

Sama', literally "listening" in Arabic, refers to both the technique of active and attentive listening that Sufis employ in their ceremonies and the ceremony itself (During 1988; 1993). According to ethnomusicologist Jean During, sama' first appeared among the Sufis in Baghdad in the ninth century and was elaborated in traditions and treatises that spread to the larger Islamic world (During 1993). It is still employed today in such places as Turkey, Africa, the Middle East, South Asia, Europe, and the United States.

Sufis believe that the activity of spiritual audition, or sama', polishes the heart, purifying the disciple and thereby making space for the love of God to inhabit the whole being. As the leader of the singing group in Paris writes:

> Sama' or spiritual audition is, with Dhikr (the invocation), a major pillar in Sufi education. The content of poems, the rhythm of singing and the whisper of melodies elevate the soul to the subtle presence of the divine Light. This saving Light purifies the soul from its imperfections, which progressively transform the vision we have of the world and the creation. The practice of sama' reveals the presence of God in anything and by the same fact invites the aspirant to nobleness of the character. It is in this sense that the sama' is considered, in Sufism, a universal message of love and peace for all humanity. Moulay Mourad al-Qadiri Boudchich [leader of Tariqa Qadiriya Boutchichiya Sama' and Madih group].[14]

For Moulay Mourad al-Qadiri Boudchich, *sama*' is a pedagogy whose practice benefits not only the individual but society at large. It is a means of purification, a way of unveiling the secrets of the divine to the self and for the community. *Akhlaq*, good acts or ethics, is one of the stated goals of the Sufi in community, and the *dhikr*, or remembrance of God ceremony, polishes the heart so that right conduct and ethical behavior prevail. Part of this active cultivation of the ethical self is done through music. As one member of the order put it, "The pedagogy is in the songs. In the [Sufi] order, one learns through the music. Each song carries its own secret [within it]." It is not only the meaning of the words that creates community, however, since many of the members do not understand Arabic. Rather, the bodily technique of attentive listening cultivates an affective stance toward themselves and others. The meaning is of course important, but the power of the words does not depend on intellectual understanding. Rather, the songs live independent of any one interpretation. They are the vehicles of the *sirr*, the secrets of initiation. Learning the liturgy and the songs, the Sufi female devotees with whom I work (called *faqirat*, "the poor ones") enter into a new community, one wherein ethics are learned, comportment is proscribed, and even marriages are made.

Of course initiates do not hear everything and repeat it right away. Like most initiations, the technique of active listening is learned in stages. As the liturgy begins with the prayers, the *faqirat* also begin there, repeating only the initial words of each phrase. Slowly they add the endings of the phrases, and little by little the middle of the phrase is added, until the whole phrase is learned. Some phrases are easier than others. Arabic contains a lot of parallelism, and the phrases with it are easier to repeat. The high level of prosody in the liturgy aids the listener in its memorization. The process is not unlike second language acquisition in that French North African and French converts to Islam are immersed in an aural ritual all at once, one they do not understand referentially, but one they come to know intimately by repeated listening (Kapchan 2008). Foucault has provided a rubric for understanding this restructuration of the senses—namely, technologies of the self, "which permit individuals to effect by their own means or with the help of others a certain number of operations on their own bodies and souls, thoughts, conduct, and way of being, so as to transform themselves in order to attain a certain state of happiness, purity, wisdom, perfection, or immortality" (Foucault 1988). Foucault's definition assumes autonomy of the subject. However, he understands that such technologies of the self are always imbricated in other power relations—of class, sociopolitical context, gender, and culture. Indeed, technologies of the self are often performed in common.[15] Listening attentively becomes one such performance.

The repetition of the names of God is common among all Sufi groups. A rhythm is created in the beginning that remains fairly stable, though accelerations occur incrementally. This repetition and consequent phonetic parallelism is instrumental in changing the initiate's "state" (al-hal) from a quotidian consciousness to an enraptured and trance-like condition that they equate with divine communion. Indeed, experiencing al-hal is one of the effects of the dhikr. What is interesting is that each devotee has her own hal. It goes a bit like this: The women are seated in a circle on the floor. They begin chanting vigorously: allah, allah, allah, allah. Between each utterance many actively push the air from their diaphragms in a kind of pumping motion. This makes their breath audible. All of a sudden, one of the women breaks with this rhythm. She calls out "allah" loudly, almost a scream. She has broken with the rhythm of the other chanters and is now punctuating their repetitions with short staccato exclamations. They seem to rise up from her body, to actually take possession of her with a volition of their own. She is in al-hal, the state. Now things "heat up" so to speak. Another woman breaks from the rhythmic repetition moaning allah in long tones over the voices of the others. She rocks back and forth. Meanwhile, some women in the group have raised the pitch of their chanting by a semitone. Another woman is a full fourth above the majority. Although the goal is to chant with one voice, the women are in fact producing an aharmonic, chromaticized melody, creating overtones as well as counterrhythms as they go into al-hal. This state is very personal; indeed, it is considered an intimate state to be experienced only in sex-segregated rituals among initiates. Nonetheless, this state, this hal, is the very heart of the Boutshishiyya Sufi dhikr insofar as it represents a culmination of musical, emotional, and spiritual dimensions. It is also a key element in understanding how Sufis learn to listen, for despite the intensity of ecstatic performance, a subtle but very present auditory responsiveness remains acute. One hal brings on others. Punctuated cries respond to spontaneously clapped rhythms. Swoons are echoed around the circle.

The repetition of the names of God in a regular ostinato rhythm provides the basis for collectively attaining a state of divine inspiration, but more singular "states" (ahwal) emerge in the spaces between the words. Sometimes a faqira might swoon and call out for God, sometimes another falls completely silent. Yet, at all points, the group is listening attentively.

There is no explicit discourse about al-hal (it is thought to be a spontaneous and individual expression of unity with God), but there is a rich fabric of sounds that result from the dhikr. The faqirat take these lessons in listening and apply them to learning the more difficult and less repetitive liturgy. Not only do the repetitions of the names of God get faster and rise in intonation, but the occurrence of *al-hal* sparks a kind of chain reaction wherein women's sporadic exclamations, their swoons and cries, respond to the exclamations of others. Attentive listening is the foundation of this improvisational performance. After three hours, the *wadhifa* ends with a prayer, the women kissing each other's hands and saying, *allah y-qbal*, may God accept [your prayers].[16]

LISTENING ACT III: SACRED SONG IN PUBLIC PLACES

A Sufi ritual is called a *wadhifa*. Literally a liturgy, the word comes from the root *wa dha fa*, or labor. According to Lévinas, liturgy is a work performed for the community, a labor in common (Lévinas 1982). In the Sufi liturgy, listening is part of this labor. It is an act that not only transforms the state of the listener but also the affective resonance of the group. As with many such endeavors, listening together holds a promise. In this case it is a promise of transcendence, a "messianic promise" to be sure, and one that, like all promises, is performative (Derrida 1985). Whether or not the promise is fulfilled, the very promissory character of the event effects social change. Among other promises, listening together in Sufi ritual holds the promise of community (Kapchan 2008).

CREATING A SONIC COMMUNITY IN PUBLIC VIEW

For the women in the Boutshishiyya order, the promise of community is enacted every time a song is sung. Community with other Sufis is an essential aspect of this religious practice. And the level of attentive listening employed in the ceremony imprints the body and its memory, so that merely hearing the sounds in one's head is a thread that ties the listener to God, to the *shaykh*, and to the community as well (Kapchan 2009). The sounds take up residence in the body, and the Sufi can listen to them simply by "remembering" them (*dhikr* is that, "remembrance of God").

What happens then when these practices and these sounds travel outside the private sphere of the liturgy, particularly in a place like France where notions of secularism (*laïcité*) are so pronounced? How do individual and collective acts of listening turn into forms of "sound knowledge" in the larger public sphere?

Sufi music is a well-known and recognized genre in the world music market. This has several effects. The circulation of Sufi music—on stages, in festivals, on the Internet, and on compact discs—creates a niche and provides a means for sacred music to circulate in nonsacred spheres of listening. Musicians as diverse as the Gnawa of Morocco, as well as emerging female vocalists like Iraqi Sahar Taha, employ the adjective "Sufi" to describe their music. That Moroccan Gnawa music—music that usually accompanies trance possession ceremonies in Morocco—accompanies a YouTube video entitled "Sufi Music from Senegal" that portrays not Sufi ceremonies, but images of Senegalese mosques, is only one of the many ironies in the usage and misusage of the category of "Sufi music."[17]

The women in the Boutshishiyya Qadiriyya order in France have two singing groups. The first, *Ensemble Rabia*, is a group of French and French North African women whose repertoire is mainly drawn from the songs sung in the order, though they borrow from West African repertoires and take creative liberty with the songs. These women do not veil.[18] The second is *Silsila*, a group primarily based in Paris whose repertoire is more conservative, remaining in the canon of Moroccan Sufi song without taking much creative liberty in stylistic innovation.[19] These women do veil. Both these groups sing on stages and at festivals in France, places such as the Institute of Muslim Culture in Paris,[20] the Lenche Theater in Marseille,[21] and the Chatelêt Theater in Paris.[22] Ensemble Rabia has produced two compact discs—*Fleurs du Sirr* (Flowers of the Secret), and *Isma*ʿ ("Listen").

The affect created in the labor of collective listening is tangible. Taken on stage it is also visible. The audiences for these concerts are diverse. They may be students, lovers of world music, people curious about Sufism, or friends of friends in the band. The concerts are free. I have attended a concert at the Nîmes Community Center with a very mixed audience, including spiritual seekers who stayed after the concert to eat the sweets provided by the women of the group, and I have been instrumental in organizing a concert at New York University's campus in Paris, whose audience was composed of other Sufis, and of a few students and faculty or administrators at NYU Paris, one of whom was scandalized by the performance of what she considered a sacred ritual in the secular space of the university (Kapchan 2013).

The young women in the group were all wearing long pink djellebas with matching headscarves. While this did not present a problem for me, I realized later that it might have been offensive to some audience members who were sympathetic to the French policy of not displaying any sartorial signs of religiosity in public institutions.

Most audience members were members of the Sufi order. First and second generation North African men in casual pants and jackets, entered the [NYU] mansion, greeting each other and mingling. There were some French women converts in western dress talking with the singers and helping to set up. The grandson of the shaykh himself, Sidi Mounir, arrived in a formal blue suit. Only four of the audience members were NYU students, and three were NYU-affiliated faculty and administrators.

The Sufis sang, the soloist employing a high nasal vibrato, the chorus answering in smooth harmonies. The Sufis in the audience began closing their eyes and swaying. As is often the case in the Middle East and North Africa, the audience expressed their appreciation of particular virtuosic turns of phrase by exclaiming "God!" (allah!).

After the concert, I overheard a conversation. Apparently one of the NYU-Paris administrators, a French woman, was outraged that what she thought was going to be a musical performance had turned into a sacred ritual. Indeed, I had noticed her unease during the concert, as the Sufis in the audience were more and more transported by the music. Clearly a border had been transgressed between the secular and the sacred as performed in a public space. But listening practices were also at play. It was the ability to listen deeply that contributed to the ambiance in the room. The Sufis had exhibited the effects of listening as an active performance—namely, the creation of a sacred and public affect that was palpable. Given music's ability to inhere (in-hear) in bodies and space, the intersubjective act of listening together actually sacralized the space, much to the chagrin of the secular audience members present.

That this kind of affective response was possible at all speaks to the palpable religious emotion generated not only by the sacred sounds, but by the listening acts of the community. Listening here was itself a performance, and it transmitted a "sound knowledge" that made at least one French administrator very uncomfortable. The Sufis, in their songs and in their listening acts, had re-partitioned the aesthetic system at play in the public realm. This, I assert, is a form of sound knowledge, one that is quite political in its assertion of difference in the public realm. While it is easy to agree that minorities enjoy equal rights in the public sphere, the encounter with difference happens most poignantly when symbolic minorities become substantive minorities—that is, when not only "identities" but actual persons with their accompanying aesthetic systems inhabit public spaces (Appadurai 2006). When these aesthetic systems are marked as "sacred," however, the encounter with a public that has deep affective ties to forms of secularity puts both aesthetic and political systems into stark relief.

CONCLUSION

In this chapter, I have demonstrated how listening acts transform individual and collective forms of being that then move into the public and political sphere. "Sound knowledge"—a nondiscursive form of affective transmission resulting from conscious acts of listening—is one example of what Jacques Rancière calls a "redistribution of the sensible," that is, an encounter with difference that is deeply aesthetic and that creates politics (Rancière 2010).

Sama^c is an aesthetic training and entrainment that moves easily across borders, and yet the challenge for the future is to be able to inhabit not only the same public space, but to be able to admit multiple aesthetic systems into that space without recourse to claims of ownership or propriety. While listening to European sacred music—Gregorian chant or the Bach B-Minor Mass—poses no threat in the public spaces of the French secular state, Muslim voices and listening practices often find no aesthetic "home" in the French public sphere. Perhaps the Sufis have something to teach in this regard: that there are as many ways to listen as there are ways to sing. Sound knowledge travels not just in the voice, but in the ear. To enact politics is to listen carefully.

NOTES

1. See Habermas 2008. "Notes on a Post-Secular Society," SignandSight.com, http://www.signandsight.com/features/1714.html. Accessed 6 February 2013.

2. An ideology that may even threaten forms of religiosity.

3. Euro-Islam cites the *New York Times* as saying that the number of converts in France has doubled in the last twenty-five years. This article is reactionary, however, and finds conversion rates high in prisons and in ghettos. My work with Sufis, while neither quantitative nor statistical, demonstrates that conversions take place among middle-class French populations as well. http://www.euro-islam.info/2013/02/06/number-of-converts-to-islam-rises-in-france/?utm_source=February%208%20-%20Euro-Islam&utm_campaign=Euro-Islam%20Feb%208&utm_medium=email. Accessed 13 May 2015.

4. Ewing 1997, 2003, 2005; Hirschkind 2006; Mahmood 2005.

5. To listen deeply involves an affective stance that, according to anthropologist Judith Becker, is qualitatively different than other kinds of listening. For those who are able or trained to listen deeply, music evokes a profound emotional experience akin to trance, one that is often (though not necessarily) experienced in a group situation. According to composer Pauline Oliveros, who first coined the term, deep listening is a self-conscious and active listening that unlocks "layer after layer of imagination, memory and meaning down to the cellular level of human experience" (quoted in Becker 2004: 2; see http://www.deeplistening.org/. Accessed May 2014.

6. See Ewing 2008; Werbner 2002, 2003.

7. In France the women's "somatic modes of attention"—"ways of attending to and with the body" were different than those in Morocco.

8. I take up the other terms (*dhikr, sirr, tawajjuh*) in the larger manuscript on this research (Kapchan in progress).

9. Si le Samâ^c ou «l'audition spirituelle» ou «le chant soufi» ou encore «Qasâïd» est un vin dont s'abreuvent les esprits, les oreilles sont autant de coupes servant à cette ivresse divine." http://www.saveurs-soufies.com/index.php?option=com_content&view=article&id=110:sama-chant-spirituel&catid=12:le-tassawuf-soufisme&Itemid=39. Accessed 12 May 2015.

10. Sabeg and Méhaignerie 2004, http://www.conventioncitoyenne.com/documents/oubliesdelegalite.pdf. Accessed 13 May 2015.

11. "Le Soupçon du Ramadan" *Libération* 11 (September 2008), http://www.liberation.fr/contre-journal/010188996-le-soupcon-du-ramadan. Accessed 13 May 2015.

12. The French Court at first upheld the annulment, but then recanted. "Mensonge sur La Virginité: Ils Sont Rémariés." 17 November 2008. *Libération*. http://www.libelille.fr /saberan/2008/11/mariage-annul-p.html. Accessed 6 February 2013. "Hymen Rompu, Mariage Récousu" *Libération* (18 November 2008), http://www.liberation.fr/societe/01012 66843-hymen-rompu-mariage-recousu. Accessed 13 May 2015.

13. "Quand la Publicité Se Met à l'Heure du Ramadan," 18 July 2012. *Advertising Times*, http://www.advertisingtimes.fr/2012/07/quand-la-publicite-se-met-lheure-du.html. Accessed 13 May 2015.

"À l'approche de ramadan, la bataille publicitaire pour le marché du halal bat son plein. "France24 Actualité Internationale" (August 2010), http://www.france24.com/fr/20100805 -france-ramadan-bataille-publicitaire-marche-halal-expansion-islam. Accessed 13 May 2015.

"Les grandes surfaces fêtent le ramadan sans le nommer" (August 2011), *Le Figaro*, http:// www.lefigaro.fr/actualite-france/2011/08/01/01016-20110801ARTFIG00355-les-grandes -surfaces-fetent-le-ramadan-sans-le-nommer.php. Accessed 13 May 2015.

14. http://www.saveurs-soufies.com. Accessed 13 May 2015.

15. Think of the yoga craze in cosmopolitan areas such as New York, for example, or social movements like veganism or anticonsumerism that are based on material practices.

16. Kapchan 2009.

17. http://www.youtube.com/watch?v=ENwWAhiLrTc. Accessed 13 May 2015.

18. http://www.ensemblerabia.net. Accessed 13 May 2015.

19. http://www.groupesilsila.com/index.php?view=article&id=2:presentation-&format =pdf. Accessed February 18, 2013 http://www.groupesilsila.com/index.php. And Facebook, http://www.facebook.com/pages/Groupe-Silsila/117191991646094. Accessed 13 May.

20. http://www.soufisme.org/site/spip.php?article222. Accessed 13 May 2015.

21. http://www.theatredelenche.info/spip.php?article519#. Accessed 13 May 2015.

22. http://www.nme.com/nme-video/youtube/id/TMebKR3GiJU.

REFERENCES

Appadurai, Arjun. 2006. *Fear of Small Numbers*. Durham, NC: Duke University Press.

Asad, Talal. 1993. *Genealogies of Religion: Christianity, Islam, Modernity*. Baltimore: Johns Hopkins University Press.

———. 2003. *Formations of the Secular*. Palo Alto: Stanford University Press.

Balibar, Etienne. 2004. Dissonances within Laïcité. *Constellations* 11, no. 3: 353–367.

Becker, Judith. 2004. *Deep Listeners: Music, Emotion, and Trancing*. Bloomington: Indiana University Press.

Benbassa, Esther. 2012a. "Cessons de voir en l'islam un ennemi!" *Le Monde*, 26 January 2012.

Bowen, John R. 2004. "Muslims and Citizens: France's Headscarf Controversy." *Boston Review* (February/March): 3135. http://bostonreview.net/BR29.1/bowen.html.

———. 2007. *Why the French Don't Like Headscarves: Islam, the State, and Public Space*. Princeton: Princeton University Press. New York Times Book Review *Editors' Choice*.

———. 2008. *Religions in Practice: An Approach to the Anthropology of Religion*. 4th rev. ed. Needham Heights, MA: Allyn and Bacon.

———. 2009. *Can Islam Be French? Pluralism and Pragmatism in a Secularist State*. Princeton: Princeton University Press.

———. 2010. *Religions in Practice: An Approach to the Anthropology of Religion*. 5th rev. ed. Needham Heights, MA: Allyn and Bacon.

———. 2011. *L'Islam à la Française*. Paris: Steinkis/Flammarion (French trans. of *Can Islam be French?*).

Bull, Michael and Les Black. 2003. *The Auditory Culture Reader*. New York: Berg.

Casanova, José. 1994. *Public Religions in the Modern World*. Chicago: University of Chicago Press.

Casey, Edward. 1987. *Remembering: A Phenomenological Study*. Bloomington: Indiana University Press.

Csordas, Thomas. 1993. "Somatic Modes of Attention." *Cultural Anthropology* 8, no. 2: 135–156.

Derrida, Jacques. 1985. *The Ear of the Other*. New York: Schocken Books.

De Vries, Hent, and Lawrence E. Sullivan. 2006. *Political Theologies: Public Religions in a Post-Secular World*. New York: Fordham University Press.

De Vries, Hent, and Samuel Weber. 2002. *Religion and Media*. Palo Alto: Stanford University Press.

During, Jean. 1988 *Musique et Extase: L'Audition Mystique dans la Tradition Soufie*. Paris: Albin Michel.

———. 1993. "Samâ." *Encyclopedia of Islam*. Leiden: Brill.

Ewing, Katherine Pratt. 1997. *Arguing Sainthood: Islam, Modernity, and Psychoanalysis*. Durham, NC: Duke University Press.

———. 2003. "The Sufi and the Mullah: Islam and Local Culture in Pakistan." In *Pakistan at the Millennium*, edited by Charles Kennedy, 169–198. Karachi: Oxford University Press.

———. 2005. "Immigrant Identities and Emotion." In *A Companion to Psychological Anthropology: Modernity and Psychocultural Change*, edited by Conerly Casey and Robert B. Edgerton, 225–240. Oxford: Blackwell Publishing.

———. 2008. *Stolen Honor: Stigmatizing Muslim Men in Berlin*. Palo Alto: Stanford University Press.

Foucault, Michel. 1988. "Technologies of the Self." In *Technologies of the Self: A Seminar with Michel Foucault*, edited by Luther H. Martin, et al. Amherst: University of Massachusetts Press. Republished in Michel Foucault. 1997. *Essential Works: Ethics, Subjectivity and Truth, Vol. I*, edited by Paul Rabinow, 225. New York: New Press. http://pages.uoregon.edu/koopman/events_readings/cgc/foucault_technologies_self_vermont.pdf. Accessed 3 July 2013).

Frischkopf, Michael. 2014. "Music as Debate: Social Forces Shaping the Heterodoxy of Sufi Performance in Contemporary Egypt." In *Music, Culture and Identity in the Muslim World: Performance, Politics and Piety*, edited by Kamal Salhi. London: Routledge.

Hirschkind, Charles. 2006. *The Ethical Soundscape: Cassette Sermons and Islamic Counterpublics*. New York: Columbia University Press.

Howes, David. 2003. "Foretaste." In *Sensual Relations: Engaging the Senses in Culture and Social Theory*, 1–16. Ann Arbor: University of Michigan Press.

———, ed. 1991. *The Varieties of Sensory Experience: A Source Book in the Anthropology of the Senses*. Toronto: University of Toronto Press.

Jakobsen, Janet R., and Ann Pellegrini, eds. 2008. *Secularisms*. Durham, NC: Duke University Press.

Kapchan, Deborah. 2007. "A Colonial Relation Not My Own: Coming Home to Morocco and France." *Ethnologia Europaea: Journal of European Ethnology* 37, nos. 1–2: 115–117. Edited by Orvar Löfgren and Regina Bendix. Special Issue on "Double Homes."

———. 2008. "The Promise of Sonic Translation: Performing the Festive Sacred in Morocco." *American Anthropologist* 110, no. 4: 467–483.

———. 2009. "Singing Community/Remembering in Common: Sufi Liturgy and North African Identity in Southern France." *International Journal of Community Music* 2, no. 1: 9–23.

———. 2009a. "Learning to Listen: The Sound of Sufism in France." *World of Music* 59, no. 2: 65–90.

———. 2013. "The Aesthetics of the Invisible: Sacred Music in Secular (French) Places." *Theater Drama Review: The Journal of Performance Studies* 57, no. 3: 132–147.

———. 2015. "Body." Keywords in Sound Studies, edited by David Novak and Matt Sakakeeny. Durham, NC: Duke University Press, 33–44.

———. in progress. Slow Ethnography, Slow Activism: Listening to the Islamic Sublime.

Lévinas, Emmanuel. 1982. *En Decouvrant l'Existence avec Husserl et Heidegger*. Paris: Vren.

Mahmood, Saba. 2005. *Politics of Piety: The Islamic Revival and the Feminist Subject*. Princeton: Princeton University Press.

Nelson, Kristina. 2001. *The Art of Reciting the Qur'an*. Cairo: American University of Cairo Press.

Rancière, Jacques. 2010. Dissensus: On Politics and Aesthetics, translated by Steven Corcoran. London and New York: Bloomsbury Press.

Rasmussen, Anne. 2010. *Women's Voices, the Recited Qur'an, and Islamic Music in Indonesia*. Berkeley: University of California Press.

Santos, Boaventura De Sousa. 2011. "A Postcolonial Conception of Citizenship and Intercultural Human Rights." https://www.youtube.com/watch?v=Ref8zloyaPA. Accessed 19 June 2015.

Taylor, Charles. 2003. *Modern Social Imaginaries*. Durham, NC: Duke University Press.

———. 2007. *A Secular Age*. Cambridge, MA: Belknap Press of Harvard University Press.

Weber, Max. 2002. *The Protestant Ethic and the "Spirit" of Capitalism*. New York: Penguin.

Werbner, Pnina. 2002. *Imagined Diasporas among Manchester Muslims: The Public Performance of Pakistani Transnational Identity Politics*. London: James Currey.

———. 2003. *Pilgrims of Love: The Anthropology of a Global Sufi Cult*. London: Hurst.

CHAPTER 2

ISLAMIC POPULAR MUSIC AESTHETICS IN TURKEY

MARTIN STOKES

THIS CHAPTER EXPLORES the art of a popular religious vocalist in Turkey, Mehmet Emin Ay.[1] It explores him both as product, and shaper, of a significant moment of change. The moment of change is a long one, stretching over the last two decades. It is conventionally understood in terms of the rise to power of Recep Tayyip Erdoğan's AKP and its—currently highly conflicted—relationship with Fethullah Gülen's Hizmet movement.[2] It is a period in which the secular state has been in retreat, and religion has crept into most areas of public life—including the popular cultural field. It has also been a period of globalization and unprecedented economic growth. This chapter focuses on a handful of YouTube sites and Facebook pages featuring Mehmet Emin Ay's singing. It explores the connections between emerging senses of religious community, contemporary mass media, and the aesthetic domain. And it explores the idea that the aesthetic—understood here as the quest for beauty—might have a more productive and contributory role to social and political transformation, particularly in the Muslim world, than is usually considered to be the case.

Consider the following scene, by way of introduction. It took place in 1991. It involved a young teacher, Orhan, who became a friend during an extended visit to a small industrial city in the south of Turkey. It was a particularly unsettled moment, in retrospect. Local industry, dominated by a large iron and steel works, was at a standstill, a casualty of the first Iraq war. The national political scene had been dominated for years by rudderless coalitions, still cleaving to an official secularism that had been enforced by the military coup of 12 September 1980. The Islamist movement had yet to emerge as an electoral force. The town was festooned with banners supporting the MHP,[3] an extreme right wing nationalist party. It was clearly a moment of opportunity for them. But most people I met seemed gloomy and unhappy. Orhan was amusingly vocal in his distaste for the current state of affairs. And he seemed to be at a bit of a loose end, doing administrative chores at the local technical college while waiting for his summer leave to begin. Inevitably, I hung out with him quite a lot that summer.

I knew, from earlier conversations, that Orhan was a devotee of Said Nursi (1878–1960), a modernist mystic, known in Turkey primarily through his extensive writings.[4] The Nur movement had been outlawed early in the years of the secular republic, but its latter-day followers were then reputed to be controlling cliques within the military, government, and academia. Orhan had, at some point during our brief friendship, given up on his earlier efforts to convert me. But I like to think he enjoyed the opportunity to chat about religion and politics in Turkey as much as I did. He would hand me booklets of Said Nursi's writings every now and again. I struggled to understand them, but we nonetheless attempted to discuss them at subsequent meetings.

A copy of Mehmet Emin Ay's *Donulay* cassette was presented to me in a similar manner. I dutifully listened to the cassette. It was like nothing I had heard in Turkey before—popular in style, in Arabic, and unambiguously religious—and I didn't know what to make of it. I looked forward to an interesting discussion when we next met. But this didn't happen, exactly. Though a talkative man, Orhan had little to say, and what little he did showed signs of struggle. It was *"güzel bir ses,"* "a beautiful voice" he said, repeatedly. He liked the elegance of his Arabic diction, in particular. He had a vague sense of the singer's popularity, and of newness, of change in the air, both political and cultural. But he just didn't seem to know how all these things connected. He seemed to assume that I—specifically, perhaps, as a musician—would clarify his thinking.

This was an odd position to be in. As an ethnographer, I did not want to put words or ideas into his head. And yet here I was, being drawn into a conversation, my input solicited, and I couldn't simply sit back. I attempted to steer the conversation in simpler and more factual ethnographic directions: where he had found the cassette, what he knew about Mehmet Emin Ay, what other similar music he knew about, who he thought listened to it. But even here I ran into a brick wall.

I did scribble a few lines in my diary about this puzzling encounter, which I was to come back to, and ponder, in subsequent years. It struck me, eventually, that more had been going on in our repeated nonconversation on the subject of Mehmet Emin Ay's cassette than I had initially realized. The difficulty of the conversation, and our persistence with it probably, in fact, spoke volumes. It spoke, for instance, of a long history of religious reaction to Turkey's authoritarian secularism, of the limits of an unpersuasive nationalism, of the frustrations of relatively poor but educated young men such as Orhan stuck in the provinces at a time of rapid and divisive change. It said something, as well, about the emergence of a religious *counterpublic* in Turkey at the time, well before an official Islamist opposition to the mainstream political parties had emerged. Charles Hirschkind's exploration of cassette sermonizing and religious counterpublics in Egypt, a book I read much later, definitely rang a bell (Hirschkind 2006). Of particular interest was his explanation of why the *da'wa* movement in Egypt cultivated *listening*—listening enabled and facilitated by cassettes—at the heart of its ethical and political project. Listening drove this community, pushed it into self-awareness and action. Something similar had clearly been going on here.

This puzzled, but persistent encounter with Mehmet Emin Ay's music in 1991 also said something, in retrospect, about the role of mass media in the transformation of modern religious culture. It has been common to regard capitalism, cities, and the Industrial Revolution among the driving forces of western secularism.[5] But, as Weber showed long ago, the calculating and instrumental attitudes that shaped capitalism had their roots in "the Protestant spirit" (Weber 2002). Capitalism has, most emphatically, not banished religion. It has, rather, relied on it. So we should not be particularly surprised that the return of religion to public and political life in the late twentieth century, more or less globally, was prompted by neoliberal political programming.[6] Religious revivals everywhere have assumed forms consonant with it. That is to say they have focused on an intimate morality and ethics, on the family, and on forms of compassion and charity that neoliberals hoped would replace state welfare systems.

"Small media" technologies have generally facilitated this return over the last four decades, whether cassette recorders, personal computers, or smartphones.[7] They have mystified, effaced, and reduced the scale of the social. They have supplied compensatory imaginations of autonomy (the self at the center of a network of "friends" or of fabricated social worlds). They have enabled new forms, however limited, of spiritual, ethical, and aesthetic participation (approval by "liking" on Facebook, written response to YouTube clips, and so forth), and thus of community. They have also provided new spaces for the witnessing and affirmation of religious visions and miracles, as Paulo Apolito shows in his important study, *The Internet and the Madonna* (Apolito 2005). Such witnessing and affirmation thrives on the Internet, like other small media, which, in his view, makes "everything true to the degree that it is present," neutralizes the control of religious hierarchies, and animates all sorts of popular movements and pilgrimages. Apolito shows that the mutual entanglement of religious movements and new media technologies is far from new. Neoliberalism has simply intensified it.[8]

One element of this scene escaped my subsequent efforts to explain and understand it, efforts that had taken the form of various kinds of useful (if, by now rather conventional) social-scientific terms. This was the question of beauty. For at least some of Orhan's motivation to reach out to like-minded people, to proselytize to people like me, to try to understand and change himself, lay in the act of listening to this cassette and pondering the beauty of the voice. The qualities of beauty in this voice were not, as we have seen, immediately obvious or transparent to him. But this was not a particular problem. For Orhan, the cassette was not just a sign of his involvement with the Islamist movement, a token, as it were, of his membership in an already-existing club. Nor was it simply an object of contemplation. It, and the beauty he was reaching for, was a more unsettled and dynamic affair. It prompted further listening, conversation, reading. It played some role in *driving*, one might say, his ethical self-fashioning and sense of participation in this new political community.

A problem here is that the category of "aesthetics" is still intimately associated with the West, with high art, and with secularism. It continues to be quite difficult to talk about "aesthetics," to think about "beauty" in a Middle Eastern and Islamic context. There is the legacy of orientalism, which reduces all Middle Eastern and Islamic aesthetics (visual, musical, literary) to a kind of antiaesthetics, the aesthetics of the ornament. This was long, and mistakenly, assumed to be a response to the proscription on visual representation. From it flowed a conception of all Middle Eastern art as a response to Qur'anic proscription, as a compensation for the denial of art's "natural" representative functions and pleasures, as a symptom of a society and culture that prefers repetition and tradition to development and critical thinking, as — at the most general level — a sign of lack. The representational elements of "Islamic ornament" thus escaped western art historians for a very long time, as did complex fields of Islamic scholarly discussion and debate about it, as did the political significance of its diverse forms.[9]

Beauty is difficult to talk about in the West, too, as social scientists. The term usually implies detached contemplation, the autonomy of the artwork, the artist as creative genius. But there are other places to start. Rancière, for instance, describes the aesthetic revolution of the late eighteenth century — the construction of an overarching field of values, where, before, one appreciated a beautiful mass, a beautiful salt cellar, or a beautiful ceiling painting in rather separate, functionally distinct, ways — as a wholesale "redistribution of the sensible" (Rancière 2004). This was, as Rancière succinctly observes, "a paradigm for revolution." Beauty now could be wrought, and experienced, anywhere, even, or particularly, where one least expected to find it. The aesthetic, in Rancière's view, connected artistic production directly with the political claims of the republic, with the ideals of egalitarianism, and with the self-actualization of "the people."

This strikes me as being a useful way to think about Orhan's questions about this voice. The sensory order of the secular republic was being overturned, "redistributed" by a new generation of politically conscious musicians, artists, activists, and consciousness-raisers associated with the emerging Islamist movement. Before, art, literature, and music had had a drab, unremarkable presence on the remote peripheries of Orhan's field of vision, on the state radio and television, in galleries, concerts, and expensive bookstores in big cities. But something had happened to upset that scheme of things. "Beauty," something Orhan had clearly found laughably remote from this deeply depressed little industrial city, had suddenly found its way into his everyday world in the banal yet entirely unexpected form of a borrowed cassette. It contributed to his sense of change on the air. It also drove him to participate in it. The act of sharing it, discussing it, and drawing a complete stranger into conversation about it—myself—was a simple instantiation of exactly this kind of participation.

How, then, do such fleeting and micro-participatory quests for beauty in a small Turkish city connect with the mobilization of a religious movement that would win elections, dominate Turkey, and oversee a period of unprecedented regional power? Once the political work of this new religious pop was done, did it disappear, or run out of creative energy, or become routinized, part of a new status quo? Did it spawn other genres, or continue to mobilize emergent, and perhaps dissident, communities? The questions are not easy to answer, but they hang over this field of popular cultural mobilization, in Turkey, as elsewhere. Bear them in mind as I discuss, in the next section, some aspects of Mehmet Emin Ay's life, his music, and the responses of his listeners.

MEHMET EMIN AY

Mehmet Emin Ay was born in Van, in the far east of the country, in 1963.[10] His father was a state-appointed Qur'an reciter in this predominantly Kurdish city. He grew up with the sounds of Istanbul's Qur'an reciters in his ears—Halis Albayrak, Fatih Çollak, Mustafa Öztürk—a tradition he still maintains. After graduating from Van's Imam-Hatip high school,[11] he moved with his parents to Bursa in the west of the country. He completed his studies there, writing a PhD at Bursa's Uludağ University on Islamic pedagogy, and, in due course being appointed professor at the Faculty of Theology there. In 2011 he was appointed to the Bursa *müftülük*, a post involving responsibility for state religious policy across the province. In recent years, he has gained a reputation as a preacher at Bursa's Edebali mosque. The picture is, then, one of a provincial but educated, well-connected, upwardly mobile, media-savvy cosmopolitan; very much, in other words, a product of the AK Party years.

His recording career began with a few one-off cassette hits in the 1990s, such as *Imam Hatiplim* and *Dolunay* containing Arabic and Turkish *kaside* (sung poetry).[12] He founded Beyza Yapım with Mustafa Demirci in 1998 for the purposes of recording and distributing their own music.[13] The two musicians tend to think of their work as a mixture of Turkish classical music and *tasavvuf* music ("mysticism," meaning, in this context, popular and connected with the Sufi lodges). They have emphatically rejected association with Turkish Arabesk, meaning, in their understanding, folk-derived mass-mediated music for the urban *lumpenproletariat* loosely modeled on Egyptian originals (see Stokes 2010 for a recent discussion of "the Arabesk debate"). But their vocal style and studio sound clearly owes something to Arabesk: lively rhythm, large string choruses, a rich array of western and Middle Eastern instruments in the mix, an emotional vocal style. And like Arabesk, this is music that is put together in a recording studio and generally reaches listeners via mass media.

Mehmet Emin Ay and Mustafa Demirci's songs are generally strophic, interspersed with vocal improvisations (*kaside* or *gazel*). They use a relatively circumscribed set of musical modes (*makam*), drawing from a repertoire that echoes that of the Arabesk-dominated market. Meters are generally duple, as in Arabesk. The agglutinative or "additive" meters common in Turkish folk and classical music are, in other words, not to be found. And as with Arabesk, too, the spoken word is prominent. Many of the CDs, such as the "Taleal Bedru Aleyna" track on *Dolunay* or the first track on *Nûru'l-Hüdâ*, have long spoken introductions, translating, explaining, or contextualizing the lyrics.

Musicians who take themselves seriously in Turkey all have to distance themselves from Arabesk, even as they embrace its stylistic norms as a basic condition of intelligibility and marketability. What *is* surprising in this context, though, is the depth and extent of Mehmet Emin Ay's engagement with the Egyptian popular repertoire of the 1950s and 60s—the music of Umm Kulthum, Muhammad 'Abd al-Wahhab, and 'Abd al-Halim Hafiz. As with many who grew up in Turkey's border regions, where Turkish state broadcasting does not enjoy a monopoly, and as with many of the key names in early Arabesk such as Orhan Gencebay, he has a lively understanding of and familiarity with the musical cultures of Turkey's southern and eastern neighbors. This knowledge informed his pronunciation of Arabic, his vocal improvisations, his intonation of *makam*-s and his sense of what, musically speaking, stirs, excites, and moves. On some CDs, such as *Nûru'l-Hüdâ*, this Egyptian frame of reference is quite explicit, prompting extensive discussion in our interview. Though firmly grounded in Turkish classical music, popular hymn (*ilahi*) singing and the popular styles that had held sway in Turkey since the 1980s, this was music that located itself self-consciously in a broader Middle Eastern and Islamic context.

The Beyza Yapım project also has a consistently didactic tone. The lyrics in Mehmet Emin Ay and Mustafa Demirci's compositions come from diverse sources, often exploring, or reviving, a particular verse form.[14] Others focus on specific devotional practices, such as *tesbîhât* (prayers recited with prayer beads, or rosary).[15] Yet others thematize the work of a particular poet, such as Seyyid Osman Hulûsî (1914–1990), or Mevlana Celalettin Rumi (founder of the Mevlevi Sufi order, known to the West as the "whirling dervishes").[16] Listeners are, among other things, being taught about their, that is, the Turkish, religious musical, and poetic heritage, and shown how it might be made meaningful in a contemporary media context.

Mehmet Emin Ay told me that one of the rationales for *Nûru'l-Hüdâ* was the feeling that many in Turkey are ignorant of the rich heritage of Arabic spiritual poetry—a consequence of nationalist secularism. A great deal, he felt, could be achieved by presenting some well-chosen selections in a familiar and popular musical idiom. In a similar vein he spoke about how few people in Turkey actually knew of Mevlana Celalettin Rumi's poetry, despite claiming him as a national treasure. Rumi's poetry had, arguably at that point, become the highly rarified preserve of a handful of scholars in Turkey with a Persian-language literary training. *Aşkın Kanatları: The Wings of Love*, was an attempt to popularize Rumi's work in a Turkish musical context. Mehmet Emin Ay's compositions on this and other CDs popularize, translate, and inform a listenership assumed, in the early years of AK party power, to be inclined to Islamic mystical culture but badly in need of instruction.

This describes the broad musical, historical, and political context of the Mehmet Emin Ay project. What, though, does it mean to those who listen? What are its particular qualities of beauty, enchantment, emotional engagement? How have such qualities related to piety, community, and the Islamist movement in Turkey? And through what performative means were such qualities forged, attributed meaning, and connected with the movement and the community? Cassette technology, as we have already seen, was important early in the process, meaning private and discrete circulation, relatively unsupervised by the state. In recent years, file sharing on the web, and more recently, social networking sites have constituted the most important sites of music consumption. The lengthy conversations attached to YouTube clips and Facebook pages, complex as they are as a source of information, provide a vital snapshot of these performative processes.

A YOUTUBE CLIP

By way of a relatively early example, consider a YouTube clip of Mehmet Emin Ay's "O Gece Sendin Gelen" (It Was You Who Came That Night).[17] This highly popular song, dating from a few years before, has had over a million-and-a-half views since it was posted on YouTube on 18 September 2006. The words are by Cengiz Numanoğlu, a retired army officer also resident in Bursa. The instrumental backing is provided by frame drum, keyboard, strings, and *fasıl kemençesi* (a classical fiddle). The musical structure comprises an ascending verse and a descending sequence (the words, translated from the Turkish: "He whose name is written in light on the domes of the throne of God / He whose name is "Ahmed" in heaven, and "Muhammed" on earth"). The next verse is in a higher register ("As torrents of light descended from the seven heavens / it was you who came, from eternity / As the angels announced the good news from the Truth / it was you who came, O Prophet Muhammed"). The lyrics express devotional thoughts in simple rhymes, referring to the Miraç, the Prophet's mystical journey into the heavens. The visuals show birds, insects, flowers, clouds, trees, waterfalls, historic mosques, and praying hands. It is a well-crafted song with a catchy tune and a warmly emotional style of delivery. It is not hard to see why it has been so popular and generated a relatively large amount of online commentary—some 305 comments, a great deal of "liking" and sharing, and tribute performances uploaded from mobile phones from as far afield as Turkmenistan. A significant rise in viewing figures from 2009 onward, and an intensification of online commentary, probably reflects mobile phone downloading.

This commentary has two important dimensions. One might be described as constituting community through the act of listening together online. Many comments locate the listener by mentioning place, or name, or locating oneself through language. Listeners indicate, for example, that they are from Bosnia, Germany, Iraq, and elsewhere. Turkish is the medium of communication, but clearly not always as a first language, and not necessarily Istanbul Turkish. Others simply respond with prayer formulae, a direct way of affirming moral presence common in everyday social interaction. These range from short ("*allah razı olsun kardeşim,*" "May God accept it, brother") or "*elhamdülillah*" (roughly, "Praise Be!" or "*amin,*" "amen"), to more elaborate formulations ("There is no God but God and Muhammed is his prophet, thousands of prayers for the Lord of Creation"; "Peace be with you. May the enlightenment of these days be with you, their mercy on your past, their blessings on your house, their light on our life in eternity, and their warmth fill your homes. May your *Kandil* festival be blessed").

Often listeners engage in direct conversation with one another. Sometimes this takes the form of arguments. "Frknyesilyurt" evokes an old debate: "It is a sin to listen to *ilahi*[18] with instruments. Please don't forget that this is a sin and try to share *ilahi*-s '*muziksiz*,' 'without music' (i.e., musical instruments). "Fatihunal" immediately replies, "Dear God, grant harmony and cooperation to my Muslim brothers, grant victory over the unbelievers, do not give those who wish to create strife an opportunity to do so" (i.e., "please let's not argue about this"). "Umahta54" writes "I guess I'm some kind of atheist or something, but, man, this really is a very beautiful *ilahi*." This draws an immediate response from "orhan nusret," who chides this person for declaring himself an atheist when he is so clearly and evidently moved by religious verse and music. "Listen and maybe you'll discover something about yourself," he suggests. "Monodias" launches into dense theological discussion, complete with reference to the hadith commentaries of Buhari and Muslim, of the idea of intercession (*Şefaat*). To call on the Prophet in the way this song does, "Monodias" implies, is to invest the Prophet with a capacity to intercede on the Day of Judgment, which in his view is "*ARACILIK, SIRK, KÜFÜR*" ("mediation, idolatry, nonbelief," upper case letters in the original). "YeniCheery" and "Murat Yüksel" are quick to contest this, with hadith references of their own. "Murat Yüksel," for his part, concludes that denying the Prophet's example of mercy is itself a kind of *küfür*, and warns: "*Çok ince bir çizgidesin dikkat!!!*" (roughly: "You're on thin ice here, be careful!!!"). A crescendo of argument follows, in uppercase letters, the song itself clearly little more than an excuse to argue about other things.

Some simply acknowledge the contributions of those writing in: "a beautiful melody. May God accept it and be pleased with those singing and those adding comments here . . ." Others reflect on the collectivity of the project more generally, and in ways that include the commentator-listeners as well as the musicians, like "Mehmet Bozkürt" "May God accept it; amen from all those who have given voice and contributed their labor . . ." Many of these comments constitute a kind of phatic communication, in other words, less an exchange of information or ideas than a means of establishing the presence of ethically and conversationally engaged co-auditors. Other responses describe emotional and aesthetic states. Some are short and simple, communicating terms of aesthetic engagement. These range from simple expressions of appreciation—"*tek kelimeyle super*" (in a word, superb), or "*muazzam*" (fab), "*Harika Ses . . . Harika Yorum . . . Harika Müzik . . .*" (Great Voice . . . Great Interpretation . . . Great Music . . .), "*ağzınıza*" or "*yüreğinize sağlık*" (Good health to your mouth, or your heart), to more emphatic and lengthy declarations, such as "Mehmet Emin Ay, you are superb, you sing so beautifully that you put people into a trance . . ." Some refer to specific qualities of voice: "forgive our sins O Lord . . . a wonderful voice and a wonderful wailing (*haykırış*) . . ."; "Yes, a very beautiful *ilahi*, besides which Mehmet Emin Ay's voice is gentle (*yumuşak*) and really suits these *ilahi*-s." Others note the singer's purity of heart: "good health to his mouth and his pure (*temiz*) heart, may God accept it, may God accept those who give us the opportunity to hear such beautiful *ilahi*-s, my brother."

A number refer explicitly to emotional states and particularly the act of weeping while listening. "Excellent . . . I couldn't stop crying while listening. May God accept it" (i.e., either the song or this person's tears). "I was really touched (*etkilendim*). May God accept it." "Cry, soul, perhaps you'll come to your senses." "May God forgive us all our sins. Amen. I never got tired of this and wept while listening. A song I'll never get bored of." A contributor who refers to herself as "Moslimkiz" (Muslimgirl) writes in twice: "The *ilahi* is superb, you know, may God accept it. I listen to it at least twice a day and weep." "Greetings. Happy Regaip Kandili to you all, my brothers, may God hear your prayers. May God accept it, a really beautiful song. Every time I listen to it my eyes fill with tears. O Muhammad—peace be upon him!— O Prophet!" "Kurt Koni" says s/he has become "*mesd*" (i.e., Turkish "*mest*"); filled with a kind of sentimental, tearful, sadness, a word often used in a secular context; as if noticing this, s/he immediately adds "May God accept it."

These early online exchanges configured an aesthetic and ethical field intimately linked to the emergence of the Islamist movement in Turkey and AK party governmentality. The key aesthetic and ethical terms, to step back slightly from the dense conversational and argumentative tone of the YouTube commentary, are love (*sevgi*), soulfulness (*gönül*), sincerity (*temizlik*), tears (*gözyaşları*), remembrance (*zikr*), and the beauty (*güzellik*) of composition (*ezgi*) and voice (*ses*). To a certain extent, these are traditional terms, terms with a long and deep history in Turkish Sufism.[19] But new meanings and usages are being forged in these exchanges, and being attached to new musical styles and new media technologies in a spirit of curiosity, excitement, and inquiry. YouTube commentary, I've suggested, provided a convenient space in which this could happen, allowing not just the circulation of the song, but public debate and discussion to take place in ways that left a trace and a record. Community, and a sense of aesthetic and ethical mission, takes shape in the process.

A FACEBOOK PAGE

Was this to continue into the Facebook era? In the eight years since the You-Tube posting of the "O Gece Sendin Gelen" video, Mehmet Emin Ay has risen impressively in national academic and religious hierarchies. It is not surprising, then, that Facebook commentary on his Edebali Mosque Facebook page, has a different feel.[20] It usually addresses him directly, whether to praise the song or the singing, or to ask questions about the music, for example. No longer is the music simply an opportunity to emote or argue or pursue general questions about musical aesthetics and spiritual legitimacy.

Some of the questions are amusingly trivial. On Mehmet Emin Ay's "Asr-i Şerif" page, "Cebrail Yigit" writes in to tell the singer that he can't download the file. Eight minutes later, he has written in again to say that he now figured out how to do it. Others make requests for old songs to be put up on the site. Yet others ask for information about Mehmet Emin Ay's "*sohbet*-s" (informal online sermons, or "conversations") related to some theme or another in the song. A more prosaic tone prevails, in other words. The language used to describe spiritual, emotional, and aesthetic reaction is also relatively limited. Appreciative comments often comprise little more than "*Allah razı olsun*," "may God accept it." The novelty of online comment has, as that of the music itself, perhaps worn off, and the number of accumulated responses is significantly lower. There is a great deal of "liking" and "sharing," on the other hand, both constituting easy and routine ways of reacting emotionally and aesthetically, and extending one's reactions to the community. So one no longer encounters the rich, extensive, and expressive web of commentary and emotionality that characterized the YouTube response to "O Gece Sendin Gelen."

In other ways, though, the musical content of these Facebook pages is significantly richer. Gathered under "Mehmet Emin Ay's videos" on the Facebook page, one finds Qur'anic recitations, *naat-i şerif*-s, television interviews, sermons, *sohbet*-s, clips from concerts, and songs old and new. 4G technology, now ubiquitous in Turkey, has made lengthy high-resolution recordings the norm, and has enabled people to circulate clips between television sets, personal computers, and the smartphones in their pockets. Facebook brings this together for users in a conveniently gathered format. Instead of embarking on a rambling and serendipitous search via Google and YouTube sidebars, one can now find as many examples of Mehmet Emin's vocal art as one could possibly desire simply by following a few links from the Edebali mosque's main Facebook page.

This has provided a very different contextualization and framing of Mehmet Emin Ay's religious pop songs. They are now gathered in a broader field, comprising unambiguously legitimate vocal practices such as sermonizing (*vaaz*), Qur'anic recitation (*tilavet*), and vocal praise forms such as *na'at*. Doubts about the legitimacy of the music, or questions about the theological implications of the lyrics, are thus more difficult to sustain. The visitor to the Facebook page is met by an unambiguously respected and senior figure, shown lecturing, or being interviewed, or preaching. Religious pop in Turkey no longer appears to be a curiosity, a provocation of secularists, or an experimental practice, constantly in need of justification and commentary. It is simply one form of outreach and consciousness-raising among many.

Religious pop is also now embedded in live performance practice. Performance practice earlier in the life of this popular religious song movement was often fraught with difficulties. On stage, it could be difficult to control showbusiness elements, cued by an audience's enthusiasm and applause. Audiences themselves might not be sure exactly how to react, given the newness of this genre. Sound recording engineers could not always be relied on to mix the sound in a way that foregrounded voice (and thus message) and kept backing instruments (which might obscure the message and thus always be morally dubious) in check. Backing instrumentalists, often professionals from the secular world, could not always be relied on to present an appropriately spiritual demeanor in the performance itself (see Stokes 2013).

The Facebook page features a clip from a concert promoting some of his and Mustafa Demir's *Aşkın Kanatları* CD material, probably late in the 2000s (posted in 2011). The song featured is "Sultanım" (My Sultan), a sentimental number, in a somewhat westernized form. A jazzy piano and string quartet are prominent at the opening; the sound of *ney* (flute), *kanun* (zither), and *'ud* (lute) take over in the verse sections, with more of an Arabesk/Turkish pop feel. Having seen them in performance—and in a performance that had clearly dissatisfied them—in 2006, I was struck by how far live concert performance of this genre had progressed. The singers seem relaxed and confident. The studio audience is warm and enthusiastic but appropriately restrained. The backing musicians are disciplined and seem to know exactly what they are doing. Performance practice conventions had clearly materialized by the time of the clip, in other words. So Facebook allows Mehmet Emin Ay to circulate an example of good practice, one that—he must have felt—had successfully negotiated the potential problems of religious musical performance, controllable in the studio, but much less so in live situations.

Finally, one is struck by the relative localness of response to clips. A number of postings request information about local events and even what busses to catch to the Edebali mosque. Facebook response seems to be far less absorbed by the question of *place* than the YouTube responses. When place is mentioned, the tone is pragmatic and factual. There are various postings from people in migrant communities. "Meryem Kabaagac," for instance, attaches a message to the "Sultanım" clip expressing the hope that the vocalists might visit their (migrant) community in Belgium and honor them with a live performance. One occasionally hears from listeners elsewhere in the Turkish-speaking world, something one can determine from names and the way in which Turkish words are romanized. But the overall impression is much more local. Non-Turkish commentators do not draw attention to their non-Turkishness, as was the case in the YouTube commentaries.

There are various possible reasons for this. Mehmet Emin Ay has clearly become something of a local celebrity, with a strong local following. Professional responsibilities mean less time, and less need, to travel, to give concerts, to work the media. Bursa is the center of his world. No longer is he quite the cosmopolitan he once was, eliciting the same kind of cosmopolitan response. The genre no longer has the novelty value it once did. Others have been working in similar or related fields, particularly on Islamist media. The arguments have settled. So there is no longer quite the sense of *national* discussion about this music, a discussion that might provoke acts of location within the nation and its diasporas. And finally, Facebook members are placed and place-able by the system. One simply clicks on a name to have access to profile pictures, timelines, likes and dislikes, places of birth, study, and occupation. If one wants to know more, one can send a friend request. Routine statements *locating* the speaker—texting, Tweeting, e-mailing, and Facebook posting, as many of us do day and night—now feel surplus to requirements, a waste of time and energy. So in this particular media space, the community of fellow listeners has become implicit and increasingly invisible, not explicit and visible.

Mehmet Emin Ay's music still circulates online and brings a community into being. But it circulates in different ways. No longer is it debated and discussed. No longer does it involve an insistence on place. No longer does it elicit responses stressing emotion and tearfulness. An element of routine has evidently crept in. Experimentalism has shifted to other areas of musical life in Turkey, to Islamic psychedelia, Islamic trance and electronica, Islamic metal. The Facebook page suggests a moment of political, cultural, and technological accommodation, one that has made this music, and its ethical project, more or less invisible once again.

CONCLUSION

The Islamist movement has been the major dynamo of Turkish social, cultural, and political life over the last twenty years. It has drawn its strength, buoyancy, and legitimacy from a sense of participation, and of cultural dynamism. The music of Mehmet Emin Ay has been an integral part of this. I have tried to show, in this chapter, how the music has not simply functioned as a sound-track to a political and economic transformation. It has been part of that very transformation, forging community and senses of participation. A component of that transformation, I have tried to suggest, has been an aesthetic quest, a quest for beauty in the drab hinterlands of Turkish modernity, in the lives of people like Orhan, with whom I began.

The quest for beauty in this particular space has not been straightforward. I have tried to demonstrate how communities of listeners struggle to attach meaning and ethical value to beauty, as encountered in Mehmet Emin Ay's music, through the important medium of YouTube and Facebook pages. The struggle, I have suggested, has produced a conversation, and the sharing of thoughts and feelings. A sense of community has taken shape in this conver-sation, and in this sharing. This has been a community very much in tune with the values of the AKP/Gülen hegemony. It consequently finds support and validation in many other areas of life. These have been national values — extending, as we have seen, beyond the Turkish nation-state to Turkish and Turkic speakers elsewhere, in the diasporas of Western Europe, in Central Asia, and across Balkan and Arab lands. These have been intimate values — shaped in the imagination of families listening together over *ramazan* meals, or of lonely young people sharing virtual tears on computers in university dorms. And they have been values that attach importance to beauty, imag-ined in Islamic terms, but as an ethical, civic, community-forging project, and not (as orientalists have imagined in the past) as arabesque, ornament, and decoration.

These are conservative values, consonant with more or less global patterns of neoliberal governmentality, well adapted to the media systems and commu-nication technologies of the early twenty-first century. They shape the kinds of "docile agency" Saba Mahmood noticed some time ago in her studies of the Egyptian Islamist movement (Mahmood 2001). This is to say, agency con-ceived in terms of submission to religious ideas and the cultivation of modesty, but agency nonetheless — oriented to collective struggle and political transfor-mation. Whether in Turkey, Egypt, or elsewhere in the Muslim world, these have been conservative revolutions, achieved through consumerism and the ballot box. But revolutions nonetheless.

Culture — and the quest for beauty — rarely plays a simple role, though. We search for beautiful and moving things, but do not always find them, or agree on what we find, or know what to do when we do. The energies involved in this quest are peculiarly volatile, and peculiarly hard to understand, particularly from the point of view of social science (as Elaine Scarry argues; Scarry 2001). Long periods of time may pass in which the quest for beauty is captured by the status quo, a capture aided by communication technologies that routinizes argument and discussion, and that limits alternative visions and mobilizations. This might, indeed, be said of religious pop on YouTube and Facebook during Turkey's AKP/Gülen years. But such "capture" is the product of a historical moment. It is not immune to pressure. People retain memories of earlier moments, moments of sensory redistribution—recall Rancière's characterization of the aesthetic—when new sounds, in unexpected places, generated excitement, comment, and conversation. Communication technologies change, opening up new spaces of conversation that can quickly become dissent. Hegemonies weaken as a result of internal contradictions. Religious pop in Turkey may have played a role in consolidating the AKP/Gülen hegemony in recent years and may well have become a commonplace, routinized, and unremarkable aspect of it. But the aesthetic and ethical values that motivated it may well lead in different directions in the future.

NOTES

1. I am grateful to Mehmet Emin Ay for spending time with me in 2006, answering my questions graciously, and discussing a draft of an earlier article I wrote about him (Stokes 2013). I am also grateful to Mustafa Demirci for making time to chat with me in the Beyza Yapım studios and for giving me a set of all of their CDs.

2. The Adalet ve Kalkınma Partisi, led by Recep Tayyip Erdoğan, came to power in the national elections of 2002. The Hizmet movement, led by Fethullah Gülen, a preacher turned media magnate currently based in Miami, is, loosely, an offshoot of the Nur movement discussed elsewhere in this chapter. It is a conservative nationalist piety movement, strongly represented in various areas of the Turkish state apparatus and particularly in the education system.

3. The *Milliyetçi Hareket Partisi*, the National Action Party, founded in 1969 by Alparslan Türkeş. It was banned at the time of the 1980 military coup but reformed and renamed itself before eventually coming back to its old name in 1992. At the time of writing it is the third-largest political party in Turkey.

4. For the definitive sociological account, see Mardin 1989.

5. Marx and Engels considered, for instance, that slum life in the industrial cities would mean that the working class would more quickly come to understand the exploitation they shared, and thus shed the mental bonds that held them in place, primarily religion. See, in particular, *The Communist Manifesto* (Marx and Engels 1848/2011).

6. By neoliberalism, I mean, roughly, the prioritization of global finance systems, the dismantlement of state welfare systems, and the relentless evocation of threats to "security." See Balakrishnan on the "market state," Balakrishnan 2003.

7. See Manuel 1989 on cassette culture in India. On new media and mobilization in the Middle East, see Eickelman and Anderson (eds.) 1999.

8. Important religious movements in the Muslim Middle East early in the twentieth cen-

tury have not so much reacted *against* modern, administrative, and mass-mediated senses of the self and of the community as, themselves, employed thoroughly modern, administrative, and mass-mediated modes of organization and proselytizing. See Gilsenan's study of the Hamidiyya al-Shadhiliyya in Egypt (Gilsenan 1973), and Mardin's study of the Nur Movement in Turkey (Mardin 1989).

9. See, in particular, Necipoğlu 1995, Gonzalez 2002, and Grabar 1992 for important contributions to the debates over ornament and geometrical design in Islamic aesthetics.

10. This and the next section are a condensed and updated version of sections in Stokes 2013.

11. Imam-Hatip Lycees were state institutions developed during the late 1980s, providing secondary education with an emphasis on religious training.

12. *Kaside* (Arabic *qasidah*) in this context means free rhythm vocalizations on religious poetry couplets, usually in Arabic.

13. Beyza Yapım also marketed some non-Turkish musicians, such as Sami Yusuf, and a variety of Turkish talent oriented to the pious market (including, for example, Taner Demiralp, Hakan Oral, Ceyhun Çelik, Başar Dikici, Göksel Baktagir).

14. For example, *nât*-s (or *nât-ı şerifler*, songs praising the Prophet, which feature in the *Nât-ı Şerifler: Gül-i Ruhsâr* and *Güle Sevda: Nât-ı Şerifler* CDs) or *münacaat*-s (a musical prayer or supplication, which feature in *Beyaz Dilekçe*). Neglected verse forms are revived, such as the Ottoman *kaside* by Sultan Abdülhamit I, to be found on *Nûru'l-Hüdâ*.

15. Litanies based on God's ninety-nine names, the *esmâ'ül-hüsna*, as featured in the *Namaz Tesbîhâtı* and *Aşkı Mevlâ: Esmâ 'ül-Hüsna* 99 CDs.

16. As in *Hulûs-i Kalb*, or Mevlana Celalettin Rumi, as in *Aşkın Kanatları: The Wings of Love*. On contemporary Mevlevi music, see Vicente 2014.

17. http://www.youtube.com/watch?v=J5lPbibKpqU. Accessed on 9 February 2014.

18. Roughly, "hymns," *ilahi* are popular strophic songs for communal singing, usually in Sufi or other devotional context, though never during official prayers. Mehmet Emin Ay's compositions are usually referred to with this term.

19. See, on Bektashism, Birge 1937, on Mevlevism, Vicente 2013.

20. https://www.facebook.com/media/set/?set=vb.137060336342925&type=2. Accessed 9 February 2014. For Mehmet Emin Ay's official web page, see https://www.facebook.com /mehmeteminayhoca. Accessed 9 February 2014.

REFERENCES

Appolito, Paolo. 2005. *The Internet and the Madonna*. Chicago: Chicago University Press.
Balakrishnan, Ghopal. 2003. "Algorithms of War." *New Left Review* 23. http://newleftreview .org/II/23/gopal-balakrishnan-algorithms-of-war.
Birge, John. 1937. *The Bektashi Order of Dervishes*. London: Luzac Oriental.
Eickelman, Dale, and Jon Anderson. 2003. *New Media and the Muslim World: The Emerging Public Sphere*. Bloomington: Indiana University Press.
Gilsenan, Michael. 1973. *Saint and Sufi in Modern Egypt: An Essay in the Sociology of Religion*. Oxford: Clarendon Press.
Gonzalez, Virginia. 2002. *Beauty and Islam: Aesthetics in Islamic Art and Architecture*. London: IB Tauris.
Grabar, Oleg. 1992. *The Mediation of Ornament*. Princeton: Princeton University Press.

Hirschkind, Charles. 2006. *The Ethical Soundscape: Cassette Sermons and Islamic Counterpublics*. New York: Columbia University Press.

Mahmood, Saba. 2001. "Feminist Theory, Embodiment and the Docile Agent: Some Reflections on the Egyptian Islamic Revival." *Cultural Anthropology* 16, no. 2: 202–236.

Manuel, Peter. 1993. *Cassette Culture: Popular Music and Technology in India*. Chicago: Chicago University Press.

Mardin, Şerif. 1989. *Religion and Social Change in Modern Turkey*. Albany: State University of New York Press.

Marx, Karl, and F. Engels. 2011 (1848). *The Communist Manifesto*. Harmondsworth: Penguin.

Necipoğlu, Gülrü. 1995. *The Topkapı Scroll: Geometry and Ornament in Islamic Architecture*. Santa Monica, CA: The Getty Center for the History of Art and the Humanities.

Rancière, Jacques. 2004. *The Politics of Aesthetics*. London: Continuum.

Scarry, Elain. 2001. *On Beauty and Being Just*. Princeton: Princeton University Press.

Stokes, Martin. 2010. *The Republic of Love: Cultural Intimacy in Turkish Popular Music*. Chicago: University of Chicago Press.

———. 2013. "New Islamist Popular Culture in Turkey." In *Music, Culture and Identity in the Muslim World: Performance, Politics and Piety*, edited by K. Salhi. London: Routledge.

Vicente, Victor. 2013. *Dancing for Rumi: The Cultural, Spiritual, and Kinetic Dimensions of the Global Sufi Music Phenomenon*. Saarbrucken: Lambert Academic Publishing.

Weber, Max. 2002 (1905). *The Protestant Ethic and the Spirit of Capitalism and Other Writings*. Harmondsworth: Penguin.

CHAPTER 3

THEATER OF IMMEDIACY: PERFORMANCE
ACTIVISM AND ART IN THE ARAB UPRISINGS

MARK LEVINE AND BRYAN REYNOLDS

TARIQ AL-TAYIB MUHAMMAD BUʿAZIZI (hereafter referred to by the more common French spelling "Bouazizi") was a street vendor in the provincial Tunisian town of Sidi Bouzid whose self-immolation on 17 December 2010 sparked the Tunisian Revolution and the collection of uprisings, revolutions, counterrevolutions, and civil wars that have rocked the Arab world for the last four years. After surviving in a coma for eighteen days with severe burns covering almost his entire body, he died on 4 January 2011.

We will never know for certain how Bouazizi understood the act of pouring gasoline over his body and lighting himself on fire. What is clear is that Bouazizi's self-immolation became an highly inspirational example of radical anti-government performance activism,[1] one staged in response to the emotional and allegedly physical injury he suffered at the hands of a corrupt and brutal government embodied, in this instance, in the guise of a municipal official named Faida Hamdi. According to the now legendary story, she and two policemen attempted to extort money from him. When he complained, she slapped him, and they confiscated his cart and scales.

Immediately after the altercation, Bouazizi went to the office of Sidi Bouzid's governor to complain and request the return of his possessions. The governor refused to see him, even after, according to witnesses, he declared, "If you don't see me, I'll burn myself." Ignored, he soon departed but quickly returned with a can of gasoline. Standing in the middle of the road, he drenched himself, shouted "How do you expect me to make a living?!," and set himself ablaze.[2] All the events, from Bouazizi's confrontation with police and municipal officials to his self-immolation, occurred in less than an hour. News of what happened spread like wildfire throughout Sidi Bouzid, and within hours angry protesters riddled the streets. Given that Bouazizi's self-immolation was in fact the third one within the space of a few weeks across Tunisia, many have wondered why his act sparked a revolution whereas the previous public suicides did not.

One reason is that his act was photographed by someone with a mobile phone camera and then mass-circulated via cell phones and the Internet in a swift flurry that completely escaped the control of the Tunisian government, then one of the world's most notorious regulators of Internet access.[3] The images of the flaming man captured in the now iconic photos (see figures 3.1 and 3.2) were quintessentially "auratic," which is to say, exhibiting an affective energy that forges solidarities between all those experiencing them: the power of the photos literally leapt from cell phones and computer screens, demanding a response from those who encountered it commensurate with the courageousness and agony of the victim/performer.

Bouazizi's self-immolation prompted many other men and women to carry out similar acts across the Arab world, including at least one Moroccan woman, Fadoua Laroui, who became known as the "Moroccan Bouazizi."[4] Perhaps none were more important than that of Bouazizi's friend, Hussein Lahsin Neji. Just a few days after Bouazizi's suicide, he went to a protest at the local offices of the UGTT (Union générale tunisienne du travail, Tunisia's state-sponsored labor union), snuck behind a police line, climbed to the top of an electricity pylon, and electrocuted himself spectacularly in protest against the governmental system that had done nothing to recognize the meaning of his friend's sacrifice.[5] While Bouazizi gets most of the attention—and resentment as well—it could be argued that it was Neji's equally dramatic self-"martyrdom" (as many Tunisians describe these actions) that added enough heat for the revolutionary fire to catch.

At the same time, the mise-en-scène of Sidi Bouzid, a nondescript town in the heart of the poorest and most agriculturally focused region of Tunisia, provided the protests with much greater saliency than would have accrued to them if they had occurred in the capital, Tunis, or another major urban center. It was precisely the intimacy of the act, occurring in a small town where, as one activist put it, "everyone is someone's cousin," that helped engender such anger and sympathy for the victims.[6]

In the weeks and months after Bouazizi's and Neji's deaths (and they were preceded and followed by other, lesser known self-martyrdoms, many of which were acts of self-immolation), all sorts of phrases and intentions were attributed to their actions and to the protesters that took to the streets in defense of their memory. Bouazizi is supposed to have shouted "*shughul, huriyya, wa karama wataniyya!*" ("work, freedom, and national dignity!"), as he took his final steps, whereas the chants of the protesters that grew in the wake of

3.1. Mohamed Bouazizi in flames. Photographer unknown.

3.2. Mohamed Bouazizi visited by President Ben Ali. Getty Images.

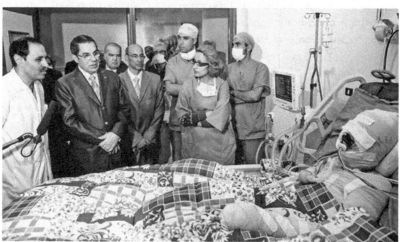

their deaths marked the first utterances that people around the world can re-member of the now celebrated demand that became the mantra that reverber-ated heroically throughout the Arab uprisings beginning with the first protests in Tunisia: "The people want the downfall of the system" ("*ash-sha'ab yurid isqat al-nizam*").

But even these actions and slogans were not merely spontaneous bursts of political genius. Rather, they were the result of a deep wave of societal maturation, which saw a new generation come of age in Tunisia, Egypt, and to a sometimes tragically lesser extent, elsewhere across the Arab world, which was no longer afraid of its aging and progressively more out-of-touch leaders. In the weeks between Bouazizi's self-immolation and his death, protests became increasingly aggressive and violent, and after he died they rapidly spread throughout the nation, including the wealthy areas of the capital. By 14 January, a half-century old political order had largely collapsed; as President Zine El Abidine Ben Ali fled the country with his family after supposedly being tricked by the head of his presidential security team into thinking a coup was imminent.[7]

As their significance amplified through the media, Bouazizi's actions continued to inspire many self-immolations across the Arab world and Europe, with one hundred and seven taking place in Tunisia alone within the six months following his death.[8] In Egypt, at least three self-immolations occurred in the weeks after Bouazizi's, including one in Cairo by a restaurant owner named 'Abdu 'Abd al-Mon'im Ja'afar (his name is also reported as Abdo Abdel Hameed), whose Bouazizi-modeled self-immolation was rooted in a failure to get much needed food coupons for his restaurant. As he burned, Ja'afar purportedly screamed, "The security of the State of the State Security, my right subconscious is lost by air (inside) of the State."[9] This was a powerful if seemingly unintelligible—and yet, if read a certain way, comprehensible—attack on the manner in which a government imposes a "state of exception" upon the vast majority of the population, which is when the government suspends the laws normally constraining its use of coercion and violence on the citizens. In effect, the citizens' continued entanglement with and dependence on the state often becomes fiercely schizophrenic.

As a result of being pulled in two or more directions at once, such as for and against the government, this schizoid dynamic moves the population toward the kind of break that, at least for a moment, has revolutionary potential.[10] A direct and major consequence of this action was to motivate a young 6 April Youth Movement activist named Asmaa Mahfouz to record a YouTube video that is famous for advancing the Egyptian Revolution. It challenged Egyptians to "have some courage" and join her protest in Tahrir on 25 January 2011.[11]

PARAMETERS OF ENGAGEMENT

The spectacle of Bouazizi's self-immolation is undoubtedly a uniquely powerful—although in fact not singular—example of the type of cultural performance that has come to define the Arab uprisings. Yet such highly charged performative individual acts are part of a continuum of performance activism that have also included more organized acts of protest, from the aggressive and sometimes violent actions of the anarchistic Ultras and the Black Bloc tactics they deploy,[12] to street art, theater, and music produced for and often in the midst of revolutionary movements and at some or even great risk to the cultural creators behind it.

We conceive of these modes of performance activism as embodying, enacting, and reflecting what Reynolds terms transversal poetics,[13] which is simultaneously a socio-cognitive theory, mode of performance, and method of analysis. Transversal poetics function as what can be described as a "traveling epistemology,"[14] constantly morphing as it moves through and between experiences and events; between virtual and material/physical spheres of publicness; between what Jürgen Habermas problematically but importantly delineates as dramaturgical and communicative action; between what scholars of space such as Henri Lefebvre, Gilles Deleuze, Edward Soja, and others would describe as state-centric, striated, and hardened spaces and, alternatively, the nomadic, rhizomatic, and fluid spaces of experience and representation.[15]

We approach such performances of dissidence in the cultural, sociopolitical, and economic environments of the Arab world through the prism of what we term "theater of immediacy." We define theater of immediacy as cultural (often, but not necessarily artistic) creation and performance for an intended audience that is not merely emergent—that is, in the process of formation—but what we refer to as "emurgent" (emergent + urgent): developing rapidly and in the context of intense sociopolitical struggle that destabilizes and even reconfigures previously dominant, congealed structures and networks of power and identity. It is, to borrow a concept from Walter Benjamin, a space and experience in which performance becomes "auratic,"—that is, its affective/emotional power is such that it extends far beyond the immediate location of the event, literally to move (emotionally and/or physically) a significant number of people—and ultimately transformative.

In these terms, it is not surprising that a politically motivated suicide started a chain reaction; if such actions can often cause copycat suicides, clearly, they can clearly also trigger intense episodes of performance activism and theater of immediacy, utilizing a variety of media, from street self-immolations to live music to vlogs; together these create a highly flammable political atmosphere in which a revolutionary explosion becomes all but inevitable.

Not every emergent performance constitutes a theater of immediacy, but emergence is a necessary condition of this theater because only performativity of that degree of force—open and transversal, and potentially revolutionary—can overcome the *necropolitics* of late authoritarian states. It can lead people beyond the increased subjugation of citizens to the power of state-sanctioned imprisonment, torture, death, and other "states of exception" by states that rely increasingly on violence and domination to maintain the hegemony they possess within society and thus open new conduits for what we identify as open, transversal, and revolutionary power.[16]

A crucial characteristic of theater of immediacy, as we conceive of it, is its experience both live and in real time. It is quickly produced (created, brought forth, staged) and so embodies and reflects the imminence and urgency of a particular, often radical, moment. Yet "live" and in "real time" in the era of digitally mediated globalization can also mean recorded, uploaded to YouTube, and replayed anywhere on anyone's computer or phone. Theater of immediacy recognizes and accounts for the elasticity of space and time—especially the here and the now—in contemporary globalized emurgent performance activism.

Moreover, theater of immediacy is transversally empowered, as it stimulates individual or group transformations that defy, exceed, or undermine established political and even epistemological systems. It subverts the subjective territories, official culture, and the sociopolitical conductors that work together, separately, and reciprocally to maintain societies' governing structures.[17] These qualities make theater of immediacy powerful, yet they also create confusion between its fleeting nature and the need to have a more lasting impact and affect in order to reshape networks and flows of power and social and political energy toward its ends. That is, theater of immediacy must at the same time be a singular and an emulatable act, one achieving the emulative authority to inspire others to copy it.[18]

In this sense, the widely circulated images of the badly beaten body of Egyptian computer aficionado Khaled Said, whose death helped spark the dissident efforts that led to the 25 January 2010 Tahrir protests, possess a similarly transversal power to those of Bouazizi. Yet it is less clear whether his public murder by police officers on a day-lit street constitutes a theater of immediacy. While his local activism (he supposedly monitored local police corruption) seemingly led to his torture and murder by corrupt police, the act itself was devoid of agency on his part. At the same time, while his public beating and execution by police had elements of spectacle and even theater to it (it was clearly "staged"), it cannot be defined as theater of immediacy since its goal was to preserve existing systems of power rather than challenge and transform them. In other words, whether or not the media coverage, communication, and responses generated by Khaled Said's story achieved, like Bouazizi's, the status of what we term an "articulatory space," which is a fluid multifaceted, primarily abstract, spatiotemporal realm in which disparate concepts and sentiments converse, ideational streams, discourses, and performances negotiate and aggregate meanings, redefine their trajectories, boundaries, and strategies, while at the same time orbiting and informing subjects of critical speculation, what became "Khaled-Said-space" never resonated with the immediate or enduring force of "Bouazizi-space," itself an articulatory space that transformed into multiple spaces of becomings-something different—of willful *becomings-x*—of seizing agency out of objectification, marginalization, and alienation. Such transversally infused articulatory spaces must contend with a resurgent "SCAF-space," "ElSissi-space," or "Assad-space," which are often more powerful than the "Zine El Abidine Ben Ali-space" and "Hosni Mubarak-space" that—with different qualities—preceded and passed through the revolutions in Tunisia and Egypt.[19]

Although ordinary people can, if they are distressed or motivated enough, attempt to emulate Bouazizi's extraordinary act of performance activism (some did so, although with less impact), artistic creation and production are of a different order. On the one hand, artistic productions are the product of a level of skill, training, and to a certain degree talent, abilities that are generally not cultivated by nonartists. This makes them harder to emulate and singularly powerful, in the manner that Benjamin described the work of art in the pre-techno-industrial age of reproduction as uniquely auratic.[20] And yet, certain types of artistic production—for example, songs, films, theater, poetry—can be sung, screened, read, or otherwise publicly performed repeatedly, and by others besides the creator(s). This enables the production of repeated theater of immediacy that generates a level of what we term "theatricity" (the artistically generated current flowing through the staged performance) crucial to sustaining and strengthening the power of collective protest.

FROM SOCIAL MOVEMENTS TO MOVEMENT AS SOCIAL

We believe that theater of immediacy contributes to a focus in social movement theory on elucidating the motives, constraints, and strategies of subaltern groups, such as workers and women.[21] It does so not by exploring social movements as a category describing various types of group organization and political action, but rather by exploring social movement as an epistemology of action. It allows us to look at the mutually implicate relationship between performativity and culture, specifically the experience of culture as a performance of publicness rather than culture as a static and controllable sphere in which dialog and interaction take place.

From our experience exploring theater of immediacy in locations as diverse as Baghdad, Lagos, Port Harcourt, Gaza, Nabi Saleh, Cairo, and other zones of intense social and political conflict, the role of spontaneity and individual or small group action (as opposed to well-organized and well-conceived collective action) is crucial to harnessing the collective power of social movements and conducting them directly against the state machinery, both ideological and repressive. That is, theater of immediacy produces the kind of transversal moments and movements that allow the reframing of social and political consciousness, the re-calculus of opportunity costs, and allocation of resources away from the long-term "war of position" against a hegemonic or at least dominant state.

It is the tension between spontaneity and maturity, between the improbable—a young man so desperate that he sets himself ablaze across from city hall and an unknown musician writing the anthem of the Arab Spring twelve hours after arriving at Midan Tahrir[22]—and civil society groups laboring for years to build an infrastructure of resistance, that enabled the initial burst of energy represented by Bouazizi's theater of immediacy to be harnessed and channeled into revolutionary action.

CHALLENGING STATE NETWORKS, CONDUITS FOR REVOLUTIONARY ACTION

Theater of immediacy and *emurgent* action are vital to the early phases and long-term resiliency of revolutionary action because they provide the initial torrent of energy that enables the rechanneling of power through society. According to transversal poetics,[23] power flows throughout society via "sociopolitical conductors" (familial, religious, juridical, media, and educational structures that interconnect a society's ideological and cultural framework), which affect the circulation of three types of relationally implicated and contested power: "open power," "state power," and "transversal power." Various groups within society struggle to control these conduits; in so doing they tap into or syphon off some of the power (political-economic voltage, so to speak) for themselves. It is in this movement that open, state, and transversal powers are connected, however conflicted their manner of interaction.[24]

Each of these types of power has the capacity to promote or oppose hegemonic ideologies. Open power is any force that has yet to be activated, related, contextualized, or differentiated as it flows through society. Open power is power before it has taken on a sociopolitical valence.[25] State power is any force that works in the interest of coherence and organization among any variables, such as words in a sentence, images on stage, or actions in the streets, and it therefore builds and reinforces structures, whether semantic, material, social, cultural, governmental, or political. Transversal power is power that challenges, subverts, and potentially upends state power. When it flowers through theater of immediacy, such power takes the essentially disciplinary and self-amplifying nature of modern power—usually although not exclusively directed by state systems of governance—and redirects it, activating and hardening once docile bodies and readying them for battle, for the violence and resilience necessary to struggle against the dominant power holders in a society.

When open and transversal power converges through specific conductors, they create conduits or networks for revolutionary activity that states find difficult to repress. Thus, for example, on the one hand, the municipal official, Faida Hamdi, with whom Bouazizi had the confrontation on 17 December 2010, was a sociopolitical conductor who failed to reinforce effectively the official territory of Sidi Bouzid, specifically, and of Tunisia, generally. The official territory of the town of Sidi Bouzid, as of all local municipalities, was a vertically integrated subset of Tunisia's overall state machinery.

On the other hand, Bouazizi proved to be a conductor of both open and transversal power; strong enough in fact, by ripple effect, to disaggregate and pull apart the networks of power that comprised the existing Tunisian state. Hamdi's power, or rather the power that flowed through her, was too weak to enforce itself adequately upon Bouazizi, while his power—the power, it should be recalled, of an ostensibly powerless person (approximating *bare life*)—was self-amplifying transversally to the point of generating a revolutionary force. But, when compared with countless others who have rebelled against the state on an individual basis, Bouazizi achieved a rare form of power, what we term a "revolutionary singularity"; his power self-amplified into an antistate virus, went airborne through various media as an articulatory space and emurgent formation, and infected corrosively the larger system.

In this regard, Bouazizi became a paradigm, a channeler of transversal power through his conduction of historical self-immolation as performance activism, which enabled his transduction from individual to international celebrity and cultural-political icon. Credited for the inspiration of Arab uprisings, and a legacy of streets and plazas named after him, stamps with his photo on it, shirts, caps, and buttons that say "We are all Mohamed Bouazizi," films about him, and accounts of him in history books (see figure 3.3), Bouazizi and the discourses and byproducts generated about and around him ensure that Bouazizi-space will remain potent for years to come, even when the actors or actions that created them have lost their power or faded from view.[26]

What is crucial to all these transversal and revolutionary spaces is they are products of overcoming fear: fear of pain, fear of death, fear of humiliation. Such transcendence of fear is a crucial factor in pushing movements, which began as sub- or countercultures and evolved into public cultures, through a gradual mastery of various levels of publicness, from grassroots organizing

3.3. A T-shirt sold on www.zazzle.com reads "We are all Mohamed Bouazizi."

and claiming public space to expertise at producing and disseminating media that remain beyond government control, beyond that liminal point where they can be reabsorbed into the hegemonic system without significant violence (as occurred in countries such as Morocco or Oman), and toward more fully revolutionary cultures and publics as occurred in Tunisia, Egypt, Libya, Yemen, Bahrain, and Syria.

The power of acting beyond fear is clear from the famous vlog of 6 April activist Asma' Mahfouz that she uploaded to YouTube less than a week before the commencement of the 25 January uprising, which is credited with motivating tens of thousands of people to join the protests:

> Four Egyptians have set themselves on fire to protest humiliation and hunger and poverty and degradation they had to live with for 30 years. Four Egyptians have set themselves on fire thinking maybe we can have a revolution like Tunisia, maybe we can have freedom, justice, honor and human dignity.

I posted that I, a girl, am going down to Midan Tahrir, and I will stand alone. And I'll hold up a banner. Perhaps people will show some honor. I even wrote my number so maybe people will come down with me.

If you have honor and dignity as a man, come. Come and protect me and other girls in the protest.

Don't be afraid of the Government, Fear none but God!

ART AT THE EDGE

Acts of extreme performance activism such as the public suicide of Muhammad Bouazizi are among the most powerful types of theater of immediacy imaginable — the citizen with no hope for life seizing from the necro-state the power at least to control his own death. Under the right circumstance, such as those enabling the widespread dissemination of the iconic imagery of Bouazizi's self-sacrifice, or Asma' Mahfouz's declaration to fellow Egyptians of her willingness to suffer a similar fate, such actions take on an auratic, transversal, and revolutionary power. But such singular occasions of performance activism are not the only or even most common forms of transversal cultural performance. Artists have long possessed a similar power to inspire and mobilize fellow citizens.

Indeed, the surpassing of fear that is a crucial trait for activists is also a sine qua non for politically engaged art. There can be little doubt as to the importance of art for revolutionary action. Marx, for example, reminds us of its power in the wake of the failed revolutions of 1848, declaring that successful social revolutions "cannot take [their] poetry from the past but only from the future." What's more, "the content [of the poetry] must go beyond the phrase"[27] — that is, the message conveyed by artistic production must be far deeper and more authentic than the hegemonic cultural and political discourses against which it is deployed.

For Theodor Adorno (Marx's most aesthetically attuned heir) all art has this potential; thus he describes art as essentially an "uncommitted crime"[28] against existing societal norms and ideologies. When the content of a work of art exceeds the mere musical or lyrical phrase, when it directly challenges existing networks and conductors of power under emurgent political conditions, the crime is committed, and both artwork and artist can expect to face censorship or worse.

This is precisely what has occurred to "revolutionary artists" across the region, particularly in Tunisia, Egypt, and Morocco. Here we recall the debate nearly three quarters of a century ago between Benjamin and Adorno over whether the "mechanical reproduction" and mass-commodified circulation of art destroyed the "aura" that previously surrounded the singular work of art. In contrast to Benjamin's more positive view of the emancipatory potential of nonauratic, mass-produced art, Adorno argued that the aura lost to commodified production and distribution would be replaced by an even more powerful and politically disempowering aura of style. We argue, however, that in the digital era, in which art can be produced, circulated, and consumed endlessly without the need for commodification and outside the control of official, political, or economic networks of power, there is renewed possibility for a return of the aura in art that inspires, motivates, and mobilizes people en masse to confront the full force of state power and institutions.[29]

We can see the power of such auratic performances in the examples of Tunisian rapper El Général, whose song "Ra'is Lebled" ("President of the Country"), written, recorded, uploaded, and circulated virally on the Internet in a matter of days, is credited with helping to launch the Tunisian revolution, as thousands of young Tunisians took to the streets in protest after his arrest. "Ra'is Lebled" demonstrates the possibility of creating theater of immediacy through artistic production rather than an immediate and spontaneous act.[30] The video was uploaded on the anniversary of Prime Minister Ben Ali's coup against Habib Bourguiba, the country's independence leader and first president. The words, which plaintively inform Ben Ali that "your people are dying . . . eating from garbage . . . We are living like dogs," capture all the anger and desperation of the majority of Tunisia's population. The music, with its ominous minor melodies and bass line and hauntingly sparse arrangement, equally captures the instability and unease of life on the (still then unbeknownst) edge of revolution.

Similar to Bouazizi's self-immolation, "Ra'is Lebled" was not the first example of the specific performance activism that it exemplified. And without previous examples to lay a phenomenological, epistemological, and aesthetic[31] foundation for its reception, there is little doubt that "Ra'is Lebled," like Bouazizi's self-immolation, would not have had the valence they did. But for both timing was perfect, as other sociopolitical conductors, a weakening economy, an increasingly bold and fearless youth generation, an experienced cadre of activists, the release of the Tunisian Wikileaks ("Tunileaks") files, and Libya's expulsion of thousands of Tunisian workers earlier in the year all supplied the groundwork so that El Général's missive to Ben Ali became a sonic, visual, and political symbol of the revolution that was bubbling over at the end of 2010. Indeed, the song became increasingly popular after Bouazizi's self-immolation. As protests began to spiral out of control, El Général was arrested, on 6 January 2011. During the three days he was in jail his fame and the fame of the song grew exponentially, making his release inevitable.

Both El Général as a person and "Ra'is Lebled" the song functioned as emurgent sociopolitical conductors during the revolution, forming an articulatory space, what could be termed "Ra'is Lebled-space." As with Bouazizi's image, the circulation of the video on social media, and its increasing prevalence at protests, served as a vector for expressing and channeling public dissent, making the rapper's voice in many ways more powerful than the President's. It was, in essence, a virtual theater of immediacy that helped mobilize and physically bring together a critical mass of people in the same space and time.

The experience of Ramy Essam, the "singer of the Egyptian revolution" (see figure 3.4), was somewhat different than that of El Général. Arriving at Midan Tahrir on 31 January 2011 as an unknown wannabe pop singer with nothing but an old acoustic guitar and a sleeping bag, within twenty-four hours he had absorbed the words, and as important, the rhythms of the protesters' chants in Tahrir, and composed "*Irhal*!" (Leave!), the song that quickly became the anthem not just of the Egyptian Revolution, but of the Arab uprisings from Morocco to Bahrain.

If El Général was arrested (which in Tunisia, immediately raises the specter of torture or other forms of abuse), Essam was seriously injured during the heat of the fighting for Tahrir on 1–2 February. Despite bandages on his head and mouth, he sang his increasingly popular song as often as possible to the crowd in Tahrir, helping to keep spirits high and mobilize new protesters as they began to flood into the Midan. It was the evening that protesters finally pushed all government forces out of Tahrir that a video was made, shot from the stage in the darkness into a nearly invisible crowd, which first brought to the world's attention the power of "*Irhal*." "That was the first day for me to take the license to be the 'singer of the *Midan*,'" Essam explains, "because everyone already saw me not just on stage with bandages, but on the front lines of the big battles. They knew."[32] Within days, the video had tens of thousands of views, spreading the words of the song not just throughout Egypt, but globally as well.

Whereas Bouazizi's suicide took place in the blink of an eye, and El Général's power lay fundamentally in the virtual dissemination of his music, Essam's power stemmed from his continued physical presence in Tahrir, not merely during the eighteen days of the 25 January uprising, but during most every day of every occupation from that time until the summer of 2013.[33] It was his physical presence and the constant repetition of the songs that helped drive the revolution to ever larger crowds that overcame any possibility of government control or repression of the music, the message, or the messenger. And when he was brutally tortured by regime forces less than two months after the

3.4. Ramy Essam performing at Tahrir Square in January 2011. Photo by Mark LeVine.

revolution, the numerous scars on his body, which were displayed to the world in several video interviews (including on the leading US news program *60 Minutes*), made him an even more powerful symbol of fearless opposition to the system, the physical embodiment of Asma Mahfouz's vlogged call-to-arms.[34]

The experience of both Ramy Essam and El Général demonstrates how in times of intense sociopolitical conflict, politically engaged artists can function as sociopolitical conductors, either virtually through the Internet or physically through public performances—as Essam puts it, their job is to "listen to all the things [people] are saying, distill them into their essence, and share it as widely as possible."[35] The combination of powerful lyrics, the right musical aesthetic, social media, and performance before large crowds—the same in-gredients for making any artist famous—can also unite and mobilize masses of people toward political ends. What is equally important, however, is that in the balance between Internet and physical presence, it is the latter that is crucial for the long-term success and power of both the artists and the move-ments they help to define.[36] That so many artists have been arrested, impris-oned, tortured, and even murdered for their art demonstrates their impact as sociopolitical conductors and the seriousness with which the state machinery takes the challenge they pose.

THE PROMISE OF MULTI-PRESENCE

Whether functioning as or creating theater of immediacy, artists like El Général and Essam achieved a "multi-presence," in which the virtual and material/physical, spontaneous and pre-recorded, synergistically reinforced the aura of each. Being present in multiple localities and discourses at the same time pro-vided them the capacity to enable and affect auratic power expansively, across multiple articulatory spaces. Ultimately, this multi-presence gives theater of immediacy not merely emurgent power, but, at least potentially, the power to sustain revolutionary solidarities and potential after the streets have become empty of protesters and the joy of revolutionary exuberance becomes the grind of struggle against counterrevolutionary forces that have learned from the mis-takes that led to the original outbursts and therefore will do everything pos-sible to ensure that the theater of revolution goes dark.

This is no easy task, however. The experience of Bouazizi's posthumous position in Tunis, and the postrevolutionary career trajectories of most revo-lutionary artists, including El Général and Ramy Essam, reveal how difficult it is for transversal, auratic events or artists, to retain their emurgent power over long periods. Bouazizi may have put Sidi Bouzid on the map,[37] but within a few months his family became the object of much jealousy and ridicule, as they were accused by other residents of profiting from his death and not sharing the wealth. El Général's career took a confusing turn after the im-mediate excitement of the revolution died down. He became more identified with the Islamist trend, and while he received numerous international invi-tations, within Tunisia he was not a major force in the development of the hip-hop scene. Even the groups that have retained a more distinct political or revolutionary message have found it much harder to reach an audience as the transition to democracy proceeded.[38]

On the other hand, in Morocco, where the power of the 20 February movement was ostensibly redirected by the king and elite, the lack of substantive political and economic progress has given rise to a potentially explosive situation vis-à-vis the country's youth, for whom a local rapper, El Haqed (L7a9ed—The Enraged or Indignant One), has become one of the most important political voices in the country. His songs, such as "Klab adDawla" (Dogs of the State) and "Wallou" (Nothing) have led to his repeated imprisonments and physical mistreatment by the government.[39] In countries in the midst of extreme violence, such as Syria, Libya, and, increasingly Iraq, the power of theater of immediacy is overwhelmed by the power of violence to close off most every avenue of publicness, virtual as well as material, that could challenge or transcend it with a more holistic vision.

As for Ramy Essam, the "singer of the revolution," he was forced to leave Egypt in the fall of 2014, his career stymied by the government and threats to his safety increasing to the point where exile had become the only realistic option. The writing was on the wall already in the summer of 2013, when the military removed President Muhammad Morsi from power. As he lamented only days before, roughly one thousand supporters of the deposed president were murdered by the military, "The new people protesting in support of the coup in Midan Tahrir don't know the words to my songs. They don't even know who I am anymore." By the time the third anniversary of the 25 January uprising came around, Essam could not leave his apartment, only blocks from Tahrir, for fear of being attacked by pro-military crowds that had long since taken over Tahrir.[40]

Essam's experiences remind us that even the most powerful songs will have little political valence if they are not able to be experienced in real time by mobilized and mobilizing citizens under emergent and transversal conditions, especially when "the system of fear is back. And is showing its teeth," as an Egyptian activist declared right around the time of Essam's departure.[41] And yet, it cannot be forgotten that the Arab uprisings began when fear left the heart of one seemingly ordinary man.

Muhammad Bouazizi's sacrifice inspired millions to shed their fear as well, through a poetry of protest that has profoundly transformed and inspired vocabularies of protest worldwide (as seen in the #OccupyCentral protests in Hong Kong), and also the deeper discourses, conduits, and practices of power and resistance at the heart of modern political subjectivity.[42] The immediacy of Bouazizi's action, and the music, poetry, theater, and graffiti of the Arab uprisings' revolutionary artists, still echo across the region, even though their power has waned. When new bodies and voices rise to shake off the fear again, the auratic, transgressive, and ultimately transcendent power that defined theater of immediacy during the Arab uprisings will once again shape public consciousness across the Arab world, and beyond.

NOTES

1. We differentiate performance activism from political or politicized performance. Performance activism, as epitomized by Bouazizi's self-immolation, has clear political implications but does not have to be engaged with clear political goals. Politicized performance is more organized, ideologically or politically motivated, goal-oriented, and usually less spontaneous.

2. Bob Simon, "How a Slap Sparked Tunisia's Revolution," CBSNews.com, 22 February 2011. http://www.cbsnews.com/stories/2011/02/20/60minutes/main20033404.shtml. Accessed 20 September 2014.

3. Account of the spread of the photo was provided to Mark LeVine by activists in Sidi Bouzid, July 2011.

4. Laila Lalami, "Fadoua Laroui: The Moroccan Mohamed Bouazizi," *The Nation*, 27 February 2011. http://www.thenation.com/blog/158878/fadoua-laroui-moroccan-mohamed -bouazizi. Accessed 7 September 2014.

5. For a description of Neji's death and the larger context in which it occurred, see Mark LeVine, "What a Difference a Decade Makes," *Al-Jazeera*, 11 September 2011. http://www .aljazeera.com/indepth/opinion/2011/09/201191174753518987.html. Accessed 2 February 2014.

6. Interviews with local residents and activists by Mark LeVine, Sidi Bouzid, September 2011.

7. This was reported by many news outlets based on an Associated Press story that ran on 11 June 2011. See, for example, "Ben Ali says he was duped into fleeing Tunisia," Radio France International, 20 June 2011. http://www.english.rfi.fr/africa/20110620-ben-ali-says -he-was-duped-fleeing-tunisia. Accessed 2 February 2013.

8. "Tunisia One Year On: New Trend of Self-Immolations," BBC News, 12 January 2012, http://www.bbc.co.uk/news/world-africa-16526462. Accessed 8 September 2014.

9. This quote was reported on numerous blog aggregators on 17 January 2010 (http:// wlcentral.org/node/967). It was part of an Agence France Presse report published by al-'Arabiyya ("Egyptian, Mauritanian set themselves on fire," published the same day, which after electronic publication edited this quote from the story, likely because of its ostensible incomprehensibility.

10. On "bare life" see Giorgio Agamben, *Homo Sacer: Sovereign Power and Bare Life* (Palo Alto: Stanford University Press, 1998); Achille Mbembe, "Necropolitics," *Public Culture* 15, no. 1 (Winter 2003): 11–40.

11. Asma Mahfouz's video was uploaded first on 18 January 2011 and is available on numerous YouTube videos, including http://www.youtube.com/watch?v=unG5WAdksQM. Accessed 9 March 2014. The video immediately went viral and is credited with one of the key moments launching the Egyptian Revolution.

12. These include self-initiated and organized and decentralized actions involving indirect confrontations with and sometimes violence against the police and destruction of property.

13. Transversal poetics was developed by Bryan Reynolds and a number of collaborators primarily in the fields of literary, cultural, theater, and performance studies, and is further developed by us here. See Bryan Reynolds, *Transversal Subjects: from Montaigne to Deleuze after Derrida* (Basingstoke: Palgrave Macmillan, 2009); *Transversal Enterprises in the Drama of Shakespeare and his Contemporaries: Fugitive Explorations* (Basingstoke: Palgrave Macmillan,

2006); *Performing Transversally: Reimagining Shakespeare and the Critical Future* (New York: Palgrave Macmillan, 2003); and *Becoming Criminal: Transversal Performance and Cultural Dissidence in Early Modern England* (Baltimore: Johns Hopkins University Press, 2002).

14. We take the idea of a traveling epistemology from Diana Taylor's notion of an "epistemology that travels," as discussed in her book, *The Archive and the Repertoire: Performing Cultural Memory in the Americas* (Durham, NC: Duke University Press, 2003).

15. See Henri Lefebvre, *The Production of Space* (London: Wiley-Blackwell, 1992). Alberto Melucci in John Keane and Paul Mier, eds., *Nomads of the Present: Social Movements and Individual Needs in Contemporary Society* (London: Hutchinson Radius, 1989).

16. Achille Mbembe, "Necropolitics," *Public Culture* 15 (Winter 2003): 11–40; Giorgio Agamben, *State of Exception* (Chicago: University of Chicago Press, 2005). The term "state of exception" (Ausnahmezustand in German) was originally developed by philosopher Carl Schmitt and is based in the state's ability to abrogate its own laws and/or place citizens outside the protections of the law (and thus open to exceptional violations of fundamental rights (life, liberty, etc.) in the name of security, the public good, or a public emergency.

17. For more on transversal poetics and the associated terms, "subjective territories," "official culture," and "sociopolitical conductors," as well as terms that will be introduced later in this chapter, "transversal power," "state power," "open power," "articulatory space," "state machinery," "conceptual territory," "transversal movement," "becomings," "emulative authority," and "pressurized belongings," see the following works by Reynolds: "The Devil's House, 'Or Worse': Transversal Power and Antitheatrical Discourse in Early Modern England," *Theatre Journal* 49, no. 2 [1997]: 143–167; *Becoming Criminal: Transversal Performance and Cultural Dissidence in Early Modern England* (Baltimore: Johns Hopkins University Press, 2003), 1–22; *Performing Transversally: Reimagining Shakespeare and the Critical Future* (Baltimore: Johns Hopkins University Press, 2002), 1–28; *Transversal Enterprises in the Drama of Shakespeare and his Contemporaries: Fugitive Explorations* (Basingstoke: Palgrave Macmillan, 2006); *Transversal Subjects: From Montaigne to Deleuze after Derrida* (Basingstoke: Palgrave Macmillan, 2009). *Transversal Subjects* includes a "Glossary of Transversal Terms."

18. Stuart Hall and Tony Jefferson, *Resistance through Rituals: Youth Subcultures in Post-War Britain* (London: Routledge, 1990); Victor Turner, *The Ritual Process: Structure and Anti-Structure* (Chicago: Aldine Transaction Publishers, 1995).

19. Perhaps the iconic depiction of the negative power of "Ben Ali-space" is archival footage of the then president frightening a young school boy, which was used in the introductory scene of the song "Ra'is Lebled" by the rapper El Général, discussed below.

20. Walter Benjamin, "The Work of Art in the Age of Mechanical Reproduction," 1936, Internet version available at marxists.org.

21. Perhaps the most telling example of possibilities and limits of social movement theory is Joel Beinin and Frédéric Vairel, eds., *Social Movements, Mobilization, and Contestation in the Middle East and North Africa* (Palo Alto: Stanford University Press, 2011). Here we are deploying Gramsci's well-known concepts of "war of position" versus the "war of maneuver" as the two primary modes of conflict between states and political elites, and the subaltern classes in capitalist and fascistic societies. For a short but useful analysis of how traditional social movement theory relates to analyses of the Arab uprisings, see Cédric Dupont and Florence Passy, "The Arab Spring or How to Explain those Revolutionary Episodes," *Swiss Political Science Review* (October 2011). See also Steven Buechler, "New Social Movement Theories," *Sociological Quarterly* 36, no. 3 (Summer 1995): 441–464.

22. Tahrir is often referred to as a "square" in English, but in fact it is a roundabout; we use the Arabic name for it in this chapter.

23. See supra note 12.

24. Normally, the groups and institutions that have managed to direct the majority of power to flow through them are understood as the "state," although criminal enterprises and networks are engaged in precisely the same activities, often with the collaboration of state actors. Thus, as Charles Tilly has observed, state making does not just resemble but actually is organized crime.

25. In this context, the power of Bouazizi's theater of immediacy was open before he activated it. That is, all the energy that would be released following his act was already flowing through society amorphously, but it had not been concentrated and directed before he became the conduit.

26. To borrow a term from Jameson, Bouazizi represents a "vanishing mediator" of a historical moment, through whom the dominant trajectories, flows, and conduits of power were pulled apart and, at least for a time, realigned and organized (Fredric Jameson, "The Vanishing Mediator; or, Max Weber as Storyteller," in his *The Ideologies of Theory*, 2 vols. (Minneapolis: University of Minnesota Press, 1988), vol. 2, 3–34.

27. Karl Marx, *The 18th Brumaire of Louis Bonaparte*. http://www.marxists.org/archive /marx/works/1852/18th-brumaire/ch01.htm. Accessed 8 October 2014.

28. Theodor Adorno and *Minima Moralia, Reflections on a Damaged Life* (London: Verso, 2006 [1951]), 111.

29. In so doing, music, and other forms of auratic art such as street theater, graffiti, guerrilla filmmaking, etc. become immanently critical of the society at large, and also crucial to bringing people together in large numbers toward the taking down, and even transcendence, of the existing system. LeVine develops this idea in "New Hybridities of Arab Musical Intifadas," *Jadaliyya*, 29 October 2011. http://www.jadaliyya.com/pages/index/3008/the-new -hybridities-of-arab-musical-intifadas. Accessed 8 March 2014.

30. El Général was not a well-known figure in Tunisia, even among rappers, when on 7 November 2010, he uploaded "Ra'is Lebled" to Facebook. See Hishaam Aidi, "The Grand (Hip-Hop) Chessboard: Race, Rap and Raison d'État," *Middle East Report* (Fall 2011).

31. Aesthetically, hip-hop had already been encoded as highly political in the Arab world, which made for greater receptivity of songs like "Ra'is Lebled" when they were released.

32. Interview with LeVine, Cairo, April 2012.

33. "If I were just a singer coming to the Midan and then leaving, it wouldn't have had the same impact," Essam explained to LeVine in an August 2014 interview.

34. Interview with LeVine, Helsinki, Finland, September 2014. As Essam explained after being tortured by the military, he was "happy" to have undergone this ordeal because "now they can't touch me. There's nothing left they can do" (LeVine, interview with Egyptian singer Ramy Essam, Cairo, April 2011. Moroccan rapper El Haqed has described the same feeling to LeVine, interview, Amman, January 2014).

35. Interview with LeVine, Cairo, April 2012.

36. On the other hand, it's important to note that while Egypt has an effectively open Internet—from Ramy Essam to hardcore pornography, and most anything is accessible without filters—without the ability to create a physical presence along with one in more traditional media (particularly in a country such as Egypt where radio and television are still by far the most important vehicles of communication), the long-term power of any artist or activist will likely be constrained.

37. At least internationally. In fact, even ten months after the outbreak of the revolution the only indication that one was approaching the town from the main highway was a spray-painted name on the existing sign.

38. Even as artists like Armada Bizerta, Binderman, Lak3y, and El Weld 15 (who was jailed for over a year for his song "Boulicia Kleb" (Police are Dogs) have continued the focus on political rap, the difficulties of earning a living as an artist, or even finding any kind of job, has drained the scene of some of its energy.

39. See Mark LeVine, "Meanwhile, In Morocco . . ." *al-Jazeera English*, 30 June 2012. http://www.aljazeera.com/indepth/opinion/2012/06/201262613325323191 9.html. Accessed 10 October 2014; Mark LeVine, "The Day the Music Died in the Arab World, *al-Jazeera English*, 26 May 2014. http://www.aljazeera.com/indepth/opinion/2014/05/day-music-died -arab-world-201452562751510993.html. Accessed 10 October 2014; El Haqed, "My Journey to Rap, Politics and Prison," *al-Jazeera English*, 6 October 2014. http://www.aljazeera.com /indepth/opinion/2014/10/my-journey-rap-politics-prison-201410671050228296.html. Accessed 10 October 2014.

40. His only consolation was the popularity of a new and very aggressive antimilitary video, "Mahnash min dol" (We are not from them), which received 100,000 views in less than 24 hours after he uploaded it the evening of the 25th (Mark LeVine, interviews and field notes with Essam, July–August 2013, January 2014, Cairo).

41. Vivienne Matthies-Boon, "Strangers in the Crowd," MERIP *Blog*, 5 September 2014. http://www.merip.org/blog. Accessed 7 September 2014.

42. For the manner in which these processes have transformed political subjectivity across the Arab world, see Mark LeVine, guest editor, "Theory and Praxis of the Arab Uprisings," special issue of *Middle East Critique* 22, no.3 (Fall 2013).

PART II

ARTISTIC PROTEST AND THE ARAB UPRISINGS

THIS SECTION FOCUSES on the role of popular culture in the contemporary Arab uprisings and their aftermath. Revolutionary moments came along with an immense creativity in images, sounds, and words and deeds alike. Poetry, music, visual culture, and other genres of popular culture were important sources of creativity and agency in the formulation of democratic claims. This section analyzes the relationship between diverse genres of popular culture—music, visual arts, and poetry—and claims for democracy and social justice during the Arab uprisings.

Nina ter Laan's chapter focuses on the role of Islamist *anashid* singers in the Moroccan protests and the transformations their musical practices underwent during this period. Within the 20 February protest movement, an artistic scene emerged where theater, music, and plastic arts became vehicles for political messages as well as sites of political action. Ter Laan analyzes the musical contributions of the Islamist Jamaʿa al-ʿAdl wal-Ihsan to the 20 February movement. In spite of puritan attitudes toward music, over the last two decades the Jamaʿa increasingly accepted music as a tool for religious proselytization, mainly propagating Islamic virtues and glorifying God and the Prophet. After the Jamaʿa joined the 20 February movement, however, several singers started to produce protest songs with explicit political messages that were performed at street demonstrations. Despite the transformations in the settings, the lyrics, and the audiences, the artists themselves hold that the meaning of their music did not change. The *anashid* singers felt they were already engaged in the political arena in which discourses on ethical behavior revolving around communal values competed. Therefore, they regard the changes in their music as a continuation of the same ethical project: one that searches for a different kind of political ethos and for an alternative form of citizenship in which Islam serves as a moral compass.

Cynthia Becker's chapter uses contemporary visual art to trace how politically engaged artists involved in the North African Berber movement counter national narratives that they feel impose an Arab-Islamic identity upon them. As the indigenous people of North Africa, many Berbers felt marginalized by their national governments, who, after colonial independence declared themselves Arab-Islamic states with Arabic as the official language, even though Berber speakers account for approximately 40 percent of the population in Morocco and 25 percent in Algeria. For the last several decades an activist movement has developed to fight for their political rights. They rejected the term Berber as a pejorative label and preferred the term "Amazigh." Amazigh activists claimed a space for themselves within the protests by referring to them as the "Amazigh Spring." This chapter analyzes the way symbols visualizing the Amazigh pre-Islamic past, the Judeo-Berber heritage, and gender equality serve to link Amazigh activists from Morocco to Libya, contributing to a sense of Amazigh unity across economic, gender, and political boundaries. These transnational visual symbols promote an Amazigh ethno-consciousness and convey their self-proclaimed values of tolerance, pluralism, and egalitarianism.

Samuli Schielke's chapter looks at the relationship of poetry with social and political change in Egypt during "the stormy season" of the revolution and its aftermath. During the 25 January revolution in Egypt, poetry, the most popular genre of literature in the Arab world, has played an important role in the events, with poets performing at demonstrations and the events themselves often taking a poetic quality. Schielke raises the question what effect, if any, a poet's voice has in the time of an uprising. The power or powerlessness of words is discussed with Egyptian poets who supported the revolution in Egypt. Accordingly, the chapter provides vernacular theories on the relationships between literary fantasy, dreams, and the material world. The theories about creativity and agency as inherently intertwined with material conditions were revised en face of overwhelming powers and the volatile fortune of the revolution. Poetry has become part of the cycle of polarization that holds Egypt in its grip since the spring of 2011.

This section thus highlights the power as well as powerlessness of popular culture to forge changes depending on the face of those who have the power to make a difference. To quote one of the poets of Schielke's research: "The revolutionaries never stopped dreaming. In no country has the military ever understood poetry and dreams."

CHAPTER 4

"ISLAM IS THERE TO MAKE PEOPLE FREE": ISLAMIST MUSICAL NARRATIVES OF FREEDOM AND DEMOCRACY IN THE MOROCCAN SPRING

NINA TER LAAN

AT THE END OF December 2010, a stream of civil uprisings and popular protests spread across the Middle East and North Africa, profoundly affecting the political landscapes of countries in the region. This series of protests, known as the "Arab Spring," have brought forth a wide variety of artistic productions. Differently positioned artists across the Middle East have used their art to reinforce claims for political change, social justice, and democracy. Artistic productions emerging from the protests have inspired an increasing interest in contemporary art from the Arab world among journalists, the art world, and academics alike. However, the majority of the publications that address the role of artistic expressions in the Arab Spring tend to focus on westernized art styles and overlook those coming from Islamist groups (Wright 2011). The lack of attention to Islam-inspired art forms in the wake of the Arab Spring derives from the common idea that the protests were largely about "democracy" and "freedom," and that Islamism[1] and democracy are incompatible. "Democracy" is usually tied to a western cultural model and "Islamism" is associated with extremism and cultural restrictions (Shilton 2013).

This chapter aims to draw attention to the role of Islamist artists and their artistic activities in the context of the Arab Spring through the lens of vocalists affiliated with a prominent but illegal Islamist organization in Morocco, the Jamaʿa al-ʿAdl wal-Ihsan (Justice and Benevolence Association/JBA). Through a detailed analysis of a specific case study drawn from my ethnographic fieldwork, I discuss the role of Islamist *anashid*[2] singers, dubbed *munshidin*,[3] in the Moroccan protests, and the transformations their musical practices underwent during the protests. In tracking these changes, I relate them to their previous repertoires, as well as to the changing political landscape in Morocco. Such an analysis illustrates how Islamist artistic activities produced in the context of the Arab Spring can articulate and engender notions of "democracy" and "freedom" as an Islamic ethical project. The chapter starts by presenting an ethnographic description of an event to which I was invited, organized by the Moroccan popular protest movement, the "February 20th movement." Then I provide some background about the Arab Spring in Morocco. Next, I discuss musical practices before and during these protests. The chapter ends with an analysis of the shifts that occurred in the musical practice of JBA vocalists.

ISLAMIC HYMNS IN A MARXIST HEADQUARTERS

It is 30 October 2011. It has now been seven months since the Arab Spring arrived in Morocco. Each week demonstrations are held nationwide, also in Casablanca, where the majority of activists are seated. I am about to visit a political artistic event to which I was invited by a *munshid* I have been working with for quite some time. As a committed member of the JBA, he had become actively involved in the Moroccan protests, ever since they joined the February 20th movement. The event I was invited to was organized by the artistic committee of the February 20th movement, and was dedicated to the liberation of "Lhaqed" or "El-Haqed" (meaning "hateful" or "malicious"), the artist name of a young rapper from Casablanca. Lhaqed was arrested a month ago, for allegedly assaulting a regime loyalist during a street demonstration in Casablanca. But according to the organizers, the real reason for his arrest is the release of a song in which he changed the country's slogan from "God, Country, King" to "God, Country, Freedom." Diffusing such a song is unthinkable in Morocco where the king is the supreme leader and both head of state and state religion. The location where the event is held is the headquarters of the United Socialist Party (PSU), an old Marxist party and one of the leftist organizations that joined the February 20th movement. It is the third time in a week the organizers have tried to set up the event. On each previous occasion the police had canceled it. I see no police and decide to enter the PSU building. Once in the building, an exhibition of cartoons hanging on a wall in the hallway catches my eye. They emanate from the Arab Spring and comment on the monarchical state (*makhzen*). Some cartoons critique the state-controlled and censored media, others address matters of corruption, the lack of proper healthcare and education, unemployment, the waste of public funds, and the control exercised by the Moroccan state over musicians.

Heavy hip-hop beats come from a room across the hallway where a young rapper performs the song of Lhaqed. When I enter the room, I see an unusual mix of people: neo-hippies, hip-hoppers, Islamists, people of youth organizations, aging Marxists, hip upper-middle-class youngsters, and some garbage collectors coming off their shifts, still in their working clothes. Some of these groups are longstanding ideological adversaries, such as Islamists and leftists,

4.1. *Anashid* band performing at the "Free Lhaqed event," in Casablanca. Photo © Author 2011.

who have been repeatedly involved in confrontations with one another on university campuses since the 1960s and 1970s. But tonight they are gathered in the same room listening to a mix of artists of various genres, demanding the liberation of Lhaqed. After every song, the audience chants slogans similar to the ones I heard at street demonstrations: "Long live the people!" and "The people want the fall of the *makhzen*!" A young woman enters the stage and starts to perform a song entitled "'Aliw as-sawt" (Raise your voice). The song is by the hand of Rachid Gholem, a well-known Moroccan *munshid* and a prominent member of the JBA. He composed the song "'Aliw as-sawt" especially for the Arab Spring. The song is a call to the Moroccan people to let go of their fears and raise their voices against political oppression and social inequality. The song "'Aliw as-sawt" has become popular among activists of all tendencies, in spite of the composer's Islamist background.

Next is a vocal ensemble, whose members are affiliated with the JBA. Six men in dark suits and matching ties pick up their microphones and instruments. There is a man playing an 'ud,[4] another playing a synthesizer. The rest are on vocals. They perform *anashid*, songs that address Islamic themes and seek to encourage their audiences to lead a pious life. This vocal genre is normally performed in domestic settings such as family celebrations in the homes of pious families. But today they perform a different repertoire, at a different setting, for a very different audience. The restrained and rhythmically slow style typical for *anashid* is maintained, but the lyrics address completely new topics. Instead of their usual songs of praise to the prophet (*amdah*), they now sing revolutionary songs demanding freedom, democracy, and justice. Some of the songs are newly composed, others are musical reworkings of old poems from the 1950s, written by members of the Egyptian Brotherhood. Everyone in the audience responds strongly to the performance of the *anashid* band. At the end of the concert, when the singers receive a standing ovation, they stand in a line and make the victory-freedom sign with their right hands.

MOROCCAN SPRING?

The February 20th movement is a popular protest movement, that emanated from a Facebook group called *Mouvement liberté et démocratie maintenant au Maroc*. This Facebook group was launched in January 2011 and served as a platform uniting young activists. In the beginning of February 2011, they started to release announcements and mobilize online for major demonstrations to be held on February 20th, 2011, across the country. With success, thousands of people answered their call and took to the streets in different cities in Morocco (Rahman 2012: 4).

The February 20th movement attracted a wide variety of sympathizers and provided public visibility and audibility to a diversity of marginalized people and organizations with distinct and sometimes contradictory agendas. Examples are the AMDH (*Association Marocaine des Droits Humains*), leftist splinter parties, Islamist groups such as the banned Justice and Benevolence Association, committed secularists such as the members of MALI (*Mouvement Alternatif pour les Libertés Individuelles*), and the Amazigh (Berber) movement. Although they differ in ideological viewpoints they managed to formulate and agree on several key demands such as a new constitution, a democratic parliament, an independent administration of justice, punishment of corruption and power abuse, the right to work, and the raising of minimum wages. The activist groups that joined the February 20th movement already existed before the uprisings. They are civil society organizations, operating outside the political system, and they hold a long tradition of activism (Cohen and Jaïdi 2006). They challenged the Moroccan political system long before the Arab Spring.

Morocco's political system is centered on a monarchy in which the king has a historical monopoly over both the religious and the political field (Geertz

1968, Munson 1993, Waterbury 1970). His religious legitimacy is linked to his genealogical descent. The king belongs to the *Alawite* dynasty, which has been ruling Morocco for over four hundred years, and whose members claim to be descendants of the Prophet. This gives him the status of *Amir al-Mu'minin*, meaning "Commander of the Faithful." This status makes the king the supreme leader of the country who is placed above the constitution, the legislative, and the executive power, and puts Islam at the center of the political structure and state legitimacy. Moreover, his status is secured in the constitution and makes him both sacred and inviolable, making public criticism of him or his family illegal. Next to the monarchy, the country has a multiparty system with a parliament and a prime minister. However, political parties enjoy little trust of the Moroccan population and actual power lies with the *makhzen*, a longstanding sociopolitical system of power distribution centered on the monarchy (Daadaoui 2011, Geertz 1968). The relations between the people in parliament and the elite surrounding the king are largely based on a patron-client relationship in which gifts, privileges, and influential positions are given in exchange for political loyalty (Driessen 1994, Hammoudi 1997, Waterbury 1970).

Despite this undemocratic system of rule, the protests in Morocco were not aimed at the resignation of the country's leader, as in neighboring countries, but concentrated on political reforms and the resignation of central figures in the political field and the private sector belonging to Morocco's ruling elites. By contrast, the current king Mohammed VI, enjoys a significant level of public support from the Moroccan people. He owes his popularity to his attempt to distance himself from the repressive political rule of his father King Hassan II, also known as the "years of lead," during which political violence and the torture and disappearance of political opponents were the order of the day (Slymovics 2005, Vermeeren 2009). Upon his ascent to the throne, Mohammed VI initiated a far-reaching program of political, social, legal, economical, and religious reforms, promoting a more secular model and the pursuit of modernization and democratization (Elahmadi 2010, Maghraoui 2009: 143). He undertook some highly visible projects, such as the realization of large infrastructural projects, the enactment of a new family code (*mudawwana*) granting women more rights, the release of old political prisoners, the creation of the Equity and Reconciliation Commission (IER), tasked with researching human rights violations under Hassan II, and the liberalization of the national media landscape. The arrival of the young monarch thus raised the hopes of many Moroccans who saw his plans as a development toward liberalization and democratization of the Moroccan public sphere.

But, despite the relaxation of government restrictions, the authoritarian foundations of the political system and the unequal distribution of power persisted. The *lignes rouges*, the "red lines" of "God, country, king" still cannot be crossed. Anyone who questions the king's religious legitimacy or competes with the official narrative of Islam is still considered a threat by the Moroccan authorities. The people of the February 20th movement decided not to demand the overthrow of the monarchy or the departure of the king. This was probably because they were aware that would have meant a loss of a big part of their public support.

In the midst of the Arab Spring, the Moroccan government was eager to present itself to the outside world as an "exception" in a region of turmoil. On 9 March 2011, the king responded to the demands by giving a speech on national television announcing constitutional reforms, an "expansion" of civil and human rights, and a newly elected parliament. A few months after the protests, the king, in his habitual role of arbiter, initiated a new constitution drawn up by a commission personally appointed by him. A referendum followed, that, despite boycotts by the February 20th movement, pushed the new constitution through. It was duly promulgated by the king on 29 July 2011, and national elections were moved up to 25 November 2011 and won by the moderate Islamic Party of Justice and Democracy (PJD). Yet, according to critics the reforms do not go far enough, since the final power still remains vested in the king. A spokesperson of the February 20th movement claims that the reforms set in motion under the king mainly served to generate a facade of democracy and modernity for the benefit of foreign media and to secure international relations, but did not serve the Moroccan people who still struggle with everyday survival.[5]

THE *JAMA'A AL-'ADL WAL-IHSAN* AND MUSIC

Although the February 20th movement claims to be a nonreligious movement, the connection of many groups to Islam could not be ignored. Notable in this spectrum was the illegal Islamist organization, the JBA, that joined the February 20th movement between 20 February and 18 December 2011. The JBA is one of today's most influential Islamist organizations in Morocco. Unlike the main Islamic political party, the PJD, it does not participate in the political field due to their refusal to acknowledge the religious legitimacy of the king. As a consequence of their participation in the February 20th movement, the organization not only provided a large number of protesters to the movement, but they also made significant musical contributions to the protests.

Despite their earlier disapproval of music due to its controversial status within Islam, over the last two decades, the JBA has gradually allowed music into the movement. In longstanding theological debates, Islamic scholars discuss whether performing and listening to music is allowed according to Islam (Shiloah 1995; see also Otterbeck and Alagha in this volume). These debates mainly revolve around the dangerous power of music, the question of what kind of instruments are permissible, and in what settings it is acceptable to perform music (Faruqi 1986). Despite the moral ambiguity surrounding music, Islamic movements throughout the Muslim world, who previously held hostile attitudes toward musical entertainment, have increasingly started to accept and incorporate music as long as it abides by and propagates Islamic virtues and morality. This has resulted in the increasing acceptance of music within and outside Islamic movements (Barendregt 2011, Haenni and Tammam 2003, Van Nieuwkerk 2013).

These developments have also affected the JBA's stance on music. The organization nowadays attributes an important role to music with the goal of enhancing religious experience, to offer a moral alternative to secular forms of art and entertainment, to revive the Islamic faith, and to integrate and mobilize people into the movement. Its charismatic and recently deceased leader 'Abdessalam Yassine[6] claimed to be a musician himself, and he encouraged music to be used to integrate the JBA into Moroccan society, attract followers, and challenge official negative cultural representations about their organization and Islam in general. Pedagogical intent is also important, in the sense that the music performed is meant to teach and educate the audience about the proper way of leading a Muslim life. The JBA includes many vocalists and has a well-developed musical network of singers, producers, studios, and festivals. A committee judges the vocalists during underground festivals on artistic quality, purity of voice, spirituality, and political impact. They have their own network of producers and musical experts who have developed manuals for the correct performance of Islamic music according to the ideology of the JBA.

One of JBA's most popular genres propagating Islamic ethics is *anashid*, literally meaning "chants" or "recitations." Traditionally, *anashid* is a term that refers to Islamic vocal music that is either sung a cappella or accompanied by light percussion instruments. *Anashid* is not considered "music" and therefore is approved as Islamic entertainment. It is not regarded as music because it distinguishes itself from profane music in that it does not use melodic instruments and only refers to Islamic topics. With the development of an artistic scene within the Islamic Revival movement starting in the 1970s in Egypt, over the last twenty years, melodic instruments (like violins and synthesizers) and also the use of lyrics revolving around worldly themes in addition to religious subjects, were gradually added to the originally minimal repertoire. In order to reach a wider and younger audience, the boundaries of *anashid* became increasingly flexible, as long as the aesthetics matched the Islamic ethics on the level of form, content, performance, and purpose (see Jouili 2012). Yet, contemporary *anashid* are still the subject of heated debates among scholars, the public, and artists.

The Islam-inspired music that is practiced and performed by artists in the JBA not only consists of *anashid* but also includes *amdah* (songs of praise to the Prophet and his family), *ibtihalat* (supplications of God), and songs in classical Arab styles (Frishkopf 2000). A typical musical performance features a vocal soloist called *munshid* assisted by a small or large chorus. The chorus sings in unison and accompanies the *munshid*. Most of the music is performed with only voice and some modest percussion, but sometimes melodic instruments are added. Some singers who have been trained as professional singers of Arabic-styled music genres give concerts with entire orchestras, of which perhaps the best-known example is Rachid Gholem.

JBA's *munshidin* operate both on professional and amateur levels and perform either solo or as part of a vocal group. They perform within the context of the JBA but also commercially for both other Islamist groups and conservative segments of society. Many vocal ensembles affiliated with the JBA work in a small cultural urban niche of Islamic entertainment, where they are hired by conservative families that wish to celebrate religious and family occasions in accordance with their Islamic lifestyles. The families that invite them are not necessarily sensitive to political Islam. Rather they are generally interested in a more devout lifestyle. The majority of concerts take place in private settings of family homes, but cultural festivals at university campuses or youth community houses, organized by Islamic organizations, are common settings as well.

CULTURAL POLITICS TOWARD ISLAM
AND MUSIC IN MOROCCO

The JBA's brand of pious entertainment has not been taken up on state stages for musical activities and religious entertainment in Morocco. This can partially be explained by the antiroyalist positioning of the organization. Another reason is that their musical style and especially their *anashid* is generally linked to "Islamism," which over the last decade has been increasingly stigmatized by the Moroccan state. *Anashid* are generally traced back to the Muslim Brotherhood and Islamic student activism in Egypt (Barendregt 2011: 235, Frishkopf 2000, Van Nieuwkerk 2011, 2013, Tammam and Haenni 2003). Under the influence of the Islamic Revival, *anashid* emerged in Morocco on university campuses in the late 1970s and early 1980s (ter Laan, forthcoming). After 9/11, and especially since the bombings in Casablanca on 16 May 2003, which were attributed to Islamist groups, the Moroccan authorities came to see Islamism as a potential threat to the stability of the country. With the support of the international community, a series of counterterrorism strategies were initiated, putting the brake on the country's democratization process. It was believed that democratization would give too much space to political Islam.

Hostility toward Islamism was also reflected in the state's cultural policies concerning religious entertainment and music. After 9/11, and particularly the Casablanca bombings of 2003, the liberalization of the audio-visual landscape and cultural arenas, which were set in motion under King Mohammed VI, were increasingly used to provide a counterweight against Islamism and to impede negative western representations of Islam. This resulted in a twofold strategy. On the one hand, the state became involved in the sponsoring and organization of major music festivals featuring prominent western artists, as well as young Moroccan performers of western-style music (like hip-hop and metal) that had been previously excluded from official platforms (Belghazi 2006; Boubia 2008; see also Salois in this volume). Some saw the inclusion of the Moroccan youth music scene on official stages as an opening of the national cultural field. Others, however, saw it as a way for the state to control potential subversion and cynically use this policy to build and advance the democratic reputation of Morocco (Boum 2012). Such festivals[7] hold an important function in the display of cultural markers typically associated with western democracy to international communities, and present Morocco as a crossroad of cultural and religious diversity (Kapchan 2008).

On the other hand, the Moroccan state set out to reformulate Sufism as the banner of "moderate" Islam. Sufism was articulated as part of a Muslim religiosity that encourages interfaith dialogue, universalism, tolerance, peace, and democracy (Shannon 2011).[8] Such "Sufi-values" are explicitly linked to a discourse of modern citizenship, national identity, and traditional Moroccan cultural heritage. Values such as "tolerance" and "diversity" are increasingly emphasized as common attributes found in both Sufism and Moroccan cultural heritage (Langlois 2009, Becker 2009). After 9/11 and the Casablanca bombings, more and more cultural expressions encouraged by the Moroccan state have been classified in close relation to such values and to Sufism in general. This discourse has also been enacted musically. Sufism, which is generally described as an esoteric or mystical dimension of Islam, uses repetitive music and chanting to reach nearness to God (Schimmel 1975). Therefore, it lends itself very well to the dissemination of music in conjunction with Islam. Where restrictions on music making have become associated with Islamism, Sufism has come to represent a "moderate" Islam that combines faith with music. It is within this discourse of cultural politics that Sufism as a musical category has become the banner of moderate Islam and Muslim tolerance (Shannon 2011).

The national religious TV and radio channel *Assadissa* (created in 2004) broadcasts liturgical recitations, songs of praise, and hymns from various Moroccan Sufi orders. Also, the Moroccan state encourages the organization of international music festivals concentrating on "sacred" or Sufi music. Festivals such as the Fez Festival of Sacred World Music or the Fez Festival of Sufi Culture offer settings where Sufi orders from across the world perform Sufi rituals in which disciples recite religious poetry, adapted to staged settings, attracting mostly Moroccan elites and tourists (see also Kapchan in this volume).

In contrast to the public promotion of Sufi music and westernized music styles, Islamist musical practices such as *anashid* are associated with Islamism. Performers of these musical genres, especially when affiliated with Islamist groups such as the JBA, are obviously not welcome as guests in these official cultural arenas.[9] *Munshidin* and their musical practices thus enjoy little visibility in official cultural representations of Islam and have received hardly any state support. Nonetheless, *anashid* as a genre of Islam-inspired music has gained popularity as an alternative to some forms of state supported entertainment. Some of JBA's *munshidin* have even successfully performed abroad and attained celebrity status. Through its increasing presence and diffusion via alternative musical circuits such as privately owned satellite channels and new media platforms such as YouTube, websites, and social network sites, the genre has become much in demand among pious publics who reject the musical entertainment offered by state-funded media and festivals.

ART AND POPULAR CULTURE AS A SITE OF POLITICAL CONTEST

Morocco's state cultural policies have an impact on what types of music are heard on national media channels and what types are not heard. Artistic expression in Morocco can also serve as a powerful tool to challenge these official perspectives. For example, one of the ideas motivating the *munshidin* is their critique of the western-oriented festivals supported by the Moroccan state, which they deem un-Islamic. In the context of the Arab Spring, their art was, then, used to raise awareness of state repression.

The role of cultural production in shaping political meanings can be described in terms of a concept of "cultural politics." This points to the entanglement of cultural production and ideology and understands culture as an arena in which social, economic, and political values and meanings are created and contested.[10] Many artists in Morocco who were involved in the protests used their art with the purpose of changing power relations within society. By using symbolic vocabularies and repertoires in their artistic expressions, they aim to influence ideas and to mobilize sentiment and action. For example, bloggers of the Moroccan activist portal *mamfakinch* (Moroccan Arabic for "we won't give up") argue that art emanating from the uprisings serves to encourage Moroccans to participate in the protests and revolt.[11]

Musically speaking, a wide range of artists participated in the protests: hip-hoppers, hard rockers, and *sha'bi* artists,[12] but also *munshidin* participated to agitate against state repression and urge for social justice and democracy. Some of JBA's musicians who joined the February 20th movement were represented in an artistic committee that aimed to use art to support and transfer political messages. The artistic committee, made up of artists from various disciplines and political-religious orientations, used their particular art forms and styles as a weapon in the struggle for more democracy. They engaged in the creation of protest slogans, the organization of artistic activities accompanying protest events, and generally called for artistic freedom as a human right, something they felt was lacking in Morocco. Some *munshidin* started to compose songs dedicated to the Arab Spring with explicit political messages that they performed at street demonstrations. These musical practices differed from their earlier musical practices with reference to performance setting, audiences, and lyrics.

MUSICAL TRANSFORMATIONS

Prior to the Arab Spring, the repertoires of the JBA-affiliated *munshidin*'s songs concentrated on Islamic themes and were mainly performed in family settings before a pious audience. In the wake of the Arab Spring protests, some of these vocalists started to produce and perform songs that differed strikingly on many levels from their earlier musical practices. I address here three kinds of shifts in sonic practice that accompanied these musical transformations.

The first shift in the musical practices of JBA's *munshidin* concerns a change in performance setting. Whereas *munshidin* mostly perform in private settings such as family houses, and enjoy little visibility in the Moroccan public sphere, the protests provided them with a context to perform their music in public as well as to exhibit their presence and their connection with the February 20th movement message. The move from a domestic to a street environment was accompanied by changing performance styles. In addition to the usual concert settings of *anashid* groups using instruments, microphones, and audio equipment, some *munshidin* started to appear in street demonstrations where they gave solo performances in which they alternated the chanting of protest slogans with singing protest songs through megaphones. The backdrop of street demonstrations also featured in numerous songs and revolutionary video clips launched on YouTube, blogs, and the media portal of the February 20th movement, *mamfakinch*. These video clips and songs were edited to sounds and images of protesting people, protest slogans written on banners, and violent police interventions.

The second shift the musical practices of JBA's *munshidin* underwent under the influence of the protests occurred on the level of audiences. *Munshidin* largely appeal to audiences of devout middle-class educated men and women who wish to partake in leisure activities without offending Islamic ethical norms. These people might be members of Islamist movements, but this does not necessarily have to be the case. However, the diverse mix of activists at the "Free Lhaqed event" I attended in Casablanca differed greatly from the *munshidin*'s usual pious, conservative audience. A considerable part of the audience consisted of secular leftists, who would never have imagined themselves listening to *anashid*, let alone cheering *munshidin* belonging to the JBA. Nonetheless, *munshidin* now found themselves performing for a diverse assembly of ideologically opposed activists, each with their habitual taste for different musical styles, who actively listened to *anashid*.

But the *anashid* these *munshidin* performed differed strikingly from their usual repertoire. The third and final shift pertains to the repertoire and lyrics. With the outbreak of the protests, *munshidin* started to bring out a completely different repertoire of songs. Although similar in style, the lyric content contrasted sharply with the *munshidin*'s previous repertoire, which consisted of songs and poems addressing Islamic topics such as God and the Prophet and urged the listener to live according to the principles of Islam. These songs were almost always sung in classical Arabic. Songs such as "Kun ma' Allah" (Be with Allah) by the well-known Moroccan solo vocalist Rachid Gholem or "Ya Rabbi Sali 'Ala Muhammad" (Oh Lord Muhammad), written and composed by the amateur *anashid* group Al-Nur (the Light), are examples of the regular repertoire sung by *munshidin* before the protests.

O LORD MUHAMMAD

O lord Muhammad, bless us with the green turban
People have visited Muhammad [his grave] but for me, he is living in my heart
People use vehicles to visit him, for me, I will go to him by feet
I came to visit the grave of my lord, the Arab messenger
Ask the angels, ask Gabriel, ask the throne porter [angels]
Ask the tablet keepers,[13] my heart is fond of the Qorashi

GROUP AL-NUR, TRANSLATED BY ABDISSAMAT AÏT DADA

During the protests, songs emerged that, by contrast, were totally devoid of religious words, topics, or references in the lyrics. Instead, the songs overtly criticized the Moroccan political system, encouraging people to raise their voice against state repression. Moreover, many of the protest songs used *darija* (Moroccan Arabic) instead of *fusha* (modern standard Arabic), the language most often used in *anashid*. In interviews most *munshidin* indicated they turned to *darija* to increase the accessibility of the content of the protest songs for a large public.[14] For example, the song "Raise your voice," written by Rachid Gholem on the occasion of the Arab Spring, was the first song that he wrote and performed in *darija* and addresses explicitly political subjects.

ʿALIW AS-SAWT (RAISE YOUR VOICE)

Be powerful, even when things are difficult.
It takes a lot of courage and perseverance to succeed.
But eventually there will be freedom.
The people will strengthen their voice despite state repression,
And muffled voices will be heard.
"No," against constitutions without the participation of the people.
Behind the walls of fear, the people will underline her will,
Because people might appear alive, in reality they are dead.
All the tears, pain, and sacrifices are not in vain,
Change is going to come, just hang on.
Chorus:
For my country, and the people of my country
And my children, our children and the future generations
Raise your voice
ARTIST: RACHID GHOLEM, TRANSLATED BY JOSEPH ALAGHA

Comparing the lyrics of "Oh my lord Muhammad" with "Raise your voice" demonstrates a turn from religious topics to the explicit discussion of political subjects such as state repression, freedom, censorship, and change. In "Raise your voice" for example, there is an open declaration against the new constitution that was drawn up by a commission entirely appointed by the king. The song not only critiques the absence of civil participation in the creation of the new constitution but also comments on a general lack of involvement of Moroccan citizens in the political process. This judgment was widely carried throughout the February 20th movement. At street demonstrations, banners with the slogan "citizens not subject!" were often carried. This slogan, on the one hand, commented on the situation in which the monarchical system dis-tributes rights and responsibilities to civilians, making them subjects. On the other hand, it called for a juridical regulated system in which citizenship is secured. By incorporating such calls for civil participation in Moroccan so-ciety into their protest songs, Islamist singers not only criticize the current state of affairs but also contribute to alternative visions of citizenship in Morocco.

DEMOCRACY AS AN ISLAMIC ETHICAL PROJECT

Taken together, what do these three shifts in practice mean? How can they be interpreted?

Interviews I conducted with singers about the changes in their musical practices during the protests revealed that, although the settings, lyrics, and audiences were different, to them, the meaning of their music was not. The fol-lowing interview fragment with Rachid Gholem, conducted after the release of his song *"Aliw as-sawt"* suggests as much:

> There might be no explicit references to Islamic topics in my lyrics any more, but to me they nonetheless have a religious meaning. Islam is there to make people free. The biggest problem of the despotism of the *makhzen* is that there is no freedom. Take the name *al-ʿAdl wal-Ihsan*. It means "justice" (*ʿadl*) and "benevolence" (*ihsan*). "Justice" in the sense of change, political change, eco-nomic change and also social change. "Benevolence," meaning to do good in the world and to develop the will to change. My previous songs emphasized this spiritual side of life, but that doesn't mean I cannot make songs about justice. I actually did sing about societal matters before, but always in an indirect way.[15]

This interview fragment shows that whether the ideas expressed in the music revolved around themes referring explicitly to Islamic subjects or to topics that reflect political consciousness and commitment to social justice, Rachid Gholem classifies the musical practices as two sides of the same coin. For him they are part of the same ethical space. To understand his perspective, I use Saba Mahmood's notion of politics as intrinsically connected to ethical practices of pious self-cultivation (Mahmood 2005). The Islam-inspired music of JBA's *munshidin* can be considered an example of such ethical practices closely related to larger debates about ethical behavior and morality. During interviews, many of the *munshidin* indicated that their motivation to perform Islamic music was to enhance moral thought, feelings, and behavior within the listener with the intention of stimulating an ethical transformation within society at large. To them music is a site through which moral virtues can be awakened (or, indeed, jeopardized), but is also a tool to develop the right inward dispositions in themselves and their listeners. In the context of the protests, these same sensibilities were invoked through music, not simply with the aim of producing pius Muslims, but to raise broader ethical concerns guided by Islamic morals.

Besides, the music of JBA's *munshidin* was already politicized. The national cultural policies influenced by antiterrorism strategies generated a discourse about a "moderate" as opposed to a "radical" Islam, embedded in notions of a "locally embedded culture and tradition" (Silverstein 2012) that are musically enacted by encouraging certain cultural-religious leisure activities over others. Even though their lyrics merely addressed religious themes and contained no political topics prior to the nationwide protests, their music was construed in opposition to official state-formulated representations of Islam. This space of opposition has been described by Charles Hirschkind through the concept of the "counterpublic," which he defines as "a domain of discourse and practice that stands in a disjunctive relationship to the public sphere of the nation and its media instruments" (Hirschkind 2006: 117). Like Mahmood, Hirschkind also turns our attention to popular culture as a medium that can cultivate sensibilities based on Islamic morality.

So, although it is tempting to explain the musical transformation as a shift from "religious" to "political," to JBA's *munshidin*, there was, quite simply, no change. This helps us see that the *munshidin* and their music were *already* engaged in broader competing discourses of ethical behavior revolving around communal values, in a political arena. They themselves justified the changes they made in their music as a continuation of the same ethical project: one that wishes to promote pious sensibilities in search for a different kind of political ethos and the formulation of alternative forms of citizenship in which Islam serves as a moral compass.

CONCLUSION

In this chapter I have demonstrated that in the context of the Arab Spring, art and music have become a vehicle for political messages as well as a site for debate and reformulation of politico-ethical values and discourses about freedom, democracy, and citizenship. Through a detailed analysis of a case study in Morocco, focusing on *munshidin*, affiliated with the Islamist Jama'a al-'Adl wal-Ihsan, I have shown how the Arab Spring and the Moroccan February 20th movement have produced a space providing public visibility and audibility to a wide variety of marginalized people and organizations. This

music has both reflected, as well as engendered alliances, between oppositional forces. With leftist-secular activists and Islamist *munshidin* sharing and
exchanging repertoires and performing in the same venue, formations could
be created surpassing ideological differences, emphasizing shared claims and
broader calls for democracy and justice. These observations hold true in the
spur of the revolutionary moment, but it remains to be seen whether this cross-
over coalition will continue.[16]

Nevertheless, the fact that JBA's *munshidin* did not experience the shifts
in their musical repertoires as a turn from religious to political, but as two
sides of the same coin, continues to challenge commonly held representations
of boundaries between ideological groups, like binaries as religious versus
secular activists. Moreover, it illustrates the roles Islamist artists occupy in re-
formulating notions of "democracy" and "freedom" within Islamic frames: as
an ethical project. More broadly, exploring Islamist artistic initiatives and the
settings of display in the Arab Spring shows us the complex constellations of
differences and communalities between sets of religious and secular orientations involved, as well as different notions of ethical and moral values guiding
notions of "democracy" and "freedom" (Hirschkind 2012). Calls for democracy no longer solely revolve around opposed political ideologies but are increasingly formulated in terms of moral values and ethical principles of governance accommodating people of different ideologies. Concepts like "freedom"
and "democracy," but also "justice," and "dignity," once notions reserved to
liberal-secular idiom, have become shared ethical notions playing a key role
in the formulation of alternative discourses of citizenship.

NOTES

The specific data I used for this chapter is part of my PhD project on Muslim devotional
music and cultural politics in Morocco. The data were gathered at the time the protests were
at their height.

1. The terms "Islamism," or "political Islam," cover a wide array of phenomena. Generally, Islamism is described and analyzed as a movement of activist groups putting Islam to use
for political purposes, with the goal to establish an Islamic state (Roy 2004: 29; Hirschkind
2012; Lauzière 2005: 241; Zeghal 2008: xv).

2. *Anashid* is the plural form of the Arabic word *nashid* or *inshad*, which can loosely be
translated as "chanting" or "reciting."

3. The word *munshidin* is plural for *munshid*, which in Arabic means "the one who recites." It is a larger term for performers of Islamic songs. When I use the term *munshidin*, I
specifically refer to the vocalists affiliated to the *Jama'a al-'adl wal-ihsan*.

4. An *'ud* is a pear-shaped stringed lute used in Arabic music.

5. "The Sweet Illusion of Democratic Change, February 24th," 2011, blog by Zineb el-
Razhoui at the website http://en.qantara.de. Accessed 23 October 2013.

6. Sheikh Yassine passed away on 13 December 2012, at the age of 84.

7. Examples of such state-supported festivals are *Mawazine* held every May in Rabat, *Timitar* held every June in Agadir, and the Festival of *Gnawa* music held in June in Essaouira.

8. This was not only the result of post-9/11 rhetoric but also part of a recent government initiative to restructure the entire religious scene in Morocco (Elahmadi 2010, Maghraoui 2009).

9. Like Rachid Gholem, who claims to be forbidden from performance in his own country due to his adherence to the JBA.

10. Definition derived from http://culturalpolitics.net. Accessed 26 January 2012.

11. 4 April 2011, "20 Février: l'art au service de la contestation et de la mobilisation," https://www.mamfakinch.com/20-fevrier-lart-au-service-de-la-contestation-et-de-la -mobilisation. Accessed 11 October 2011.

12. *Sha'bi* music is a popular genre of Moroccan folk music.

13. Muslims believe that Allah wrote the content of the Qur'an on a tablet.

14. Due to a high illiteracy rate (33 percent in 2011), only a few Moroccans read, speak, and write Modern Standard Arabic. CIA World Factbook, https://www.cia.gov/library /publications/the-world-factbook. Accessed 27 December 2013.

15. Personal interview with Rachid Gholem, 5 May 2011.

16. At this point, there are very few protests. The February 20th movement lost much momentum over the years. The JBA pulled out of the protest movement on 18 December 2011, shortly after the Islamic political party, the Justice and Development Party (PJD), won the national elections held in November 2011. The withdrawal of the JBA resulted in a weakening of the February 20th movement. The reason indicated by the national press was that the JBA, after the election victory of the PJD, no longer wanted to be in a protest movement that fought a government led by Islamists (Karim Boukhari, Telquel, 24 December 2011). Also the implementation of a new constitution and the early elections held in November 2011 signaled a sign of change, which drove many supporters of the protest movement to withdraw from the streets (Ahmed Charaï, L'Observateur, 25 March 2013).

REFERENCES

Barendregt, B. 2011. "Pop, Politics and Piety: Nasyid Boy Band Music in Muslim Southeast Asia." In *Islam and Popular Culture in Indonesia and Malaysia*, edited by A. N. Weintraub, 235–256. London: Routledge.

Becker, C. J. 2009. "Art, Self-Censorship, and Public Discourse: Contemporary Moroccan Artists at the Crossroads." *Contemporary Islam: Dynamics of Muslim Life* 3 (2009): 143–166.

Belghazi, T. 2006. "Festivalization of Urban Space in Morocco." *Critique: Critical Middle Eastern Studies* 15, no. 1: 97–107.

Boubia, A. 2008. "*L'enjeu politique des festivals de musique au Maroc*." MA thesis, Institute for Political Studies, Paris.

Boum, A. 2012. "Youth, Political Activism and the Festivalization of Hip-Hop Music in Morocco." In *Contemporary Morocco: State, Politics, and Society under Mohammed VI*, edited by Bruce Maddy-Weitzman and Daniel Zisenwine. London: Routledge.

Cohen, S., and L. Jaïdi. 2006. *Morocco: Globalization and Its Consequences.* New York: Taylor & Francis.

Daadaoui, M. 2011. *Moroccan Monarchy and the Islamist Challenge: Maintaining Makhzen Power*. New York: Palgrave Macmillan.

Driessen, H. 1994. "De aura van de monarch." In *In de ban van betekenis: Proeven van symbolische antropologie*, edited by Henk Driessen and Huub de Jonge. Nijmegen: SUN.

Elahmadi, M. 2010. "Modernisation du champ religieux au Maroc 1999–2009." In *Une decennie de réformes au Maroc (1999–2009)*, edited by C.d.é internationals, 117–140. Paris: Karthala.

Faruqi, I. R., and L. L. Faruqi. 1986. *The Cultural Atlas of Islam*. New York: Macmillan.

Frishkopf, M. 2000. "*Inshad Dini* and *Aghani Diniyya* in Twentieth-Century Egypt: A Review of Styles, Genres and Available Recordings." *Middle East Studies Association* 34, no. 2: 167–183.

Geertz, C. 1968. *Islam Observed: Religious Development in Morocco and Indonesia*. Chicago: University of Chicago Press.

Haenni, P., and Tammam. 2003. "Chat Shows, Nashid Groups and Lite Preaching. Egypt's air-conditioned Islam." *Le Monde Diplomatique*.

Hammoudi, A. 1997. *Master and Disciple: The Cultural Foundations of Moroccan Authoritarianism*. Chicago: University of Chicago Press.

Hirschkind, C. 2006. *The Ethical Soundscape: Cassette Sermons and Islamic Counterpublics*. New York: Columbia University Press.

Hirschkind, C. 2012. "Beyond Secular and Religious: An Intellectual Genealogy of Tahrir Square." *American Ethnologist* 39, no. 1: 49–53.

Jouili, J. 2012. "Halal Arts, What's in a Concept?" *Material Religion. The Journal of Objects, Art and Belief* 8, no. 3: 402–403.

Kapchan, D. A. 2008. "The Promise of Sonic Translation: Performing the Festive Sacred in Morocco." *American Anthropologist* 110, no. 4: 467–483.

Laan, N. ter. Forthcoming 2015. "Dissonant Voices: Music, Islam and Cultural Politics in Morocco." PhD thesis, Radboud University, Nijmegen.

Langlois, T. 2009. "Music and Politics in North Africa." In *Music and the Play of Power: Music, Politics and Ideology in the Middle East, North Africa and Central Asia*, edited by Laudan Nooshin. Farnham, Surrey: Ashgate.

Lauzière, H. 2005. "Post-Islamism and the Religious Discourse of Abd al-Salam Yasin." *International Journal of Middle East Studies* 37, no. 2: 241–261.

Maghraoui, D. 2009. "The Strengths and Limits of Religious Reforms in Morocco." *Mediterranean Politics* 14, no. 2: 195–211.

Mahmood, S. 2005. *Politics of Piety: The Islamic Revival and the Feminist Subject*. Princeton: Princeton University Press.

Munson, H. L. Jr. 1993. *Religion and Power in Morocco*. New Haven: Yale University Press.

Rahman, Z. 2012. "Online Youth Political Activism in Morocco: Facebook and the Birth of the February 20th Movement." *Journal of New Media Studies in the MENA*, issue no. 1 (Winter).

Roy, O. 2004. *Globalized Islam: The Search for a New Ummah*. New York: Columbia University Press.

Schimmel, A. 1975. *Mystical Dimensions of Islam*. Chapel Hill: University of North Carolina Press.

Shannon, J. 2011. "Suficized Musics of Syria at the Intersection of Heritage and the War on Terror." In *Muslim Rap, Halal Soaps, and Revolutionary Theater: Critical Perspectives on*

Islam and Performing Arts, edited by Karin van Nieuwkerk. Austin: University of Texas Press.

Shiloah, A. 1995. *Music in the World of Islam*. Detroit: Wayne State University Press.

Shilton, S. 2013. "Art and the 'Arab Spring': Aesthetics of Revolution in Contemporary Tunesia." *French Cultural Studies* 24, no. 1: 129–145.

Silverstein, P. 2012. "In the Name of Culture: Berber Activism and the Material Politics of 'Popular Islam' in Southeastern Morocco." *Material Religion. Journal of Objects, Art and Belief* 8, no. 3: 330–353.

Slyomovics, S. 2005. *The Performance of Human Rights in Morocco*. Philadelphia: University of Pennsylvania Press.

Van Nieuwkerk, Karin, ed. 2011. *Muslim Rap, Halal Soaps, and Revolutionary Theater. Artistic Developments in the Muslim World*. Austin: University of Texas Press.

Van Nieuwkerk, Karin. 2013. *Performing Piety: Singers and Actors in Egypt's Islamic Revival*. Austin: University of Texas Press.

Vermeeren, P. 2009. *Le Maroc de Mohammed VI: La transition inachevé*. Paris: Éditions la découverte.

Waterbury, J. 1970. *Commander of the Faithful: The Moroccan Political Elite; A Study of Segmented Politics*. London: Weidenfeld and Nicolson.

Wright, R. 2011. *Rock the Casbah: Rage and Rebellion across the Islamic World*. New York: Simon & Schuster.

Zeghal, M. 2008. *Islamism in Morocco: Religion, Authoritarianism, and Electoral Politics*. Princeton: Markus Wiener.

CHAPTER 5

VISUAL CULTURE AND THE AMAZIGH
RENAISSANCE IN NORTH AFRICA AND
ITS DIASPORA

CYNTHIA BECKER

DURING THE SO-CALLED Arab Spring protests, Berbers called for their national governments to acknowledge their historic and cultural contributions to North Africa and to recognize their language, Tamazight, as an official language on a par with Arabic. As the indigenous people of North Africa, many Berbers felt marginalized by their national governments, who, after colonial independence declared themselves Arab-Islamic states with Arabic as the official language, even though Berber speakers account for approximately 40 percent of the population in Morocco and 25 percent in Algeria.[1] For the last several decades an activist movement has developed to fight for the political rights of the Berber population. Most activists have rejected the term Berber as a pejorative label given to them by outsiders, from the Greek and Roman words for "barbarians," preferring the term "Imazighen," which means "the free people," or "Amazigh," which is the singular adjectival form.[2]

Amazigh activists claimed a space for themselves within the protests by referring to them as the "Amazigh Spring," "Democracy Spring," or simply "North African Revolutions." In order to distinguish themselves, Amazigh protesters from Libya to Morocco waved a blue, green, and yellow flag with a large red emblem in the center (figure 5.1). This flag, originally created by a small group of largely male Amazigh activists in 1997, has developed into an international identity symbol for the Imazighen. In fact, over the years, many such identity symbols have emerged, including ancient pre-Islamic icons as well as newly created ones, such as the Amazigh flag. Activists adopted self-consciously secular symbols and use them to declare their identity as unique from Arabs. They carry them during protests, paint them as graffiti, and post them on activist websites. This chapter uses interviews and participation in Amazigh cultural events in North Africa and its diaspora to demonstrate how these visual symbols have contributed to a pan-Amazigh Renaissance. As

5.1. Imazighen protesting in Libya (2011). Photo courtesy of Libyan Amazigh 101.

this chapter demonstrates, visual arts seen during protests, on the Internet, and at Amazigh cultural celebrations have permeated popular culture. Such visual symbols serve to link Amazigh activists from Morocco to Boston, contributing to a sense of Amazigh unity across economic, gender, and political boundaries.

AMAZIGH FLAG: ACTIVISTS AND THE AMAZIGH DIASPORA

One of the most ubiquitous symbols used by members of the Amazigh linguistic and cultural movement is the Amazigh flag, created in 1997 at a meeting of the Amazigh World Congress in the Canary Islands. Activists created a blue, green, and yellow flag to symbolize Amazigh solidarity and devotion to a transnational identity movement. According to the Amazigh World website, the Amazigh flag serves as:

a symbol of reawakening, a password for all Imazighen, wherever they are found. A symbol whose colors and design are drawn from our past, and at the same time guides our destiny, guaranteeing that our children will hoist it permanently wherever a brethren arrives.[3]

Its stripes refer to the sky, pastures, and the desert, referencing the natural environment and, by extension, the transnational Amazigh homeland that extends across the Mediterranean coast to West Africa.

The color red of the flag's central motif, a letter from the ancient Berber alphabet called *tifinagh*, represents the blood of struggle. The *tifinagh* script, possibly related to the ancient Phoenician alphabet or Libyco-Berber alphabet, dates back to the fourth century BCE. It was used to write administrative texts and funerary inscriptions in a widespread area from the Canary Islands to modern Libya (Casajus 2001).

Although *tifinagh* went out of use centuries ago in North Africa, many activists revived the use of individual *tifinagh* letters as identity markers. For example, the *tifinagh* symbol in the center of the flag is known in Tamazight as *yaz* (English /z/) or an *aza*. This letter (equivalent to the English letter "z") serves as one of the primary visual symbols of the Amazigh community. This letter is the central character in the word "Amazigh," which means, "free man." In contrast, flags used by contemporary North African nation-states often feature colors and symbols that refer to Islam. For example, the crescent moon and five-pointed star, internationally recognized symbols associated with the Islamic faith, can be found on the Algerian, Libyan, and Tunisian national flags.

In addition to being flown by protestors across northern Africa, the Amazigh flag is commonly hung at cultural events organized by Amazigh activists in the United States (figure 5.2). Due to their economic and political marginalization in their homelands, many Berbers migrated outside of northern Africa, moving to France, the Netherlands, and, more recently, to the United States. In Morocco, Arabic became the only official language recognized in the 1962 constitution. Since the Arab language represents Islamic legitimacy and Arab ethnicity, Amazigh activists viewed this act as a refusal to acknowledge Morocco's indigenous population (Silverstein and Crawford 2004: 44). A similar situation existed in Algeria where Amazigh activists, unable to defeat the Arabization policies of their national governments, founded nongovernmental institutions abroad to promote their heritage (Silverstein 2007: 109–120).

In 1967, for example, intellectuals from Algeria founded the *Académie Berbère* in Paris to preserve and promote Berber culture and the Tamazight language. One of their actions was the creation of a standardized *neo-tifinagh* script that was a phonetic notation of Kabyle, one of the Berber languages spoken in northern Algeria. As explained by Salem Chaker, the Algerian professor of Tamazight and director of the Berber Research Center (CRB) in Paris, their effort was well intentioned but done by a group without any linguistic

5.2. Three generations of women (from right to left: Soumia Ait El Haj, her grandmother, and mother) hold the Amazigh flag at an Amazigh New Year Celebration, Everett, MA, 2010. Photo by author.

training. Instead, Chaker and other Algerian scholars have dedicated themselves to developing a pan-Amazigh script using Latin characters.[4] Many believe that since the Latin script is more widely accessible to those outside of North Africa, it will allow Tamazight to become a truly transnational language (Ilahian 2006: 124–125).

Despite the push by Algerian scholars to use the Latin script, *tifinagh* has made a recent resurgence in Morocco. This is largely due to the creation of the Royal Institute for the Study of Amazigh Culture (IRCAM) by the Moroccan king in response to internal protests and demands made by Amazigh activists. By 2003 IRCAM made the controversial decision to write Tamazight using a *neo-tifinagh* script, rejecting both the Arabic script and the Latin script (the latter for fear of Islamist reprisals for appearing pro-western). Many Amazigh activists, especially those in Algeria, rejected IRCAM's decision, claiming that the *tifinagh* script was purposefully chosen to exoticize the Berber language and make it more difficult to learn.

Regardless, the decision by IRCAM to use the *tifinagh* script led to its proliferation into mainstream Moroccan society. IRCAM has published numerous books, including school textbooks in *tifinagh*, and many public buildings feature signs written in Arabic, *tifinagh*, and Latin scripts. The *aza*, in particular, has developed into a popular decorative symbol. In fact, Amazigh activists have transformed the *aza* into a three-fingered hand gesture where the first three fingers are raised and parted, while the remaining fingers are clenched. The three raised fingers evoke the three vertical projections at the top of the *aza*, and activists state that they represent three concepts central to the Amazigh movement: *awal* (language), *akal* (land), and *afgan* (people).

VISUAL SYMBOLS OF A PRE-ISLAMIC PAST

Despite the proliferation of *tifinagh* in Morocco, Berbers in Algeria reserve its use for brief messages or short slogans on banners and walls. For example, at the entrance of a small Berber village outside of the city of Tizi Ouzou, the capital of Amazigh activism in Algeria, an artist wrote a poem in Kabyle, the Berber language spoken in the region, written with the Latin script. Locals also adorned its white walls with geometric symbols once common to clay pottery made in the region and also painted various portraits that they labeled with *tifinagh* (figure 5.3). On the far bottom right, an anonymous artist painted a profile portrait of Jugurtha, the illegitimate grandson of King Massinissa, who is pictured to his right. Massinissa ruled an ancient North African kingdom called Numidia as an ally of Rome from 206 BCE until his death in 148. Under Massinissa, Numidia extended from the contemporary nation of Morocco in the west to eastern Libya. Jugurtha boldly usurped the throne from Massinissa's legitimate heirs, taking power around 117 BCE and waging war against the Roman Empire for eight years. Eventually Jugurtha was captured, brought to Rome in chains, and executed in 104 BCE (Camps and Chaker 2004: 3978). The linkage of Amazigh activists to figures from ancient history, such as Jugurtha, suggests an Amazigh inherent sense of rebellion and opposition against external oppression (Maddy-Weitzman 2011: 177). Jugurtha was in reality a ruthless ruler, who readily sacrificed friends, family, and counselors to strengthen his power, but, in recent years he has emerged as a Berber hero, who embodies fearlessness and resistance (Camps and Chaker 2004: 3977). This association of Jugurtha with bravery and courage is further expressed in the name written under the portrait seen in figure 5.3. The graffiti artist used *tifinagh* script to write the word "Yugurten." According to the scholar Salem Chaker, this was the original Berber form of the king's name, and this phrase is still used among Berbers in North Africa, meaning "he exceeds them," with "them" referring to "the enemies," further referencing Jugurtha's heroic nature (Camps and Chaker 2004: 3978–3979).

5.3. Close-up of graffiti painted on the entrance to a Kabyle village located outside of the city of Tizi Ouzou. Photo by author (2006).

VISUALIZING GENDER EQUALITY

In addition to celebrating heroic Berber men, the Amazigh movement also recognizes the achievements of notable Berber women. In general, Amazigh activists state that Berber women were historically emancipated and enjoyed greater freedom than their Arab counterparts. They hold up an ideal image of Tuareg, an Amazigh group who lives in the Sahara and Sahel. Tuareg women own their own livestock and nomadic tents and exert considerable influence over domestic matters. While Tuareg men wear turbans that they use to cover their mouths and noses, women do not cover their faces with veils. These factors contribute to the view by North African Berbers that Tuareg represent a less-Arabized and more pure version of Amazigh culture that gives considerable freedom to women. Therefore, Amazigh activists use this as evidence that prior to the arrival of Islam, Berber women carried considerable power and status, often claiming that Berber society was once matriarchal (Becker 2010: 207–208).

The role of women in Amazigh society as guardians and carriers of Amazigh identity has been translated into a powerful visual trope commonly employed by the Imazighen. For example, the graffiti seen in figure 5.3 features the figure of a woman on the left. The graffiti artist wrote the word "Dihya" underneath this female figure referring to the name of a mythological Berber queen who led the resistance against invading Arabs in the late seventh century. Commonly called "the Kahina," believed to derive from the Arabic word *kahin*, meaning "seer" or "priestess," oral histories recount that she belonged to a Judaizied Berber group who lived in the Aurès Mountains of contemporary Algeria. According to legend, she led a resistance movement that at first defeated the attacking Arab army. As she waited for a renewed Arab assault, the Kahina ordered nomadic Berbers to destroy the crops, herds, and towns of sedentary Berbers in order to make the land less appealing to the conquerors. This scorched earth policy did not thwart the invaders and resulted in her loss of the support of sedentary Berbers. The returning Arab army quickly defeated her sometime between 693 and 702 CE (Maddy-Weitzman 2011: 23). For Amazigh activists the Kahina remains a legendary figure in the Berber struggle against Arabization (Hannoum 2001).

During the French colonial period, for example, the legend of the Kahina leading the Berbers in resistance against Arab invasion was used by the French to legitimize French colonization, framing it as the liberation of Berbers from their oppressors. Ironically, the sketch of Dihya on the wall of the Kabyle village in figure 5.3 probably derived from an 1870 painting by the French orientalist artist Charles-Émile-Hippolyte Lecomte-Vernet. Although the current location and original title of the painting by Lecomte-Vernet is unknown, his painting of a female figure, known by the current title *Berber Woman*, has been reproduced on dozens of Amazigh websites and blogs to represent the mythological figure of the Kahina (figure 5.4). Painted in the hyperrealist style typical of nineteenth-century orientalist art, Lecomte-Vernet painted the bare arm of this female figure to exude a sense of strength, while her sidelong glance suggests that she is assessing a threat—a glance also captured by the contemporary graffiti artist of Tizi Ouzou. Her red garment suggests courage and sacrifice, while she wears Berber-style jewelry, including a silver headpiece, brooches (*fibulae*), and silver bracelets. The desert background suggests the geographic setting of northern Africa, yet it is removed enough from any particular historical or social context that Amazigh activists can use this painting to illustrate the story of this powerful female warrior, that activists commonly refer to as "The Berber Queen."

Numerous scholars have written about how nineteenth-century European paintings, such as the one by Émile Lecomte-Vernet, reveal orientalist stereotypes and reflect colonial ideologies. However, further layers of meaning concern the postcolonial afterlife of these images and how Imazighen reclaim them to suggest a new empowering discourse. Such imagery influences the performance of identity, especially gender roles, and contributes to a pre-

5.4. Charles-Émile-Hippolyte Lecomte-Vernet, French painter (1821–1900), *Berber Woman* (1870). This photo was accessed from http://youzero1 .blogzoom.fr/53221/Histoire-du-Kahina/ on 8 November 2013.

vailing idea held by Amazigh activists that boldness, bravery, and the ability to serve as political leaders characterized Berber women in the pre-Islamic past.

In addition to orientalist paintings, colonial photographs of Berber women proliferate Amazigh websites. One of the most prominent photographs, taken by the renowned photographers European Rudolf Lehnert and Ernest Landrock in the early twentieth century, was published in *National Geographic Magazine* in October 1922 (figure 5.5). It was among a group of sixteen photographs published in *National Geographic* under the title "Peoples and Places of Northern Africa" with the caption:

> Where the Gold of Many Lands Becomes a Wedding Dowry. Among the Ouled Nails, sentiment has little place. In their early youth these girls migrate to the Mediterranean ports, where, as dancers, they entertain the stranger and the wealthy native, and acquire ornaments of gold coins. When their glittering dowry is finally saved, they return to the desert and become dutiful wives in the tents of their own people (Author unknown 1922: 368).

Most colonial-era publications characterized so-called Ouled Nail women as "indescribably picturesque," women that were "somewhat careless, to put it mildly, so far as their morals are concerned" and dedicated to the "profession of pleasing men" (Powell 1912: 22–24). These women, who did not consider themselves prostitutes in the western sense of the term, were classified as such by the French, who literally imprisoned them in cafés or small windowless rooms where they performed for French soldiers, often providing sexual services in exchange for remuneration. They became tourist attractions and were used to promote Algerian tourism by French travel agencies (Limoncelli 2010: 124). Brought to Paris as part of the Universal Exposition of 1900, these women danced for the French public in the Algerian pavilion. Afterward, the designation "daughter of Ouled Nail" became a common expression used to designate a prostitute or courtesan (Clancy-Smith 2006: 28). Photographs of Ouled Nail women bedecked in layers of jewelry immediately captured the imagination of the European and American public—especially the image in figure 5.5, which was recently republished in a recent collection of *National Geographic Magazine's* greatest photographs (Jenkins 2012: 110).

With the development of photography, colonial photographs were not only published in magazines, they were mass-produced and widely circulated in the form of postcards, as seen in figure 5.5. Between 1900 and 1930, such postcards were mass-produced to be disseminated throughout Europe. Postcards documented scenes of historical colonial visits, landscapes, architecture, and people. One important project of these early photographers was

5.5. Rudolf Lehnert and Ernest Landrock, photographers. Postcard published by Lehnert and Landrock, early twentieth c., collection of the author.

scène et type photographs that classified colonial inhabitants deemed to be colorful or exotic according to ethnic or tribal categories (Geary 2008: 146–147). A massive amount of scholarship has deconstructed such postcards as revealing western stereotypes and imperial discourse (e.g., Alloula 1986, Belmenouar 2007). However, an alternative manner of interpreting the photographic images on them was suggested by the art historian Christraud Geary, who writes that scholars should consider photographic subjects from Africa as agents who actively asserted views of themselves and represented their personal, social, and religious identities through particular props, clothing, and poses, even if the photographer was European (Geary 2002: 20). Can the woman in figure 5.5, who was most likely a paid model, be seen as a victim of colonial policy or a woman expressing pride in her heritage?

Amazigh activists interpret such photographs of the Ouled Nail as images of empowerment. Amazigh activist websites highlight what is evidently a tattoo motif on the forehead of the woman in figure 5.5 as a representation of an *aza*—a symbol associated with freedom. The closely cropped photograph in addition to the woman's direct gaze and facial tattoos are interpreted by activists as suggesting bravery and strength, contributing to the popularity of this image and its circulation among Amazigh activists. For Amazigh activists, such imagery verifies their claim that unveiled powerful women dominated Berber society, contributing to their own version of history.

TRANS-SAHARAN REFLECTIONS AND AFRICAN INDIGENEITY

While the decorated female body remains a powerful visual metaphor associated with the values of liberation and the perseverance of Berber culture, Amazigh men are less likely to dress in "authentic" Amazigh dress, choosing to express their heritage by wearing T-shirts, baseball caps, or scarves decorated with the Amazigh flag. An exception is the region of southeastern Morocco where local tour guides commonly present themselves as the "blue men of the Sahara," dressing in indigo turbans and gowns also worn by Tuareg men in the Sahara and Sahel. These Berber men, who live on the edge of an erg filled with rolling sand dunes near the small town of Merzouga, take tourists on short treks across the dunes in colorful caravans.

These Berbers display an image of themselves to tourists as Tuareg nomads living an idyllic nomadic existence free from the influence of Arabization. They intensely market Tuareg culture to European and American tourists, and locals have opened small hotels with names as "Kasbah Le Touareg" and "Les Hommes Bleus." A musical group called Imoudda, which means "nomad" in Tamazight, performs in the style of the popular Tuareg band Tinariwen, a Tuareg band famous for its protest songs that supported Tuareg rebellion against the Malian state in the 1990s. The Moroccan band Imoudda wears Tuareg-inspired indigo blue turbans and gowns when they play for tourists as well as local events.

For Amazigh activists in Merzouga and elsewhere Tuareg represent the Noble Savage—the pure Imazighen uncorrupted by Islam and Arabization—freely crossing borders and living in harmony with nature in a pristine cultural state (Becker 2009: 87). The marketing of Tuareg culture in southeastern Morocco as an ethno-commodity also influences their self-perception. Even when they are not working with tourists, men continue to dress in this fashion. As noted by the Comaroffs in their book *Ethnicity, Inc.*, "the producers of culture are also its consumers, seeing and sensing and listening to themselves enact their identity," becoming the "authentic," the "original" (Comaroff and Comaroff 2009: 26).

Indeed, the nomadic ancestors of this Berber group in southeastern Morocco historically led caravans into the Sahara, typically wearing white turbans and hand-woven wool clothing. By the 1950s, colonialism enforced national borders, stopped trans-Saharan trade, and most had settled into adobe houses, founding numerous small towns. However, their appropriation of Tuareg popular culture, such as music and indigo blue clothing, allows them to give visual form to a transnational Amazigh identity. It also represents what might have been if national borders had not been created, their ancestors had not settled down, and Berber culture had not been "tainted" and "corrupted" by Arabization.

These young men represent themselves as Tuareg in order to recapture an authentic ethnic identity for themselves, since for North African Berbers they represent a less-Arabized, more pure form of Amazigh culture. In addition, such ethno-connections are used to stress pan-Berber imaginings of a unified homeland they call Tamazgha that encompasses many postcolonial nation-states. Tamazgha comprises the territory from the Nile to the Canary Islands and from the Mediterranean Sea across the Sahara into West Africa, including the contemporary nations of Mali, Niger, and Burkina Faso. Activists refute the popular claim heard in North Africa that the Berbers originated in Yemen and Syria, giving them a common Middle Eastern origin with Arabs. In a recent article published in the left-leaning, secular magazine *TelQuel*, printed in French, Ahmed Assid, the Moroccan Amazigh activist and researcher at IRCAM, stressed the indigenous African roots of Berbers, stating that Berbers are both African and Mediterranean:

Archeology shows us that the origins of Amazigh society are not oriental. They are African. Here we're talking about a period going back as far as 200,000 years. Amazigh is undoubtedly an African language. It is also valid to argue that the Tifinagh script shares a common origin with other written scripts from Africa. The official historical account supports the notion that the Amazigh alphabet is of Phoenician origin in order to give it the appearance of originating in the Orient. We are African, even when we shake our hips to the beat of the AHOUACHE dance or we see our mother take the reigns at home. The Amazigh share their music with sub-Saharan Africa as well as a matriarchal system.[5]

Assid's statements are meant, in part, to repudiate Arab nationalist claims that Berbers originally came from Yemen in order to give Berbers and Arabs a common Middle Eastern origin. Berbers themselves stress an indigenous territorial connection to North Africa. Amazigh activists, such as Assid, reinforce claims to their indigenous status by emphasizing connections between themselves and sub-Saharan Africans, who they consider "authentic" Africans. They also claim a pre-Islamic utopian world ruled by women in opposition to the oppressive, patriarchal culture they associate with Arabs and Islam.

YENNAYER: A BERBER HOLIDAY

In order to further their claims to indigeneity, Amazigh activists pay homage to what they believe to be the first manifestation of Berber civilization in recorded history: the conquest of Pharaonic Egypt in 950 BCE by Sheshonk I. Ancient Egyptian texts refer to the Libu, a North African group from which the name Libya derives, who joined with another tribe, the Meshwesh, and invaded Egypt. Sheshonk I, the leader of the Libu-Meshwesh, founded a dynasty that conquered and ruled Egypt for more than two hundred years (Maddy-Weitzman 2011: 15). In 1968, the Paris-based *Académie Berbère* memorialized this early mention of a group that Amazigh activists identify as their ancestors. They decided to begin their newly established Berber calendar with the year 950 BCE, creating the holiday of Yennayer and establishing a Berber calendar distinct from an Islamic one.

The creation of Yennayer, taken from the Tamazight word for "January," is recognized as a secular New Year celebration and ancient agrarian holiday. It is celebrated differently in various parts of North Africa but typically involves large family dinners. Yennayer serves as one of the few occasions that unites Amazigh activists in the diaspora and reinforces the creation of family-like bonds between immigrants in a new land. It gives Amazigh immigrants in Europe and the United States the opportunity to teach their foreign-born children about their Amazigh heritage. As noted by the scholar Bruce Maddy-Weitzman, the celebration of Yennayer provides Amazigh activists with a forum to illustrate the deep-rooted history of the Imazighen and to fashion a "coherent and usable historical narrative, complete with commemorative rituals" (2011: 207). More important, the recognition of Sheshonk I as an Amazigh ancestor allows Imazighen to present themselves as active agents capable of large-scale organization and political mobilization rather than as victims of Arab conquest (Maddy-Weitzman 2011: 16).

VISUALIZING JUDEO-BERBER HERITAGE

In addition to connecting themselves to ancient Egypt, Amazigh activists express the importance of religious plurality and acknowledge the friendly relationship between Berbers and Jews as an important part of Amazigh history. As explained to me by Meryam Demnati, a researcher at IRCAM in Morocco: "we [Imazighen] have lived a long time with Jews and with Christians. My father always brought me to Jewish festivals. There was conviviality with each one accepting the religion of the others. Today our children are taught to hate other races and other religions."[6] Demnati, as many other Amazigh activists, feels that since colonial independence and the rise of pan-Arabism, North Africans have become increasingly intolerant of religious and cultural differences.

In addition to recognizing the friendships and mutual respect that existed between Berbers and Jews, some Amazigh activists stated that since Jewish communities existed in North Africa since at least 70 CE and maybe even earlier, Berbers practiced Judaism, converting to Islam after the arrival of Arabs. While it is true that Jewish communities existed among Berbers, who also spoke Tamazight, it is unknown whether Berbers historically converted to Judaism or whether Jews, who came to North Africa from elsewhere, were acculturated as Berbers.

The Moroccan artist Chaimae Mechtaly explored the shared history of Berbers and Jews in her portraits of women, which were inspired by colonial era postcards of Jewish women (see figures 5.6 and 5.7). Mechtaly recently found family documents written in both Hebrew and Tamazight that led her to discover that her paternal grandfather, who was originally from southern Morocco, was of Judeo-Berber heritage.[7] Mechtaly began painting as a means to understand her lost Judeo-Berber heritage. When she learned about the legend of the Kahina, she began to copy early twentieth-century

1019. DEBDOU (Maroc) - Jeune femme Juive

5.6. Chaimae Mechtaly displayed her paintings at Yennayer, Everett, MA, January 2013. Photograph by author.

5.7. Photographer Unknown, *Debdou (Maroc) Jeune Femme Juive*, ca. 1910. Postcard published by Éditions Roumendil. Collection of the author.

photographs of Moroccan Jewish women. She felt this exercise helped her deal with "questions of colonialism, exploitation, religion, pan-Arabism and ethnic and gender marginalization."[8]

Mechtaly displayed her paintings at a recent Yennayer celebration in the United States, where the recognition of a shared heritage between Jews and Berbers causes less controversy than in North Africa. The identification of Imazighen with Jews and their amenability toward Judaism has drawn harsh criticism that Berbers are unwilling to support the Arab world in its struggles against Israel (Maddy-Weitzman 2011: 146). Such a controversy arose when the film *Tinghrir-Jerusalem: Echoes of the Mellah* by the French-Moroccan Berber filmmaker Kamal Hachkar was screened in Morocco.

The film dealt with Hachkar's rediscovery of a Judeo-Berber culture through a journey that took him from France, to his ancestral village of Tinghrir in southern Morocco and eventually to Israel. Hachkar's journey allowed him to locate Jews in Israel who still spoke Tamazight and reminisced fondly about their Moroccan homeland and the friendly relationships they shared with their Berber neighbors. The message of his film was one of a religiously plural and tolerant society where Jews and Muslims co-existed in harmony. Many of the Moroccan Jews Hachkar interviewed stated that they regretfully left Morocco. Some left due to religious convictions but others feared that the Arabization and Islamization policies of the postcolonial state might lead to the intolerance of religious diversity.

When this film was screened at the Moroccan National Film Festival of Tangier in February 2013, a few dozen protesters gathered to call for the cancellation of the film. Some Moroccans, especially officials from the ruling Islamist party, Justice and Development (PJD), criticized the film because they believed that it called for the normalization of relations with the state of Israel.[9] The film was not cancelled, and, instead, served as a platform to test Morocco's new democratic principles and overturn the previous culture of censorship that existed. The Amazigh activist Mounir Kejji explained to me that Hachkar's film "touched a taboo topic here in Morocco, but Judaism is a component of North Africa that can not be erased from history, and we should have a dialogue about it."[10] Hachkar's film won the festival's prize for best work by a new filmmaker.

After a screening of his film in the United States, the filmmaker explained that although pan-Arabists and Islamists often attacked his film, it was not meant to be controversial; rather it simply showed that Moroccan Muslims and Jews lived together in peace. Hachkar explained in an online interview: "With the 'Arab Spring' we are seeing an obscurantist political Islamism emerge. This intolerant Islam is not mine, it is not our grandparents' either, who lived in

Tinghrir. Today an ideological battle is being waged."[11] Hachkar, who figures prominently in the film speaking Tamazight, Moroccan Arabic, French, and Hebrew, explained that although there is no longer a Judeo-Berber culture flourishing in Morocco, alliances can be forged between Berbers and Jews in order to re-experience a pluralistic society.[12]

Hachkar's film also carries a pro-Amazigh message. It reveals that the Judeo-Berbers from Tinghrir, who left for Israel, faced prejudice similar to that experienced by rural Imazighen in postcolonial Morocco. During the 1950s and 1960s, the postcolonial nations of Morocco, Algeria, Tunisia, and Libya refused to acknowledge the Tamazight language. Berbers in many parts of North Africa experienced ethnic, linguistic, and social marginalization, as the Tamazight language was associated with peasantry and provincialism. When Judeo-Berbers who spoke Tamazight moved to Israel, they faced similar discrimination. Hachkar's film reveals how Berber-speaking Jews often abandoned Tamazight and embraced a Judeo-Arab identity. Arabic was associated with such urbanity, and, because urban dwellers were considered to be more sophisticated and urbane than those from the Berber countryside, many Jews hid their Berber roots. Therefore, to avoid prejudice Judeo-Berbers did not teach their children the Tamazight language. Hachkar captures the shared histories of hardship and discrimination experienced by both Judeo-Berbers in Israel and Berbers in postcolonial Morocco. He contributes to a new visual language made to promote an Amazigh ethno-consciousness that conveys the values of cultural and religious tolerance and the celebration of plurality.

SECULARISM, ISLAM, AND THE ARAB SPRING

As expressed by Hachkar, Amazigh activists view conservative strains of Islam as threatening to artistic freedom and human rights. Instead, some Moroccan Amazigh activists admire the Zionist movement as a model for the Amazigh struggle, since Zionists assert their rights at all costs against what they view as an antagonistic Arab and Muslim world (Maddy-Weitzman 2011: 146–147). Some have founded Judeo-Berber friendship associations and have begun projects to reconstruct the abandoned Jewish quarters (*mellah*) of rural Moroccan villages (Silverstein 2012: 343). Such actions demonstrate how most activists present themselves as tolerant progressives and believe that the Amazigh culture and language can only thrive in a democracy where cultural and religious difference is accepted.

Some activists have gone as far as demanding the secularization of North African national governments as an alternative to political systems based on Islam. They argue for the separation of religious authority from political life and the relegation of religion to the private domain (Ben-Layashi 2007: 159, 161; Maddy-Weitzman 2011: 189). In Morocco, Ahmed Assid received considerable backlash for his public statements on secularization and, in particular, his claim that Moroccan school textbooks contain information that may lure youths to engage in violent acts in the name of Islam. In an interview with me, Assid explained that he strived to fight fanatical Islam since the Amazigh culture could only thrive in a situation where a democracy was accepted and value was given to human rights. The majority of Moroccans are Muslim, but secularity, according to Assid, could successfully coexist with Islam and be based on a uniquely Moroccan model that looks to Amazigh history. Assid stated that, "Imazighen adopted Islam to their own local culture that remained separate from the ruling dynasties, even if that dynasty was Amazigh, such as the Almohad Dynasty, since they borrowed many of their ideas from the Middle East. Moroccan Islam should not impose a view from the Middle East and impose *shari'a* law or fanaticism. We should draw from our own localized Amazigh traditions, which support cultural and religious diversity."[13]

Despite their call for secular political governments, many activists recognize the importance of religious practice to their individual daily lives, especially those who live in socially conservative rural areas. These activists have begun to promote a form of Islam permeated with Berber cultural beliefs that involves such actions that would be rejected by Islamists as pagan survivals. These involve pilgrimages to Muslim Sufi shrines and the wearing of masks during Islamic holidays. Amazigh activists condone such practices as representing a unique Berber form of Islam that represents respect for diversity and open-mindedness, rather than a "rejection of piety or a denial of Islam as a core identity diacritic or everyday practice" (Silverstein 2012: 344). Rather than view these practices as pagan survivals, the scholar Paul Silverstein writes that Amazigh activists view them as "modern indexes of a threatened Berberness," allowing them to use Berber culture to present a tolerant form of Islam and combat religious fundamentalism (2012: 346–347).

Amazigh activists put aside their distrust of Islamists and Arab nationalists and joined them on 20 February 2011 to protest on the streets of Morocco. Men and women from various political, religious, and ethnic affiliations demonstrated together during what Moroccans later named the February 20th movement. Amazigh activists converged with Islamist activists in their mutual critique of the government. After years of struggling and small concessions made by the king, these protests finally pushed King Muhammed VI to declare Tamazight an official language of the state alongside Arabic in the Moroccan constitution.

Similar protests occurred in Algeria, where demonstrators protested unemployment, the lack of housing, the rise of food prices, and governmental corruption. In the Kabyle region of Algeria, an area that has historically engaged in violent protests against their national government, protesters have demanded that the status of Tamazight be upgraded from a "national language" to that of an "official language." In August 2013, hundreds of activists in the Kabyle region organized a public lunch during Ramadan to call for the secularization of the Algerian state. In Algeria those who do not fast during the Muslim month of Ramadan can be arrested for engaging in anti-Islamic activities, since the government makes the Ramadan fast mandatory for all Algerians. In this instance the government ignored the protestors.

CONCLUSION

While Amazigh activists continue demonstrations in the Kabyle region of Algeria, protests in Morocco have diminished. The Moroccan Amazigh activist Mounir Kejji explained to me that an alliance between Amazigh activists and other protesters, especially Islamists, was not in the best interests of Imazighen. He said, "Can we [Amazigh activists] really construct a state with people with whom we are diametrically opposed. Are we really cooperating with them? We [Amazigh activists] cannot join with someone who will be with you one day and suppress you the next."[14]

After the fall of Qaddafi in 2011, Amazigh activists from across North Africa and Europe traveled to Libya to advise Berbers on how to integrate themselves into their nation's new constitution. Qaddafi's government largely oppressed Berbers, arresting community leaders and accusing them of undermining Libya's social unity. The basic goal of Amazigh activists was to encourage the new Libyan government to recognize the Berber language. For example, Meryam Demnati, a researcher at IRCAM, advised Libyan teachers on how to develop pedagogical material to be used in the classroom, since, as with Morocco, the goal of Amazigh activists in Libya was to write and teach Tamazight using a *neo-tifinagh* script.[15] However, they still struggle for official recognition in Libya, as the nation's post-Qaddafi Transitional National Council (TNC) made no mention of Tamazight as an official language in its August 2011 constitutional declaration. While they recognized Arabic as the only official language, they did declare cultural rights for all the components of Libyan society, recognizing all languages as national languages. This angered many Imazighen who insist on the constitutional recognition of the Tamazight language as an official language of Libya and feel that the constitution discriminatorily grants them minority rather than equal status.[16]

Despite these difficulties, local Amazigh activists in western Libya started a radio station that broadcasts in Tamazight, and, for the first time in four decades Tamazight has been spoken over Libyan airwaves.[17] Libyan Berbers began forming cultural associations and organizing celebrations, such as Yennayer, for the first time. Many have incorporated symbols associated with the transnational Amazigh movement into their daily lives. Amazigh activists in the United States, for example, recognizing that the Amazigh flag was not readily available in Libya, mailed some flags to activists there. Such visual imagery contributes to a sense of a collective consciousness that crosses national boundaries. However, even in countries such as Morocco, where activists successfully protested and gained the official recognition of Tamazight by the king, activists cautiously guard their newly won official status. During Mawazine, a public music festival in the Moroccan capital of Rabat, dozens of activists waved the Amazigh flag during a performance by the Tuareg band Tinariwen in May of 2013. At the same festival a few days later, police confiscated all Amazigh flags and detained some flag-holders during the performance by the Moroccan group Izenzaren, a band that sings in Tamazight. Such uneven treatment of Amazigh activists by the government suggests that their status remains precarious.

Like all vibrant, living ethnic movements, the transnational Amazigh movement continues to define itself and to negotiate its status. Across North Africa and in the Amazigh diaspora, activists wear T-shirts that feature images of Numidian kings and paint such images as graffiti to publically proclaim their deep pre-Islamic history. They recycle colonial photographs of tattooed, jewelry-clad and unveiled women to suggest liberation from Islam, which they associate with patriarchy and female oppression. They explore the precolonial rapport that existed between Muslim and Jewish Berber-speakers, considering their relationship in film and in painting. They feature such images on their political banners and the dozens of Amazigh-centric websites dedicated to their cause. Since Amazigh activists associate the Arabic language with an Arab nationalism that excluded Berbers, they write in Tamazight—often using the *tifinagh* script. These transnational visual symbols, which are recognized by activists from Morocco to Libya, promote an Amazigh ethnoconsciousness and convey their self-proclaimed values of tolerance, pluralism, and egalitarianism.

NOTES

1. Approximately 8 percent of the population in Libya and 1 percent in Tunisia speak the Tamazight language and consider themselves Imazighen.

2. Considerable variation exists among scholars and activists concerning terminology, as Amazigh activists, especially from Algeria, sometimes refer to themselves as Berberists.

In this essay, I use the terms Imazighen (singular: Amazigh) to refer to activists and the Amazigh movement to refer to their cause. I use the terms "Berber" and "Tuareg" to distinguish between related populations living in North Africa (the term Berber is used) and in the Sahel/Sahara (the term Tuareg is used). The origin of the word "Tuareg" remains unknown and many Tuareg prefer to call themselves Kel Tamasheq, referring to their language.

3. http://www.amazighworld.org/history/modernhistory/articles/flags.php).

4. http://www.tamazgha.fr/Professor-Chaker-Speaks-Out-on-the-Tifinagh-Script-Issue ,427.html.

5. http://www.telquel-online.com/En-couverture/Enquete-Africains-mais-pas-trop/555.

6. Interview with the author, 27 May 2011.

7. Unpublished interview with Chamae Mechtaly by Eden Alkalilah, 5 April 2013. I also spoke to Mechtaly on numerous occasions about her paintings.

8. http://thebrandeishoot.com/articles/12925.

9. http://kamalhachkar.com/actualites/.

10. Interview by author with Mounir Kejji, Rabat, 27 May 2013.

11. http://jewishrefugees.blogspot.com/2012/07/moroccan-film-maker-accused-of-zionism.html.

12. *Tinghrir-Jerusalem: Les Echos du Mellah*, 2012. Released by L'Harmattan/Les Films d'un jour.

13. Interview by author, Rabat, Morocco, 26 May 2013.

14. Interview by the author, Rabat, Morocco, 27 May 2103.

15. Interview by author, Rabat, Morocco, 26 May 2013.

16. http://www.temehu.com/imazighen/berberism.htm.

17. http://news.nationalpost.com/2011/07/11/ancient-language-renewed-in-libyan-rebellion/.

REFERENCES

Alloula, Malek. 1986. *The Colonial Harem*. Minneapolis: University of Minnesota Press.

Al-Rumi, Aisha. 2009. "Libyan Berbers Struggle to Assert Their Identity Online." In *Arab Media and Society*, issue 8, http://www.arabmediasociety.com/?article=713. Accessed 24 February 2013.

Author unknown. 1922. "Peoples and Places of Northern Africa." *National Geographic Magazine* 42, no. 4: 368.

Becker, Cynthia. 2009. "Matriarchal Nomads and Freedom Fighters: Transnational Amazigh Consciousness and Moroccan, Algerian, and Nigerien Artists." *Critical Interventions* 5 (Fall): 70–101.

———. 2010. "Deconstructing the History of Berber Arts: Tribalism, Matriarchy, and a Primitive Neolithic Past." In *Berbers and Others: Beyond Tribe and Nation in the Maghrib*, edited by K. Hoffman and S. Miller, 195–220. Bloomington: Indiana University Press.

Belmenouar, Safia. 2007. *Rêves mauresques: De la peinture orientaliste à la photographie colonial*. Paris: Hors Collection.

Ben-Layashi, Samir. 2007. "Secularism in the Moroccan Amazigh Discourse." *Journal of North African Studies* 12, no. 2: 153–171.

Camps, Gabrielle, and Salem Chaker. 2004. "Jugurtha." *Encyclopédie berbère* 26: 3975–3979.

Casajus, Dominique. 2001. "Déchiffranges: Quelques réflexions sur l'écriture libycoberbère." *Afriques (online): Débats, Méthodes et Terrains d'Histoire*, http://afriques.revues.org/688.

Clancy-Smith, Julia. 2006. "Le regard colonial: Islam, genre et identities dans la fabrications de l'Algérie francaise, 1830–1962." *Nouvelle Questions Féministes* 25, no. 1: 25–40.

Comaroff, John L., and Jean Comaroff. 2009. *Ethnicity, Inc.* Chicago: University of Chicago Press.

Geary, Christraud. 2002. *In and Out of Focus: Images from Central Africa, 1885–1960*. Washington, DC: National Museum of African Art.

Hannoum, Abdelmajid. 2001. *Post-Colonial Memories: The Legend of Kahina, a North African Heroine*. Portsmouth, NH: Heinemann.

Ilahian, Hsain. 2006. *Historical Dictionary of the Berbers (Imazighen)*. Lanham, MD: Scarecrow Press.

Jenkins, Mark Collins. 2012. *National Geographic 125 Years: Legendary Photographs, Adventures, and Discoveries that Changed the World*. Washington, DC: National Geographic Society.

Limoncelli, Stephanie A. 2010. *The Politics of Trafficking: The First International Movement to Combat the Sexual Exploitation of Women*. Palo Alto: Stanford University Press.

Maddy-Weitzman, Bruce. 2011. *The Berber Identity Movement and the Challenge to North African States*. Austin: University of Texas Press.

Powell, E. Alexander. 1912. "Sirens of the Sands." *The Metropolitan* 36, no. 1: 22–24.

Silverstein, Paul. 2007. "Islam, Laïcité, and Amazigh Activism in France and North Africa." In *North African Mosaic: A Cultural Reappraisal of Ethnic and Religious Minorities*, edited by N. Boudraa and J. Krause, 104–118. Cambridge: Cambridge Scholars Press.

———. 2012. "In the Name of Culture: Berber Activism and the Material Politics of 'Popular Islam' in Southeastern Morocco." *Material Religion* 8, no. 3: 330–353.

Silverstein, Paul, and David Crawford. 2004. "Amazigh Activism and the Moroccan State." *Middle East Report* 233: 44–48.

CHAPTER 6

CAN POETRY CHANGE THE WORLD?
READING AMAL DUNQUL IN EGYPT IN 2011

SAMULI SCHIELKE

WHAT A SILLY QUESTION . . . Of course poetry cannot change the world. Poetry is about the work of metaphors and symbols, the rhythm and music of language, and the play of mind, moods, and meanings. How could it possibly make any difference in a world where the power of the strongest prevails, where guns and drones speak loudest, and where brainwash by mass media and black-mail by secret police are the most compelling forms of spoken and written word?

In 1975, the Egyptian poet Amal Dunqul (1940–1983)—a communist, militant nationalist, and drunken Bohemian who cultivated the attitude of principled opposition in his life and literary work (Elreweny 1992)—published the poem *From the papers of Abu Nuwas* (*Min awraq Abi Nuwas*) in which he lets the medieval Arab poet Abu Nuwas (see Kennedy 2007) speak about the asymmetry between the power of the word and the power of money and violence. In one part of the long poem Dunqul, who was famous for his use of Arabic, Islamic, Roman, and Hellenic history and myths, relates to Islam's most powerful story of martyrdom: The massacre of the Prophet Muhammad's grandson al-Husayn and his followers in an ambush by the Omayad caliph Yazid ibn Muʿawiya:

> *I was in Karbala*
> *The old man told me: al-Husayn*
> *died for the sake of a mouthful of water*
>
> . . .
>
> *I asked how the swords could prey on the noblest family*
> *The one whom heaven had gifted with sight answered*
> *that it was the gold that glittered in every eye*
>
> . . .
>
> *If the words of al-Husayn*

and the swords of al-Husayn
and the majesty of al-Husayin
fell without saving the truth from the gold of the princes
How could the truth be saved by the babbling of poets?
While the Euphrat is a tongue of blood that does not find the lips![1]

كنتُ فـي الـكـربـلاءِ

قـال لـيَ الـشيـخُ : إن الـحسيـنْ

مـاتَ مـن أجل جرعة مـاءْ

....

وتساءلـتُ كيف الـسيـوفُ استبـاحت بنـي الأكـرمـيـنْ

فـأجـابَ الـذى بـصّرتـهُ الـسمـاءْ

إنـه الـذهبُ الـمـتـلألـئُ فـي كـلّ عيـن

....

إن تـكـن كـلمـاتُ الـحسيـنْ

وسيـوفُ الـحسيـنْ

وجلالُ الـحسيـنْ

سَقَطَتْ دون أن تُـنقـذ الـحق مـن ذهب الأمـراء

أفـتـقـدر أن تـنقـذ الـحق ثـرثـرةُ الـشعـراءْ؟

والـفـراتُ لـسانٌ مـن الـدم لا يـجدُ الـشفـتيـن!

And yet Amal Dunqul was not deterred from writing poetry that was strongly committed to ideals of national and revolutionary struggle. He left behind a powerful and innovative oeuvre that glorifies uncompromising struggle and combines it with a deep pessimism. In 1962, in the early years of his career, his poem *Spartacus' Last Words (Kalimat Shartakus al-akhira)* caught the tragedy of revolutionary struggle in a way that has lost nothing of its validity today. Its opening lines take up the Biblical and Qur'anic story of Satan's fall from grace, and turn it into a symbol of tragic heroism:

Glory to Satan, god of the winds
Who said "no" to the face of those who said "yes"
who taught Man to tear apart nothingness
He who said no, thus did not die
And remained a soul eternally in pain[2]

المـجد لـلـشيطان .. مـعبـود الـريــاخْ

مـن قـال "لا" فـي وجهٍ مـن قـالـوا "نَـعَمْ"

مـن عَلْم الإنسـانَ تـمـزيق الـعـدمْ

مـن قـال "لا" .. فـلـم يَـمُثْ،

وظل رُوحـاً أبـديـة الألَـمْ !

In 1976, not long before Sadat's famous visit to Jerusalem and the Camp David treaties, Amal Dunqul took the murder of the pre-Islamic Arabian tribal leader Kulayb in 494 CE, which resulted in the forty-years-long Basus War (see Hoyland 2001) as the foil for *Don't Reconcile (La tusalih)*, one of the most powerful anti-peace poems ever written. This is its beginning:

Don't reconcile
. . . even if they granted you gold
What if I gouged out your eyes
and replaced them by jewels . . .
Will you see?
These things cannot be bought . . .[3]

لا تُصـالـخ

.. ولـو مـنحوك الـذهبْ

تـرى حين أفقأ عـيـنيكَ،

ثـم أثـبت جوهرتـين مكـانـها..

هل تـرى..؟

هي أشيـاء لا تـشتـرى..

For a long time, Dunqul's work was appreciated only in small leftist and intellectual circles. His poems were too avant-gardistic in style to be sung and memorized the way more popular genres of poetry are. Strongly oppositional in content, they were also a thorn in the eye of the Egyptian authorities. They were not forbidden, but they rarely got reviews or other mention in state-controlled media. The situation changed quite suddenly with the outbreak of the 25 January revolution that was accompanied by a revival of politically committed leftist poetry from the 1960s and 1970s. Especially Ahmed Fouad Negm's (1929–2013) witty and rude colloquial poems and songs gained enormous popularity and circulation, but also many of Amal Dunqul's verses entered the corpus of revolutionary citations. However, while Ahmed Fouad Negm's poetry with its commitment to colloquial orality was more suitable for songs and slogans, Dunqul's poetry was more likely to find its ways to graffiti, discussion circles, and quotes on social media (for graffiti, see images 6.1 to 6.3; see also Nicoarea 2013; Roters 2011).

Already in autumn 2010, a graffiti artist sprayed a passage from *Spartacus' Last Words* on the seafront boulevard in Alexandria in protest against the expectation that Hosni Mubarak's son Gamal would soon follow in his footsteps:

Do not dream of a happy world
Behind every Caesar who dies, there is a new Caesar[4]

لا تحلموا بعالم سعيد

فخلف كل قيصر يموتُ: قيصر جديد!

As citations from Dunqul's works circulated, they also gained independence from their original political context. In 2011 and 2012, especially the line "Don't reconcile"—originally written in anticipation of a peace treaty with Israel—became a widely cited expression of determined struggle against the first period of military rule by the Supreme Council of the Armed Forces (see images 6.2 and 6.3), and was sprayed on many walls as a call to not give in and to make no compromises. "We are those who said no" became the title of a social media group[5] established in 2011 in reference to the constitutional referendum of March 2011. The opening lines of *Spartacus' Last Words* were sometimes cited (although often without mentioning Satan) by proponents of a no-vote in the constitutional referendum in December 2012. In November 2011, I encountered a group of young men with literary interests who were having a tea break on the lawn of one of the green spaces of Tahrir Square late one evening, in the aftermath of the street battles of Mohamed Mahmoud Street. They had one book with them: the collected works of Amal Dunqul

6.1. Graffiti in downtown Cairo depicting Rami al-Sharqawi, who was killed by security forces during demonstrations at the Council of Ministers on 17 December 2011, with a passage from *Spartacus' Last Words*: "I hang from the morning's gallows / My forehead lowered by death / Because alive, I did not lower it!" (Translation by Suneela Mubayi 2012). Photo by Shady Basiony Marei, April 2012.

(Dunqul 2005), which they were reciting and discussing. It was as if some of those poems had been written just for that moment.

Of course poetry does not change the world, and yet the sudden popularity and timeliness of Amal Dunqul's work in 2011 show that the question about poetry and change needs to be asked—the more so since many Egyptian poets and writers have been asking the same question. And they have some quite interesting answers to offer.

WHAT THIS CHAPTER IS ABOUT AND WHAT IT IS NOT ABOUT

This chapter looks at the relationship of poetry with social and political change in Egypt during the stormy season[6] of the nation's most recent revolution. It is not an attempt to give a general overview of the tremendous amount of important poetry and literature involved, nor can it account for the important and ambiguous role of intellectuals and writers in Egypt's politics and

6.2. Graffiti at Tahrir Square in Cairo with the line "Don't reconcile" surrounded by portraits of martyrs of the revolution (in light colors) as well as both revolutionary and counterrevolutionary figures (in dark colors). Photo by Shady Basiony Marei, December 2011.

6.3. Graffiti outside Alexandria University, showing a portrait of field marshal Hussein Tantawi and the lines "Don't reconcile" (below the portrait in the middle) and "Down with military rule" (on the left). Signed (on the right) by "the We Must campaign" (Hamlat Lazem), a small leftist/liberal group. Photo by Samuli Schielke, October 2012.

society. Those themes are dealt with in very good and useful manner by, for example, Lewis Sanders IV and Mark Visoná (2012), Richard Jacquemond (2008), Elisabeth Kendall (2006), and Mounah A. Khouri (1971). In this chapter I take up a different set of questions: What power could the poet's words actually have in social and political conflicts and transformations? Are they actually effective in planting visions and stances in people's minds? Or are they merely the soundtrack of history? And does it make sense anyway to think about poetry as something that is separate from the world?

These questions do not only concern Egypt's and other Arab countries' revolutionary experience. The same questions have arisen on other occasions in, for example, Europe and Latin America and probably in every other part of the world as well. And they will rise again and again because in certain moments in history, the link between literary fantasy and political struggles becomes tangible and urgent. The experience of Egyptian poets is important beyond the country and the time in which they live.

These questions were asked and discussed by a group of writers and literature enthusiasts gathered in a café in the eastern outskirts of Alexandria, and it was Amal Dunqul in particular whose work they frequently mentioned in the course of this discussion. In this chapter, I do not try to provide an overview of different theoretical approaches in the international academia to these questions. Instead, I try to make use of the theories offered by the people involved: a group of living poets from Egypt in the middle of a revolution. They have a specific perspective that is due to their role as writers and readers of poetry that have a history of experience and reflection on the relation of literature and life. Their perspective also represents a much wider section of the society that played a key role in the revolutionary process: a vast social class of urban inhabitants who are excluded from the comfort of the bourgeois classes (often misleadingly described as "middle classes") but who by the means of their education and their work as civil servants or salaried workers nevertheless manage to aspire, work, and live above the poverty line.

Another thing that I will not do is make a distinction between religious and secular poetry or poets. Although a distinction between religious and secular ideology and politics does indeed mark one of the many social conflicts in Egypt, it would not do justice to the poets discussed here (it might still do justice to others, of course—see Furani 2012). There are three reasons for that.

The first reason is that the creed, language, and symbolism of Islam are present in Arabic poetry regardless of the poets' personal religious stances. One cannot think about eloquence in Arabic language without reference to the Qur'an. And no matter what one's personal religious commitments may be, the topic of martyrdom and heroic defeat invites the analogy with the martyrdom of al-Husayn. Amal Dunqul's poem cited above, in which Abu Nuwas reflects how the swords could prey upon the majesty of al-Husayn, is a case in point. More recently, the colloquial poet Mustafa Ibrahim transferred the tragedy of al-Karbala to the clashes of Mohamed Mahmoud Street that shook Egypt in November 2011 in his poem *I saw today* (Inni ra'ayt al-yom), written as a film script that concludes:

I saw today—the image from outside
I said: Al-Husayn still—once again will die
I saw today—as a revolutionary sees
that over al-Husain's body—soldiers gathered
thrashing him with sticks—every time he stood up
and that people stood by the side—crying instead of helping
and that the flag was turned into a sieve—by bayonets and birdshot
and that the path was laid out—with blood all the way
I saw today—blood on the soldier's belts
I saw that al-Husayn is us—
However much he's killed—he lives[7]

إنـى رأيـتُ اليـوم .. الصـورة مـن بَـرُّه

وقُـلت الحسـين لِسُّه .. هيمـوت كمـان مـرُّة

إنـي رأيـتُ اليـوم .. فيمـا يـرى الثـائر

إن الحسـين مَلمـوم .. فـوق جُثتـه عسـاكر

بـيدغدغوه بـالشوم .. كُل أمّـا يـيجي يقـوم

وإن البشـر واقفـة .. تبكـي بيـدَال مـا تحـوش

وإن العـلم مصفـاة .. م السـونكي والخرطـوش

وإن الطريـق مَفـروش.. بـالدَّم لـلآخر

إنـي رأيـتُ اليـوم .. الـدَّم ع الآيـش

وان الحسـين إحنـا ..

مـهمـا اتقـتل.. عـايش

The second reason might seem counterintuitive in light of the first but in fact flows directly from it: there is a separation between revelation and poetry that was established in the first years of Islam. The Qur'an in clear terms states that it is not poetry. God's message and poetry belong to two different genres of speech even if they overlap in terms of form and grammar. Although Islam inspirits poets and their words, and although there are venerable genres of explicitly religious devotional poetry, there is also a long-standing Arabic tradition of poetic licence—probably as old as Arabic poetry itself. The language of revelation is a language of ultimate truth, while the language of poetry is marked by a scope of relativity, explorative freedom, and, indeed, licence. And it is worth remembering that Arabic poetry is also written by poets of Christian and other faiths, some of it devotional and committed, and some of it not. In a sense, poetry has no religion.

The third reason is that in Egypt today, there exists a tangible split between two takes on literary production: one committed to a tradition of *adab* (meaning both the cultivation of fine manners as well as literature in general) according to which good literature must go hand in hand with good purpose, a didactic unity of aesthetic pleasure and ethical learning (Jacquemond 2008: 10); and another committed to the tradition of poetic licence, a vision of poetry and literary imagination as a site of exploration and experimentation (see, e.g., Kennedy 2007). Importantly, this split does not follow political or religious divides. Straightforward didactic or propagandistic poems are written by leftists, Islamists, and old regime loyalists alike, by Muslims and Christians, by pious and impious writers—and so are experimental, daring, and even potentially blasphemic ones.

Literary aesthetics does have a political dimension to which I return in the next section. And yet in the circles where I do research, I have found revolutionary leftists, Muslim Brotherhood sympathizers, and Salafis alike emphasize that good poetry must be free from the didactical restrictions of immediate purpose. On one occasion in autumn 2012, I was invited to a gathering of poets in a café in Victoria, a district in eastern Alexandria, where friendly exchange about poetry turned into a heated political debate. Some of the poets in attendance were Islamists of either Salafi or Muslim Brotherhood orientation, while others saw themselves as leftists or liberals. This was a time of increasing polarization between supporters and opponents of political Islam, and the debate rapidly turned into an angry exchange of mutual accusations, with no possibility to reach an agreement. Eventually, one of the poets (recognizable as a Salafi by the fashion of his beard) replied to the accusation that Islamists considered their opponents as infidels (*kuffar*) by pointing out that he himself had written a poem that according to Salafi doctrine would constitute unbelief (*kufr*), featuring the gods of Olymp and telling about inner struggle and ambivalence. Others asked him to recite it, and as the tempers calmed somewhat, he and others began to recite their poems. As suddenly as it had begun, the heated political tension disappeared, and instead the poets were reciting, listening, enjoying, and praising each other's work. Regardless of their irreconcilable political differences, they took pleasure in the aesthetic quality and the existential and subjective take of each other's poems—an accomplishment in its own right at a time when Egyptians often found it very difficult to find any sort of shared language. Poetry with a clear didactical message would hardly be able to accomplish that.

Regardless of their take on commitment and poetic license, however, poets (except those who only write for themselves) all hope that their works are heard and are capable of affecting their audiences. So while they may have misgivings about clear statements of didactic purpose, in the ongoing revolutionary situation that they found themselves since spring 2011, they were compelled to reflect on the relationship poetry may have with conflicts and transformations, be they political, social, spiritual, or intimate.

A VERY COMPACT OVERVIEW OF ARABIC POETRY AND EGYPT TODAY

Poetry is the most popular genre of literature in the Arabic-speaking world. People who may never have read a novel in their life, nevertheless often memorize poetry and may have written some themselves. While the market and readership of books of fiction and poetry is extremely low, Arabic poetry enjoys wider circulation because, unlike in Europe and North America, it remains strongly grounded in the spoken word—and therefore is also often circulated through audiovisual media (see, e.g., Miller 2007). This is reflected also in the way most Arabic poetry currently in circulation continues to rely on rhyme and meter. More experimental styles of free-rhyme poetry exist and are produced and consumed in more dedicated literary circles, but poetry as a popular art remains strongly committed to a recognizable rhythm and a musical quality of language. Obviously, poetry has a strong link with music. In pre-Islamic poetry, poetry and song were inseparable (Adonis 1990). Today, there are no clear borders between poetry and song. But there is, of course, a material difference between the written and the spoken word, and some poems are better for singing, while others are better suited for reading and graffiti.

Poetry in Arabic language has a long and magnificent history (see, e.g., Kennedy 2007; Adonis 1990; Jayyusi 1977; Badawi 1975; Khouri 1971; Furani 2012). The oldest known Arabic poetry was in circulation long before the rise of Islam and was collected in written form in the first centuries of Islam. This "poetry of the age of ignorance" (*al-shi'r al-jahili*) remains the ultimate standard of Arabic poetic expression until today, and an Arabic literary education invariably must begin with those first poets, and then proceeds through the establishment of meters and genres, theories of rhetorics and poetics, the works of classical poets across centuries—and finally perhaps contemporary poetry. The poetry that is written or spoken in a place such as Egypt today, however, is different from that heritage. Contemporary poems seldom use the double verse of classical Arabic poetry. They have a narrative unity that encompasses the entire poem—unlike in classical Arabic poetry where there is a narrative unity of the verse but not of the poem. Contemporary poems are also often strongly subjective, spirited by a romantic theory of the author expressing her or his authentic self—in contrast to ancient Arabic poetry in which eloquence of expression was crucial while originality of meaning was not. An ever-larger part of contemporary poetry is written or spoken in colloquial Egyptian Arabic, which differs from classical Arabic in morphology and syntax, and also in rhetorical registers. As a result, there has emerged a divide between classical Arabic as the language for more highbrow, more serious, and either decidedly conservative or decidedly avant-gardistic poetry, and Egyptian Arabic as the language of more popular, more humorous, and more down-to-earth poetry. There are interesting exceptions to this distinction— for example, free-rhyme poetry in Egyptian Arabic, which was launched by a group of young writers in the 1990s and is associated with avant-gardist literary aesthetics.

Literary aesthetics often has a political resonance. The classicist style of *'amudi* ("columnic") poetry has today become associated with either a socially conservative stance or conservative uses such as devotional poetry. "Prose poetry" (*qasidat al-nathr*), that is, poetry that does not rely on meter or rhythm, is often associated with leftist or liberal stances and bohemian lifestyles and not recognized as proper poetry by more conservative audiences. The currently most proliferated poetic styles of free-verse poetry in meter (*taf'ila*) and of colloquial poetry influenced by *zagal* (traditional, often improvized colloquial poetry close to song) are not as clearly marked in political terms and have been used to express fundamental discontent sometimes, and to praise presidents at other times.[8]

The politics of poetic aesthetics is not a straightforward ideological matter, however. Rather, the politics involved is better understood as a general attitude to existence whereby affirmation of authority (be it religious, national, or other) resonates better with a conservative style, while a critical attitude of nonconformity goes along with a search for new ways of expression. For example, the Alexandrian poet Shaymaa Bakr, whose poetry I quote at the end of this chapter, identifies herself as a Salafist and a pan-Islamist, but her personal attitude to life is one of nonconformity and rebellion. Her verses are a free variety of *taf'ila* that builds on the innovations in poetry established by the generation of Amal Dunqul. Her poems develop themes of desire and discontent. Her ideological stance notwithstanding, her literary aesthetics and her attitude to poetry and life appear much closer to leftist avant-gardism than to the classicist *'amudi* poetry of romantic heroism that is written and circulated by Jihadists in Iraq and Syria today (see Creswell and Haykel 2015). Their poetry, in turn, is much closer in style (though not in message) to the socially and aesthetically conservative poetry that is promoted by television shows and literature prizes in the Arab Gulf states.

In any case, poetry has a strong presence in life, and many people quote poetry to express their feelings, to argue for a point, and to make sense of a situation. And most visibly in the last few years, poetry has become intertwined with the language of political conflict and dissent.

In winter 2010–2011 and during the following spring and summer, a series of revolutionary uprisings shook the Arab world. They marked the beginning of a stormy season of political confrontations, chaotic shifts of mood and coalitions, and general societal turmoil. The enthusiastic days in the beginning were a poetic moment in two senses. First, poetic verses turned into chants and slogans were an important way to mobilize for the uprisings and to express their demands (Colla 2012). Second, there was a poetic quality to the moment of uprising itself:

> A revolution is in itself a poetic event insofar as it is about taking the ordinary things, otherwise evident and transparent like the words of prose, and playing with them, wondering about them, not taking them for granted, putting them together in a new configuration. . . . If in ordinary days the work of fantasy precedes action by opening the space to think of alternatives, in the time of a revolution, action runs ahead of imagination and forms it. This was the original revolutionary moment: the birth of a sense that something to date unimaginable is in the process of being realised." (Schielke 2015: 180)

It all turned unimaginably more complicated, frustrating, and violent in the course of the following years. As this chapter goes to press in summer 2015, the catastrophic failure of almost all those revolutions (with the potential exception of Tunisia) is now evident. The fantastic quality of those days seems, in hindsight, to belong to the field of fantasy. Or—a more disturbing thought—the fantastic quality of those days may in some way have contributed to the bloody mess that followed.

Writing about the poetry that was recited and produced during the first days of the Egyptian Revolution, Lewis Sanders IV and Mark Visonà (2012) describe poetry as "the soul of Tahrir" and grant it the power to give shape and name to what was emerging in that moment. They also point out that the nation and the body of "the people" (al-sha'b) were at the heart of those poems that reflected and gave direction to a vision of the uprising in terms of national liberation and unity. It was an ambiguous direction though, and the openness of the claim to speak in the name of "the people" makes it available for revolutionary and counterrevolutionary slogans alike (Colla 2012). This nationalist grounding of the uprising—and its ambiguity—went at first unnoticed by many academics and media observers, who were paying perhaps too much attention to the Islamists, who at the time appeared to be the main winners of the uprising. But religious politics, rather than being able to unite Egyptians, turned out to be so extremely divisive that it provided the occasion for a counterrevolution in 2013 that was emphatically and explicitly framed in nationalist terms as "the people" against "the terrorists." The spirit of heightened nationalism and patriotic unity that was shaped in Tahrir 2011, became, in 2013, the ground of faith for a new military regime that entered an extremely violent confrontation to eradicate its Islamist contenders.

Many of the prominent literates of the capital emphatically sided with this nationalist turn, and in different nuances supported the new military leadership and the brutal suppression of its opponents in the name of a "war against terror." Novelists such as Alaa El-Aswany and Sonallah Ibrahim and poets such as Abdel Rahman el-Abnudi and Ahmed Fouad Negm, who in 2011 had spoken out loud for the revolution, after summer 2013 spoke out for what they believed was a revolutionary cleansing of Egypt from antipatriotic terrorist elements (Azimi 2014; el-Abnudi 2014; Lindsey 2013; CNN Arabic 2013; Negm 2013). On the other side of the struggle, less prominent poets sympathetic to the cause of the Muslim Brotherhood have produced texts that give words to their struggle, and sometimes also expressed their frustration about so many people turning into what they see as "slaves of the military boot" (see, e.g., Mossa 2013). Yet others have taken an outsider position, supporting neither military rule nor the Muslim Brotherhood, frustrated and marginalized in the face of an extremely destructive circle of confrontation and violence (see, e.g., Shehata 2013). Many poets who are associated with such a third stance—notably so the above-mentioned Mustafa Ibrahim—fell into a lengthy period of silence or stopped addressing political topics, leaving the stage of critical commentary to comedians like Bassem Youssef and satirical writers like Belal Fadl.[9]

So when we ask whether poetry can change the world, it is a question that concerns an ambiguous change. There is no escape to the arrogant certainty of Jean-Paul Sartre (1949: 63–64) who in his call for engaged literature claimed that of course good literature and good cause were united. The question needs to be asked in a different way: What kind of relationship could the poetic word have with this world we live in?

A DISCUSSION WITH POETS, WHERE AN ANSWER BEGINS TO TAKE SHAPE

Since 2010, I have been doing ethnographic fieldwork together with the novelist Mukhtar Shehata[10] about people who write poetry, short stories, and novels in different literary and social milieus in Alexandria, Egypt's second-largest city. In autumn 2011, I started meeting with a circle of friends from a low-class informal settlement in the east of Alexandria, all of them male schoolteachers in their late thirties or in their forties. In those days, they used to gather in the small garden of a café at the outskirts of the neighborhood to discuss politics, poetry, and life. Most of them are active writers, and some of them can claim a name in the literary circles of the city. Literature is for them not a profession but a passion that they pursue as a sort of parallel life next to their ordinary lives as schoolteachers and family fathers.

One of our meetings with this circle took place in October 2011 in the presence of the poets Kamal Ali Mahdy, Muhammad Mahmoud Mousa, Ashraf Dossouki Ali, and Hamdy Mosa, as well as Nazih (who describes himself as a passionate reader but not as a writer), Mukhtar, and myself.[11] This was a time when the future course of the Egyptian Revolution was still unclear, when continued optimism was becoming mixed with increasing frustration and pessimism, and when many of the political divisions that later would pit people against each other had not yet taken full shape. All the men in the circle were staunch supporters of the revolution, but in the following years they have taken different paths in political matters.

The original topic of the discussion was poets' search for fame and immortality, but the topic shifted when the effect of two poets on the Egyptian Revolution was mentioned, one of them Amal Dunqul, the other the Tunisian Aboul-Qacem Echebbi (Abu al-Qasim al-Shabbi, 1909–1934), whose poem, *The Will to Live* (Iradat al-hayah), originally written against French colonialism, had become something of a refrain of the revolutions in Tunisia and Egypt.

In a previous meeting a week earlier, the poet Kamal Ali Mahdy had mentioned that Amal Dunqul had "shaken up" the society with his poetry and with provocative verses such as "Glory to Satan" and "Don't Reconcile." Now, Kamal took up Amal Dunqul's poetry again to point out that good poetry can gain new life and relevance decades after it was written. This resulted in a discussion about poetry's capacity to move people and to change the world.

It was a long discussion, and I quote it in almost full length. The reason is I want to give the poets a space to develop their ideas so that you can think together with them and also make up your own mind about their arguments. Anthropologists often translate their ethnographic data into the academic jargon that is in fashion, and explain it by theories that are in use in their academic institutions. This is often the most boring part of anthropological writing. We usually owe the best of our ideas not to the theories we read elsewhere, but to encounters in the field with people that have good theories of their own about their own situation. That evening in the café was one such encounter of inspiring conversation and generous sharing of ideas. And now, the poets in the café wish to share the following with you:

KAMAL: The lasting genius of Amal Dunqul is that he shook up the society and made a change in it. That is the genius that gave his work permanence. It is the genius of something nobody else had done, shaking up Egyptian society. . . .

MUHAMMAD: I believe that poetry is like different seeds. Every seed sprouts and grows, flourishes and thrives in a specific soil. So when a poem finds specific conditions that suit it, it flourishes. When did the poetry of Amal Dunqul become famous? In the January 25 Revolution, because he was a revolutionary. And a strong romantic poem can become famous if the society comes to a rest and the material conditions of life improve, then the poems in circulation will be romantic poems. Why is Amal Dunqul famous now? Why not five or six years ago? Why do we talk about him now? Because of the January 25 Revolution.

NAZIH: When Aboul-Qacem Echebbi said:

If one day the people will to live / Then Fate must an answer give . . .[12]

إذا الـشعبُ يـومـاً أراد الـحيـاة   فـلا بـد أن يـستجيب الـقـدرُ

In the period of the French occupation [of Tunisia], that verse fitted very well. Then a period followed when it didn't fit. In the current period it fits very well again. So there does not need to be permanence, it depends on its period. Look and you see: the verse changes the world. Why? In this atmosphere, people are effected by it. They want change. They find this verse and are affected by it.

MUHAMMAD: If the necessary conditions are there and the society rises up in revolution, then you will find the poetry of Amal Dunqul revived.

SAMULI: Do you mean that the revolution is an occasion to read Amal Dunqul, but that Amal Dunqul did not cause the revolution?

MUHAMMAD: No, he is not a cause of the revolution. But his poems were written in a revolutionary state of mind. So everytime the people rise up in revolt, they will find a poem by Amal Dunqul that suits them. Otherwise, where was Amal Dunqul for the last thirty years when Hosni Mubarak ruled and there was no revolution? Nobody mentioned Amal Dunqul then.

KAMAL: I mean that Amal Dunqul as a contemporary of the defeat of 1967[13] said something that shook up the society. He refused the reality. I don't mean that he was only protesting against the defeat of 1967 . . . If he had lived in the days of the revolution [of the Free Officers] in 1952, he might have been against the revolution itself. And if he had lived before 1952 [during the monarchy] he might have been a revolutionary against the king, and so on. . . . His genius is in the way he takes up rejection, and convinces us to join him in rejection, to go along with him in that direction.

HAMDY: I support what Kamal said, but I want to take it to another direction. The poet is an anarchist and a buffoon. He strives to establish himself and his character through difference and opposition. Amal did that. He demolished the traditional structure of poems and strove for a different vision altogether, new idea and new technique. Through difference and opposition he wants to say: "I'm ingeniously different from the others." With his genius he reached a different level and delighted the reader with his stance of difference. . . . But poetry does not change the reality of society. I even say that the Qur'an itself does not make a change. The Sublime and Exalted God is the one who makes a change. Let me tell you something. When I sit in a cafe and they play recitation of the Qur'an on the loudspeakers, I'm well aware of the meaning of the verses, and I'm aware of commanding the right and forbidding the wrong— yet despite knowing all that I continue doing whatever I'm doing. Therefore the noble Qur'an did not change me because the will to change by the Sublime and Exalted God was not there. And that is the highest book of all.

NAZIH: That you didn't change is not the Qur'an's fault. But it does change others.

HAMDY: It changes others because it is accordance with the will of God.

NAZIH: But everything is in accordance with the will of God.[14] If a car would hit me now, would it not be in accordance with His will?

HAMDY: Look, maybe Aboul-Qacem Echebbi didn't originally speak out his verse as a political protest like we imagine. Maybe he was addressing a particular issue of social injustice. But when a revolution occurs, there is what rhetoric calls speech in accordance with the circumstance. In the circumstances of a specific time, that verse is in accordance with a specific mental state. Therefore it gained a dimension that wasn't imagined by Aboul-Qacem Echebbi.

NAZIH: A question if I may: Why did the Prophet, peace and blessings be upon him, include one like Hassan ibn Thabit[15] to the work of da'wa? Hassan was just a poet, what did he change in the Islamic society so that the Prophet included him?

At this point, Nazih and Hamdy entered a detailed debate about what the role of poets was for spreading Islam in the age of the Prophet. Hamdy maintained that it was merely to react to poetic insults (hija') against the Prophet, while Nazih detailed examples in which poets had compelled polytheists to recognize the supremacy of Islam. This prompted Hamdy to clarify his argument:

I say that something changes when it is in accordance to the will of God. I did not rule out the role of poetry in shaping life. But in light of the current culture of the society, it is a relative change in the relation of one to a million.

NAZIH: Currently or generally?

HAMDY: Since a very long time. I gave you an example: The most eloquent books in existence are the Qur'an and the Bible, that is, the divinely revealed books. They are the highest in poetic expression and wisdom. But the increase of the numbers of Muslims, Christians, and Jews is only proportional to the increase of the population of the world.

ASHRAF DOSSOUKY ALI: Maybe Hamdy entered an issue that belongs to the invisible realm [ghayb], which is beyond my power, and it is a different topic. But to get back to the discussion about ibda' [creative practice, creation of literature, art, or music], one of the elements of ibda' is asala [originality, authenticity], and the other is fluency and skill. . . . If you are an original [asil] poet or writer and you master your technique and your talent, and possess a vision, then you can initiate a change, and you can do it across time and space. There is a poet whose capacity is limited to making a change in the framework of his tribe, or his nation in the modern era; and there is another poet who can claim to be universal, or global, and who can change others in a radical way. A radical change does not mean that it involves everybody. We say that the Egyptian people all went out in the January 25 Revolution. But that does not mean 80 million Egyptians did it. Those who had a concern for the problem of change did. . . . If you are an authentic poet or writer, you are capable of addressing the supreme shared grounds of humanity. When I write a poem and it reaches a greater number of people, when it reaches the Egyptian, the European, the American, this means that I have been able to touch a shared human element that we all have, because we all descend from Adam. . . . As for a poet who does not initiate a change, he is one who only expresses his own self, his internal problems. But when he speaks about a problem that touches others, this means that he is capable of reaching the shared ground of humanity.

NAZIH: That's the question I want to ask: Why are poets right now unable to change anything? Is it the poetry's fault? Or is it the poets' fault?

MUHAMMAD: It's the society's fault, a society that does not enable people to read. And politics has participated in alienating the society from reading. The poet has ended up writing for himself.

NAZIH: Our society is useless. How else could have someone like Hisham Al-Gakh[16] made it to fame?

MUKHTAR: Hisham Al-Gakh is merely a vocal phenomenon, nothing more.

NAZIH: But he made it.

I have given this discussion so much space because the four poets provide key theoretical answers to the question that frames this chapter. The discussion boils down to essentially two theoretical answers. According to one theory, which is argued for in different nuances by Muhammad Mousa and Hamdy Mosa, we take recourse to words and ideas that convey the situation in which we are. If there is a revolution, then people revive revolutionary poetry to express their situation, but poetry itself had no power to initiate a revolution. Hamdy goes even so far as to deny that divine revelations have the power to change people's minds. Such power, he argues, is God's alone and therefore beyond any worldly causality. Later the same evening, he added that poetry can affect individuals through the power of aesthetic pleasure but that whatever change this may involve remains entirely on the individual level.

According to the other theory, which is argued more cautiously by Kamal Ali Mahdy and more strongly by Nazih and Ashraf Dossouki Ali, poetry does have the power to provide people with models for emotions and actions. According to Kamal, Amal Dunqul's poetry has unsettled values that have been taken for granted and has also helped establishing the attitude of rejection as an affect and a moral virtue—something that has been instrumental for the revolutionary process (see Schielke 2015, chapter 9). Nazih and Ashraf go further and argue that poetry can have the power to enter the minds and hearts of people, to persuade and to provide inspiration for solutions—a view that is also echoed in many chapters in this book (for example in Bryan Reynolds' and Mark LeVine's point about "open power" and Deborah Kapchan's analysis of the affective effect of listening).

While the poets in the gathering disagreed about the theoretical problem of the power and powerlessness of words, they unanimously agreed that in practice, poetry has less power than it should because people do not read and because only second-rate crap (such as the poetry of Hisham Al-Gakh) gains wide popular appeal. This is a characteristic predicament of all artistic and creative production: the more nuanced and sophisticated the creative production, the more it becomes a distinctive property of a dedicated and cultivated few and the less likely can it reach wider audiences. Especially in Egypt, there is a stunning gap between the social and moral authority writers claim (and sometimes gain), and the actual readership of literary works (Jacquemond 2008: 6). Poetry that can shake up that which is taken for granted, can only do so among those whom it reaches in the first place and who are interested in such play of mind—which is mostly identical with dedicated literary circles. There are exceptions, however—rare occurrences like the January 25 revolution when the avant-gardistic work of Amal Dunqul suddenly gained a wider audience. But even then, what reached public consciousness were one-liners and not full-length poems.

THE QUESTION NEEDS TO BE REPHRASED, AND THE ANSWER IS PARADOXICAL

Inspired by this discussion, Mukhtar Shehata developed during the following days a theory to unite the two theories and to show how literary fantasy might indeed make a difference, and why that power was always limited. The outcome was what he describes as a dialectical triangle of fantasy, dreams, and choices. Fantasy (*khayal*, here in the sense of an imagination that is conscious about the nonreality of the imagined), in this theory, is a space of freedom where one can imagine and explore ideas without having to consider their practical possibility or feasibility. One is not, however, free to have an unlimited scope of fantasies. So this is not a liberal theory according to which people just need to dare to imagine something and to pursue it. On the contrary, the scope of the imaginary is a scarce resource that is available to different people in different degrees. Fantasy, Mukhtar argues, is in turn linked with dreams (*ahlam*, here in the sense of imaginations that are linked with the expectation that they can and need to be realized). What on the level of fantasy was a play of mind, can as a dream be a pursuit and a plan. Such dreams, finally, can be the ground of choices people make, concrete actions that have a material effect, change the reality in one way or another. And that reality, in turn, is the ground that determines the scope of dreams and fantasies. But it is an unpredictable process, Mukhtar points out: the revolution was in part marked by the way some people were able to turn impossible fantasies into concrete actions, but these actions are not finite. They initiate a new circle of choices, dreams, and fantasy, and as long as the circle is not complete, we lack the scope of imagination to anticipate its consequences.

In light of this theory, it becomes clear that the question whether poetry can change the world was posed in a misleading way for two reasons. First, poetry is not separate from the world to start with, and therefore cannot have external causality. Instead, poetry is part of the world as it changes, with fantasies becoming the ground of dreams and actions, and actions and experiences feeding and limiting the scope of the imaginable. Fantasy, too, is a scarce resource. Second, the question has been posed in a too megalomanic fashion, as if only great and dramatic events were important. Such megalomania was compelling in Egypt in 2011. Talk about "change" (*taghyir*) was in the air, and it did not mean just any change. It meant sweeping, fundamental, holistic transformation of humanity, politics, and society. This grand vision of change neglects processes where some things change but only for a handful of people. And it also neglects the possibility of change going wrong.

More often than not, the productive relationship of fantasies, dreams, and actions is limited to intimate, personal change and makes little or no difference in regard to wider relations of power. As Amal Dunqul reminded us in *From the Papers of Abu Nuwas*, the gold of princes remains far more powerful than the babbling of poets. This is how Mukhtar saw the situation more than two years later when he shared with me his bitter frustration about the course of the events:

> Poets only make a change in their imaginary world that is parallel to the real world of frustration. There is no real change happening. If anything changes it is through force, deception, and manipulation. The dreamers and poets are simply used, their sweet words are spread to beautify the picture. Change is made by those with realistic interests. The poets and dreamers spearhead the change in a dream world that has no relationship with the real world, but they are being used [by the powerful for political ends]. The Muslim Brotherhood never liked Amal Dunqul. The revolutionaries never stopped dreaming. In no country has the military ever understood poetry and dreams.

This is the gist of Mukhtar's sceptical revision of his theory in January 2014: Those who actually have the power to make a difference do not care about poetry, but they do know how to exploit sweet words to beautify their crimes. The original, authentic change that is involved in poetry only reaches few crazy dreamers and remains in a parallel world.

This is a widespread view among poets and writers I have spoken with, many of whom always have been highly sceptical about the idea that their writing could make a difference in society. However, they do think that writing can make a difference—for the writer. The only ones who are tangibly changed by literature are the literates themselves—and perhaps also some of their close friends, family, and some people who search for their company because they are drawn to the different world they embody.

In this vein, the Alexandrian poet Shaymaa Bakr contested the very idea of an anthropological study of writers and poets:

> Why do you as an anthropologist study poets? Anthropology should be about the whole of society. Poets are outsiders, they are exceptional and discon-nected, they do not express or represent the society.

She is right, of course. Poets are among the most unrepresentative people an anthropologist can study. She is the living proof of her own argument, uniting in her person some extraordinary ideological and religious contradictions in a decidedly idiosyncratic manner.[17]

However, it is precisely her idiosyncrasy—and the idiosyncrasy of so many other writers—that raises interesting questions about poetry as a part of the world. As with many other poets, Shaymaa thinks of herself as too exceptional to be of any sociological relevance, but at the same time she has the urge and the skill to speak about issues that need to be said and heard. The question about poetry's place in the world, in this sense, is one about the role of idio-syncratic and strange people and ideas in the making of a society.

The answer can only be paradoxical. Between 2011 and 2012, Shaymaa Bakr recorded her sceptical vision of the revolutionary dream of change in her poem *I Say* (*Aqul ana*), which she describes as a "rebellion against rebel-lion." The following is my translation of a short passage from her much longer poem:

> *We had to grab for the wind*
> *The sheep had to reject being skinned*
> *after it was slaughtered*
> *Brothers of ours had to die . . .*

so that the open graves . . .
can promise to us that we haven't died yet
that there is a killing that does not kill us
But we should not have
raised our ambition so that it can devour us
We had to set fire
into all the dry wood
without afterward demanding from time
that it may turn the earth green again
Who would trust his feet if he staggered
if one step
tried to change its pace
on the same futile road

كـان لابـد أن نـقبض الـريـخ

لابـد لـلشاة أن تـرفض الـسلـخَ

مـن بـعد أن ذبـحت

أن يـموت لـنا إخوةً ..

فـالـقبور الـتى فُـتحت ..

سوف تـُنْـبئوَنا أنـنا لـم نـمت بـعدُ

ومـن الـقتل مـا لـيس يقتلـنا

إنـما لـم يكن يـنبغى

أن نـربى الـطموحَ لـيأكلـنا

كـان لابـد أن نـشعل الـنارَ

فى كـل هذا الـهشيم

ثـم لا نـسأل الـوقتَ

أن يـُرجعَ الأرض خضراءَ

مـن ذا يـصدق أقدامـه لـو تـرنـّحَ..

لـو جرُبت خطوةٌ

أن تـغير إيقـاعـها

فوق نـفس الـطريق الـعقـيم .

I Say is an interesting vision of the dilemma of those Egyptian revolutionaries who according to Mukhtar "never stopped dreaming," who spearheaded the idea of change, contributed to a political rupture, but failed to realize any of their aims and ends. Shaymaa Bakr points out that the problem is not just that they were defeated. More gravely, she tells us, their vision of radical change created a struggle that is structured so that it cannot be won. We set the dry wood on fire and expect earth to turn green again. We try to change the pace of our steps, but we are still on the same road. The revolutionary dreamers, who indeed were spirited by crazy fantasies and unlikely dreams, transported some of those dreams from the closed circles of the dedicated few to the streets of Egypt. They failed, and yet they left their mark on history. Their struggle was effective but not liberating.

This is why I think that it would be too optimistic to think of poetry and poets, literates, artists, and other dreamers and misfits as simply powerless when they face the sturdy power of oppression. It might even be too optimistic to think of them as useful idiots who unwittingly provide the powerful with an ideological cover. There is a third, more disturbing possible consequence.

Kamal Ali Mahdy argued that Amal Dunqul taught Egyptians to consider rejection a virtue, a value in its own right in spite of likely or certain defeat. Only very few Egyptians actually were affected, and the part played by Amal Dunqul's poetry may not have been particularly great. But those very few belong to a radical political minority that, since 2011, has indeed fashioned rejection as a political principle with important practical consequences. Their stance of a principled "no" comes with a radical vision of change as a value in itself, and implies a claim for uncompromising purity and struggle. They are by all counts far too weak to ever gain power, but they have been over and again able to stir the political situation and to disrupt the foreseen path of events. And more than once they have—sometimes unwittingly, sometimes quite willingly—aided more powerful forces to seize the day.

This is by no means unique to Egypt. Poetry, along with songs and slogans derived from poems, has been strongly present in probably all the recent Arab uprisings. Some poetry—especially Aboul-Qacem Echebbi's *The Will to Live*—has traveled across the Arab world and become ingrained in the language of protest and revolt (see Colla 2012). At the same time, revolt has proven to have ambiguous consequences. It may be liberating. It is very likely to be destructive. This is not a new insight, of course. Albert Camus argued in 1951 that philosophical rebellion is a fundamental human trait that over time results in real revolutions. But, Camus adds, the problem is that revolutions are, by definition, murderous.

Amal Dunqul promised eternal torment to those who say no. But it is not only the torment of futility and defeat that Mukhtar expressed. It is the torment of consequences. Not without a reason did Dunqul set "Don't Reconcile" in the historical event of a murder that unleashed a war of vendetta so deep and bitter that it continued for forty years. As the principle of rejection has entered the daily life of Egypt, it has also become part of a world where compromises are considered treason and where confrontation appears as the only moral choice. Poetry, too, is part of the vicious circle of polarization that haunts Egypt since spring 2011.

NOTES

Acknowledgements: This chapter is based on a shared research project together with Mukhtar Saad Shehata. Furthermore, I am grateful to Ashraf Dossouki Ali, Hamdy Mossa, Mohamed Mahmoud Mosa, Shaymaa Bakr, Amr Khairy, Abdelrehim Youssef, Fares Khidr, and the editors and peer reviewers of this book for their ideas, critique, and help.

Note on transliteration: There are numerous ways to transcribe Arabic with Latin letters, and all of them are inadequate in one way or another. In this chapter, poetry is cited in the Arabic original, accompanied by English translation. For proper names, the spelling used by the persons themselves is used. Otherwise, simplified Arabic transcription rules of the International Journal of Middle Eastern Studies are used.

1. Dunqul 2005, 334 (my translation). Recital by the author: http://www.youtube.com/watch?v=Tf9inqeTevU. Most of Dunqul's poetry is also freely available online as are many original recitations by the author.

2. Dunqul 2005, 91; English translation by Suneela Mubayi 2012. Recital by the author, http://www.youtube.com/watch?v=YuInA7MCLq4.

3. Dunqul 2005, 347 (my translation; for other translations, see, e.g., Roters 2011, Hegazy 2007). Recital by the author: http://www.youtube.com/watch?v=uF5OHwLqOhg.

4. Dunqul 2005, 93 (my translation).

5. *Ihna illi qulna la'*, https://www.facebook.com/No4everythingisWrong.

6. I find "the Arab Spring" a highly misleading seasonal metaphor for the events that began in 2011. If one wants to use a seasonal metaphor for the years of revolutions and counterrevolutions, then the Coptic month of Amshir (8 February to 9 March) that in Egypt is characterized by stormy, unpredictable weather, is definitely more fitting than "spring."

7. Ibrahim 2013, 138 (my translation).

8. Classical and classicist Arabic poetry has a characteristic verse structure where a pair of half-verses together forms the narrative and structural unit of the verse (*bayt*). Poetry with this structure is known as *'amudi*, i.e., "columnic" because in written form, poems made up of double verses appear as two columns. For example, the verse "If one day the people will to live / Then Fate must an answer give" by Aboul-Qacem Echebbi, cited on page 137, is a classicist double verse. In contemporary poetry, single verses have become the norm. Of the poems quoted in this chapter, Mustafa Ibrahim's poetry represents colloquial rhymed poetry influenced by the modernist *taf'ila* and the traditional *zajal* alike. The poetry of Amal Dunqul (as well as that of Shaymaa Bakr) represents a more experimental form of *taf'ila* that has a complex and free structure of verses and that is built on a rhythmic structure on changing meters and sometimes rhyme. On classic and modern poetics see Furani 2012.

9. Pioneer of a style of satirical writing that became extremely popular in a short time

before 2011 (see, e.g., Fadl 2005), Belal Fadl became an important third-current voice until January 2014 through his column in the daily newspaper *Shorouk*, although his influence was of course far more limited than that of the TV comedian Bassem Youssef. See Fadl 2014; *Mada Masr* 2014. For an overview of Belal Fadl's columns in Arabic, see http://www .shorouknews.com/columns/BilalFadl.

10. See Shehata 2010, 2014. For an overview of his essayistic work online, see http:// www.ahewar.org/m.asp?i=6026.

11. For their published works, see Ali 2007, 2008; Mahdy 2005; 2007; Mossa 2012a, 2012b, 2013.

12. Aboul-Qacem Echebbi, *Iradat al-hayah* (The Will to Live), English translation by Sanders and Visonà 2012: 229. This poem is also the source of the slogan, "The people want the toppling of the regime."

(الـشعب يــريــد إسقـاط الـنـظـام)

That was originally coined in Tunisia in December 2010 and has been repeated in all uprisings in the Arab world since 2011. For a history of the poem's different readings and uses, see Colla 2012.

13. In 1967, the Arab armies of Egypt, Syria, and Jordan were defeated by Israel in a humiliating manner in the Six-Day War. This event became central to much of Amal Dunqul's literary work.

14. Ashraf is making implicit use here of an Islamic theology of freedom and destiny according to which humans are free to act, but they act out the predestined will of God. According to this theology, human intention, cause, and effect are real, but they only take place in accordance with the will of God, as Hamdy agrees in the following course of the discussion.

15. For his biography and poetry, see Hassan ibn Thabit 1994.

16. Some years before 2011, Hisham Al-Gakh had made it to considerable fame with very straightforward colloquial poetry that addressed the worries and frustrations of ordinary Egyptians. Poets who move in dedicated literary circles commonly love to hate Hisham al-Gakh's populist style. For a translation of one of his poems, see Sanders and Visonà 2012, 227–228.

17. Since she keeps her writings and her private life strictly apart, I cannot get into the details.

REFERENCES

el-Abnudi, Abdel Rahman. 2014. *Mish kull waraga titmidi*. Poetry recital on CBC+2 TV channel, 9 January. http://www.youtube.com/watch?v=vBrkIokHY5c&feature=youtube.

Adonis. 1990. *An Introduction to Arab Poetics*. Translated by Catherine Cobham. London: Saqi Books.

Ali, Ashraf Dossouki. 2007. *Wasawis wa al-sabab Layla: Diwan*. Alexandria: Silsilat Alwan Ibda'iya.

———. 2008. *Laysa al-an: Diwan*. Alexandria: Silsilat Taghyir/Change.

Azimi, Negar. 2014. "The Egyptian Army's Unlikely Allies." *New Yorker*, 8 January. http:// www.newyorker.com/online/blogs/newsdesk/2014/01/why-egypts-liberal-intellectuals -still-support-the-army.html?mbid=social_retweet&mobify=0.

Badawi, M. M. 1975. *A Critical Introduction to Modern Arabic Poetry*. Cambridge: Cambridge University Press.

Camus, Albert. 1991 (1951). *The Rebel: An Essay on Man in Revolt*, translated by Anthony Bower. New York: Vintage Books.

CNN Arabic. 2013. "Negm: Matkhafush ʿala Masr wa al-Ikhwan yighuru." 30 November. http://archive.arabic.cnn.com/2013/entertainment/11/30/nejm.amman/.

Colla, Elliot. 2012. "The People Want." *Middle East Report* 263. http://www.merip.org/mer/mer263/people-want.

Creswell, Robyn, and Bernard Haykel. 2015. "Battle Lines: Want to Understand the Jihadis? Read Their Poetry." *New Yorker*, 8 June. http://www.newyorker.com/magazine/2015/06/08/battle-lines-jihad-creswell-and-haykel.

Dunqul, Amal. 2005. *Al-Aʿmal al-Kamila*. Cairo: Maktabat al-Madbuli.

Elreweny, Abla. 1992 (1985). *Al-Ganubi: Amal Dunqul*. Al-Kuwayt and Cairo: Dar Suʿad Al-Sabah.

Fadl, Bilal. 2005. *Bani Bajam*. Cairo: Merit.

———. 2014. "The Political Marshal of Egypt." *Mada Masr*, 2 February. http://madamasr.com/content/political-marshal-egypt.

Furani, Khaled. 2012. *Silencing the Sea: Secular Rythms in Palestinian Poetry*. Stanford: Stanford University Press.

Hassan ibn Thabit. 1994. *Diwan Hassan ibn Thabit*, edited by Abd A. Ali Mihanna. Beirut: Dar al-Kutub al-ʿIlmiya. http://ia600401.us.archive.org/6/items/waqdwaween1/32476.pdf.

Hegazy, Nada. 2007. *No Amends*. http://noamends.blogspot.com/2007/06/no-amends.html.

Hoyland, Robert G. 2001. *Arabia and the Arabs from the Bronze Age to the Coming of Islam*. London: Routledge.

Ibrahim, Mustafa. 2013. *Al-Manifesto: Diwan bi-l-ʿammiyya al-masriyya*. Doha: Bloomsbury Qatar Foundation Publishing.

Jacquemond, Richard. 2008. *Conscience of the Nation: Writers, State, and Society in Modern Egypt*. Cairo: American University of Cairo Press.

Jayyusi, Salma Khadra. 1977. *Trends and Movements in Modern Arabic Poetry*. Leiden: Brill.

Kendall, Elisabeth. 2006. *Literature, Journalism and the Avant-Garde: Intersection in Egypt*. London: Routledge.

Kennedy, Philip F. 2007. *Abu Nuwas: A Genius of Poetry*. Oxford: Oneworld.

Khouri, Mounah A. 1971. *Poetry and the Making of Modern Egypt (1882–1922)*. Leiden: Brill.

Lindsey, Ursula. 2013. "A Voice of Dissent Joins the Nationalist Chorus." *Mada Masr*, 6 October. http://madamasr.com/content/voice-dissent-joins-nationalist-chorus.

Mada Masr. 2014. "Belal Fadl Leaves Al-Shorouk Following Censorship of Article." 2 February. http://madamasr.com/content/belal-fadl-leaves-al-shorouk-following-censorship-article.

Mahdy, Kamal Ali. 2005. *Rajul min Yahmum*. Cairo: Kutub ʿArabiya.

———. 2007. *Yawm yakun al-raʾi: Shiʿr*. Cairo: Supreme Council for Culture.

Miller, Flagg. 2007. *The Moral Resonance of Arab Media: Audiocassette Poetry and Culture in Yemen*. Cambridge, MA: Harvard University Press.

Mossa, Hamdy. 2012a. *Al-Qatira tuʿabbiʾ al-ahlam sawb al-muntaha: Diwan shiʿr*. al-Mansura: Dar al-Islam li-l-tabaʿa wa-l-nashr.

————. 2012b. *Halib al-shams: Riwaya*. al-Mansura: Dar al-Islam li-l-taba'a wa-l-nashr.

————. 2013. *Lamma' al-biyada*. http://www.youtube.com/watch?v=HWhWDJ3ku4Y.

Mubayi, Suneela, trans. 2012. *Amal Dunqul: Spartacus' Last Words. Jadaliyya* (23 August). http://www.jadaliyya.com/pages/index/6998/amal-dunqul_spartacus-last-words.

Negm, Ahmed Fouad. 2013. Interview on Mehwar 2 TV Channel. 3 December. http://www .youtube.com/watch?v=v-W50dYhL1M.

Nicoarea, Georgiana. 2013. "Graffiti and Cultural Production in Contemporary Cairo: Articulating Local and Global Elements of Popular Culture." *Romano-Arabica Journal* 13: 261–272. http://www.academia.edu/3776871/Graffiti_and_Cultural_Production_in_Con temporary_Cairo_Articulating_Local_and_Global_Elements_of_Popular_Culture.

Roters, Daniel. 2011. "Khaled Saeed—Die Toten mahnen die Welt." *Sawtuna* (19 June). http:// arabistikwwu.blogspot.nl/2011/06/khaled-saeed-die-toten-mahnen-die-welt.html.

Sanders, Lewis IV, and Mark Visonà. 2012. "The Soul of Tahrir: Poetics of a Revolution." In *Translating Egypt's Revolution: The Language of Tahrir*, edited by Samia Mehrez, 213–248. Cairo: American University of Cairo Press.

Sartre, Jean-Paul. 1949 (1947). *What Is Literature?*, translated by Bernard Frechtman. New York: Philosophical Library. https://archive.org/details/whatisliterature030271mbp.

Schielke, Samuli. 2015. *Egypt in the Future Tense: Hope, Frustration and Ambivalence, before and after 2011*. Bloomington: Indiana University Press.

Shehata, Mukhtar Saad. 2010. *La li al-Iskandariya*. Cairo: Arabesque.

————. 2013. "Ana Jaban . . . wa anta al-shuja' . . . hadhihi kull al-hikaya!" *al-Hiwar al-Mutamaddin* (27 July). http://www.ahewar.org/debat/show.art.asp?aid=370559.

————. 2014. *Taghribat Bani Saber*. Alexandria: Dar Kalima.

PART III

ISLAM: RELIGIOUS DISCOURSES
AND PIOUS ETHICS

THIS SECTION ELABORATES the Islamic discursive tradition—both Sunni and Shiʿa—with regard to popular culture in general and music in particular. In addition, it illustrates how contemporary pious discourses have developed among artists and have been translated into ethical practices and aesthetic forms.

Jonas Otterbeck's chapter presents the complex relation of Sunni Islamic discourse to the practice of music making and listening. The chapter illustrates how a multitude of voices compete about formulating the Islamic answer to the key issue of its permissibility. By first dealing with the issue "what is music" and next by analysing the concept of "authority in Islam," Otterbeck is able to provide a contextualized approach to the contestations that have been ongoing since the earliest days of Islam and have been particularly intense during the last decades. Otterbeck distinguishes between prominent trends such as the moderate position, the liberal position, and the hardliners and he sketches the proponents' main arguments and social settings. The chapter thus offers a contextualized explanation why a certain idea might seem plausible at a time or in a place when other ideas might circulate and be seen as heretic or simply wrong. Otterbeck examines the complexity and contradictions inherent in Islamic discourse and shows that interpretations relate to discursive power and are not a-historically givens.

Joseph Alagha's chapter focuses on Shiʿa debates on Islam and performing arts. Like Otterbeck, this chapter also shows that Islamic law (*shariʿa*) is a socially constructed phenomenon and "Islam" is a social practice that is constantly undergoing revision. Alagha highlights the differences between classical and contemporary methods of reasoning on the performing arts between Shiʿa and Sunni sources and scholars. It particularly examines the preponderance of moderate views surrounding music within the contemporary Shiʿite tradition. This is related to a specific method of reasoning based on the jurisprudential concept of *maslaha* (interest, advantage). Alagha explores how the concept of *maslaha* has been used in the cultural field by Shi'ite religious scholars, in particular by movements such as Hizbullah, and reveals how the concept of *maslaha* as understood by Hizbullah's leaders and cadres is translated into flexible cultural politics and artistic practices in Lebanon.

Jessica Winegar's chapter explores a new trend in Egypt: the emergence of self-avowed Islamic visual artists among a younger generation of art students. For many of these religious students and professors, art is key to the process of becoming a better Muslim, for reaffirming Islamic and Egyptian "identity," and to creating a stronger and more "developed" Islamic society. They form joint student-faculty groups that are committed to creating art that does not violate what they understand to be the principles of Islam but also to creating art that serves Islam and God. This art school, which was once a bastion of self-avowed secularists, is now the site of influential clubs that perform community art works dedicated to promoting Islamic values among themselves and in lower-class communities. The chapter highlights that these pious Muslims view art as absolutely critical to their lives and their work as modern and cosmopolitan Egyptians. These views challenge dominant modernist assumptions that contemporary art is or should be against institutionalized religion or at least critical of it. The chapter thus also questions underlying conceptual frameworks that equate youth and arts with secularism.

Karin van Nieuwkerk's chapter also traces the development of pious art and Islamic aesthetics by following the career of an Egyptian Islamist producer, actor, and playwright Ahmad Abu Haiba over the last thirty years. His career shows the strong dialectical relationship between Egypt's sociohistorical transformations and the field of art. The chapter analyzes how in the 1980s, Egypt witnessed a growing revival of religiosity, a time when many artists stepped down from art for religious reasons. From the late 1990s onward a pious market for leisure and art emerged. There developed an extensive field of religiously inflected art accommodating religious sensibilities and promoting a culture of diverse pious taste. Such cultures of the affluent classes were also influenced by global cosmopolitan forces coming from both the West and the Gulf. Abu Haiba and other artists have been on the vanguard of these developments. The chapter thus shows that art not only reflects social change but also helps to bring it about. Sociopolitical developments have a strong bearing on the field of art, whereas the field of art simultaneously shapes the sociopolitical landscape and its ongoing transformations.

This section thus highlights not only the historical and contextual character of religious discourse on art and its ensuing artistic practices but also the importance of the field of art to study these ongoing transformations.

CHAPTER 7

THE SUNNI DISCOURSE ON MUSIC

JONAS OTTERBECK

O, Umaiyads, avoid singing for it decreases shame, increases desire, and destroys manliness, and verily it takes the place of wine and does what drunkenness does. But if you must engage in it, keep the women and children away from it, for singing is the instigator of fornication. ROBSON 1938: 27

THIS HARSH STATEMENT MADE, according to the hadith[1] scholar Ibn Abi al-Dunya (d. 894), by the Umayyad Caliph ibn Walid (d. 744) summarizes much of the forbidding attitude of some Islamic scholars[2] regarding music. Still today, some scholars promote this understanding. Others praise music and consider it an important aspect of both general and religious culture. But as with most discourse on religion, things are not that simple. For example, the Persian Sufi al-Huwairi (d. 1073) wrote that "Audition [i.e., listening to music] is like the sun, which shines on all things but affects them differently . . . : it burns or illumines or dissolves or nurtures" (al-Huwairi 2001: 512). His message is echoed in much Islamic writing: Be careful with music, it is powerful.

This chapter maps out the discourse on music within Sunni Islamic thinking (for Shiʿite views, see Alagha, this volume). Rather than providing an Islamic answer to the relation Muslims should have to music, this chapter attempts to illustrate how a multitude of voices compete about formulating the Islamic answer. This contestation has been ongoing since the earliest days of Islam and has been particularly intense the last decades. To be able to do this, some concepts that might seem easily understood, such as music, Islamic scholar, and Islam must first be discussed.

WHAT IS MUSIC?

A direct equivalent of the word "music" did not exist in Arabic during the time of Muhammad in seventh-century Arabia. The Arabic word *musiqa* (or *musiqi*[3]) is a loan word from Greek, likely incorporated into Arabic during the eighth or ninth century, and was primarily used when discussing music in philosophy, not performed music. The philosophical discourse on *musiqa* is speculative and fascinating (discussing among other things music and cosmology) but barely connected to everyday religion or to the Islamic discussions about the legality of music, rather to cosmology (Shehadi 1995). Instead, the music performed in real life was described as *ghina'* (singing), *sama'* (listening), *sawt* (voice, song, sound), *'alat al-tarab* (musical instruments), *al-tarab* (enchantment[4]), or more slighting as *malahi* or *lahw* (distraction, diversion). Here, I will use music as a generic term but use the relevant Islamic terminology when quoting and discussing specific instances.[5]

Islamic scholars argued for a difference between religious tonal expressions (chants, the call to prayer, melodic recitation of the Qur'an, etc.) and other expressions that could be called music (or any relevant term of the above). This had the apologetic aim of protecting the religious use of music from critique. For example, Hanbali scholar Ibn Taymiyya (d. 1328), who pleaded for a restrictive attitude to music, contrasted the *sama'* (the listening) to music, which he considered illegitimate, with the *sama'* to the word of Allah in melodic Qur'an chanting (*tajwid*), which he considered essential (Shehadi 1995: chapter 6; al-Faruqi 1985: 7). One prominent idea was that there is a difference between a natural musicalness and a schooled musicality, the first being approved of and used for example in Qur'anic chanting, the other, used when singing or playing instruments, had a dubious status (Shehadi 1995: 151; Sabri 1910/1995).

For many Islamic scholars, musical performances were associated with singing and dancing girls (and boys) at taverns where wine was consumed and prostitution flourished. Such places are never popular in the moral discourses of religious scholars, but an additional problem within Islamic discourse is the idea of gender segregation and the importance of covering the individual *'awra*, the private parts.[6] According to some Islamic scholars, *'awra* included the female voice, especially the singing voice. The singing (in extreme interpretation even the speech) of women was perceived as indecent to men. This line of reasoning was more common before the proliferation of audio-visual media. Opinions have changed about where the limits of female decency may be drawn. Still today, female singers cannot get a license to make officially distributed records in Saudi Arabia (Urkevich 2005). However, using digital home recordings and web pages such as MySpace circumvents this. For example, Saudi pop group The Accolade (with a female vocalist), active on MySpace, had a minor underground hit, "Pinocchio," in Saudi Arabia in 2008 (see web pages: *Accolade*; *New York Times*). However, in most Muslim countries, female artists are not censored in this fashion.

Islamic scholars are prone to interpret the male gaze on female performers (or on *al-murdan*, the beardless male youth) as potentially sexual or even as sexual by definition. In any case, seeing and hearing the female (or effeminate) performer uprooted the gender segregation system meant to minimize social contacts between unrelated men and women.

As a result, in many Muslim societies performing artists have held unclear social positions and been suspected of immoral living. For example, the most renowned female singer of religious songs in Egypt in the nineteenth century was al-Hajja al-Suwaysiyya. According to Virginia Danielson (1997: 209): "She appeared wearing a long black wrap, head covering, and face veil, with her husband, son, and brother as accompanists." Al-Suwaysiyya was part of a class of respectable female performers called *'awalim* (learned women) in Egypt. Still, she needed to mark her respectability through clothing and company (see also van Nieuwkerk 1995: chapter 2).

The premises and mechanisms for music making and playing have changed rapidly from the late nineteenth century and onward. These changes include the possibility to record, the emergence of a music industry, new instruments, the adding of electricity and amplification, radio broadcasts, new concert venues, new ideas about performance as such, music in theaters and on film, and also new ways of consuming and listening to music (see Bohlman 2002). Further, in many Muslim societies, these changes were part of a process of westernization quickly internalized as part of daily life, especially by the elite (Armbrust 1996). There were few reasons for Islamic scholars to praise this development. New musical styles and new technologies were viewed with suspicion. Religious specialists, of any religion, are not famed for being the cultural vanguard hailing the newest foreign cultural trends. Rather, a certain amount of conservatism may be expected, even though exceptions do exist. Consequently, musicians have been accused of destroying the national cultural heritage and corrupting the youth by introducing novelties (Otterbeck 2004; LeVine 2008a).

Thus, the discourse on music is far from homogeneous, and music was and still is being associated with ideas and practices that might compromise it, the artist, and the consumption of it. Throughout history we find different approaches that overlap and contest each other. For example, one finds writing from the Islamic world on music theory (dealing with scales and the very elements of music), *shari'a* discussions on the legality of music, a high cultural defence of music written by learned Muslims, and a Sufi discussion on the power and usage of music in ritual (including apologetic defenses thereof).

AUTHORITY AND THE ORDER OF ISLAM

Who has had an authoritative opinion on the relation between Islam and music, and can all writings by Muslims be considered to be Islamic? Some of the best-known historical tracts on music were not written by scholars that were primarily writing from an Islamic starting point. For example, the edifying text on morals *al-iqd al-farid* (The Unique Necklace) was written by Ibn ʿAbd Rabbihi (d. 940), a poet and intellectual at the Umayyad court in Andalusia. Still, in the text, religious arguments are put forth and discussed. At the time, being educated was synonymous with having a deep knowledge of religion. Since Ibn ʿAbd Rabbihi knew his views to be contested by some Islamic scholars, but embraced by others, he consciously made a discursive intervention (Asad 1993: 164) writing against the forbidding attitude, promoting the virtues of music.[7]

Even though most writing has a relation to religion, much has little to do with the legal scholarly debate. What then counts as Islamic? As in most traditions, Islamic scholars try to impose their interpretations as authoritative and genuine. They use powerful discursive mechanisms trying to exclude voices deemed as unqualified, deviant, or mad and discipline others who may participate in the discourse. But, from the perspective of the anthropology of Islam, not only intellectual, theological positions are acknowledged as interpretations of Islam. Established oral traditions, local—sometimes curious—ideas and practices with or without a long history may also count as Islamic. In fact, intellectually expressed ideas and local customs are frequently embedded in each other, and one cannot be understood without the other. Still, the proponents of the different views and practices might be in open conflict with each other. But regardless if views are in dialogue or conflict, they are in a relation to each other forming the conditions of the discourse. Regarding music, discussions may address singing, dancing, and music making at tombs, celebrations, and other gatherings such as *mawlids* (celebrations commemorating a holy person) or *naʾat* singing (religious chants) after the *jumaʿa* prayer (the noon Friday prayer) in a Barelvi mosque, or other popular practices. Some scholars, especially those of the Hanbali school, deem these practices illegal *bidʿa* (innovations). Still, the practices might be supported and seen as seminal locally by a scholar, *shaikh* or *shaikha*, and especially by the common believer.

Anthropologist Talal Asad (1986) called the generated interpretations of Islam over time a discursive tradition. Evidently, not everything said and done by Muslims is part of that discourse. Ideas and interpretations must have a relation to Islamic discourse in some way, but not a very determined way. It does not, for example, have to be intellectual. Seen this way, Islam becomes the aggregated product of discursive struggles over time. Some of these contestations and their followers are isolated from each other, others fight bitter battles about what Islam means. Yet others are content with a plurality as long as no one quarrels. In this great drama in time and space, certain persons stand out as religious specialists.[8] Note that "specialist" is meant to be an economic category. Religious specialists have their livelihood from religion; it is what they produce—not crops or silver rings. A religious specialist in Islam (or in any other tradition) does not have to be a theologian ('alim) or trained legal scholar (faqih). It may as well be a self-taught person locally perceived as holy. Religious specialists are especially interesting since they exercise power by verbalizing and enacting interpretations of Islam from an enhanced social position. But, they are not the majority. What the common believers do, accept, or believe holds great power through sheer numbers.

If Islam is understood as a discursive tradition and if the discourse on music is heterogeneous, how do we describe the Sunni discourse on music over time? Below I describe three positions in the present and point at their use of and connection with the past.

THE MODERATE POSITION: FROM CULTURAL CONSERVATISM TO PURPOSEFUL ART

The moderate position is that music in itself is not a problem. It is the lyrics, the style of performance, and the company in which it is performed, and possibly the timing of the performance that might be problematic. Classically, these possible restrictions were addressed as zaman (time), makam (place), and ikhwan (brothers, metaphor for company) as for example in the well-spread Sufi manual al-risala al-qushayriya fi 'ilm al-tasawwuf (The Qushayriya Epistle on the Knowledge of Sufism) by the Shafi'i scholar and Sufi master Abu al-Qasim al-Qushayri (d. 1074) (Knysh 2007). The believers were encouraged to take those three elements into account when judging whether listening to music (sama') was appropriate or not. Contemporary discussion often stresses that lyrics should be decent. Love and longing for a beloved are respectable topics according to most, but dirty lyrics are not.

Moderate interpretations have deep historical roots and have dominated in several of the Muslim empires. Today one finds several different main strands of this position. There is the jurists' argument, the Sufi argument, and what can be called the wasatiyya call for a fann al-hadif (purposeful art).

WHAT IS NOT FORBIDDEN IS ALLOWED

One of the Islamic scholars best known for a lenient attitude to music is Yusuf Al-Qaradawi. He is often referred to both by proponents and critics of this position. The Egyptian-born scholar, residing in Qatar, was propelled into world fame through his TV-show *Shari'a wa-l-hayat* (*shari'a* and life) on al-Jazeera. He was already well known for authoring many books (Zaman 2004: 145 f.). Al-Qaradawi has on several occasions, in writing and in speech, addressed the issue of music. Making reference to Andalusian scholar Ibn Hazm (d. 1064), al-Qaradawi maintains a classical principle in *fiqh* (jurisprudence): What is not explicitly forbidden is allowed. Even though giving credit to the forbidding attitude to music by pointing out its historicity (al-Qaradawi 1995: 32), he argues that it is what accompanies music that makes it *halal* (legal) or *haram* (forbidden). When singers use dirty language or incite to sexual transgressions, for example, through movements, then music becomes problematic. He connects his interpretation to classical Islamic standpoints on morality targeting slanderous talk, excess, irresponsible sexuality, and so forth. He also adds another argument well founded in Islamic history expressed by, for example, the Sufi sheikh Abu Hafs Umar al-Suhrawardi (d. 1234):

> Music does not give rise in the heart, to anything which is not already there. So he, whose inner self is attached to anything else than God is stirred by music to sensual desire, but the one who is inwardly attached to the love of God is moved, by hearing music, to do his will. (Quoted in Schimmel 2001: 12)

According to al-Qaradawi, the individual believer will have to judge by his or her reaction to music if it is suitable or not. If the music increases love and mercy to Allah and your dear ones, no objections can be made, but if it makes you want to do drugs and have illicit sex it is *haram* for you (al-Qaradawi 1997: 299).

For al-Qaradawi, morality should be integrated in all aspects of society, also in art (Zaman 2004: 145). Religious specialists like al-Qaradawi only defend culturally decent music. Where the limits of decency should be drawn is a different question. Examples tend to be safe, such as expressing admiration for Fairuz. When Islamic scholar Sheikh 'Adil ibn Salam al-Kalbani from Saudi Arabia caused a big fuss by proclaiming music as primarily legal in June 2010, he defended himself from criticism by saying that he was not referring to indecent songs such as those of Lebanese artists "Nancy Ajram and Hayfa Wehbe" (Otterbeck 2012). Apart from the comical pinpoint accuracy of the examples (he obviously knew about these artists), it shows the moderate position's proponents' preferences for music that does not rock the boat. No Islamic scholar has, to my knowledge, discussed, for example, heavy-metal lyrics saying that if they make youth reflexive about religious symbols and myths, it is *halal*—a logical extension of al-Qaradawi's line of reasoning.

In classical theology, it is often stressed that a hadith says: "God has not sent a prophet except with a beautiful voice." This has been interpreted as meaning that Allah blessed all prophets with a pleasing and melodic voice. This in turn was taken to mean that tonal expressions were allowed and promoted, for example, by the Shafi'i scholar and Sufi Abu Hamid Muhammad ibn Muhammad al-Ghazali (d. 1111) in his seminal work *Ihya 'ulum al-din* (Farmer 1942: 22; al-Ghazali 1901: 209). However, Islamic scholars such as Ibn Taymiyya have exposed the argument to devastating criticism for drawing parallels between the voices of prophets and music (see Shehadi 1995).

THE POWER OF *SAMA'*

One of the most referred to stands on music is the Sufi discourse on *sama'* (listening to music). Several prominent Sufi intellectuals have addressed the topic, and their arguments resonate in the contemporary moderate position. The eleventh-century Sufi Sheikh al-Qusayri wrote in length on *sama'*. Even though referring to both Qur'anic verses and hadiths in his writing, the core of his argument—in which he is passionate—is found in his rendering of the tales and sayings of former Sufi masters. In these, music is presumed to be extremely powerful, bringing out feelings of fear, love, and sadness. It has the ability to render men unconscious and even kill animals and men (whether death is primarily symbolic or not is unclear). The stories are didactic and tell of music (and *sama'*) as a blessing for the mature Sufi, but a danger to the inexperienced. Time, place, and company for the *sama'* should be right, otherwise it may give rise to base feelings instead of touching the heart of the devout, the heart being the key metaphor for the Sufi followers' possibilities to find the secret truth (*sirr*) hidden in the soul of men by Allah. The Sufi defense of *sama'* cannot be disassociated from Sufi ritual and the relationship between *murshid* (guide) and *murid* (guided). The classical Sufis never defended worldly music of the taverns; in that sense it was elitist. The classical Sufi position on *sama'* is repeated today with very similar words.

Today, some Sufis have entered the world music scene, presenting their music as spiritual and offering it on the market to anyone regardless of their understanding of the Sufi path. Artists like Nusrat Fateh Ali Khan and the Sabri Brothers (Pakistan), Al-Kindi Ensemble (Syria), or Kudsi and Süleyman Erguner (Turkey) all participate in the commercialization of what Shannon (2011) calls Suficized[9] music. To the proponents of this development, the music may draw people to the Sufi way and make them curious about it, and in this there is more gain than harm.

FANN AL-HADIF (PURPOSEFUL ART)

Most likely it was the movement called al-*wasatiyya* (the middle way) originating in Egypt that inaugurated the present discussion on *fann al-hadif* (purposeful art) in Sunni Islam, the idea being that music as a powerful expression should be put to the service of Islam (Baker 2003; Otterbeck 2008; Van Nieuwkerk 2011). *Al-wasatiyya* is an intellectual trend among Islamic scholars trying to develop a balanced, neither extremist nor indulgent, way to understand Islam in the present (see further Van Nieuwkerk, this volume). Among the first prominent sheikhs to take to the barricades on this issue was Sheikh Muhammad al-Ghazali (d. 1996). Al-Ghazali had a long-standing interest in the arts and had both promoted, for example, the modern Egyptian novel,[10] but also voiced strong opinions on the immorality of elements in modern Egyptian art. When famed novelist Naguib Mahfouz suffered a nearly fatal knife attack in October 1994 (Baker 2003), Al-Ghazali immediately rushed to the defence of Mahfouz and strongly condemned the use of violence.[11] He, and others of *al-wasatiyya*, saw the vicious deed as an attack, not only on the novelist, but on art as such, well aware of the harsh attitudes of reactionary Islamic scholars over the last decades. Instead, al-Ghazali strongly proposed a new discourse on arts. Some of this discourse was already in place, for example, in Muhammad 'Imara's[12] *al-islam wa-al-funun al-jamila* (Islam and the Belle Arts, 1991) and in parts of earlier work by al-Ghazali himself, such as the book *Mustaqbal al-Islam kharij ardih: kayfa nufakkiru fih* (The Future of Islam beyond Its Main Region: How Do We Think about It, 1984) and in the rich production of Yusuf al-Qaradawi. Two important points of this discourse were that art in itself and artists themselves are not inherently blameworthy and that art should be in an active relation with Islam and be inspired by it and give back inspiration. The Islamic scholars of *al-wasatiyya* are more interested in discussing what good art, including music, would mean, rather than engage in explaining, yet again, why lyrics encouraging drinking and casual sex really cannot be called Islamically sound.

A moderate voice promoting *fann al-hadif* is Egyptian Internet- and TV-preacher 'Amr Khaled. Khaled is a former accountant (not a trained theologian) who started his religious career preaching in mosques in well-off areas in Cairo. Khaled actively supports the production of modern Islamic music as a counterdiscourse to, so-called, offensive songs promoted through sexualized video clips. On his TV show, in his books, and on his webpage, Khaled is calling for a modern *da'wa* (call to Islam), using the artistic expressions of the present. "What is needed are arts and culture that will propel youth toward work, development, and production," Khaled (2005) writes. Art should, according to him, be useful and moral. For example, during Ramadan 2004 Khaled started to promote the deeply devout artist Sami Yusuf, whose music had recently become popular in Egypt, on his Iqra TV show (*Sunnaa al-hayah*, Life Makers) (Kubala 2005; Armbrust 2005).

The idea of a purposeful Islamic art reminds us of the discussion in Marxist and socialist circles about the function of art. Art was commissioned to propel the citizen, especially youth, into action for the cause. Further, good art was didactic and edifying, not nihilistic or bourgeois. In Marxist and socialist writing on art and society from the late nineteenth and early twenty century, art was seen as an important tool for making the workers see the world with new eyes, leaving their false consciousness (Solomon 2001). In this, Islamic scholars and socialist scholars share a vision, though the content of the messages promoted differ radically. Islamic scholars worldwide engage in and promote the production of purposeful art and consumption culture. The last twenty years has seen the birth and the rise of Islamic films, children's TV programs, video games, comic books, novels, paintings, design, couture, and not least music.

THE LIBERAL POSITION: FROM COMPETITION TO A CALL FOR FREEDOM

Only few Islamic scholars have developed a liberal position about music, if by liberal it is meant that one either ascribes to an understanding that competing worldviews and life style options are good for Islam or develops a postmodern ethics and aesthetics with a high tolerance for artistic discourse and preparedness for complex symbolic and ironic playfulness. While I have found a few scholars arguing for the former, I have not found any promoting the latter. I turn to a few Muslim artists inspired by Islam who have promoted the latter.

ISLAM IS COMPETITIVE

Lebanese Sheikh Ibrahim Ramadan al-Mardini posits arguments in his book on music in line with, he claims, established Sunni scholars in Lebanon (al-Mardini 2001; Otterbeck 2008). In interviews, al-Mardini explains that according to him the role of the *faqih* (Islamic jurist) is primarily advising the believer, not policing and censoring. Instead, he stresses that cultural expressions are central to any societal development; it is not the role of religious leaders to restrict these. Still, not all music is *halal*—for to promote Satanism can never be Islamic. But until it is proven that a piece of music is illegitimate, it is to be understood as permissible (al-Mardini 2001: 46). Instead of banning music, he thinks it important that cultural expressions find their own outlet, while the

Islamic scholar advises the believers about the better way. Youth might have poor priorities at times, but if scholars, in a positive way, can show that Islam provides a better path, al-Mardini is certain this will lead many to religion. But if scholars promote the censoring and banning of music, people will become alienated.[13] In his book al-Mardini argues that there is no clear condemnation of music in the Qur'an and that most of the hadith that has been put forth as proof of music being illegitimate are weak hadith.[14]

It should be pointed out that al-Mardini's book has not been hailed and gained influence. In fact, religious authorities in Lebanon have not allocated him a mosque to preach in (which is common when having a higher degree from a *shari'a* faculty); instead, when I met him, he was making his living as a pharmacist.[15]

FREEDOM OF EXPRESSION IN MUSIC

People arguing that Islam has room for any musical expression may be found outside the realm of Islamic scholars. Of course, many Muslims make music, but not necessarily because of their Islamic conviction. But others try to make convictions and music making meet. An example is Salman Ahmad, guitarist of well-known Pakistani rock band Junoon. In his autobiography (2010) he argues that his so-called "Sufi rock" is deeply spiritual and does not in any way contradict his faith, even though he is a rock star and has devoted fans of both sexes. Rather, he sees his striving for peace between India and Pakistan and his efforts to inspire youth to dare to formulate critique against society and partake in it as built on Islamic ethics. Apart from a general idea about a positive faith, Ahmad has also participated in a movie called *The Rock Star and the Mullahs* (2003) in which he takes the discussion about the legality of music head on with some hard-line Islamic scholars and their students in Pakistan. When I met Ahmad in Sweden, while promoting the movie, he stressed that the continuous opposition toward music he had met over the years had forced him to speak out against the hardliners.[16] Ahmad, who is a medical doctor, well versed and an intellectual in his own right, will not accept authoritarian reasoning. "I still have not met anyone who has convinced me that music is *haram*," he said.

An altogether different example is Aki Nawaz, the creative force behind the British band Fun-da-Mental who in his art has pushed the boundaries of the possible. Nawaz has during his career often used provocations to get his message across, for example in the song "Goddevil" (because of the clever layout readable as both God Devil and Good Evil), and "Cookbook DIY" in which Nawaz enacts the role of an Islamist terrorist making dirty bombs but also an American scientist making clean bombs, forcing the listener (and viewer) to make a comparison. Nawaz, who is a strong proponent of freedom of speech and critique of corruption, also claims to be deeply spiritual in his art. For example, the album *There Shall Be Love* (2001) is, in part, a celebratory album to Sufi Qawwali music. What is interesting is that Nawaz as a public figure aspires to the right to have a say about what art a person considering himself Muslim may produce. It is not formulated as theology but as lived ethics with a backdrop of Muslimness (see further Swedenburg 2010).

A final example that might seem odd to label liberal is the different expressions of Islamic punk. Not always, but often enough informed by anarchism, Islamic punk calls out for freedom of personal lifestyle choices, freedom from oppression, and freedom of religious interpretation (Fiscella 2012). This urge for freedom connects it to liberal discourse. Some punk has an Islamic agenda, such as the taqwacore bands in the United States that, during their growth period, wanted to be viewed as a possible expression (or maybe more correct, extension) of Islam. Their ideas were inspired by the novel *The Taqwacores* (2004) by Michael Muhammad Knight. Fed up with the restrictions on Islam he encountered as a convert, Knight was on the verge of leaving Islam when he conjured up his dream team of anarcho-Muslims sharing housing and wrote a novel about them. Soon young American Muslim punks sought contact and wondered if there was such an environment that they would fit in. From there grew the *taqwacore* scene.[17] *Taqwacore* does not present carefully crafted theology; rather it consists of conscious (and quite often informed) provocations against the guardians of the theological discourse. For example, on an open-stage evening at the yearly conference of ISNA (The Islamic Society of North America) in 2007, the *taqwacore* band Secret Trial Five took the stage and broke every taboo imaginable, including a rule of the ISNA conference that women were not allowed to sing on stage. They were cut off and thrown out. But their intervention led to change as women were allowed to sing the following year (The film *Taqwacore: The Birth of Punk Islam* 2010, Fiscella 2012). Thus, the band actually participated in the discussion of the *halal* and *haram* of music in Islamic environments.

THE HARDLINERS: FROM RESTRICTIVE ATTITUDES TO REACTIONARY CALLS

To the hardliners, music is problematic. At the bottom of the rejection lie some basic assumptions. As the moderates, hardliners presume that music is emotionally powerful, but instead of seeing the potential, they spot the danger. Music arouses passion, but not for Allah, but to the emotions themselves and the artists performing. As a consequence, time (and money) is wasted on music—instead of turning to Allah. The professional musician is criticized for spending too much time practicing (amateurs may be accepted by certain more "moderate" hardliners), time is also spent listening, which becomes associated with a particular societal abomination called *lahw* (implying, in hard-line discourse, spending time on diversions and meaningless chatter) and with pleasure-seeking sinfulness in bad company interconnecting music with singing, dancing, joking, gambling, drinking wine, and fornicating. There might be pleasure in listening to music, but it is there only because the Devil uses it to lure people astray (Otterbeck 2004). An additional argument found in later texts is that excessive interest in music playing and listening is a particular Western ill that should be shunned. Chauvinist warnings against cultural erosion are common among the hardliners of today.

RESTRICTIVE INTERPRETATIONS

An article from Mustafa Sabri (d. 1954), former *Shaikh ul-Islam* (the highest religious authority) to the Ottoman state, provides a good example of a restrictive interpretation. The article was originally published in 1910. Almost a century later Sabri's text was reprinted in translation in the journal *Anadola*—not as a historical text on music but as an authoritative text on the topic.

> Perhaps Islam does not see right to remain indifferent to music because it knows how delightful music is to our nature and how strong it is on our feelings. Our religion has an exceptionally good view in any case, in discovering the hidden dangers which might be inherent in the sweetest and most pleasurable things. (Sabri 1910/1995)

With this warning, Sabri presents one of the main arguments of the hardliners. He further explains that music awakes passion in people and makes them see reality in a more extreme way, increasing happiness for the glad and sorrow for the miserable. But the most problematic issue is that "music has a tremendous effect in agitating the feelings of romance and love" (Sabri 1910/1995). Thus, music opens up the uncontrollable in people by warping their perceptions. And Islamic guidance promotes control and the remembrance of Allah and the listening to Qur'anic recitation, not to admittedly skilled musicians and composers. Sabri also establishes that music is a "useless activity" and that some are led astray by western influences and let their daughters spend time learning instruments.

Sabri wrote from the perspective of a trained Islamic scholar who was well aware of new social patterns he considered to be influenced by the West. The article bridges classical and new writing and touches most themes that will be repeated during the coming century. Today, similar conservative and forbidding attitudes on music can be found on several web pages where for example Islamic pop music, elevator music, cell phone ring tones, music connected to computer games, and so forth are discussed or dealt with in fatwas.[18]

Wahhabi scholars and Salafi activists are particularly well represented on the Internet. One of the earliest fatwa services, set up in 1997, was the Wahhabi web page "Islam Questions & Answers," run by Saudi Sheikh Muhammad Salih al-Munajjid.[19] Al-Munajjid both writes himself and compiles possible answers from other scholars, preferably from Saudis or from the Hanbali school of law. Some texts might seem odd to the outsider but they have an internal logic of interest. For example, fatwa no. 7577 deals with what to do if the family of your bride to be is insisting on hiring musicians for your wedding. Al-Munajjid advises the groom to try to talk them out of it by reasoning or by calling in a respected mediator. If the groom's will is not respected he should not marry the bride (if she is not in total disagreement with her family's wishes of course). Two things need to be explained. First, even though the advice might seem unreasonably harsh to most, it follows an established Wahhabi/Salafi logic called *al-wala' wa-al-bara'* (associating with Muslims and disassociating with infidels). If mixing with people who like to party, you will compromise yourself and risk leading yourself astray, better to cut all relations and turn yourself to Allah. Second, it is the role of the mufti to enlighten the believer about the straight path; it is the believer's call to decide on which sins to indulge in and which to avoid. The scholar knows that the believer will err now and then. Therefore, it is important to understand the Islamic concept of compensation for sins through prayer, pilgrimage, and good deeds. That is, the believer may commit sins but if he or she keeps track and honestly repents (makes *tawba*), the believer can balance them. This is not to claim that Muslims do not feel guilt when erring, or that all sins may be ignored or negotiated. Some sins are considered *al-kaba'ir*,[20] the great ones, and should not be taken lightly even though Allah may forgive the honestly remorseful.

Another key concept for hardliners is *lahw* (diversions) also found in another related form, *al-malahi* (instruments of diversion). According to early exegesis traditions, some of Muhammad's companions (for example Ibn Mas'ud, d. 653) and some of the earliest Muslim intellectuals (for example al-Hasan al-Basri, d. 728) claimed that the words *"lahwa al-hadith"* from the Qur'an (31:6) imply music, among other things. These words are difficult to translate but "idle tales" is indicating that narratives (diversions) distract people. At best, these tales are harmless; at worst they may lead believers astray. To the hardliners the latter is not only a possibility but also the likely outcome. Proponents of a restrictive interpretation address music as *lahw*, often making references to the Saudi Wahhabi scholars Ibn Baz (d. 1999), Muhammad ibn Salih al-ʿUthaymin (d. 2001), and Abdulaziz al-Sheikh, or the Jordanian hadith scholar al-Albani (d. 1999).

REACTIONARY INTERPRETATIONS

While the above might be uncompromising, it does not explicitly advocate violence against those who engage in music. But this can happen. This attitude has a history, for example, the Shafiʿi scholar Ibn Hajar al-Haythami al-Makki (d. 1567) claimed he had broken musical instruments and brought musicians to court (Shehadi 1995: 116). Other scholars have made similar boasts.

In modern times, religio-political movements referred to as Islamist are prone to always have at least two issues on their agenda: first, to restrict women's freedom of dress and movement; and second, to censor and quell, with violence if necessary, musical expressions, musicians, and music listening. Reactionary interpretations seek legitimacy in *hisba*, the idea that the promotion of virtue and prohibition of vice (*al-amr bi al-maʿruf wa al-nahy ʿan al-munkar*) is a duty to Muslims who may, metaphorically, do *hisba* by thought, tongue, or hand (or by sword, another common metaphor) (Cook 2003). Note the word *munkar*, meaning "vice" or "an abominable act." A common scenario is that when a state loses control of law and order, Islamist groups come forth promoting *hisba* by hand to impose the Islamic character of society, arguing that it is an individual's duty (*fard ʿayn*) to do this (Otterbeck 2008). In this, the Taliban (Afghanistan), al-Shabab (Somalia), and the Islamic State (in Iraq and Syria, IS) all agree. Thus, reactionary interpretations legitimize violence and censorship toward music and musicians by arguing that by not restricting music evil will corrupt society. It is for the common moral good that transgressors must be punished and purged.

CONCLUSION: A DISCOURSE WITH MANY NUANCES

The goal of this essay has been to sketch prominent trends, their main arguments, and their social settings.[21] Those holding moderate, liberal, or hardline attitudes, or who oscillate between these, all contribute to the discourse on music within the Islamic discursive tradition, creating a conversation over the centuries through action, oral, and written statements that contradict and complement each other, that confront, criticize, and ignore each other. It is a discourse with many nuances; I hope this chapter has introduced some of them.

NOTES

1. A hadith is a narrative about what Muhammad or his closest companions said or did in different situations. Collected by several authors, they together form the corpus of text understood as presenting Muhammad's *sunna* (his customs, or his interpretation of Islam).

2. There are several different words for Islamic scholars specifying their trade such as *faqih* (jurisprudent), *'alim* (trained theologian), etc. Since the discourse on music is discussed by different types of Islamic scholars, I address them as Islamic scholars generally and at times specify by adding the law school (*madhhab*) they are attached to.

3. In medieval manuscripts the final letter's (*ya*) diacritical marks are often omitted leaving two possible readings, either *musiqi* or *musiqa*. In contemporary times *musiqa* is used in the same way as "music."

4. *Tarab* refers etymologically to strong feelings, literally "enchantment," but became synonymous with music since music, by definition, was considered to awaken strong emotions (Shiloah 1995:16).

5. This is an established practice used by Shehadi 1995, Shiloah 1995, al-Faruqi 1985, and others.

6. *'awra* should not be mistaken for genitals. Rather, *'awra* is what ought not to be exposed to a stranger, especially of the opposite sex, if you want to be perceived as decent and respectable.

7. For a thorough discussion of 'Abd Rabbihi, see Shehadi 1995: chapter 8.

8. The concept "religious specialist" is borrowed from Turner 1991: 87.

9. With the neologism "suficized" Shannon wants to express the character of the music certain artists have composed and recorded as Sufi music.

10. For example, al-Ghazali praised Naguib Mahfouz when he won the Nobel Prize in literature in 1989.

11. Al-Ghazali's position on violence against the deviant and heretic is somewhat contradictory, or, as indicated by some, changed during the latter part of his life, with the Mahfouz incident as a turning point. When prominent social commentator and Islam critic professor Farag Fouda was murdered in 1992 (see further Winegar, this volume), al-Ghazali seemed to be supportive of violence against some opponents (Mostyn 2002).

12. About Muhammad 'Imara, see Høigilt 2010.

13. Personal communication, al-Mardini, October 2005.

14. In this al-Mardini is supported by Maliki scholar 'Abd Allah bin Yusif al-Juda'i' (2007) who reaches similar conclusions.

15. Al-Mardini discussed this in detail with LeVine (2008b) who interviewed al-Mardini in both 2006 and 2007.

16. Personal communication, Ahmad in Malmö, 9 February 2007.

17. Personal communication, Knight in Malmö, 25 February 2010.

18. A fatwa is a statement made by an Islamic scholar about how to interpret Islam in a concrete situation.

19. http://islamqa.info/en/. The web page is translated into several languages including Urdu, Hindi, Chinese, Russian, Uygur, German, Japanese, French, Turkish, Spanish, etc.

20. There are several lists of *al-kaba'ir* compiled by Islamic scholars, both old and new. One often reproduced is ad-Dhahabi's (d. 1346) *al-Kaba'ir*. Some lists actually do include the intentional listening to music.

21. For a fuller, more ordered history, please consult Shiloah 1995 or Shehadi 1995.

REFERENCES

Ahmad, S. 2010. *Rock & Roll Jihad: A Muslim Rock Star's Revolution.* New York: Free Press.

Armbrust, W. 1996. *Mass Culture and Modernism in Egypt.* Cambridge: Cambridge University Press.

———. 2005. "What Would Sayyid Qutb Say? Some Reflections on Video Clips." *Transnational Broadcasting Studies* 14. www.tbsjournal.com/Archives/Spring05/SpringSummer 2005.html. Accessed 27 September 2005.

Asad, T. 1986. *The Idea of an Anthropology of Islam.* Washington, DC: Georgetown University, Center for Contemporary Arab Studies.

———. 1993. *Genealogies of Religion: Discipline and Reasons of Power in Christianity and Islam.* Baltimore: Johns Hopkins University Press.

Baker, R. W. 2003. *Islam without Fear: Egypt and the New Islamists.* Cambridge, MA: Harvard University Press.

Bohlman, P. V. 2002. *World Music: A Very Short Introduction.* Oxford: Oxford University Press.

Cook, M. 2003. *Forbidding Wrong in Islam.* Cambridge: Cambridge University Press.

Danielson, V. 1997. *The Voice of Egypt: Umm Kulthum, Arabic Song, and Egyptian Society in the Twentieth Century.* Chicago: University of Chicago Press.

Al-Dhahabi. 2012. *Al-kaba'ir, Major Sins.* London: Dar al-Taqwa.

Farmer, H. G. 1942. *Music: The Priceless Jewel; From the Kitab al-iqd al-farid of Abd 'Abd Rabbihi (d. 940).* Translation by H. G. Farmer. Collection of Oriental Writers on Music V. Published by the author, Bearsden, Scotland.

Al-Faruqi, L. 1985. "Music, Musicians, and Muslim Law." *Asian Music* 17, no. 1: 3–36.

Fiscella, A. 2012. "From Muslim Punk to Taqwacore: An Incomplete History of Punk Islam." *Contemporary Islam* 6, no. 3: 255–281.

Al-Ghazali, Abu Hamid Muhammad ibn Muhammad. 1901. "Emotional Religion in Islam As Affected by Music and Singing." *Journal of The Royal Asiatic Society.* [Translation and comments by Duncan B. Macdonald of book 18 of *Ihya 'ulum al-din*.]

Al-Ghazali, M. 1984. *Mustaqbal al-Islam kharij ardih: kayfa nufakkiru fih.* Amman, al-Urdun and al-Dawhah, Qatar: Mu'assasat al-Sharq lil-'Alaqat al-'Ammah wa-al-Nashr wa-al-Tarjamah.

Al-Huwairi, Ali Bin Usman. 2001. *The Kashf al-Mahjub: A Persian Treatise on Sufism.* Lahore: Zia-ul-Quran Publications. [Reprint of the translation by R. A. Nicholson, 1911.]

Høigilt, J. 2010. "Rhetoric and Ideology in Egypt's Wasatiyya Movement." *Arabia* 57, nos. 2–3.

'Imara, M. 1991. *al-islam wa al-funun al-jamila.* Al-Qahira: Dar al-Shuruq.

Al-Juda'i', 'Abd Allah bin Yusif. 2007. *Al-musiqa wa-l-ghina' fi mizan al-islam.* Beirut: Mu'assasatu l-Riyyan.

Khaled, A. 2005. "Culture: The Distinguishing Feature of a People." In *Transnational Broadcasting Studies* 14. www.tbsjournal.com/Archives/Spring05/khaled.htm. Accessed 27 September 2005.

Knight, M. M. 2004. *The Taqwacores.* New York: Autonomedia.

Knysh A. D. 2007. *Al-Qushayri's Epistle on Sufism.* Great Books of Islamic Civilization. Translated by A. D. Knysh. Reading: Garnet.

Kubala, P. 2005. "The Other Face of the Video Clip: Sami Yusuf and the Call for al-Fann al-

Hadif." *Transnational Broadcasting Studies* 14. www.tbsjournal.com/Archives/Spring05
/kubala.html. Accessed 27 September 2005.

LeVine, M. 2008a. *Heavy Metal Islam: Rock, Resistance, and the Struggle for the Soul of Islam.*
New York: Three Rivers Press.

———. 2008b. "Heavy Metal Muslims: The Rise of a Post-Islamist Public Sphere." *Contemporary Islam* 2, no. 3: 229–249.

Al-Mardini, I. R. 2001. *al-tibyan fi ahkam al-musiqi wa-al-alhan.* Beirut: Markaz beiruti li-al-dirasat wa-al-tawthiq.

Mostyn, T. 2002. *Censorship in Islamic Societies.* London: Saqi.

Otterbeck, J. 2004. "Music as a Useless Activity: The Logic behind Conservative Interpretations of Music in Islam." In *Shoot the Singer! Music Censorship Today*, edited by M. Korpe, 11–16. London: Zed Books.

———. 2008. "Battling over the Public Sphere: Islamic Reactions on the Music of Today." *Contemporary Islam* 3, no. 2: 211–228.

———. 2012. "Wahhabi Ideology of Social Control Versus a New Publicness." *Contemporary Islam* 6, no. 3: 341–353.

Al-Qaradawi, Y. 1995. *Islamic Awakening between Rejection and Extremism.* Herndon: International Institute of Islamic Thought.

———. 1997. *The Lawful and the Prohibited in Islam.* Cairo: Al-Falah Foundation.

Qur'an, the. Translated by Y. Ali.

Robson, J. 1938. *Tracts on Listening to Music.* In Oriental Translation Fund 34. London: Royal Asiatic Society.

Sabri, M. 1995. "A Topic of Dispute in Islam: Music." *Anadolu* 5, no. 4: 1–5. [Original published in 1910 in *Beyan-ul Haq*].

Schimmel, A. 2001. "The Role of Music in Islamic Mysticism." In *Sufism: Music and Society in Turkey and the Middle East*, edited by A. Hammarlund, T. Olsson, and E. Özdalga, 8–17. Istanbul: Swedish Research Institute in Istanbul.

Shannon, J. H. 2011. "Suficized Musics of Syria at the Intersection of Heritage and War on Terror: Or a 'Rumi with a View'." In *Muslim Rap, Halal Soaps, and Revolutionary Theater: Artistic Developments in the Muslim World.* Edited by K. van Nieuwkerk, 257–274. Austin: University of Texas Press.

Shehadi, F. 1995. *Philosophies of Music in Medieval Islam.* Leiden: Brill.

Shiloah, A. 1995. *Music in the World of Islam: A Socio-Cultural Study.* Detroit: Wayne State University Press.

Solomon, M., ed. 2001. *Marxism and Art: Essays Classic and Contemporary.* Detroit: Wayne State University Press.

Swedenburg, T. 2010. "Fun^Da^Mental's 'Jihad Rap.'" In *Being Young and Muslim: New Cultural Politics in the Global South and North*, edited by L. Herrera and A. Bayat, 291–308. New York: Oxford University Press.

Turner, B. 1991. *Religion and Social Theory.* 2nd ed. London: Sage.

Urkevich, L. 2005. "Saudi Arabia, Kingdom of, I. Introduction." In *Grove Music Online.* http://www.grovemusic.com/shared/views/print.html?sectionomusic.44734.1. Accessed 27 October 2005.

Van Nieuwkerk, K. 1995. *"A Trade Like Any Other": Female Singers and Dancers in Egypt.* Austin: University of Texas Press.

———. 2011. "Of Morals, Missions, and the Market: New Religiosity and 'Art with a Mission' in Egypt." In *Muslim Rap, Halal Soaps, and Revolutionary Theater: Artistic Developments in the Muslim World*, edited by K. van Nieuwkerk, 177–204. Austin: University of Texas Press.

Zaman, M. Q. 2004. "The 'ulama of Contemporary Islam and Their Conceptions of the Common Good." In *Public Islam and the Common Good*, edited by A. Salvatore and D. F. Eickelman, 129–155. Leiden: Brill.

INTERNET

Accolade, http://www.myspace.com/theaccolade.sa. Accessed 26 July 2013.

New York Times, http://www.nytimes.com/2008/11/24/world/middleeast/24saudi.html ?pagewanted=all&_r=0. Accessed 26 July 2013.

FILMS AND SONGS

Fun-Da-Mental *Goddevil*. 1996.

Fun-Da-Mental. *There Shall Be Love!* 2001.

Fun-Da-Mental *Cockbook* DIY. 2006.

The Rock Star and the Mullahs. 2003. Ruhi Hamid and Angus MacQueen, directors. Produced by Pamela Friedman.

Taqwacore: The Birth of Punk Islam. 2010. O. Majeed, director. Produced by EyeSteelFilm/D. Cross and M. Aung Thwin.

CHAPTER 8

SHI'A DISCOURSES ON PERFORMING ARTS: *MASLAHA* AND CULTURAL POLITICS IN LEBANON

JOSEPH ALAGHA

Any message, call, revolution, civilization, or culture cannot be successfully disseminated if it is not expressed in artistic form.
IMAM 'ALI KHAMINA'I

THERE IS A WIDE VARIETY of religious discourses on the permissibility of music and performing arts in Islam. As Otterbeck (this volume) shows, a spectrum of voices from hardline to liberal interpretations can be discerned. Most analyses, however, have focused on the dynamics within Sunni Islam, the religion's majority sect. This chapter explores the evolution from classical to contemporary methods of reasoning in Shi'a sources and by Shi'a scholars, and the artistic practices they enable. Whereas one might expect Shi'a discourses on music or the artistic scene in resistance movements such as the Lebanese Hizbullah to be rather restrictive, in fact there are a preponderance of moderate views surrounding music within the contemporary Shi'ite tradition. This is related to a specific method of reasoning based on the jurisprudential concept of *maslaha* (interest, advantage).

In order to understand the flexible and quite moderate Shi'ite discourses on art, it is necessary to examine the concept of *maslaha*, and its meaning in classical and contemporary Shi'ite jurisprudence. That foundation allows for a fuller exploration of how the concept of *maslaha* has been used in the cultural field by Shi'ite religious scholars, in particular, by movements such as Hizbullah. Such an exploration reveals how the concept of *maslaha* as understood by Hizbullah's leaders and cadres has allowed for an open, lively artistic cultural practice.

MASLAHA IN CLASSICAL AND CONTEMPORARY SHIʿA JURISPRUDENCE

In Muslim theology, *maslaha*, as a secondary source in Islamic law, is referred to—in the Qurʾan, the Traditions (hadith), and books of jurisprudence—as interest, benefit, advantage, good deed, and virtue.

By the mid-fourteenth century CE, there emerged a unanimity among religious scholars that Islamic jurisprudence theories had developed in three main stages, from the principles of jurisprudence to the development of maxims based on them, and finally, to the development of the purposes of the *shariʿa* (Masud 1996; al-Shatibi 2003; al-Jaziri 2001; al-Sarakhsi 1993; Mutahhari 2010, 2011, 2013; Maghniyyé 1988; Ibrahim 1998; Mahmasani 1955; Al-Murtada n.d.; Rishahri 2000).

In this regard, the most salient and widely used maxim is that the avoidance of vices is preferable to obtaining interests. This is the frame of reference or the rule of thumb that religious scholars (*ʿulama*) employ when they resort to the principle of balancing interests with vices. Another maxim is that necessities permit what is prohibited. This implies that prohibited things or social practices could become sanctioned in some favorable contexts. Then, there is a maxim that attributes things to their final causes, that is, everything has a purpose (*maslaha*) in life. Finally, the maxim of "mutual competition" (*tazahum*) states that in case of conflict of duties, then priority ought to be given to the most pressing duty over the least pressing duty, or the one deemed more important than the other (al-Shatibi 2003; al-Sarakhsi 1993; Maghniyyé 1988; Mahmasani 1955). These in turn are related to the purposes of *shariʿa*, which stipulates that Islamic law was revealed to human beings because of the interest (*maslaha*) in reinterpreting the law. Most scholars agree that these are based on natural and inalienable rights possessed by all human beings (Masud 1996; al-Shatibi 2003; al-Jaziri 2001; Mahmasani 1955; Rishahri 2000). These general maxims are used by contemporary Shiʿite religious scholars such as Imam Khumayni and Ayatullah Fadlallah, the spiritual leaders of many Lebanese Shiʿa. We can see this in the manner in which they employ the maxims and the concepts of *maslaha* and *tazahum* in the public sphere.

The late Imam Khumayni (24 September 1902–3 June 1989)—the founder of the Islamic Republic of Iran and its main ideologue—argued that *maslaha* is the result of an action in the domain of justice. In that sense, the jurisprudential concept of *maslaha* (interest, advantage) is opposed to *mafsada* (disadvantage, vice). *Maslaha* emanates from the spirit and essence of religion. Religion was revealed for the benefit and interest of the people in order to obtain happiness on earth and in heaven. Based on this reading, *maslaha* is supposed gradually to lead to perfect harmony (Khumayni 2002: 173–175).

Imam Khumayni argued that every ruling or injunction takes into consideration the jurisprudential concepts of *maslaha-mafsada* in matters of legislation and social practices. According to him, *maslaha* is a deeply rooted element of Islamic law (*shariʿa*) (2002: 175–176). He added that the negligence of *maslaha*, or its nonexecution in a righteous manner, will lead to a serious disorder in administering the affairs of the Muslim nation (*umma*). It will be a hindrance to the Muslim community's advancement, development, and prosperity. Khumayni stressed that the effectiveness of Islam and its civilizational role hinges upon the implementation of this vital element of *maslaha* (2002: 169). In line with Khumayni's 1988 edict (*fatwa*), he concluded that the *maslaha* of the Islamic order takes precedence over everything else, and everyone should strictly obey it and abide by it (2002: 169–170).

According to Khumayni, decision-making is based on the principle of *tazahum*, that is, giving priority to the most pressing or important duty over the least pressing or important one. In case of *tazahum* between moral *maslaha* and material *maslaha*, then moral *maslaha* always takes precedence. For instance, the governor or ruler has the capacity to demolish any house, or even a mosque that stands in the way of constructing a highway, after he pays an equitable price (Khumayni 2002: 172–73). Khumayni added, in case of *tazahum* between public good and private good, then public good always takes priority since it conforms to religious stipulations. For example, the government can one-sidedly annul any religious injunction agreed upon with the people, if the government deems it in opposition to the interests of the country or Islam (ibid.: 175–185).

Similarly, the late Lebanese Ayatullah Sayyid Muhammad Husayn Fadlallah (1935–2010)—the highest-ranking Shiʿite religious authority (*marjaʿ*) in Lebanon and one of Hizbullah's early ideologues—employed the concept of *tazahum*. As with Khumayni, Fadlallah explained that when a person is confronted with two rulings that require the exercise of his reason, reason (the mind) tells him that God has imposed on human beings rulings for the sake of *maslaha* and *mafsada*. In this case, what takes precedence is either the warding off of the grave disadvantage or the following of the most salient advantage. Thus, in accordance with the maxim discussed above, the ruling is carried out on the basis of waiving the less important injunction in favor of the more prominent one. Ayatullah Fadlallah went on to the extent of affirming that a religious ruling could be "frozen" under pressuring social circumstances. These social circumstances might relegate this ruling to a category of lower importance, so that it can be overridden by a ruling that has high priority or importance and takes precedence over it. Thus, the ruling remains in effect and binding, but it can be annulled under special circumstances, if necessity and interest (*maslaha*) deem it to be so (Fadlallah 2009: 82–83).

The general maxims and ideas about the concept of *maslaha* do not yet clarify the flexibility or pragmatism in its application to specific issues, such as art to which it has prominently been employed.

MASLAHA AND SHIʿA DISCOURSES ON PERFORMING ARTS

Leading religious scholars such as Khumayni and his successor Imam ʿAli Khaminaʾi agree that *maslaha* has a prominent role in contemporary Shiʿite jurisprudence, especially in relation to art. Particularly, reformist Iranian president Muhammad Khatami (1997–2005) had a pioneering contribution in this regard. He gave prominence to culture as a manifestation of *maslaha* in the Islamic Revolution. The crux of Khatami's argument is that Islam is not a normative, essentialist, elusive concept; rather, Islam is culture. From this perspective, it is interesting that Khatami's discourse was void from the use of the word "Islam." In all his speeches and writings, he employed culture (*farhang*), civilization (*tamaddun*), and religion (*din*). Thus, Khatami was recasting Islam in cultural terms in order to stress its modern, liberal, and moderate face, as opposed to its stereotyped radical image (Khatami 2001).

To a lesser extent, the current leader of the Islamic Republic of Iran and Hizbullah's "spiritual leader," Imam Khaminaʾi asserts that cultural work is always an antecedent to political and military work because, he argues, without culture no society can prosper. Khaminaʾi adds that the Islamic Revolution needs to have a strong, enriching cultural background (2009: 66, 85). He stresses that any message, call, revolution, culture, or civilization cannot be successfully disseminated if it is not expressed in artistic form (Khaminaʾi 2009: 10, 83). Whereas Khatami identifies Islam as culture, Khaminaʾi believes that culture is one of the means to achieve the aims of the Islamic revolution. In other words, he employs an instrumentalist concept of culture that is in the service of the *maslaha* of the Islamic Republic.

Khumayni repeatedly stated that the role of "genuine" art or purposeful art is realized when it takes from the core of the authentic Islamic culture, which is according to him the culture of justice and purity. He added that from an Islamic cultural perspective, art is the clear presentation of justice and dignity (ʿAqil 2008: 84). In turn, Imam Khaminaʾi argues, "since purposeful movies and theatrical works are intended as a means of awakening and knowledge production, then they are sanctioned to be filmed and shown to the public because they disseminate Islamic culture and contribute to conscience raising, especially among the youth" (Khamina'i 2004: 48). He adds, concerning purposeful dancing in weddings and folkloric events, if it is free from debaucheries, and thus intended to respect Islamic culture and the religious sensibilities of the audience, then it is sanctioned (Khamina'i 2004: 32–33).

Another voice is Ayatullah Fadlallah through his views on *maslaha* and art. Fadlallah affirmed that he does not regard purposeful dancing and singing, which preserves moral obligations, to be prohibited, especially if it takes into consideration societal restrictions.[1] Fadlallah legitimized women's participation in theaters and movies, including dancing and public performance, on the grounds of *maslaha*, as long as these professions do not contradict Islamic values. He encouraged Muslim women to engage in public performance because of its *maslaha* to the Islamic cultural sphere. In short, a woman can practice any profession and interact in the public space if she abides by the public good: Islam's ethical values, norms, and religious sensibilities.[2]

Interestingly, Fadlallah's flexibility resulted in toning down his argument, in light of the *maslaha* of the community: "Meanwhile, I think that when Muslims' conditions change and many unfamiliar habits become familiar, such issues, especially if people distinguish between legal art and the illegal one, might become familiar to them. That is why we find ourselves so far cautious about the professions of singing and dancing trying to figure out what is the *maslaha* of Islam."[3] In line with his belief that Islam is a social practice and that Islamic law is a socially constructed phenomenon, it seems that Fadlallah implied that a ruling could be revised, even overridden in light of changes in religious sensibilities and societal norms. This modern thinking is in conformity with the nature of Shi'ite jurisprudence.

Nooshin (this volume) turned my attention to the difference in the marketing, receptivity, and consumption of Khamina'i's fatwas on "purposeful art" in Lebanon and Iran, and the "culture industry" that is guided by this. According to them, Khamina'i's publications on purposeful art are indicative of the ideological (rather than doctrinal) basis of these views, to the extent that he seems to say one thing for "export" and another for domestic consumption in Iran. Thus, the context seems to be of vital importance, in addition to the content and purpose.

MASLAHA AND HIZBULLAH IDEOLOGUES' PERSPECTIVES ON ART

Religious discourses not only became available in the public sphere but also are actually appropriated and used as a strategic tool by political-religious leaders. Meftahi and Nooshin observed that the discourses available might be implemented or applied differently in different countries. For that reason, I will take the Lebanese Hizbullah's reworking on the *maslaha* and art discourse as a case study: first, to study their use of the concept; and second, to see which actual artistic practices their views enable.

The Lebanese resistance movement Hizbullah is not monolithic and is indeed divided into four wings: the military, social services/NGOs, political, and cultural politics or "resistance art." In conformity with its policy to change as circumstances themselves change, the party's internal structure allows it to operate on these various levels simultaneously (Alagha 2011b: 185).

The rapid evolution of Hizbullah from a marginal splinter group to a dominant group in national and international politics enhanced its representation of cultural and artistic productions by giving them more weight and visibility in public space—one of the core goals of the movement (Alagha 2009, 2011a). The movement has long propagated and encouraged "art with a mission," "purposeful art" (*al-fann al-hadif*), or "resistance art" (*al-fann al-muqawim*). Imam Khamina'i's recurrent statement that art is the most eloquent and effective means of Islamic propagation (2009: 6, 9, 27, 50, 83) forms the crux of the party's justification of purposeful art or, in the context of Hizbullah, resistance art. Indeed, Hizbullah is a strong supporter of resistance art and promotes it through specialized NGOs: (1) *Risalat*: "The Lebanese Association of Arts" that is concerned with performing arts; and (2) *Ibda'* ("creativity") that deals with plastic arts. Resistance art is also disseminated in Hizbullah's weekly newspaper *al-Intiqad*, its "unofficial" mouthpiece the daily newspaper *al-Akhbar*, and media institutions such as *al-Nour* satellite radio, *al-Manar* satellite TV, and the "unofficial" *al-Mayadeen* satellite TV.

Hizbullah's cultural politics is based upon and legitimized by the Shi'ite jurisprudential concept of interest (*maslaha*). Hajj Muhammad Ra'd—the current head of Hizbullah's parliamentary bloc and *Shura* (consultative) Council member—told me that there is no conflict between Hizbullah's Islamic identity and its cultural productions, since there is no big practical difference between the two. Ra'd adds that Hizbullah bases itself on the following precept: what falls within the domain of the legally prohibited (*haram shar'i*), Hizbullah endeavors to prevent from coming into being or tries to abort it; what falls within the domain of the "permitted" (*mubah*), Hizbullah does its best to find the most just implementation in conformity with its religious vision. Thus, according to Ra'd, Hizbullah's cultural politics are based upon two basic principles that offer the movement a great margin of leeway in public performance: (1) keeping away the vices (*al-mafasid*) has precedent over advancing interests (al-masalih); (2) balancing between interests and vices in order to determine a person's actual duty.[4]

Because of the importance of cultural politics to Hizbullah, the party has founded three institutional centers that deal with cultural productions and performance. These are headed by three leading shaykhs: Shaykh Akram Barakat, the director of the *Cultural Islamic Al-Ma'arif Association*; Shaykh 'Ali Daher, the director of Hizbullah's Cultural Unit; and Shaykh Shafiq Jaradi, the Rector of *Al-Ma'arif Al-Hikmiyya College*, whom I have interviewed.

As early as 1985, the concept of "purposeful art" was in circulation by the party's music bands, especially in Hizbullah's military marches and *anashid* (songs, hymns, and anthems). Over the years, Hizbullah's music bands evolved to an orchestra that produces symphonies. Although the party uses the term "The Music Theory in Islam" (*Al-Nadhariyya al-Musiqiyya fi al-Islam*), what Hizbullah is referring to is both a practice and a sociopolitical rather than scientific or standard "theory of music." Standard "music theory" is when scholars write about the mathematics of acoustics and the amplitude of sound waves (such as the precise mathematical formulae for generating the overtone series, questions of harmony and dissonance, issues of tuning, how musical instruments actually make sounds, calculating wavelengths, modal theory, etc.). Theoretically, Hizbullah's "music theory," is conveyed as such:

> Revolution is also a language that caters to a special kind of human emotions and feelings that are expressed by dignity, honour, advancement, and Islamic revival or renaissance (*nuhud*).[5] Rhetorically, revolution is always an awakening, a stimulation that comes at a time when one of the human languages stutters. Metaphorically, art and revolution are languages that coalesce and live within the human being; when one wakes up, the other ensues. When the time was ripe for action and resistance, it was inevitable for the language of art to appear on the scene and to accompany this revolution, this new eventuality in order to satisfy an urgent need, the need of intellectual pleasures at a time when many people were engaged in vices and "corruption in the land" (7:176) leading a life of degeneration and diversion into sensual pleasures.[6]

Hizbullah aims to elevate purposeful music and *anashid* to the level of professionalism, as *Risalat*'s raison d'être statement stipulates. Practically, the mission of the party's music bands or "music theory" is summarized as such:

> Hizbullah's Islamic artistic bands professionally specialize in different kinds of musical arts and believe in art as a means to realize noble aims. They abide

by the tenets of Islam and operate in complete harmony with the Resistance's project of jihad through music as a nationalist, humane option that rejects tyranny and calls for freedom of the human being and the liberation of the land in harmony with Islam's moral virtues and religious sensibilities. The music bands have been producing art with a mission, committed art, which satisfies the pious aspirations of the human savor in art.[7]

Several Hizbullah cadres discuss the theme of art as Islamic revival and cultural resistance. Shaykh ʿAli Daher is against purposeless art or "art for the sake of art"; rather, he is for purposeful art. Daher regards resistance art as a specific genre of purposeful art, which is distinguished by its content, message, and subject matter. Resistance art deals with political and social issues as well as themes such as jihad, sacrifice, patriotism, and the like.[8] Muhammad Kawtharani, the vice-president of *Risalat*, defines resistance art as the art of Islamic revival or renaissance that revitalizes the *umma* and wakes it up from its hibernation; the art that moves emotions and feelings to struggle against invasion, occupation, and oppression.[9] From this and the discussions below, it seems difficult to me to delineate a sharp line, or to set a sharp distinction between propaganda and resistance art since both concepts seem to be merged.

In conformity with Hizbullah's music theory, the revolutionary and humanistic elements of resistance art are highlighted by various cadres. Hajj Ghalib Abu Zaynab, the party's officer for Muslim-Christian dialogue, defines resistance art as social art that deals with people's humanistic and social causes, aimed at "polishing and sharpening potential skills." From this perspective, it is labeled as positive art. Resistance is a positive act: resisting oppression and crying for freedom are legitimate in order to rectify the present imbalance, but with temperance as Prophet Muhammad has commanded: "You are the *umma* of moderation (Q 2: 143)." Abu Zaynab adds that resistance art promotes ethical and spiritual beauty and stresses the concept of God's mercy. Abu Zaynab clarifies that resistance art aims at "promoting justice, meritocracy, integrity, and philanthropy." He adds, "resistance art is an embodiment of greater jihad, societal jihad, the jihad against the self and its corrupt desires." Abu Zaynab stresses that resistance art contributes to the development of society in a positive way, thus "guiding society away from darkness (evil) into light (virtues) by reforming the self and morals."[10]

More important, the three directors of Hizbullah's cultural politics institutions strongly argue that resistance art contributes to polishing human abilities. They consider leisure activities, which promote "pious entertainment" or "fun," important to the perpetuating of a self-confident, industrious, and productive human being.[11] The party's deputy Secretary General, Shaykh Naʿim

Qasim, adds that resistance art is sanctioned in its capacity as a purposeful mobilizational tool; as such, it is highly recommended as a cultural leisure activity (ʿAbbas 2009: 6–7). Hizbullah's Shaykh Akram Barakat argues that Shiʿite traditions encourage the pursuit of "purposeful fun" and leisure activities within the domain of certain religious safeguards. According to him, art, performance, and dancing are not in themselves *haram*. Further, things that were previously *haram* could become *halal* and vice versa. In other words, prohibition or sanctioning has to do with the variables of time, place, and environment. What has to be kept in mind is the aim, goal, and purpose. From here stems the justification of purposeful art or resistance art. In line with Imam Khaminaʾi (2004: 16–51), Barakat argues that Islam calls for progress in all domains: reform in art elevates human worth and values. As such, the basis of Shiʿite jurisprudence is the call for innovation and modernity in order to be up-to-date with all aspects of life. God does not judge solely on the basis of the results, rather the intentions. This notion leaves room for jurisprudential innovations, which allow certain artistic practices that were once prohibited to become sanctioned and recommended. For instance, earlier Shiʿite jurists banned chess because it was used as an instrument of gambling. When its usage changed to an intellectual tool that promotes critical thinking, the ruling changed from prohibition (*haram*) to sanctioning (*halal*).[12]

Although Abu Zaynab stresses that resistance art expresses the will of society and addresses people's sensibilities and emotions,[13] the serious practical problem of gender mixing threatened to encroach upon Hizbullah's religious sensibilities. Intensive deliberations among Hizbullah's leading cadres resulted in sanctioning this social practice within the narrow confines of pious entertainment. For Hizbullah to approve gender mixing, public performance, and acting and dancing on stage during the occasion of the birth of Imam al-Mahdi, a heated debate among the three heads of Hizbullah's cultural politics institutions ensued. The deliberations centered over the legitimacy of this social practice, and what are the religious prohibitions, safeguards that ought to be taken into account. Hizbullah's Deputy Security General Shaykh Naʿim Qasim along with Shaykh Muhammad Yazbik, head of the Religio-Judicial Council, were asked to pass judgment, and they ruled in favor.[14] Thus, Hizbullah was able to cater to the religious sensibilities of its constituency by sanctioning the mixing of the sexes in artistic productions, in spite of the religious prohibitions that usually bar many Islamists and Islamic movements from engaging in such cultural activities. In short, Hizbullah relates interest (*maslaha*) to reform, resistance, mobilization, and political struggle. For that reason, the party regards art as resistance art.

It has become clear that the main characteristic of Shiʿite discourses on *maslaha* is the generic unifying argument: an artistic practice or expression is sanctioned *if and only if* it is: (1) purposeful and (2) the advantage (*maslaha*) behind it outweighs the disadvantage (*mafsada*). This is Hizbullah's, Khumayni's, Khamina'i's, and Fadlallah's general rule of thumb, which is in turn based upon a modern interpretation of Shi'ite jurisprudence.

MASLAHA AND HIZBULLAH'S ARTISTIC PRACTICES

The discourse on art and *maslaha* has translated into actual artistic practice as well as its limits through the genre of political satire.

Hizbullah's Islamic cultural sphere is trying to emulate the above concepts and put them into practice through ideologically motivated art, or "art with a mission" (see Van Nieuwkerk 2011), or, in the context of Hizbullah, resistance art. This section offers extended examples of the emergent Islamic cultural sphere. I will show popular and cultural activities that are in line with the discourse of purposefulness and *maslaha*, in relation to music, revolutionary theater, and comedy or satire. Does every artistic expression—sanctioned in the Islamic cultural sphere—fall within the domain of purposeful art?

Hizbullah's music bands *Firqat al-Wilaya* and *Orchestra Shams al-Hurriyya* testify to this trend of purposeful art or resistance art. The party's official music group *Firqat al-wilaya* was established in 1985. It composed the party's anthem and is mainly concerned with producing Islamic *anashid* that mobilize Hizbullah's constituency to perform jihad through music. Women's Firqat al-Wilaya (*Firqat al-wilaya al-Nisa'iyya*) followed suit. Two subsidiary groups *Firqat Fajr al-Isra' al*-Inshadiyya and *Firqat al*-Radwan also branched from *Firqat al-wilaya*. Hizbullah is the only Islamic party that has an orchestra of more than one hundred musicians who play more than forty-four instruments.[15] Many Islamists—such as the Taliban (Alagha 2012)—classify these as "instruments of the Devil/Satan."[16] Conversely, Imam Khamina'i sanctions these, including the *mizmar* (single- or double-reed clarinet or oboe), the flute (*nay*), the violin, and the cello (Khamina'i 2004: 20–31).

Orchestra Shams al-Hurriyya ("Freedom's Sun Orchestra") has been producing symphonies since its founding in 2003. Unlike Hizbullah's Orchestra, which is exclusively dominated by males, Tehran's Orchestral Symphony is characterized by gender mixing, thus portraying liberal attitudes and more openness (*infitah*) than the Lebanese Hizbullah.

Nevertheless, it might be a semantic difference rather than a doctrinal one. For instance, when Tehran's Orchestral Symphony performed—at the ESCWA Theater in Beirut—it seemed to be more "liberal" than the Lebanese Hizbullah with regard to the movement of the body in public space (rhythmic movements

8.1. Teheran's Orchestral Symphony performing in Beirut on 29 September 2012. Photograph by Musa al-Husayni, from http://www.alahednews.com.lb/.

8.2. Teheran's Orchestral Symphony performing in Beirut on 29 September 2012. Photograph by Musa al-Husayni, from http://www.alahednews.com.lb/.

on stage), the strict abidance by the Islamic dress code, and more important, the mixing of the genders, in contrast to the exclusively male musicians who compose Hizbullah's orchestra. As fig. 8.1 and fig. 8.2 reveal, the ponytail of one of the women performers extended farther than her veil. More important, the woman who was performing on the cello got absorbed in her performance to the extent that she started swaying her body and "dancing" in "rhythmic movements" (*harakat-imawzun*),[17] which might not be in conformity with the standard practice in Iran, as Shaykh 'Ali Daher told me. The reason is that she was engaged in enchantment (*tarab*), which Shi'ite religious scholars (*marja's*) prohibit (Alagha 2011a). *Tarab* "can be described as a musically induced state of ecstasy, or as an enchantment, aesthetic emotion and the feeling roused by music." In short, *tarab* is "the aesthetic feeling that the music produces" (Racy 2003: 6, 229). Thus, *tarab* makes any artistic expression "fall" or degenerate from the domain of purposeful art to lowbrow art.

Hajj Ghalib Abu Zaynab told me that many religious symphonies produced by Hizbullah's Orchestra are influenced by Christian hymns.[18] It is remarkable that the revolutionary *anashid* of *Firqat al-Wilaya* were broadcasted via loud speakers from the mosques' minarets in celebration of every military victory Hizbullah accomplished against its enemies. With this practice, Hizbullah is broadening Imam Khumayni's mandate, which sanctioned broad-casting *anashid* on TV and radio: "The *anashid* that have benefit (*maslaha*)—such as mobilizing the youth to revolution and war-like activities such as the ones chanted in eulogizing martyr Mutahhari (with musical instruments)—are sanctioned." Khumayni added that a *nashid* could become an obligatory duty in some battles (Hamidi 1994: 112ff).

Two examples of revolutionary theater are the musical plays "When Do We See You?" and the artistic performance "Dawn"—both intended to com-memorate the birth of Imam al-Mahdi. In commenting on the above plays, Shaykh Khudr al-Dirani, *al-Manar*'s ombudsman or the "director of religious censorship," told me that theater should not only be based on the *word*, but the *scenes* should also speak for themselves: "it was the purposefulness of the scenes (*maslaha*) that mattered." Thus, the scene ought to be a stark indicator of the content. He stresses the punctuality and meticulousness of Hizbullah's theatrical productions. According to al-Dirani, this is the way in which Hiz-bullah's plays ought to be disseminated and construed: "this is our manner of knowledge production, dissemination, and consumption."[19] Shaykh Barakat observes that the plays as revolutionary theater are artistic expressions, as such a humanistic endeavor, not a religious one. He adds that the cultural produc-tions of Hizbullah reflect the environment in which it lives. Hizbullah has no problem with diversity; on the contrary, Islam believes that diversity enriches culture. According to Barakat, Hizbullah's cultural productions are oriented toward the realization of these goals.[20]

If we explore comedy and sociopolitical satire, we can look into the limits of the concept of *maslaha*'s flexibility. The 1 June 2006 episode of the weekly political satire program entitled "*Basmat Watan*" ("The Death of a Nation" or "The Laughs of a Nation") almost led Lebanon into sectarian fighting when one of the comedians derided Sayyid Nasrallah.

One of the comedians, dressed in a Shi'ite turban and attire, mocked Nas-rallah as a political leader, and not as a religious leader, thus trying to avoid of-fending the religious sensibilities of Hizbullah's constituency. In spite of that, they took to the streets chanting Imam Husayn's call in Karbala': "Death to humiliation," intending to go all the way to the Christian heartland to "burn" LBCI. On their way, they committed mayhem in Sunni and Christian areas, almost engaging the local inhabitants, who adhere to a diametrically opposed ideology, especially the youth residing in these areas. After Hizbullah's mem-bers of parliament and middle-rank cadres failed to contain their crowds, in an unprecedented call, Nasrallah in person, by way of Hizbullah's media, called on the demonstrators to return to their homes. Although they immediately obeyed, the riots tainted Hizbullah's image as an advocate of free speech and expression and upholder of public freedoms.

Nevertheless, the last episode of *Basmat Watan* in July 2013 did not elicit any negative reaction from Hizbullah's cadres or its constituency, since along-side Sayyid Nasrallah, the Sunni mufti of the Lebanese Republic and the Maronite Cardinal were also depicted. It might be also because the message behind the show was that of national unity and religious tolerance and co-existence, at a time when sectarian discord was rupturing the achievements of the Arab uprisings in the MENA region. However, the episode of 8 November 2013 was not well received by Hizbullah's constituency, because a comedian mocked Sayyid Nasrallah. This time, they vented their anger by blocking roads with burning tires.

Does Hizbullah have a problem with comedy shows and comedians per se? Could these also fall within the domain of pious fun and entertainment? How does this comport with the precept of practice that Hizbullah is not stringent when it comes to "fun" and does not mind political satire, and even encourages it as a purposeful art, especially in print media and as caricatures?

In response to my question: "Is there a prohibition on comedy as such in Shi'ite discourse?" Abd Al-Halim Fadlallah, the director of Hizbullah's think tank, and Shaykh Shafiq Jaradi assured me that "there are no jurisprudential reservations on comedy as such." They attributed the scarcity of comedy productions in Hizbullah's Islamic cultural sphere to the restrictive public space that "suppresses creativity and artistic innovation" out of fear of insulting or hurting religious sensibilities.[21] From the above, it seems that the sensitivity toward comedy might be toward the likelihood of insulting the sensibilities of Hizbullah's senior religious figures and, by extension, the Shi'ite tradition they represent. Muhammad Ra'd clarified that Hizbullah considers such political comedies and satires as "purposeless lowbrow art that do not respect the religious sensibilities of the Shi'a."[22]

Nevertheless, Ayatullah Fadlallah holds another view, which indirectly criticizes Hizbullah's practices. In a personal interview, he told me, "not a single person holding public office is immune to criticism; whether he is a political or religious leader . . . he is not infallible and he is bound to err: blessed he who does not commit mistakes." Ayatullah Fadlallah added, "we welcome any criticism, especially if it is constructive and aimed at reform; so ought Hizbullah."[23] It seems Ayatullah Fadlallah is more liberal than Hizbullah when it comes to comedy or political satire, and by extension, the freedom of speech and expression. Thus, there are divergent views between the adherents of Hizbullah and other Shi'ites who follow Ayatullah Fadlallah's rulings.

We have seen that Hizbullah does not believe in the theory of "art for the sake of art" or purposeless art. Rather, Hizbullah promotes art with a purpose, art with a noble mission, especially stressing the mobilizational and propaganda role of resistance art. In conformity with its music theory, the party does exploit certain forms of performing art, especially music and revolutionary theatrical plays, as effective means of mobilization in the service of "noble" ends such as fighting aggression and occupation in order to promote peace and justice. In the Islamic cultural sphere, purposeful art legitimizes using the mosque as a medium to disseminate revolutionary *anashid*. Hizbullah's religious authority Imam Khamina'i even sanctioned chanting religious or revolutionary *anashid*, with musical instruments, at the mosque, as long as they do not interfere with the duty of prayer. Nevertheless, the Islamic cultural sphere has its limitations. Even though there is no prohibition on comedy in itself in Shi'ite discourse, the shortage of comedy production is attributed to the limited public space allocated to it in the Islamic cultural sphere. The party censured comedy shows that might encroach upon the Shi'ite doctrine or hurt the religious sensibilities of the Hizbullah constituency. Therefore, in spite of Ayatullah Fadlallah's views that do not bar criticizing religious figures when they err, it seems that the problems of satirists started when they included Hizbullah personalities in their satires.

The concept of *maslaha* rules out certain comedies as artistic expressions, since, in Hizbullah's eyes, they seem to promote purposelessness, or since the disadvantages behind them outweigh the advantages. Thus, they may threaten the very foundations on which the Islamic cultural sphere is erected, namely, that art should be in the service of "noble human goals," as such being the main reason for the well-being of the humanistic community, as Khamina'i clarified (2009: 73).

CONCLUSION

Maslaha is a concept of jurisprudence in classical and contemporary Shi'ite thought that can be seen as at the heart of the discourses on performing arts and Hizbullah's ideas and practices.

In order to understand the specific, and quite moderate, flexible, and pragmatic contemporary understanding of Shi'ite discourses on art, it is beneficial to examine the importance and specific use of the concept of *maslaha* in Shi'ite thought as applied to artistic practices in the cultural field such as performing art, especially resistance art, revolutionary theater, and political satire. Resistance art is ideologically motivated art that caters to Muslim religious sensibilities, in opposition to "purposeless lowbrow art," which does not. Through an observance of Islamic values and norms, *maslaha* sanctions engagement in social practices and artistic expressions such as purposeful art or resistance art.

Like Imams Khumayni, Khamina'i, and Ayatullah Fadlallah, Hizbullah's ideologues have argued that there is no prohibition in the absolute on artistic expressions such as singing, dancing, music, and musical instruments. Rather, based on the context, content, and usage, prohibition or sanctioning is appropriate (Hamidi 1994: 107–108). In line with Shi'ite jurisprudence, all my interviewees have accorded that the only genre that is prohibited in artistic expressions is the one that leads to corruption, moral vices and debaucheries, or enchantment, since it is thought that desire takes control over reason, rendering man an instinctual animal. Save that, everything else is sanctioned. Thus, for Hizbullah, prohibition or sanctioning is contextual, which allows certain artistic practices that were once prohibited to become sanctioned and recommended. The same ruling applies to music, singing, dancing, and other artistic expressions in the domain of the performing arts. This is in accordance with the flexible and pragmatic use of *maslaha* as a balancing act between advantages and disadvantages, between good deeds and bad deeds.

This precept of practice seems to resonate Giddens' conclusion: "The reflexivity of modern social life consists in the fact that social practices are constantly examined and refined in the light of incoming information about these very practices, thus constitutively altering their character" (Giddens 1990: 38). Thus, in knowledge production and dissemination, one has to keep in mind that "Islam" is a social practice that is constantly undergoing revision.

NOTES

1. The Jurisprudence of Art, http://english.bayynat.org.lb/se_002/jurisprudence/art .htm. Accessed 17 July 2009.

2. Interview with author, 4 August 2009.

3. The Jurisprudence of Art, http://english.bayynat.org.lb/se_002/jurisprudence/art .htm. Accessed 17 July 2009.

4. Interview with author, 4 August 2009.

5. Cf. "Art is an obligation for Muslims. . . . We will not be able to carry out *Nahda* [Renaissance] without Art . . . art as a tool of progress" (Winegar 2008: 28–29).

6. www.welaya-hlb.com. Accessed 17 July 2009.

7. Interview with band members M. Yunis and B. Laqis, 3 August 2009.

8. Interview with author, 22 October 2009.

9. Interview with author, 15 February 2010.

10. Interview with author, 10 August 2009.

11. Interviews with author, August 2009.

12. Interview with author, 5 August 2013.

13. Interview with author, 10 August 2009.

14. Interview with Muhammad Kawtharani, 20 January 2010.

15. Such as the violin, counterbass, cello, bassoon, clarinet, flute, piccolo, piano, trumpet, trombone, French horn, tuba, alto saxophone, tenor saxophone, percussion, drums, conga (tumbadora), bass drum, cymbals, timpani, and xylophone.

16. Based on their interpretation of the hadiths (Sahih al-Bukhari: Book no. 15, Hadiths no. 70 and 72; Book no. 58, Hadith no. 268; Sahih Muslim: Book no. 4, Hadith no. 1942; Book no. 024, Hadith no. 5279).

17. Conceptually, if one looks at the indexing of Imam Khamina'i's fatwas, as they are thematically classified in his 2004 book, one finds the word "dance" (raqs), as opposed to "rhythmic movements" (harakat-i mawun), as the term is employed in Iran.

18. Interview with author, 10 August 2009.

19. Interview with author, 9 August 2013.

20. Interview with author, 16 October 2009.

21. Interview with author, 3 August 2009.

22. Interview with author, 19 December 2013.

23. Interview with author, 4 August 2009.

REFERENCES

'Abbas, F. 2009. *Zaman Al-Intasarat* [Days of Victory]. Beirut: Dar Al-Hadi.

Alagha, J. 2009. "A Tug of War: Hizbullah, Participation, and Contestation in the Lebanese Public Sphere." In *Publics, Politics, and Participation: Locating the Public Sphere in the Middle East and North Africa*, edited by S. Shami, 457–487. New York: Social Science Research Council of America.

———. 2011a. "Pious Entertainment: Hizbullah's Islamic Cultural Sphere." In *Muslim Rap, Halal Soaps, and Revolutionary Theater: Artistic Developments in the Muslim World*, edited by K. van Nieuwkerk, 149–175. Austin: University of Texas Press.

———. 2011b. *Hizbullah's Identity Construction*. Amsterdam: Amsterdam University Press.

———. 2012. "Jihad through Music: Hizbullah and the Taliban." *Performing Islam* 1, no. 2: 263–289.

'Amara, M. 1999. *Al-Ghina' wa Al-Musiqa: Halal amm Haram?* [Singing and Music: Religiously Sanctioned or Prohibited?] Series of Islamic Enlightenment, no. 33. Cairo: Dar Nahdat Misr.

———. 2007. *Al-Islam wa Al-Funun Al-Jamila* [Islam and the Fine Arts]. 3rd ed. Cairo: Dar Al-Shuruq.

Al-Ansari, M. 1984 CE. *Fara'id Al-Usul* [Obligations in the Principles of Jurisprudence]. Vol. 2. Qumm: Mu'assasat Al-Nashr Al-Islami.

'Aqil, M. 2008. *Hakadha Takalama Hurras Al-Umma* [This Is the Way the Guardians of the Nation Have Spoken]. Beirut: Dar Al-Mahajja al-Bayda'.

Calhoun, C. 2003. "The Democratic Integration of Europe: Interests, Identity, and the Public Sphere." In *Europe without Borders: Re-Mapping Territory, Citizenship, and Identity in a Transnational Age*, edited by M. Berezin and M. Schain, 243–274. Baltimore: Johns Hopkins University Press.

Fadlallah, M. H. 2009. *Al-Ijtihad Byna Asr Al-Madi wa Afaq Al-Mustaqbal* [Jurisprudence between the Shackles of the Past and the Horizons of the Future]. Beirut: Al-Markaz Al-Thaqafi Al-'Arabi.

Giddens, A. 1990. *Consequences of Modernity*. Cambridge: Polity Press.

Hafez, K. 2010. *Radicalism and Political Reform in the Islamic and Western Worlds.* Cambridge: Cambridge University Press.

Al-Hamidi, S. H. 1994 CE. *Al-Ghina' wa Alat Al-Tarab* [Singing and the Instruments of Enchantment]. Tehran: Markaz Nashr Jami'at Al-'Ilm wa Al-Sun'a fi Iran.

Ibrahim, F. 1998. *Al-Faqih wa Al-Dawla: Al-Fikar Al-Siyasi Al-Shi'i* [The Jurisprudent and the State: Shi'ite Political Thought]. Beirut: Dar Al-Kunuz Al-Adabiyya.

Al-Jaziri, A. R. 2001. *al-Fiqh'ala Al-Madhahib Al-Arba'a* [Jurisprudence Based on the Sunni Four Schools of Law].Cairo: Mu'assat Al-Mukhtar.

Khamina'i, A. 2004. *Ajwibat Al-Istifta'at* [Answers to Questions]. Second Part. Karbala': Manshurat Karbala' al-Muqadasa.

———. 2009. *al-Fann al-Islami 'inda al-Imam al-Qa'id [Islamic Art According to Imam Khamina'i].* Compiled by Muhammad Salar, cultural attaché of the Islamic Republic in Lebanon. Beirut: Dar Al-Mahajja al-Bayda.

Khatami, M. 2001. *Speeches and Activities at the United Nations.* Beirut: Iranian Cultural Center.

Khumayni, I. 2002. *Dirasat fi Al-Fikr al-Siyasi 'inda Al-Imam Al-Khumayni* [Studies on the Political Thought of Imam Khumayni]. Beirut: Al-Ghadir.

Kohlberg, E. 1991. *Belief and Law in Imami Shi'ism.* Hampshire: Variorum.

LeVine, M., and A. Salvatore. 2009. "Religious Mobilization and the Public Sphere: Reflections on Alternative Genealogies." In *Publics, Politics and Participation: Locating the Public Sphere in the Middle East and North Africa,* edited by S. Shami, 65–90. New York: Social Science Research Council of America.

Mahmasani, S. 1955. *Falsafat Al-Tashri' fi Al-Islam* [The Philosophy of Jurisprudence in Islam]. Beirut: Dar Al-'Ilmlil Malayyin. Translated by F. J. Ziadé (1961). Leiden: Brill.

Masud, M. K. 1996. *Al-Shatibi's Philosophy of Islamic Law.* Islamabad: Islamic Research Institute.

Mughniyyé, M. J. 1966. *Al-Shi'a wa Al-Hakimun* [The Shi'ites and the Rulers]. Beirut: Al-Maktaba Al-Ahliyya.

———. 1988. *'Ilm Usual Al-Fiqh fi Thawbihi Al-Jadid* [The Science of the Principles of Jurisprudence in Its New Garment]. Beirut: Dar Al-Tayyar Al-Jadid, 225–232, 363–365.

Al-Murtada, S. n.d. *Al-Shari'a fi Usul Al-Shi'a* [Islamic Law in Shi'ite Islam]. Vol.1. Tehran: Intisharat Danishkah Tehran.

Mutahhari, M. 2002. *Understanding Islamic Sciences: Philosophy, Theology, Mysticism, Morality, Jurisprudence.* London: ICAS Press.

———. 2010. *Al-Islam wa Mutatalibat Al-'Asr* [Islam and the Demands of the Age]. Beirut: Dar Al-Amir lil Thaqa fawa Al-'Ulum.

———. 2011. *Fiqh* [Jurisprudence]. Beirut: Dar Al-Wala'.

———. 2013. *The Role of Reason in Ijtihad.* http://www.al-islam.org/al-tawhid/reason-ijtihad.htm. Accessed 25 July 2013.

———. *The Role of Ijtihad in Legislation.* http://www.al-islam.org/al-tawhid/ijtihad-legislation.htm. Accessed 25 July 2013.

Al-Qaradawi, Y. A. 2004. *Fiqh Al-Ghina' wa Al-Musiqa fi Daw' Al-Qur'an wa Al-Sunna* [The Jurisprudence of Singing and Music in Light of the Qur'an and Traditions]. 3rd ed. Cairo: Maktabat Wehbé.

Racy, A. J. 2003. *Making Music in the Arab World: The Culture and Artistry of Tarab.* Cambridge: Cambridge University Press.

Rishahri, M. 2000. *Al-'Aqlwa Al-Jahil fi Al-Kitabwa Al-Sunna* [Reasoning and Ignorance in the Qur'an and the Traditions]. Beirut: Dar Al-Hadith.

Al-Sarakhsi, A. B. B. M. 1993. *Usul Al-Sarakhsi*. Beirut: Dar Al-Kutub Al-Islamiyyamu.

Al-Shatibi, A. I. I. B. M. 2003. *Al-Muwafaqat Fi Usul Al-Shari'a*. Cairo: Al-Maktaba Al-Tawfiqiyya.

Van Nieuwkerk, K. 2011. "Of Morals, Missions, and the Market: New Religiosity and 'Art with a Mission' in Egypt." In *Muslim Rap, Halal Soaps and Revolutionary Theater: Artistic Developments in the Muslim World*, edited by K. van Nieuwkerk, 177–204. Austin: University of Texas Press.

Winegar, J. 2008. "Purposeful Art between Television Preachers and the State." *ISIM Review* 22: 28–29.

CHAPTER 9

ISLAM AT THE ART SCHOOL:
RELIGIOUS YOUNG ARTISTS IN EGYPT

JESSICA WINEGAR

PIETY ON CAMPUS

ON A VERY HOT late afternoon in August 2010, fifty or so students at Cairo's College of Fine Arts, a state school, were busily setting up tables in the school's courtyard and covering them with trays of food that many of them had prepared at home. These were members of the largest student club at the college. "Al-Warsha" (or "The Workshop") boasted 1,200 members and had an associated NGO that was committed to pious arts activism—using art to cultivate students' piety and to do good for society and Islam. That night, the core members had organized an *iftar*, a dinner to break the Ramadan fast. After a morning of distributing free food to the poor, they brought more food in the overheated and congested transportation that clogs Cairo's streets in advance of the sunset call to prayer, when the entire city becomes quiet and Muslims break their daily fast together. In very modest Islamic attire, these 18- to 22-year-old artists rushed to get everything in its proper place before the *adhan*, the call to prayer that would soon be recited by a young male art student from the stairs of the arts lecture hall building that overlooked the courtyard. As soon as the *adhan* was over, students distributed dates, the traditional fast-breaking food in Egypt, as well as tamarind juice and soft drinks. The young men then went to the mosque to pray, while most of the women stayed behind to set aside food for the men and to begin eating themselves. When the men returned, the art students sat and ate in mostly gender-segregated groups, chatting and laughing. My partner at the event was a 1986 graduate of the same college, and throughout the evening he expressed surprise at the change in the student body of his alma mater. His memories of his college years, as those of his classmates I know, are filled with faculty challenging dominant values of society, faculty and students making fun of Islamist groups, horsing around in the courtyard, and romantic trysts in back hallways. "There were seeds" of this religiosity back then, he told me that evening, but pious students did not dominate the art school.

Now, twenty-five years later, the oldest college of arts in the Arab-majority Middle East, founded in 1908, is home to several initiatives, al-Warsha being the most prominent of them, that aim to better link art with Islam and to make art students better Muslims. Another popular student group, called Firsan, regularly hosts events on campus such as lectures by religious authorities that address the relationship between arts and Islam. The group called One Glimpse gathers every Friday before prayers and paints one scene together in situ as a way to explore and reaffirm Egyptian and religious identity. They frequently go to an area of the city known as "Islamic Cairo" for its famous medieval Islamic architecture. And finally, one of the most popular professors at the college has gained a significant following for his large art projects that depict scenes from the life of the Prophet Muhammad. For many of these religious students and professors, art is key to the process of becoming a better Muslim, for reaffirming Islamic and Egyptian "identity" (hawiyya), and to creating a stronger and more "developed" Islamic society. All of these groups are committed to creating art that does not violate what they understand to be the principles of Islam, but also, and more importantly, to creating art that serves Islam and God.

So how did this happen? For the greater part of the last century, this first school of modern art in Egypt was known more for having a liberal, often secular-oriented professoriate and student body, and for teaching art that emphasized national belonging and social struggle more than religious identity (Kane 2013; Winegar 2006). By the new millennium, it had become the seat of ascendant and influential pious art activity. How have definitions of art, and of the proper role of the artist in society, perhaps changed as a result? This chapter explores this new phenomenon by situating it within the history of state and Islamic discourses on the arts and the rise of the Islamic revival in Egypt (see also Van Nieuwkerk, this volume), and within the rise of neoliberalism. This historical and economic contextualization raises the additional question of how much is actually new in this new Islamic art movement.

To address these issues, this chapter takes al-Warsha as a case study to examine how members conceptualize the relationship among art, Islam, and society in their discourse and activities. By taking seriously students who dedicate copious amounts of their time to this group and its endeavors, we can gain an appreciation for how some pious Muslims view art as absolutely critical to their lives and their work as modern and cosmopolitan Egyptians, in large measure as a result of particular historical and economic conditions (not because of some Islamic "essence"). This phenomenon also challenges many dominant modernist assumptions, circulating in western precincts of the international art scene, that contemporary art is or should be against institutionalized religion or at least critical of it. In such views, art can have spiritual undertones (as in the case of Euro-American high-modernist painters), but art that advocates religious orthodoxy goes against the secularist presumptions of the modern (Asad 2003; Elkins 2004). Furthermore, the young artists at the Cairo College of Fine Arts overturn related modernist notions of the ideal artist as a social malcontent or rebel (Winegar 2006). They also force us to reconsider ideas circulating in the western press (since the Middle East uprisings began in 2011) of young Egyptians as secular revolutionaries.

A BRIEF HISTORY OF RELIGION AND
NATION IN EGYPTIAN ART EDUCATION

While many artists and professors of earlier cohorts at the College of Fine Arts might be surprised and, in some cases, disturbed, by the rise of public religiosity at their alma mater, a closer look at how the college has dealt with religious issues over the last century shows that discourses on the value of religion in relationship to art, and vice-versa, have always been present at the college, as have religiously inspired artistic practice and debate. The very founding of the College of Fine Arts in 1908 was in part made possible by a fatwa (a nonbinding religious opinion) by the main mufti of the Republic at the time, the Islamic reformer Muhammad 'Abduh. The fatwa supported the establishment of a royal college of fine arts in Cairo partly on the basis of his view that art was "one of the best educational methods."[1] Islamic reformers, other prominent intellectuals, and state arts officials at the time argued that the establishment of a modern art school was necessary for the building of the modern nation, including a nation in which Islam was the major religion. They deemed the prohibition against image making in some interpretations of Islamic texts as no longer relevant in modern society, as the danger of idol worship ceased to exist. This engagement with key Islamic texts to form opinions about art specific to time and place has been a central part of Islamic practice across centuries (Flood 2002; Otterbeck, this volume).

Throughout the twentieth century, the number of art schools, museums, galleries, and other arts institutions proliferated in Egypt. Thousands of practicing Muslims and Christians (along with Jews and at least one notable Baha'i, the famous artist Hussein Bikar) attended or taught at these institutions, with the vast majority viewing no conflict between their religious beliefs and their artistic practice. Some, albeit a minority, explored religious themes in their art—such as images of mosque architecture, popular Sufi symbols and festivals, and Arabic calligraphy—often through a nationalist framework, as an expression of a key component of Egyptian identity.

Debates peppered this history as well. In 1976, the college administration decided to prohibit live nude models for art classes, causing a ruckus between those who thought the practice was necessary for proper artistic training and those who thought that it was not necessary for students to violate local/religious mores in order to become accomplished artists and modern citizens. At times in the 1980s, 1990s, and 2000s, with the rise of the Islamic revival, Muslim students in the sculpture department would wonder if they should put holes in the top of their figurative sculptures so as not to offend what they viewed as God's prohibition against imitating his powers of creation (the holes emphasize the figure as manmade and guard against the figure taking on any human-like spirit). In response, various deans and professors scheduled lectures and workshops, often run by state-trained imams, on the compatibility of art and Islam—even in figuration—and the necessity of art to the nation, thus reiterating religious views from the early twentieth century.

For the most part during this period, the arts curriculum did not include any explicit discussion of the relationship between contemporary religion and art. Islamic art was taught as a historical subject, alongside ancient Egyptian art, historical Coptic Christian art, and western art history with an emphasis on the classical and neoclassical periods. Students were exposed to works of modern Egyptian art, which were often analyzed through a nationalist frame, as an artist's expression of a specifically "Egyptian" scene or issue. Professors encouraged students to absorb all these historical influences, then mix them with their own personal expression in order to do work that was simultaneously unique and expressive of the nation. The basic emphasis of the training at this school was in classical drawing and painting skills, with a focus on figuration and realism.

With the rising influence of the Islamic revival in the 1980s and 1990s, art professors began to promote the view that the arts were necessary to fight "backward" or "uncivilized" interpretations of Islam in modern society. Some were not against the revival per se, but most were concerned that the increase in public piety might lead to a strictness of interpretation of religion that might hamper the arts. Older professors, especially, became concerned by the appearance of new religious groups on campus. Additionally, most professors and students at the college worried about the emergence, especially in the late 1980s and early 1990s, of Islamist groups who advocated violence against the authoritarian state. The Mubarak government spearheaded, and art professors participated in, an "Enlightenment" (*nahda*) campaign that explicitly used arts and culture to fight what was viewed as religious fundamentalism (Abaza

2010; Winegar 2009). The catalogue for the 1996 Young Artists' Salon, for example, featured an article by Ahmed Rif'at Sulayman, who was a new doctoral student in art education at the time. Sulayman's piece shows that the government intended for visual arts programs to draw youth away from political Islam. Titled "The Role of the Youth in Facing the Waves of Fundamentalism," the article argues that there is a dangerous rise in the popularity of Islamic groups on art college campuses and that they perpetuate erroneous ideas—such that art, particularly figurative art, is forbidden, *haram*. Sulayman draws on the Qur'an and hadith (sayings of the Prophet Muhammad) to provide examples of the compatibility between Islam and art and to argue that art institutions have a vital role to play in steering young people away from these groups, in encouraging students to fight these trends through art.

While a fuller history of the place of religion at the College of Fine Arts has yet to be written, it is clear from this cursory discussion that religion and the arts were always intertwined in artistic practice, discourses, and debates, and that art school professors and staff have historically presented the view that art is necessary for a modern nation, that it does not conflict with Islam, and that indeed proper national modern art is necessary to combat misinterpretation of Islam. It is also clear that Islamic visual referents were mostly compartmentalized in a curriculum that emphasized them as primarily historical and only one part of a multipart national canon.

Let us return, then, to the alumnus at the *iftar*, and his statement that in the 1980s, the "seeds" of religiosity were present at the college. In a photograph of art school students from the mid-1980s (figure 9.1), a few women are wearing the kind of explicitly Islamic dress that was becoming increasingly popular with the rise of the Islamic revival since the 1970s. We can see now that it is not necessarily that religiosity was new at the time, nor were revivalist-modernist notions of Islam in relationship to the arts. What *was* striking was the *visibility* of students' piety, the insistence on particular forms of ethical behavior among unprecedented numbers of students, and the linking of both to artistic practice.

THE ISLAMIC REVIVAL: MORALITY, CHARITY, VISUALITY

This increase in visible piety and insistence on ethical behavior present in the 2000s at the Cairo College of Fine Arts is in large measure part of the rise of the Islamic revival. As Van Nieuwkerk notes in this volume, there are many reasons for the development of intensified public religious sensibilities throughout the region, and in Egypt in particular, beginning in the 1970s. These included: the devastating defeat of the 1967 war (which many attributed

9.1. Students at the College of Fine Arts, Cairo, early 1980s. Photograph courtesy of Ahmed Ragab Sakr.

to Egyptians' failures to properly worship God); the 1979 Iranian Revolution's success in deposing a western lackey; increased work migration to and from more religiously conservative Gulf societies; increased access to religious texts with the rise in literacy and proliferation of religious spaces and study groups; Sadat's support of Islamic groups in his battle with leftists; and the moral dilemmas created by the western media imports and the increase in interactions between nonrelated men and women, especially in urban areas.

In this volume and elsewhere Van Nieuwkerk (2008a, 2008b) shows how these dilemmas were particularly pronounced in the performing arts, which have generally been morally ambiguous in Egyptian society because people's bodies and potentially immoral acts are represented on stage and screen. In film and television, for example, a wave of female artists left the field in the 1980s after becoming convinced that their craft spread immorality throughout society. But by the late 1990s, as other forms of Islamic discourse emerged that stressed the positive potentials of art for religion, some of these actresses returned. They and others adopted the veil and insisted on roles that did not compromise their piety. Artists and religious figures began intensely promoting "purposeful art" or "clean art" (Alagha, this volume; Tartoussieh 2007; Van Nieuwkerk 2011) in cinema, theater, and music—both in Egypt and throughout the region. New wildly popular television preachers became key figures in this promotion of art for religion. Young, polished men such as Amr Khaled and Moez Masoud drew on many of the same discourses on art from the Islamic tradition as had muftis and imams supporting the art college, and others throughout the course of Islamic history to argue that Muslims have an obligation to do and/or appreciate art for Islam and for the nation (Winegar 2014).

And art students and junior professors were listening. These new messages reinforced a century of teaching at the art college that emphasized that there was no contradiction between being an artist and a good Muslim. But they also spoke to something these new students and younger faculty felt lacking in their arts training: an emphasis on and prioritization of Islam in their lives and careers. These messages also spoke to their concerns about rapidly increasing economic impoverishment and social decline and provided a way for them to use both art and Islam to address it.

The expansion of the Islamic revival in Egypt (and worldwide) coincided with the rise of neoliberal economic policy. This policy emphasizes private enterprise and the "free" market—that is, reduction of state regulations, trade protections, subsidies, and investments. Sadat, and especially Mubarak, enacted this policy in full force in response to pressures from international lenders such as the International Monetary Fund and the World Bank. The result in Egypt was, to put it simply, the further enrichment of the wealthy and immiseration of the poor.[2] As around the world, NGOs and charities, many of them religiously oriented, stepped in to fill the resource gap (Atia 2013). For art students, many of whom come from more modest working- or middle-class backgrounds and who attend the state-run College of Fine Arts, this neoliberal economic turn most notably meant a deterioration of their entire schooling system and the neighborhoods in which they lived, as well as economic struggles in their families. It also meant that many had significant familiarity with NGO/charity development discourses, if not actual development projects in their own neighborhoods. For example, many college students knew of, or had volunteered with Al-Risala, a very popular nationwide religious developmentalist charity begun in 2000 by youth from Cairo University, and that became a model for similar organizations.

A key component of the Islamic revival has been its visuality, analyzed by surprisingly few scholars. Deeb (2006) provides a rare analysis of how pious Lebanese (in this case Shi'a) try to change the visual aspects of public space to be more in line with Islamic ethics, through various posters and billboards and also Islamic dress. In Egypt, the Islamic revival has had a significant effect on the visual aspects of life in major cities. In comparison to fifty years ago, for example, one now sees many, many more mosques, religious advertising on signs and billboards, religious stickers and décor on the walls of public buildings or in public transportation, and Islamic dress as the main sign of piety. Art school students and young faculty in the early 2000s, who came of age in lockstep with the visual profusion of the Islamic revival, are especially attuned to the importance of visuality in everyday life. They spend their days creating and assessing visual art, and frequently lament what they see as a decline in "public taste" in the visual aspects of the urban environment in the last ten to twenty years, a period of public disinvestment in public space that in large measure led to its deterioration (Winegar 2006, 2011). With the emphasis on visual symbols of piety in urban Egypt, the simultaneous decline in the visual beauty of the built environment, and the focus on visuality in art school life, it is no surprise that religious art school students in particular would use their training to focus their efforts on linking visuality, Islam, and social development.

AL-WARSHA: A WORKSHOP FOR
MAKING WELL-MANNERED MUSLIM CITIZENS

The founder of al-Warsha, Ihab al-Tukhy, is a charismatic assistant professor who was trained as a sculptor at the College of Fine Arts in the late 1980s and early 1990s. He attended the same imam lectures as everyone else, learned from his professors how Islam and art were compatible, and how art was necessary for the continued development of the nation. He, like others in the group, also came of age at the height of the proliferation of the Islamic revival, when the majority of Cairenes were cultivating public forms of piety. He joined the growing fan base of the new television preachers who advocated a kind of technologically savvy cosmopolitan Islamic piety and who spoke about the importance of art for building a strong Muslim society and a strong nation. He also started his professional life at the exact time when the aforementioned religiously oriented charities were forming and increasingly providing social services to a population suffering with the withdrawal of state subsidies in healthcare, education, and food with neoliberalism. Growing up in a mixed-income neighborhood in central Cairo ('Abdin), he had witnessed the rapidly growing inequalities and dilapidation of the built environment during the Mubarak years. In an interview, he described this experience as teaching him the strong moral fiber of "simple people" (al-nas al-basita) but also their "limited culture" (thaqafa mahduda). He became concerned about their behavior, and particularly their forms of expression such as swearing and thuggery.[3]

All of these experiences contributed to his founding of al-Warsha student club in 2000, which he termed an "artistic charity" club (khayriyya fanniyya).

9.2. Orphans attending International Orphans Day celebration hosted by al-Warsha at the Cairo College of Fine Arts, 2010. Photograph courtesy of Ehab al-Toukhy.

It started with thirty-one members and quickly grew to be the most popular club at the school. They were dedicated to doing art that did not violate any Islamic principles and to using art to help those less fortunate in Egyptian society. They sponsored religious lectures, held clothing and food drives for the poor, and invited orphans to the college on International Orphan Day every year for traditional puppet theater performances and arts and crafts classes with the explicit intention of "reviving Islamic values" (figures 9.2 and 9.3). As the activities grew, al-Tukhy formed an NGO with the same name and rented a separate space near the campus for planning meetings and computer graphics/animation classes. Since the 2011 protests began, the NGO has rented adjacent spaces in the same building for an art gallery where they host exhibitions of student and faculty work, religious lectures, and artists' talks. They also opened an arts and crafts workshop where they hold classes and produce crafts for sale at various stores. Al-Warsha (the club and NGO) has a very active Facebook page on which members post announcements of activities as well as quotes from religious texts, and from various religious leaders. As of June 2015, this group had over five thousand members.

One of the key activities of al-Warsha is a program aimed at civilizing orphans through the arts, called "Litarda." Litarda means "to satisfy Him," and it appears in two verses of the Qur'an. Al-Warsha members who par-

9.3. Painting activity at International Orphans Day celebration hosted by al-Warsha at the Cairo College of Fine Arts, 2010. Photograph courtesy of Ehab al-Toukhy.

ticipate in Litarda do so explicitly to satisfy God, who enjoined Muslims to care for orphans in multiple verses in the Qur'an. A well-known hadith of the Prophet Muhammad also relates that those who care for orphans will be close to the Prophet in paradise, and another relates that God will count one good deed for each hair on an orphan's head that a Muslim strokes in compassion. Litarda members describe feeling that they are serving God by trying to "correct behaviors" (*ta'dil suluk*) of orphans and increase their knowledge of Islam through art, thereby making orphans better (in their view) members of Egyptian society and better Muslims. Although some members did not appear to have ready answers to my questions about which kinds of behaviors needed correcting among orphans, others specifically mentioned lying, stealing, hitting, and yelling. Art, in their view, was fun and interesting for kids and thus a great means through which to convey religious messages and to make orphans more cultured. And Ramadan was the key time in their ritual calendar to renew their commitment to this project.

The Ramadan fast-breaking *iftar* in the summer of 2010 came in the midst of a flurry of al-Warsha charity activities for the holy month, including distributing bags of food to the needy every morning in the intense summer heat. The group was just starting to plan their last charity acts for Ramadan—a visit to a different orphanage every day of the last ten days. The goal of these visits was twofold: to maximize their worship in these most special last days of Ramadan, when any evening the heavens could open to human supplication and God's willingness to recognize good acts might be greater; and to find an appropriate orphanage for the second installment of the Litarda program. The program was an eighteen-month curriculum that they developed that consisted of one moral lesson per week or two, as conveyed through a story of one of the prophets (*qisas al-anbiya'*) and accompanying art projects to illustrate the story. During the last ten days of the month and after, the core members of Litarda tried to recruit other Warsha members to the project by trying out one lesson (from the curriculum or related to it) to see if it could be successful with a particular orphanage. Success, it turned out, was judged by the potential that the group saw in having the orphans conform to their model of an Egyptian Muslim citizen, with proper behavior.

The group kicked off the first day with a morning visit to a boys' orphanage in the same mixed-income downtown neighborhood where the leader al-Tukhy had grown up. The group had already done some work in this orphanage before, and members touted it to me as an exceptionally good one with decent children. As we stood outside waiting for everyone to come, one of the women explained that not all the orphans have deceased parents. Many of them have parents who can no longer afford to keep them, she said, and it is very sad that the parents are so desperate that they have to give their kids to an orphanage. Before the group of about ten of us went up the stairs to enter the orphanage, the leader had us go around in a circle and say what our intentions were for the visit, that we needed to think carefully about intentions. Nearly everyone said they were going "for God" or "to follow the Prophet's way." (al-Tukhy answered for me, saying that I was going for "research," which he thankfully noted was a noble goal). Once we had settled on the sofas and chairs in the main living room of the orphanage, the boys, aging around nine or ten, came out in twos and threes to shake our hands. They then sat on the floor or on al-Tukhy's lap. The visit kicked off with al-Warsha members verbally quizzing the kids on their knowledge of Ramadan and whether or not they fast or pray regularly. They responded with "bravos" for all of the correct responses and for all the children who were meeting these basic requirements of Islam. The group also introduced a quiz game with a wide range of religious questions, and a game with a puzzle based on a religious theme. They also asked the students to recite parts of the Qur'an and to sing religious praise hymns.

Throughout all of these activities, several kids kept asking "when are we going to play?" and many were fidgeting or engaging in horseplay. The leader and the Warsha youth told the orphans repeatedly to sit still, to stop hitting, to stop teasing each other, and to listen to the lessons. The orphanage's supervisors, mainly lower class women, stayed silent through this whole visit. When I asked one of them about what the "behaviors" were that needed correcting, as the Warsha people had been using that term, she laughed and said she didn't know. After the group prayed the afternoon prayer together (women and men in separate rooms), the women decided to go back to the headquarters and pack the rest of the Ramadan food bags for the next days' distribution. As we were descending the staircase, the leader called down to us and excitedly told us to remember how many merits (*hasanat*) we were getting with God as a result of our visit with the orphans that day.

The sense that they were doing important work in society while gaining credit with God buoyed the Litarda members for the rest of the ten days of Ramadan. While many Egyptian college students slept in the mornings due to staying up late at night and the difficulty of making it through the long summer fast, Litarda members met every morning at a different orphanage. They exerted tremendous energy to manage crowds of rambunctious children while giving them morality lessons through activities such as coloring within the lines on pre-printed coloring book sheets and telling stories with puppets and painted storyboards (figure 9.4). They tried to teach them the importance of sitting and listening, of avoiding horseplay, of speaking to each other without teasing or "vulgar" words. They aimed to show their care for orphans, to get themselves and the orphans in God's graces in these crucial last days of Ramadan, and to test particular groups of orphans for their capacity to be reformed as proper Muslim citizens of Egypt. Repeatedly, members said they needed to "straighten" or "fix" the values and behaviors of orphans.

The Litarda curriculum explicitly emphasized these values. For example, one section focused on the story of Joseph and was intended to teach "acceptance of God's will" and the importance of "belonging." The art students had the orphans paint background panels and then act out different parts of the story of Joseph being sold into slavery and then later becoming the second in command in Pharoah's Egypt. They encouraged the orphans to paint in the same realistic style that dominates their classical training at the arts college. Through this set painting and acting, Litarda members aimed to show the children that accepting difficult circumstances is all part of God's will for you and, if trust is put in Him, could result in great things. They also take advantage of the fact that Joseph's reward takes place in Egypt to show the orphans the importance of "belonging to Egypt," as one of the organizers put it. Litarda leaders also had the children draw scenes iconic to Egypt to encourage their belonging—scenes that abound in the drawing and painting classes at the fine arts college and in school exhibitions. These included images of Egyptian vil-

9.4. On-site art lessons at a Cairo orphanage given by a team from al-Warsha, August 2010. Photo by author.

lages, streets in Islamic Cairo, and idealized pictures of peasants or people from the popular (*sha'bi*) classes. The word used for belonging in these visual lessons, *intima'*, also has connotations of loyalty, reflecting dominant notions of moral citizenship in Egypt. Other values that served as object lessons in the curriculum included patience, modesty (i.e., not being arrogant), the importance of concentration, the principles of color mixing, love of God, honesty, leadership skills, and organization. These were taught through various other artistic methods such as origami, clay molding, puppetry, and book art. Litarda members thus integrated many aspects of their training as visual art students into these lessons to get orphans to execute what were, in their opinion, the most visually compelling means and ends of moral education as Egyptians and as Muslims.

In the Litarda program and their other activities, al-Warsha members viewed art as a means of creating national and religious collectivity, and as a way of improving oneself and the collective. For them, being an artist meant accepting God's bestowal of artistic talent and using it to make oneself a better Muslim, and to help others become better Muslims, as well as Egyptians. The motivation, their intention, for visiting the orphanage that hot Ramadan day was to honor God by helping orphans do the same. In other words, art was the means, not the goal.

While al-Warsha members and other College of Fine Arts students and new faculty were busy braiding art and religion so intently, many other artists in Egypt were not. Artists exhibiting at the main contemporary art galleries in Cairo, for example, tended to be self-described secularists, or at least not advocates of this trend of purposeful art in the service of Islam. Many of these artists, such as the alumnus cited at the beginning of this chapter, were not even aware of the Warsha group and the other religious activities on campus. Those that were aware sometimes commented to me that these were somehow lesser artists, or not even "real" artists, because of the way they so closely linked art with piety.

A NEW ISLAMIC ART?

Members of al-Warsha are rewriting what it means to be an artist in Egypt and also redefining art more generally. Although their views that there is no conflict between art and Islam, and that art is key to building a modern nation, have been dominant in art education for over a century in Egypt, they insist on foregrounding the ethical dimensions of their work in new ways that emphasize Islam as a much more critical component of artistic practice than has been the case previously. And, judging by their numbers, their views are gaining ground despite the large numbers of artists who do not view art as necessary to religious practice and vice-versa, and despite vocal artists who openly oppose such interweaving of art and piety. For those, art is about personal expression, and/or national identity, and/or criticism of dominant social, political, or religious trends. The new definitions of the artist as a good Muslim activist, and of art as necessary to spread the Islamic message, appear to be gaining ground for reasons related to the history of such ideas in Islamic discourse as well as the history of national art institutions and the political economic situation in the country.

In neoliberal Egypt, the numbers of orphans and the poor grew, the visual environment became increasingly dilapidated, people bemoaned the perceived decline in morality, and charities proliferated in response. Meanwhile, nation-state institutions, such as the College of Fine Arts, continued to inculcate nationalism and promote moderate Islam as a way to produce a modern citizenry. Thus, fine arts students were, in their own education, given means to emphasize visuality and nationalist values in both profession and piety. In their artistic charitable works, al-Warsha members drew on over a century of positive discourses about the relationship between art, Islam, and society. But they also gave the project of using art to build the nation and Islam a new twist, galvanizing discourses on the arts and Islam that had recently become popular in the larger cultural sphere. "Belonging" to Egypt remained important, but now being a good Muslim and promoting Islamic values were seen as the most critical part of this nationalist project. For members of al-Warsha, doing charitable works vis-à-vis art was a way of cultivating piety, of using what they viewed as their God-given talents for the purpose of becoming better Muslims and spreading Islamic values. Yet they did not merely seek to use art to build a modern nation, or to advance moderate Islam in particular, or to reconcile art and Islam. Art, for them, was a vehicle through which to become closer to God and to bring others closer to God. In the halls of the Cairo College of Fine Arts, we thus see a new trend in contemporary visual arts—one that has connections to the past but that also contains a novel infusion of purposeful Islamic ethos.

This case has implications for our understanding of the broader trend of purposefully religious art-making across the Middle East. It suggests that participants in this phenomenon may be reworking longstanding religious and nationalist discourses about the arts, in part by linking them together in more concerted and explicit ways. Rather than religion being made subsidiary to the nation, and rather than the focus being mostly on religion's compatibility with art in order to produce the nation, it appears that artists are now engaging with religious texts and contexts much more broadly and substantively, and doing so in order to become both better Muslims as well as proper citizens. The dominant concept emerging is that one needs to be a proper citizen to be a better Muslim, and vice-versa, and that the arts are key to that goal.

This case also suggests that the dominant criteria by which many artists judge other artists, artistic activity, and art works may be shifting. When upwards of five thousand artists (or at least those interested in the arts) value those who are trying to achieve piety through art activities, one wonders if the notion of who is a "good" artist is changing such that to be included in this category one must increasingly engage, explicitly and overtly, in dominant, institutionalized, religious discourses and activities. Furthermore, what is considered necessary and/or acceptable artistic practice now appears to increasingly include charitable work through the arts. And finally, it remains to be seen whether this trend will alter the dominant frameworks by which actual art works are judged and valued, in terms of content, style, media, and message.

Although there are many variables, not the least of which are the ongoing uprisings across the region, we may be witnessing a transformation in prevailing hierarchies of value concerning the arts—and the visual arts especially.

This will particularly be the case in Egypt if and when religiously oriented artists continue to build new institutions and transform others from within. This process is likely to continue, because the religious and artistic values these artists espouse are mainstream, and because most do not participate in any religion-based oppositional politics that would be suppressed by the military regime. Like the uprisings, the global effects of this transformation could be significant for Muslim religious communities and beyond.

NOTES

1. In Rashid Rida, *Ta'rikh al-ustadh al-imam al-shaykh Muhammad ʿAbduh* (Egypt: Matbaʿat al-Manar, 1931).

2. Walter Armbrust deftly argues how this neoliberal economic policy was a key cause of the Egyptian Revolution (Armbrust 2011).

3. Interview with author, 7 March 2011.

REFERENCES

Abaza, M. 2010. "The Trafficking with Tanwir (Enlightenment)." *Comparative Studies of South Asia, Africa and the Middle East* 301, No. 1: 32–46.

Armbrust, W. 2011. "A Revolution against Neoliberalism." *Al-Jazeera*, 24 February.

Asad, T. 2003. *Formations of the Secular: Christianity, Islam, Modernity*. Palo Alto: Stanford University Press.

Atia, M. 2013. *Building a House in Heaven: Pious Neoliberalism and Islamic Charity in Egypt*. Minneapolis: University of Minnesota Press.

Deeb, L. 2006. *An Enchanted Modern: Gender and Public Piety in Shiʿi Lebanon*. Princeton: Princeton University Press.

Elkins, J. 2004. *On the Strange Place of Religion in Contemporary Art*. New York and London: Routledge.

Flood, F. B. 2002. "Between Cult and Culture: Bamiyan, Islamic Iconoclasm, and the Museum." *Art Bulletin* 84, no. 4: 641–59.

Kane, P. 2013. *The Politics of Art in Modern Egypt: Aesthetics, Ideology and Nation-Building*. London: IB Tauris.

Tartoussieh, K. 2007. "Pious Stardom: Cinema and the Islamic Revival in Egypt." *Arab Studies Journal* 15, no. 1: 30–43.

Van Nieuwkerk, K. 2007. "From Repentance to Pious Performance." In *ISIM Review* 20: 54–55.

———. 2008a. "Creating an Islamic Cultural Sphere: Contested Notions of Art, Leisure and Entertainment. An Introduction." *Contemporary Islam* 2, no. 3: 169–176.

———. 2008b. "Piety, Penitence, and Gender: The Case of Repentant Artists in Egypt." *Journal for Islamic Studies* 28: 37–65.

———, ed. 2011. *Muslim Rap, Halal Soaps, and Revolutionary Theater: Artistic Developments in the Muslim World*. Austin: University of Texas Press.

Winegar, J. 2006. *Creative Reckonings: The Politics of Art and Culture in Contemporary Egypt*. Palo Alto: Stanford University Press.

————. 2009. "Culture Is the Solution: The Civilizing Mission of Egypt's Culture Palaces." *Review of Middle East Studies* 43, no. 2: 189–197.

————. 2011. "Taking Out the Trash: Youth Clean Up Egypt after Mubarak." *Middle East Report* 259: 32–35.

————. 2014. "Civilizing Muslim Youth: Egyptian State Culture Programs and Islamic Television Preachers." *Journal of the Royal Anthropological Institute* 20, no. 3: 445–465.

CHAPTER 10

WRITING HISTORY THROUGH THE PRISM OF ART: THE CAREER OF A PIOUS CULTURAL PRODUCER IN EGYPT

KARIN VAN NIEUWKERK

The Muslim Brothers are heading towards authority, they are so influential. They have the power of the street. So, it might be useful if you are asked to be inside the cockpit. . . . On the other hand, maybe you need to be outside the focus to give them the other opinions and ideas . . . It is the dilemma of being inside or outside; which gives you a clearer vision?[1]

THUS REFLECTED Ahmad Abu Haiba as he contemplated whether to join the new media channel of the Muslim Brothers, "Egypt 25,"[2] in December 2011. Abu Haiba (b. 1968) (see figure 10.1), is an actor, playwright, and producer. In 2010, he was selected by the American network CNBC World as one of the top seven media leaders in the world. His career is intertwined with that of the Egyptian Islamist movements, influenced by them while simultaneously shaping their course through his diverse artistic and media activities. He eventually decided to enter the ring and influence the Muslim Brothers' course from within,[3] a career that would come to an abrupt end when President Mursi was ousted on 3 July 2013.

In this chapter, I analyze the sociopolitical and religious transformations in Egypt, particularly of the Islamist movements, by going into the trials and tribulations of Abu Haiba's career during the Mubarak era, which spanned three decades from 1981 until 2011. His story, along with those of other artists, provides an intimate account of sociohistorical changes in Egypt. Utilizing oral sources, biographies or micro-level stories to delve into macro sociohistorical and political development is a well-established genre of history writing.[4] The field of art, however, remains broadly under-examined as a historiographic source despite the clear advantages of using artists and their works as prisms through which to explore sociopolitical issues. Art not only reflects social change but also foreshadows transformations and helps to bring

10.1. Abu Haiba at the studio with the 4Shbab logo in the background.
Photo by author.

them about. Sociopolitical developments have a strong bearing on the field of
art, whereas the field of art simultaneously shapes the sociopolitical landscape
and its ongoing transformations.

   In this chapter, I analyze the sociopolitical and particularly the religious
transformations in Egypt through the lens of the performing arts. What can we
learn about sociohistorical, political, and religious transformations in Egypt
by studying the field of art and the life of artists? How are the contestations
about social and political issues reflected in art and vice versa? In this chapter,
I tell the story of Abu Haiba to draw a larger picture of changing life and politics in Egypt. In each section I link his biography to the broader sociopolitical
context of Egypt, and to transformations in the Islamists' discourses and attitudes toward art.

PIETY AND THE TRANSFORMATIVE POWER OF ARTS

It is a cartoon character that you are building with these music videos . . . How can you compare this to the Qur'an that comes from above! . . . Have God's words become inferior to music and women?! By Allah, this will be the downfall of Islam and the rise of western-inspired pop music. . . . Music turns people into infidels. Music ruins morality.[5]

The destructive force accorded to music by a Salafi preacher—who attacked Abu Haiba's endeavor to spread Islam by launching an Islamic music video channel—demonstrates the transformative power attributed to music. This power can be ascribed both to the artists and to the works of art they create.

In many countries artists and celebrities are perceived as icons and trendsetters. Celebrities reflect, reinforce, and have the power to transform the sociopolitical and cultural context in which they live. Stars are entertainers, but also idols, models, and educators. They legitimize certain lifestyles and have a great impact on public consciousness and debate (Turner 2004; Marshall 1997). Celebrities not only influence consumption patterns and cultural identity, they are also increasingly touchstones for discussing political, social, moral, and religious issues (Van den Bulck and Tambuyzer 2008).

The transformative power of art works is related both to the aesthetics of the art productions and their ability to move audiences. Art can evoke emotions and memories, affect the senses, and mold the audience's sensibilities (Nooshin 2009; Hirschkind 2006; Frishkopf 2011).

This neatly corresponds to the Salafi preacher's distaste of music, in the sense that he feared it would ruin morals and bring about a western-inspired taste culture.

Accordingly, the potential transformative power of the arts does not necessarily tell us anything about the direction of change. This has to be studied in a specific sociohistorical and political context. The Egyptian context has been increasingly influenced by a growing Islamization of the public sphere and the development of pious taste cultures.

Embracing a pious lifestyle usually has a radical effect on the everyday life of believers. They are encouraged to adapt their habits and way of living. The cultivation of religious sensibilities often means a profound transformation in people's everyday world, including their experience of and relationship to art.

We thus see a convergence between the deep sensory impact of artistic aesthetics as well as religious transformations on the body and the self. Pious life styles can be strengthened by enjoying pious arts and recreation. Pious art can help to inculcate religious dispositions and sensibilities into audiences (Van Nieuwkerk 2013). This makes pious arts into a profound transformative experience and a highly contested phenomenon—as is evidenced by the Salafi preacher who opposed Abu Haiba's Islamic art project.

EGYPT'S ISLAMIC REVIVAL IN THE 1980S

I can describe myself as a religious guy starting from ten years ago. Before that, I consider myself a ... fundamentalist, extremist ... just like many young Muslims. TV is forbidden, everything is haram *[illicit], the arts are* haram. *.... I just took it strong. .... Anyway it was a period."*[6]

This characterization by Abu Haiba of himself reflects a more general development in Egypt during the 1980s, that is, the growth of religiosity among large sectors of Egyptian society.

The Islamic movements were diverse, ranging from state-sponsored Islam, militant groups, the accommodationist Muslim Brothers, to the piety movement and Sufism (Sullivan and Abed-Kotob 1999: 20; Bayat 1998; Mahmood 2005). This division was not strict and showed overlap.

The enormous growth of private mosques was one of the clearest examples of the massive expansion of the Islamic sector. It was estimated that in 1970 there were about 20,000 private mosques, in 1981, 46,000 and in the mid-1990s, 140,000 (Wickham 2002: 98, 107). Also, the number of Islamic associations expanded rapidly. Alongside the private mosques, Islamic charity organizations, health clinics, and schools, a wide range of Islamic businesses developed. "Islamo-business" (Haenni 2005) also expanded into publishing and media companies as well as mass production of religious commodities. Moreover, outward signs of religiosity, such as veiling or grooming a beard, became clear visual markers of the Islamic revival.

The growth of religiousness also affected the field of art. Several celebrities, particularly women, left wealth and fame behind in order to veil and to devote themselves to God. Actress Shams al-Barudi and her husband, the actor Hassan Yusif, were the first to retire in 1982, followed by many others. These well-to-do stars were in the middle of a successful career in art when they "repented" from their "sins" and started to follow religious classes. The pious celebrities received a great deal of media attention. They provided a new role model, not only for lower-middle-class women but also for affluent ones. They started to preach veiling and piety among higher-class women and enabled the extension of the piety movement into the higher echelons of Egyptian society.

Most of these celebrities first consulted the conservative sheikh al-Sha'arawi (1911–1998) on the permissibility of art. He was an Azhari cleric, critical of the state and sympathetic to the Muslim Brothers. He did not extensively tackle the topic of art, but generally held that art is like a glass or knife. It can be used for good purposes or for bad ends. In general, the discourse on art within the Islamist movements was restrictive at the time. Religious scholars mainly fulminated against mainstream "vulgar" art and its "obscenities," and did not call for an Islamic alternative.

EGYPT'S ISLAMIC REVIVAL IN THE EARLY 1990S

I went to college. Then things became different. We started to think about . . . what is really religious wrong, what is really religious good. We decided to be more open to the people. So I started to read a lot of books. . . . These works led me to think that I should not refuse art. . . . So I started to use art to deliver the message . . . At the beginning it was just very bad plays . . . boring, . . . in fusha language[7] . . . historical plays. I remember there was a competition of play teams at the university. The judges came to our show and they actually slept during the show. They literally slept! Because it was so boring. I myself was about to sleep [laughs]. . . . We became better and . . . I started to feel that art is not just about meaning as a tool, art is something beautiful. I started to write . . . plays . . . and we won the competition in my last year. . . . Within three years we became the best . . . as an Islamic artist group. It was really marvelous."[8]

The early 1990s, and particularly 1992, was a turbulent period in Egyptian history. Egypt was targeted by a series of terrorist attacks, on Copts, policemen, intellectuals, and foreign tourists. The moderate Muslim Brotherhood moved from the periphery to the center and enhanced its influence through electoral victories in professional associations. The Mubarak regime began to hunt down "Islamists," "extremists," and "terrorists" and blurred distinctions between them (Wickham 2002: 200). In October 1992, an earthquake struck Egypt as well. The expanding Islamist service sector was the first to arrive and assist the Cairene poor, further emphasizing the state's inefficiency and negligence.

Egypt was also struck by an incessant stream of "repentant artists." From the 1990s—with a peak in 1992—the number of retiring artists increased at a staggering speed. They became objects of intense media debates. Islamists capitalized on the repentance and veiling of artists to promote their views on morality for Egyptian society. These views were contested by secularists and liberals, who feared a further Islamization of the public sphere due to the pious artists' influence.

The battle between the regime and Islamists was thus no longer limited to the military, political, and social field, but extended into the cultural arena. Militant Islamists attacked theatrical groups, performers, and video shops that they considered to produce or sell "vulgar" art (Ramzi 1994). Yet, at the same time, religiously inspired students, such as Abu Haiba, started experimenting with an alternative form of art. They were linked to the Islamist *Jama'at Islamiyya* groups at the university and developed pious art, first as a hobby, but increasingly in a more professional way.

These student-artist groups took the safe side of religious discourse by refusing to work with women and to keep a distance from music. As Abu Haiba said about the start of his career at the university: "It was without women and without music. It had a clear Islamic message. . . . When I would like to make a justification for that period, I would say the usual theater was just only about women and partly about music." After his graduation in 1991, they started to use music: "It was a strange coincidence, the biggest theater in Egypt at that time, Ramsis, was controlled by the Syndicate of Engineers. It was hired by 'Adil Imam[9] for the previous ten years. The strange coincidence was that his contract ended at the same time I graduated from the faculty. The syndicate was controlled by the Muslim Brothers, so they decided not to renew the contract. It was a historical moment; everything was just in front of me: there was a theater, and the people who controlled the theater would like to have a kind of Islamic theater. We are the winners of the festival and we are all engineers. So everything fitted." Accordingly, they started to perform in this theater. Yet, in 1995, the political fortunes that had helped them to access the theater turned against them: The Egyptian government began a crackdown on radical and moderate Islamist movements and the Muslim Brothers were kicked out of the syndicate (Wickham 2002). The team fell apart, and Abu Haiba started a career in the media.

EGYPT'S ISLAMIC REVIVAL IN THE LATE 1990S

At that time there were only religious programs on state TV such as those of sheikh al-Sha'arawi. . . . A lecture in the mosque: that was the concept of religious TV or Islamic media at the time. When I started my company I raised this question: "Why should it be so traditional? We can make good music, a good talk show." So we

started our new program "Words from the Heart." That was the
beginning of ʿAmr Khalid. But no one decided to buy the program.
... It was something new to them. This is not a religious program,
so they were afraid.[10]

The state's fierce crackdown on Islamist opposition in the mid-1990s did not
stop a further Islamization of the cultural sphere. This was partly due to the
state's own ambiguous politics. In order to counter Islamist opposition, the
state had adopted a dual image: secular-modern *and* religious-nationalist
(Mehrez 2008). The secular and modern image was important for outside consumption and with regard to the substantial Coptic minority. The secular cultural field played a crucial role in spreading this image. Many artists shared
the state's fear for militant Islam and portrayed Islamists as bearded fanatics
who were out of touch with reality (Armbrust 2002). The state's religious-
nationalist image was crucial for internal use toward the conservative Muslim
majority. In order to reach the last goal, al-Azhar, the important religious institution that is largely controlled by the state, was given space to voice conservative religious views. These views sometimes closely resembled those of
moderate Islamists. The strength of the state was also the result of the great
ideological divide between the two potential oppositional forces (Shehata
2010). The state further encouraged and strengthened this polarization.

Another important development in Egypt in the late 1990s, and particularly
influential for the field of art, was the proliferation of religious authorities.
The religious field became more competitive and fragmented, and several religious scholars who distanced themselves from the official line and preachers
without an al-Azhar background, such as ʿAmr Khalid, became active players
in the media debate. Of particular importance is the emergence of a moderate Islamist trend, the *wasatiyya* (Baker 2003). They emerged from the mainstream Muslim Brotherhood but have become an independent current. After
the death of al-Ghazali in 1996, al-Qaradawi became the most influential
representative.

Al-Qaradawi (b. 1926) is perhaps the most prolific *wasatiyya* writer on art
(1998, 2001). He states that there is no conflict between piety and moderate
entertainment. Diversion is essential to recreate, but one should find a balance
between religious obligation and recreation. The general rule is that everything is permissible except if it is clearly stated in the Qur'an or Sunna[11] that it
is *haram*. Despite their positive ideas on art in general, *wasatiyya* intellectuals
fulminated against the state of art present at their time. The discourse stopped
at the point of general claims that art is not *haram* given conditions and stipulations. Their gender discourse allowed space for women's work as long as her

primary and natural role was properly executed. Veiling was a cornerstone for female public activities. Art, though, was not deemed an appropriate field for women.

It was the lay preachers without al-Azhar training, such as ʿAmr Khalid, who became important advocates of actively using art to further the religious revival. In 1995, ʿAmr Khalid entered the religious arena without religious education. His authority and that of other new preachers was based on charisma, youthful looks, communication skills, and the use of new media (Wise 2003). Their style of preaching completely differed from that of sheikhs such as al-Shaʿarawi: it stressed personal piety instead of religious rulings, was participatory instead of authoritative and took place in a gender-mixed studio instead of the mosque. Due to its vanguard concept, this new participatory concept of preaching was not immediately successful, as Abu Haiba related.

EGYPT'S ISLAMIC REVIVAL IN THE NEW MILLENNIUM

This idea of Islamic art requires a lot of work and dedication. . . . Participating in the work of al-fann al-hadif *[art with a mission] is a vital choice for our community; if* al-fann al-hadif *does not prevail in our community, then it will be lost. Art and the media have a vital role to play in upholding the ethical values of our nation by safeguarding its ideals, ideas, and basic moral doctrines.*[12]

Thus, Abu Haiba expressed his views on an official meeting dedicated to "art with a mission." It is particularly the generation of young preachers of the late 1990s that promoted the new discourse on "art with a mission." ʿAmr Khalid, for instance, pointed at the great responsibility of artists for the community: they can spoil or edify the Muslim community.[13] He urged the artists who retired for religious reasons to come back and use their talents for the Islamic awakening. Preachers and artists, such as ʿAmr Khalid and Abu Haiba, transformed art into a mission aimed at molding society in line with the Islamic message. The "art with a mission" discourse builds upon the *wasatiyya* ideas that art is permissible but extends this view by transforming art into a project that should further the Islamic Revival.

Fann al-hadif advocates hold that Islam and art are strongly linked. They point to the imperative to beautify the mosque, by which devotion is directly connected to beauty. In the same vein they argue that the Qurʾan is the clearest example of beauty, which makes encountering beauty a religious practice. Besides, they reason that God knows the basic makeup of man, that is, reason, body, feeling, and conscience. Nothing that benefits the human being is prohibited in Islam. Islam cannot prohibit creativity or beauty, because they nurture human feeling and conscience. Moreover, the hadith "God is beauty and He loves beauty" is another indication that enjoying beauty is a devotional practice. The idea is that God created beauty and in order to thank God for this blessing it is a human's duty to enjoy it.

Religiously committed artists were inspired by this discourse and worked out actual formats and forms of art. Accordingly, from a religious discourse on art, the matter was turned into a project, and finally into pious artistic productions. Abu Haiba had in the meantime gained extensive experience in two different fields of art: Islamic theater and Islamic TV. Both fields had their own problems and adversaries. In 2000, during the Palestinian intifada (uprisings), some members of the theater company decided it was time to show their support during a special week for Palestine. Abu Haiba wrote a play, which they performed for two weeks. This motivated them to professionalize the team. After that he wrote a trilogy of "resistance theater": *Wake Up*, *Vietnam II*, and finally *The Code*. The latter was a political comedy about Egypt, a tricky play that was obstructed by the authorities and eventually closed down in 2008 due to its political sensitivity.

As a playwright, Abu Haiba faced opposition at the national level of the government and liberal journalists due to the plays' preponderant religious character. In the global media world, however, he was attacked by Salafi opponents and Saudi funders, who disagreed with his "open Islamic message" and especially with his use of "women and music." For instance, Abu Haiba was approached to start the new Saudi-owned channel *al-Risala*. Yet, his vision met with heavy resistance. After six months, it was turned into a regular religious channel with preachers only.

Beside Islamic media and theater, religious singers and wedding bands emerged and were increasingly popular. Several veiled actresses returned to produce moral-ethical productions in which they acted wearing a veil. In the beginning of this millennium, they started to reappear in overtly religious serials, on topics such as the life of sheikhs. Yet, in 2006, four celebrities also returned in social drama and serials. Abu Haiba's channel *al-Risala* was an important channel for the comeback of the veiled artists.

EGYPT'S ISLAMIC REVIVAL IN THE LATE 2000S

The problem is that certain people treat Islam as if it is their territory. . . . It has nothing to do with logic or religious knowledge, right and wrong. It has something to do with their sense of dignity: "This is our Islam." . . . I only care about whether something is really haram *or not. Is something not* haram*, but you don't like it, you feel it is outside the borders . . . I don't care . . . , these are your borders! I am not obliged to respect your borders. So the issue was not that I exceeded the limits of Islam, but that I exceeded the borders of Islam.*[14]

Thus reflected Abu Haiba when also his new endeavor to start a religious music video clip channel in 2008, 4Shbab, had failed due to Saudi views on Islam. The channel was successful and received three awards at the Arab video-clip festival. Yet, it failed with regard to funding: neither Egyptian liberal businessmen nor Salafi funders from the Gulf supported his projects. His artistic ideas to combine Islam and art in a professional and modern format, though, were becoming increasingly popular. This was due to several reasons, of which the spread of the piety movement into the affluent classes was probably the most important factor. The novel development was not the spread of piety as such, but the class component. This resulted in a broadly shared pious climate among different classes, informing leisure and lifestyle.

The new preachers have been of great importance in the emergence of new forms of religiosity that blended wealth and faith. It was mockingly called "air-conditioned Islam" (Tammam and Haenni 2003). Also the veiled celebrities and pious stars exerted influence on the affluent classes. Moreover, the returned migrants from the Arabian Peninsula were well off and had experienced religiosity in a luxurious setting. Many returned migrants settled in (upper) middle-class neighborhoods and mingled with the more secularized or passively religious Egyptian (upper) middle classes. Returned migrants introduced religious classes and preachers into elite clubs and opened businesses with a religious flavor.

The Islamization of the (upper) middle class has accordingly also resulted in a blossoming of upscale religious consumerism and a market for "modern Islamic art." However, the well-to-do classes were not only influenced by pious taste cultures but also by global flows of consumption and commoditization. Luxurious shopping malls and gated communities were developed in posh neighborhoods and on the outskirts of Cairo (Denis 2006; De Koning 2009). Although the concept of the mall and the protected city are mainly American inventions, the influence of the Persian Gulf luxury as well as morality is clearly visible. As Vignal and Denis note: "The references at first glance seem American, but passing through the Gulf imprints them with specific moral and symbolic codes" (2006: 119–120).

This intersection of global and religious sensibilities took a specific form. It is *halal* rather than religious in a strict sense. Although it is not in contradistinction with religious prescriptions, it is not produced or consumed with a religious purpose. It is "clean" in the double sense of the word: that is, first, spotless or hygienic, and second, morally respectable and appropriate. The development toward *halal* and "clean" formats can be witnessed in the field of art as well. "Clean cinema" became popular, a genre of films and serials that cater for religious sensibilities without an overtly Islamic reference. Songs were "halal-ified" by cleansing the lyrics of inappropriate wording.

In line with the fragmentation of religious authorities, discourses, and practices, there developed a diversification of art for the various religious consumer markets: from an explicitly religious format to a clean, up-scale form. Clean artworks and leisure activities have no religious reference but are in accordance with the "nice religiosity" of the (upper) middle class and enable participation in an affluent consumerist lifestyle. The *halal* form became increasingly popular, much to the dismay of the strictly religious who considered the loss of the religious message a great danger for the future of the Islamic community.

(PIOUS) ART DURING THE REVOLUTION AND BEYOND

I felt so oppressed at the time. It seems like my goals are not achievable. . . . Then I started to work as a political activist till it happened . . . the revolution . . . I was one of the people who started on the 25th of January [2011] . . . I was arrested during the morning of the 25th. . . . We were arrested for four, five hours and they released us again. We went back to Tahrir. We did not know or expect that the regime would finally respond. By the 5th of February I got connected to Ibrahim 'Issa[15] . . . I became one of his fans although he is against the Islamists . . . Ibrahim said we need to express our voice, the Tahrir voice, because the regular channels express . . . the state's point of view or the private channel expresses the businessmen's point of view. I told Ibrahim: "I can do this." . . . At my laptop I started to take the videos from the Internet from Facebook and re-edited it and sent it by e-mail to a satellite in Bahrain. . . . I prepared everything and we decided it is going to be on air on Thursday, the day before Mubarak stepped down [11 February 2011]. We came on air that day, the second day he stepped down, so actually we became the channel of the revolution. We started to broadcast everything, the people shot in the street, on Tahrir, the martyrs, interviews with activists. . . . The channel became so popular.[16]

Egypt's process of economic liberalization was accompanied by severe political deliberalization. As Mona Abaza documents: "The golden age of Egyptian liberal tycoons is paired with the regime's record for the worst human rights violations, especially after the Taba Hilton bombing in October 2005, which led to the detaining of twenty-four hundred people under inhumane conditions and torture. Egyptian security forces have been identified by Human Rights Watch as committing mass human rights abuses. For the first time in Egypt's history, women were violently sexually harassed" (2010: 38). The Mubarak regime thus began to rely more heavily on repression and on divide and rule strategies, particularly between Islamists and secularists (Shehata 2010). After the success of the Muslim Brothers in the 2005 elections, another crackdown by the regime followed. The leftist opposition was fragmented, but during the period 2000–2005 they assumed a greater visibility. The state of emergency, in force since 1981, placed any opposition party or individual under threat of persecution. Yet in 2006, 2007, and 2008, there were massive strikes in the public and private sector, particularly among textile workers of Mahalla al-Kubra (Bayat 2009: 9).

Islamists were largely absent during the initial stage of the revolution. The religious establishment of al-Azhar had ties of allegiance with the regime. Salafists condemned the protest and aligned with Saudi Arabia's Wahhabi clerics' view that "all protest movements in the Arab world are western machinations against the Muslim community."[17] The Muslim Brothers' position evolved under pressure from the street, and on the "Day of Rage," on 28 January, the Brothers started to mobilize.[18] The Egyptian *Masry al-Yawm* reporter al-Anani noted the familiar antagonism, or "Salafobia," from liberals toward the Islamists, making effective coalition-building during the months after the revolution a near "mission impossible."[19] After a transition period in which the Supreme Council of the Armed Forces (SCAF) was in power, the 2011 election indicated a victory for the Brothers and the Salafists. Eventually, Muhammad Mursi beat Ahmad Shafiq, the last prime minister under Mubarak, and was installed as president in June 2012.

Zakia Salime has argued that culture, aesthetics, and politics have never become more intertwined than during the current uprisings in the Middle East and North Africa.[20] My material is mostly collected before the revolution, but the story of Abu Haiba, whom I interviewed twice after the revolution, confirms the strong politicization of art. Besides graffiti, street theater, poetry, the revolution has also inspired the creation of new songs including the genre of "Martyr Pop."[21] Egyptian popular singers, even those initially not very supportive of the revolution, have produced a song and clip commemorating the people who were killed during the eighteen days of protest.

The unpredictable and wavering course of the revolution was reflected in Abu Haiba's endeavor with "Tahrir channel." Everything went well with the channel until September 2011. The channel attracted a lot of stars because—as Abu Haiba explains—"a lot of people wanted to be cleansed in our channel." That is, many stars working for the state-controlled media, wanted to revamp their image. Then, the channel started to suffer financially because the advertising company that bought airtime withdrew. They had to look for other funders, but the Tahrir channel had become an icon for the revolution that was not easily sold to foreigners or old-regime businessmen. He finally sold it to a businessman who was forced to deal with the former regime but was relatively clean and uncorrupted.

Although Abu Haiba longs to go back to the field of art and to produce a film, the highly politicized climate drew him into media and politics.[22] He rejected the Brotherhood's offer to run their channel at first, but accepted it in the end. Due to the strong polarization between "liberals" and "Islamists," as well as the strong anti-Mursi campaigns, he felt forced to take sides. He felt that due to his Tahrir channel past he could add "the revolution stance" to "Egypt 25" and transform it into new media in which everyone could express their opinion without hostility. He was fighting on two fronts again, against the old Mubarak forces in the mediascape as well as the Muslim Brotherhood's attitude "we are the best." He tried to bring in people from outside the Muslim Brotherhood, encouraging debate and "professionally biased" news, by which he meant taking a stance while also bringing in the other voices. Due to a shortage of money and a lack of time, the coming of power of the Muslim Brotherhood had, according to Abu Haiba, not yet meant a boost for Islamic art.[23]

A few days after I last met him, his career showed another unexpected course that reflected the ongoing struggles in Egypt: on 3 July 2013, a few minutes after general al-Sisi announced that Mursi was ousted and new presidential elections were to be held, his channel "Egypt 25" was taken off air.[24]

CONCLUSION

Through the prism of the field of art, this chapter analyzed the history of Egypt, particularly the pious Islamist currents during the Mubarak era. The career of Abu Haiba shows the strong dialectical relationship between Egypt's sociohistorical transformations and the field of art. In the 1980s, Egypt witnessed a growing revival of religiosity among large, lower- and middle-class sectors of the population, from militant to pietistic forms. Artists were just one of the groups affected by the religious spirit in Egypt in those days. They were, however, also special—not only with regard to their affluent backgrounds and life-styles, but also with regard to their influential status as celebrities. They have provided pious role models for emulation among millions of fans.

In the 1990s, we saw the ambiguous politics of the state, trying to contain, co-opt, and repress the diverse manifestations of Islamist politics and culture, increasingly blurring distinctions between them and enforcing total repression. Confrontations by the state against Islamists were also fought out within the cultural arena with the help of the secular cultural players. There were hardly any Islamic artistic alternatives. Moreover, during this period, the fragmentation of religious authorities increasingly took form in the popularity of young lay preachers, with a pleasant, "lighter" version of the Islamic message that was well received by (upper) middle classes. The post-Islamist turn by part of the Islamist movement enabled the Islamization of the higher echelons of Egyptian society. This in turn enabled the development of pious markets for leisure and art, thus facilitating the return of religious performers. The pious artists were also backed by the change in religious discourse on art, in particular by the emergence of the discourse on "art with a mission."

In the new millennium, there thus developed an extensive field of religiously inflected art accommodating religious sensibilities and promoting pious taste cultures. The religious taste cultures of the affluent classes were also influenced by global cosmopolitan forces coming from both the West and the Gulf. A pleasant post-Islamist style had in the meantime become available as an alternative to all audiences. There thus developed a fragmented market that balanced different combinations of religious missions and pleasant, un-demanding, recreation.

The revolution has given an impetus for art, particularly for forms that address political issues. Observers were not optimistic about the coming of power of the Muslim Brothers in Egypt and the collapse of the "secular" state for the field of art. Many feared for restrictions in the freedom of expression, including artistic expressions, and are happy with the fall of Mursi after one year.

These anxieties rest upon two assumptions: first, the idea that the state was the protector of "enlightened" art, and, second, that Islamists will restrict art. As we have seen in this chapter, these suppositions—although powerful discursive strategies during the Mubarak era, which are presently current as well—are not necessarily an accurate description of the realities on the ground. The former state was not only the protector of "secular-enlightened" art, but also responsible for the Islamization of the public sphere. The Islamists—without denying the existence of restrictive views on art and limited room for aesthetics outside a religious scope among some strands of Islamists—have also experienced transformations toward moderate and "clean" artistic formats among other strands.

Abu Haiba and other artists have been on the vanguard of these developments. In the polarized climate during the one-year reign of Mursi, Abu Haiba found no time and money to engage with the Islamic art and media project. After Mursi's ousting, however, he returned to art and published two novels.[25] Whatever the direction of the current political developments, it is to be expected that the field of art will closely reflect and foreshadow Egypt's ongoing transformations.

NOTES

1. Interview with author, 19 December 2011.
2. "Masr 25" is named after the date of the revolution on 25 January 2011.
3. Interview with author, 24 June 2013.
4. E.g., Kertzer (1997), Mintz (1982), Ginzburg (1980).
5. This is a fragment from the documentary by El-Mokadem "Pop Goes Islam" about Abu Haiba and the Islamic fashion model Yasmin Mohsin.
6. Interview with author, 4 November 2010.
7. Standard Arabic.
8. Interview with author, 4 November 2010.
9. 'Adil Imam is one of the most famous Egyptian actors. He is known for his anti-Islamist critiques and films mocking Islamists, such as Al-Irhabi (1994).
10. Interview with author, 4 November 2010.
11. The Sunna is considered the second most important source of Islamic Law after the Qur'an and describes the practices of the Prophet and his companions.
12. The Islamic journal for women and children, al-Zuhur magazine, had organized an annual conference on the topic "art with a mission" on 7 April 2007. Abu Haiba was one of the invited speakers.
13. The importance of culture, art, and media is addressed in an episode of his program, "Life Makers."
14. Interview with author, 4 November 2010.
15. Anchor and author, known for his anti-Salafi stance and his critiques on the Sauditization of Egypt ('Issa 1993).
16. Interview with author, 19 December 2011.
17. http://religion.info/english/articles/article_519.shtml. Accessed 24 February 2011.
18. http://religion.info/english/articles/article_519.shtml. Accessed 24 February 2011.
19. http://www.almasryalyoum.com/en/node/483504. Accessed 6 August 2011.
20. http://muftah.org/?p=1071. Accessed 20 June 2011.
21. Gilman. http://norient.com/video/martyrpop/comment-page-1/#comment-3897. Accessed 5 May 2011.
22. Interview with author, 24 June 2013.
23. Interview with author, 24 June 2013.
24. Live update at 21.12 ahramonline and personal observation as I happened to be

in Egypt during the events. http://english.ahram.org.eg/NewsContent/1/64/75594/Egypt
/Politics-/Live-updates-Egypt-tense-as-army-deadline-looms-.aspx.

25. http://www.dailynewsegypt.com/2015/03/15/review-of-novel-land-of-the-gypsies/.
Accessed 14 June 2015.

REFERENCES

Abaza, M. 2010. "The Trafficking with *Tanwir* (Enlightenment)." *Comparative Studies of South Asia, Africa and the Middle East* 30, no. 1: 32–46.

al-Qaradawi, Y. 1998. *Diversion and Arts in Islam*. Cairo: Islamic Printing and Publishing Company.

———. 2001. *The Lawful and the Prohibited in Islam*. Cairo: El-Falah.

Armbrust, W. 2002. Islamists in Egyptian Cinema. *American Anthropologist* 104, no. 3: 922–931.

Baker, R. W. 2003. *Islam without Fear: Egypt and the New Islamists*. Cambridge, MA: Harvard University Press.

Bayat, A. 1998. "Revolution without Movement, Movement without Revolution: Comparing Islamic Activism in Iran and Egypt." *Comparative Studies in Society and History* 40, no. 1 (January 1998): 136–169.

———. 2009. *Life As Politics: How Ordinary People Change the Middle East*. Palo Alto: Stanford University Press.

De Koning, A. 2009. *Global Dreams: Class, Gender, and Public Space in Cosmopolitan Cairo*. Cairo: American University of Cairo Press

Denis, E. 2006. "Cairo as Neo-Liberal Capital? From Walled City to Gated Communities." In *Cairo Cosmopolitan: Politics, Culture, and Urban Space in the New Globalized Middle East*, edited by D. Singerman and P. Amar. Cairo: American University of Cairo Press.

Frishkopf, M. 2011. "Ritual as Strategic Action: The Social Logic of Musical Silence in Canadian Islam." In *Muslim Rap, Halal Soaps, and Revolutionary Theater: Artistic Developments in the Muslim World, edited by* K. van Nieuwkerk, 115–149. Austin: University of Texas Press.

Ginzburg, C. 1980. *The Cheese and the Worms: The Cosmos of a Sixteenth-Century Miller*. Baltimore: John Hopkins University Press.

Haenni, P. 2005. *L'islam de marché: L'autre révolution conservatrice*. Paris: Seuil.

Hirschkind, C. 2006. *The Ethical Soundscape: Cassette Sermons and Islamic Counterpublics*. New York: Columbia University Press.

'Issa, I. 1993. *al-Harb bi al-Niqab* [War with the Face Veil]. Cairo: Dar al-Shabab.

Kertzer, D. I. 1997. *The Kidnapping of Edgardo Mortara*. New York: Alfred A. Knopf.

Mahmood, S. 2005. *Politics of Piety: The Islamic Revival and the Feminist Subject*. Princeton: Princeton University Press.

Marshall, D. 1997. *Celebrity and Power*. Minneapolis: University of Minnesota Press.

Mehrez, S. 2008. *Egypt's Culture Wars: Politics and Practice*. New York: Routledge.

Mintz, J. R. 1982. *The Anarchists of Casas Viejas*. Chicago: University of Chicago Press.

Nooshin, L. 2009. "Prelude: Power and the Play of Music." In *Music and the Play of Power in the Middle East, North Africa and Central Asia*, edited by L. Nooshin, 1–33. Farnham, Surrey: Ashgate.

Ramzi, K. 1994. *From Extremism to Terrorism: The Relationship between Religious Groups and the Arts*. Cairo: LRRC Egypt, http://www.geocities.com/CapitolHill/Lobby/9012/Freedom/kamalmain.htm. Accessed 18 November 1999.

Shehata, D. 2010. *Islamists and Secularists in Egypt: Opposition, Conflict, and Cooperation*. New York: Routledge.

Sullivan, D. J., and S. Abed-Kotob. 1999. *Islam in Contemporary Egypt: Civil Society vs. the State*. Boulder, CO: Lynne Rienner.

Tammam, H., and P. Haenni. 2003. "Chat Shows, Nashid Groups and Lite Preaching: Egypt's Air-Conditioned Islam." *Le Monde diplomatique*, 3 September.

Turner, G. 2004. *Understanding Celebrity*. London: Sage Publications.

Van den Bulck, H., and S. Tambuyzer. 2008. *De celebritysupermarkt* [The celebrity Supermarket]. Berchem: EPO.

Van Nieuwkerk, K. 2013. *Performing Piety: Singers and Actors in Egypt's Islamic Revival*. Austin: University of Texas Press.

Vignal, L., and E. Denis. 2006. "Cairo as Global/Regional Economic Capital?" In *Cairo Cosmopolitan: Politics, Culture, and Urban Space in the New Globalized Middle East*, edited by D. Singerman and P. Amar. Cairo: American University of Cairo Press.

Wickham, C. R. 2002. *Mobilizing Islam: Religion, Activism, and Political Change in Egypt*. New York: Columbia University Press.

Wise, L. 2003. "'Words from the Heart': New Forms of Islamic Preaching in Egypt." M.Phil., Oxford University. http://users.ox.ac.uk/~metheses/Wise.html. Accessed 28 November 2006.

CULTURAL POLITICS AND BODY POLITICS

THIS SECTION NOT ONLY discusses cultural politics of states through censorship and control over cultural productions, whether secular or Islamic, but also how the body, gender, and Islamic morality are made to embody the body politic.

Christa Salamandra's chapter explores the role of television drama as a sophisticated genre imbued with political positions, social analyses, and philosophical observations. The virtual absence of locally produced cinema, widespread satellite access, and limited markets for books, theater, and the arts all channel the nation's creativity into fictional television. Drama has become the largest platform for creative endeavor through which Syria's intellectuals and artists disseminate a secular stance that is abandoned by the al-Asad regime in its efforts to co-opt Islamic revivalism. The rise of pan-Arab stations owned by wealthy, religiously conservative citizens and states of the Gulf Cooperation Council has swelled the industry, but it has also engendered a preference for Islam inflected or religiously acceptable material. Syria's largely secular and socially progressive drama creators must please these new markets and censors. This chapter examines the various strategies Syria's drama creators adopt to cope with—and prevail in—this new media environment. Some set their works in the golden ages of Islamic empire, or the old neighborhoods of early twentieth-century Damascus, folklorizing and relegating religion to an idyllic but safely distant past. Others turn to the contemporary world, Islamizing their critiques of Islam by promoting a liberal religiosity. A few creators continue to produce social realism with little religious reference, often to critical acclaim. All reflect a paradoxical mix of complicity and critique.

Laudan Nooshin's chapter discusses the emergence of a new kind of state-sanctioned "Islamic" popular music in Iran since the 1990s. The new local pop music (*pop-e jadid*) offered musicians a public platform to open up discourses around Islam. Nooshin examines the strategies by which the artists align their music with Islamic sensitivities and shows that musicians appear to go along with the official "public transcript" while subtly contesting dominant discourses on religion without appearing to do so. The chapter analyzes the ambiguous representations of Islam in the work of Ali Reza Assar, one of the most successful "new pop" singers, and Arian, a grass-roots mixed-gender pop band. The musicians tread a fine line between expressing ideas about Islam through musical forms often regarded as un-Islamic and seeking to create a space that allows for the contestation of dominant discourses on religion itself.

Ida Meftahi's chapter sheds light on the historical formation and the aesthetic configuration of female performing bodies in Iran. The intrusion of female sexuality into the public space and onto the theater stage, especially after the unveiling of 1937, raised new moral issues in Iran, resulting in the association of female performing bodies with immorality. With the advent of the Islamic Revolution of 1979, there was an immediate disruption of the performing art forms and venues that were deemed to be improper or signifying "prostitution" and "eroticism" — most of which involved women's bodies. The postrevolutionary genre of "rhythmic movements" (harikat-i mawzun), however, introduced a new public dancing body, one whose corporeal characteristics are sublime enough to enact the values of Islam and the revolution. To overcome the difficult task of sublimating the dancing subject into a chaste performer, a range of techniques and stage elements have been deployed. The costumes used in performances of rhythmic movements have been mostly black, white, or other muted tones, and loosely fitted so as to obscure the shape of the body. Music has also been used to de-eroticize the performer of rhythmic movements and the choreography is controlled. Reinforcing the image of a "proper" Muslim through embodying the expressions of heaviness, chastity, purity, and spirituality, the "purified body" of the performer thus enacts the bio-ideology of the government.

Shayna Silverstein's chapter explores how dance traditions in Syria are a site for the production of Muslim identity among youth. Though the state continues to endorse secular Arabism in ways that are reinforced by nationalistic and secularized modes of cultural production, Islamic identity has become increasingly popular. The ways in which women negotiate Islam and popular dance helps to illuminate the particularities of Islamic identity in the Bashar al-Assad era. This chapter details the way young Muslim women participate in dabke and how they situate themselves in public discourses on the body, gender, and Islamic morality through this popular dance. Female movements are central to the production of moral, modest, and pious identities.

The chapter especially focuses on dancing (or not dancing) by young Muslim women in public and private spaces, choices that not only establish moral frameworks but also assert a sense of agency. The chapter thus demonstrates that young Syrian women draw on public and private domains to strategically position themselves in the contested moral arena of popular dance.

This section thus highlights the importance of the field of Islam and popular culture for studying cultural politics of states and the crucial and contested ways the (female) body expresses and embodies religious, moral, and political values.

CHAPTER II

AMBIVALENT ISLAM: RELIGION IN SYRIAN TELEVISION DRAMA

CHRISTA SALAMANDRA

SYRIA — ITS LILTING ARAB DIALECT, classically trained actors, and dark, satirical realism — burst onto the newly expanded pan-Arab satellite airways in what has become known as the drama outpouring (*al-fawra al-dramiyya*) of the 2000s. Once country cousin to its larger and better-funded Egyptian counterpart, the Syrian TV industry helped to shape Arab popular culture in and for the new millennium. Building on an older generation's theatrical, cinematic, and televisual forms of political and social commentary, Syrian television creators broke new ground in their nation's leading cultural export: the thirty-episode *musalsal*, dramatic miniseries.

In the absence of participatory politics in Syria and much of the Arab world, drama has become a key arena of contestation over past and present, polity and society, one involving a paradoxical blend of complicity and critique. The politics of drama production reveal a complex interplay of state control and reformist impulse, and of secularism and religiosity, which endured through the war that began in 2011, with production remaining at half its pre-conflict level. Drama is still produced despite the difficult circumstances; they air amid rumors — and some evidence — of satellite network boycotts. Although subject to state control and social censorship, drama creators have expanded the boundaries of public discussion of Islam and religiosity. They have also upheld a secular stance abandoned by the al-Asad regime in its efforts to co-opt Islamic revivalism. This position, I argue, has engendered an enduring language of secular critique.

THE *MUSALSAL* THEN AND NOW

Eagerly anticipated and obsessively followed, drama is associated with Ramadan, when new serials air on consecutive evenings after fasting ends, and audiences partake in what has become one of the holy month's most popular secular rituals.[1] In Syria, the term "drama" has become synonymous with thirty-episode serials, even if comedic. Precursors date back to 1967, when TV pioneers Ghassan Jabri, Hani al-Rummani, and Faisal Yassiri produced the first Syrian Ramadan *musalsal, The Misers (al-Bukhala')*, a dramatization of ninth-century author al-Jahiz's classic *Kitab al-Bukhala'*.[2] Over the next forty years, a distinct Syrian television drama industry developed, with its own set of conventions and a range of subgenres, including historical, contemporary social, comedy, folkloric, and the science fiction-like "fantasy" *(fantaziya)*.

Poverty proved productive for Syrian drama creators. Unlike their well-established Egyptian counterparts, the Syrians lacked studios, stars, and other elements of infrastructure that would have built a more conventional television industry. Instead, Syrians brought cinematic techniques to TV drama, using a single camera—as opposed to the three of studio-based TV production—shooting on location, and relying on ensembles of well-trained actors in place of celebrities. "Director of the first beginnings" Ghassan Jabri first took his camera out of the studio and into the streets of Damascus with *Behind the Walls (Wara' al-Jidran)* of 1979. Moscow-trained filmmaker Haytham Haqqi, finding no outlet in Syria's minuscule cinema industry, followed suit in 1994 with part one of *The Silk Market (Khan al-Harir)*. Set in Aleppo of the 1950s, and largely filmed in this city's spectacular covered suq, this drama depicted a merchant class debating the merits of unification with Egypt and the loss of an elected parliament and domination by Damascus that this would entail. Viewers read it as an allegory of the present, and its screenwriter, acclaimed novelist Nihad Sirees, found his subsequent work censored.

Najdat Anzour, who emerged from Jordan's advertising industry, privileged the visual over the political in his early serials. Most TV makers, often themselves from urban backgrounds, have evoked the city, and particularly Damascus; Anzour moved to the rural locations that had been the preserve of Syrian filmmakers. His treatment of Hanna Mina's classic novel of rural life, *The End of a Brave Man (Nihayat Rajul Shuja')*, featured spectacular sweeps of Syria's coastal landscape, and an ethnographic attention to the detail of village life. These directors and others drew inspiration from European art-house films screened in the cinema clubs active in Syrian cities during the 1970s. Each developed a discernible style, but share a dark, gritty aesthetic that recalls Soviet social realism and Italian neorealism. Haytham Haqqi single handedly served as Syria's production academy, training an entire generation of directors whose works fed the boom years of the 2000s.

Syrians produced comparatively few dramas during the 1990s, even though economic liberalization had opened the door to private production. Pan-Arab television had yet to truly take off, and satellite access remained limited. The audience—and producers' imagined viewership—remained national. Earlier research on Arab drama reflected this national scale of production and consumption. Anthropologists and others have treated serials aired on Egyptian terrestrial television of the 1980s and 1990s, examining the production and consumption of specific programs at a time when national networks united national audiences in the act of watching and responding.[3] My own research on the series *Damascene Days* demonstrated how Syrian state-produced dramas of this period also addressed a local viewership. Their narratives seemingly designed to engender Syrian nationhood instead enhanced sectarian, regional, and class divisions, fault lines that have fed a lengthy civil war (Salamandra 1998, 2000, 2004). While these serials were sometimes purchased by and aired on various state-controlled television stations across the Arab world, their target audiences remained Egyptian and Syrian, respectively. With the spread of satellite technology, the pan-Arab scale has displaced the national in content and reception, as dozens of series vie for over a hundred million viewers.

In Syria, the drama outpouring grew from the convergence of persistent authoritarianism, neoliberal reform, and the expansion of satellite channels and access. While retaining its censorship apparatus, the Ba'thist state instituted privatization in 1991, a process accelerated when Bashar al-Asad took over the presidency upon his father's death in 2000. Private TV production companies mushroomed, and many of their owners enjoyed cozy relationships with the regime.[4] Pan-Arab satellite entertainment networks such as the Saudi-owned MBC and Dubai TV began to fill their long broadcast hours with Syrian drama serials. Restrictions on freedom of expression coupled with commercial expansion proved unexpectedly generative: Syrian drama harnessed intellectual energies that might otherwise have animated party politics, social movements, journalism, or academia. The virtual absence of locally produced cinema, widespread satellite access, and limited markets for books, theater, and the arts all channeled the nation's creativity into fictional television. For Syria's intellectuals and artists, drama now represents a mainstay of employment and the largest platform for creative endeavor. As a result, the thirty-episode dramatic miniseries has grown into a sophisticated genre imbued with political positions, social analyses, and philosophical observations. Many of these reflect the secular, progressive ideologies that Arab regimes abandoned and Islamic revivalism supplanted. In their dramas, Syrian TV creators reconfigure the global artistic idiom that has long given voice to progressive concerns: social realism. This endeavor reaches fullest expression in a key form, the contemporary social drama (*al-drama al-ijima'iya al-mu'asira*). Also extended to satire, Syrian drama's signature gloomy aesthetic is immediately recognizable in a satellite bouquet channel surf. It distinguishes Syrian productions from the glittery Egyptian melodramas that had long dominated Arab fictional television. Syria's gritty realism serves as a transnational register of critical commentary on Arab politics, society, and religiosity. It has also informed the explosion of satirical media emerging from oppositional sources during the conflict.

THE SERIAL AND THE STATE

The new millennium brought a shift in the industry's relationship with the Syrian state. Upon assuming power in 2000, Bashar al-Asad forged warm relationships with actors and directors, and overturned censorship committees on their behalf. This may have reflected an attempt to maintain control over the industry amid liberalization, but it also buttressed the glamorous image that the younger leader apparently sought to project.[5] Bashar expressed pride in the drama industry, purportedly boasting that foreign leaders have commended him for airing the critical satire on state television (Salamandra 2005). In turn, drama creators projected their hopes for change onto the persona of the new president. As with other reform-minded elites, they believed transformation would occur gradually. With his western education and British-born wife, Bashar al-Asad appeared the consummate modernizer, positioned to unravel the militarized police state that had grown over nearly four decades of Ba'th Party rule. He introduced a discourse of reform that industry people hoped would turn into practice. In his 2000 inaugural speech, Bashar emphasized a "desperate need to [sic] constructive criticism" and implied a move away from the Soviet-style restrictions on cultural and intellectual production that had characterized his father Hafsiz al-Asad's rule:

Reform and improvement are certainly needed in our educational, cultural, and information institutions in a way that serves our national interests and strengthens our genuine culture that leads in turn to undermine the mentality of isolationism and passivism and addresses the social phenomena that negatively affect the unity and safety of our society.[6]

As the reform process slowed and backfired, many drama creators blamed the so-called "old guard" for the lack of progress, and saw Bashar as a thwarted democrat distinct from, and hampered by, a fossilized regime with entrenched security structures and an outmoded personality cult.

The liberalization process was one aspect of the promised reform package that did proceed unabashedly, although it served best those with links to power, who enjoyed greater access to business licenses. As private television production companies flourished, public-sector production shrank. The leadership may have thought it had outsourced propaganda to private producers. Yet drama makers circumnavigated the regime's censorship apparatus through the satellite realm. Every serial filmed in Syria must submit a script for approval. Those sold to, or commissioned by, foreign stations skip a second stage of oversight; only series aired on Syrian channels need approval of the final product. The pan-Arab media ecology has effectively, if inadvertently, undermined the Syrian state's control of content. On occasion Syrians—and other Arab satellite viewers—viewed a sliced-to-shreds episode aired on Syrian state television while its uncut version appeared on a pan-Arab network the same evening.

Money now trumps Ba'thist ideology but imposes new conditions and constraints. Most television makers must now compete for funding from, and thus please, an equally exacting set of censors in the religiously conservative Gulf Cooperation Council states.[7] Gulf stations fund most series and receive exclusive rights for Ramadan broadcast in return. On occasion, private producers, often from the GCC, will fund series and subsequently market them to stations. Syrian producers argue that the lack of state financing exposes them to the caprice of Gulf business practice. While Egypt's foreign ministry has taken up the role of distributor, marketing packages of series to Gulf channels, the Syrian state has left its television makers to fend for themselves in a competitive market for coveted Ramadan first-run airings.

Despite the lack of state support—and continuing censorship restrictions—Syrian drama sells, finds vast audiences, and is taken seriously enough to provoke social, political, and diplomatic tensions at local, national, and international levels.[8] Yet their creators complain that their power to promote secular progressive agendas is waning under GCC domination of the television market; economic liberalization without democratization leaves them vulnerable to both Syrian state censors and Gulf buyers. It is difficult to gauge how pan-Arab audiences themselves view GCC influence on fictional television. Most of the major GCC stations operate through state subsidies or private patronage; few rely solely on advertising revenues. In addition, the *musalsal*'s structure—thirty episodes airing on consecutive evenings—would render ratings obsolete as soon as they appear.[9] It is GCC station managers, themselves often Arab expatriates, who select what is aired, but they are answerable to network owners. The leading Saudi and Emirati entertainment channels represent the socially liberal end of the Gulf's ideological spectrum, and their owners often find themselves at odds with state and nonstate conservative forces in their own countries.[10] Yet Syrian drama creators, like other secular Arab elites, conflate the conservative Islam of the Gulf ruling elites, and the political Islam of movements such as the Muslim Brotherhood, as forces against modernity and the modernization process.

Such dissatisfactions reveal a nostalgia for the original Ba'thist socialist project and the accompanying Syrian state support; they also point to an underlying faith in the benefits of a strong state, a belief that deregulation leads to disaster, and a fear that the form this disaster will take is political Islam. This concern underlies the support the al-Asad regime has enjoyed among some TV makers during the antiregime uprising that began in 2011. The leader's wartime supporters include those long critical of regime abuses. It also helps explain the reluctance of other drama creators to join the opposition. Industry figures employ a mode of expression akin to what Michael Herzfeld refers to as "structural nostalgia." In Herzfeld's formulation, both state and nonstate actors refer to an edenic age of harmonious social relations, a time before social disintegration and moral decay mandated state intervention. This imagining legitimizes accommodation with the state as a necessary evil (Herzfeld 1997: 109–138). Syrian television makers invoke what might be called a structural nostalgia in reverse, harkening back to a more recent era of state support for art, cushioning cultural producers from the vicissitudes of market forces, the taste preferences of satellite television executives, and what they see as a growing Islamization of public culture. As leading social drama screenwriter Najib Nusair puts it:

Drama began here with a group of intellectuals, who were working in the arts, with state support. They set up small companies [with liberalization in the early 1990s] but because of [the new need for] capitalist investment, they were really unable to make a go of it. Then along came the Gulf investors, they went either to the sons of those in power—Khaddam, etc.—and set up production companies. . . . When we have Gulf financing, and all Syrian drama depends on the Gulf market, this means we must abide by Gulf censorship conditions, in addition to our own censorship conditions. And it's well known that Saudi censorship is the most extreme. These conditions are present throughout the Arab world, but more so in Saudi. It's the matter of religion, involving women's modesty, the relationships between women and men, no touching, alcohol, foul language, everything in life. Because of this Syrian *musalsals* are sterilized, sterilized![11]

THE RISE OF ISLAM IN THE PUBLIC SPHERE

In much of the Arab world, notions of cultural authenticity are increasingly associated with Islam. In contemporary Arab intellectual discourses, authenticity, *asala*, is associated with religion and with revivalist Islam in particular, where it refers to fundamentalism in the literal sense, to a return to a pure Islam of scripture, of Qur'an and hadith, and the era of the Prophet Muhammad (Kubba 1999: 132). The conflation of authenticity with Islam is quintessentially modern, and marks a shift in recent Islamic thought, from the jurisprudential to the cultural and symbolic. The era of the Prophet Muhammad and early Islamic history form a model to be emulated. Much revivalist Islam adopts a method of authentication, *ta'sil*, reflecting the belief that the Qur'an contains a comprehensive guide to proper conduct for individuals, organizations, and governments (Al-Sayyid 1999: 109–110).

Constructs of Islamic authenticity have become the dominant mode of anticolonial, anti-imperial critique in Syria, as in much of the Arab world. The "clash of civilization" discourse permeates the region's intellectual and political climate; Arab intellectuals—including television drama creators—face pressure to defend their secular viewpoints against charges of westernization (Huntington 1998). This trend marks a reversal for leftist and liberal thinkers, many of whom once saw Islam as an impediment to modernization.[12] Just as Islamists reconfigure Islam in nationalist terms (Asad 2003), secularists inflect secularism with Islam. Drama series compete for audiences amid a transnational satellite "flow," to adopt Raymond Williams's term for the stream of television broadcasting that includes specialized religious channels and new-style Muslim preachers (1975).

In addition to promoting religious programming, both state and nonstate forces seek to cleanse the satellite airways of material deemed antithetical to Islamic mores. For example, the leader of Saudi Arabia's Supreme Judicial Council suggested that satellite television network owners who ignore warnings to remove "immodest" programs from the airways during Ramadan could face execution.[13] Drama makers self-censor treatments that might be considered Islamically inappropriate, and heed religiosity, but their versions of religion and Muslim polity and society often clash with the puritanism of Saudi Arabia's Salafi Islam and the conservative nature of Islamic revivalism. Marwan Kraidy describes a shift in Saudi Islamist discourse about television from a rhetoric of censorship to one of critical engagement (2013). Syrian drama has followed a similar trajectory. After years of avoiding religious reference, some have adopted a range of strategies to reconcile calls for Islamic authenticity and modesty with their own, largely secular, proclivities (Salamandra 2008).[14]

ISLAM AS FOLKLORE AND COSMOPOLITAN COSTUME HISTORY

Television serials serve as an important source of history for many Arabs. Big-budget historical epics set in the golden ages of Islamic empire—complete with elaborate period sets, luxurious costumes, and thunderous battle scenes— appear aligned with much revivalist and Islam-inflected anti-imperialism: they pit good and evil, Muslim community against foreign enemy. They also seem to support authoritarianism by depicting strong, heroic leaders. Yet by invoking al-Andalus (Islamic Spain), as director Hatim ʿAli has in a series of epics, dramas recreate a cherished—and partly imaginary—instance of Muslim tolerance. ʿAli's *Hawk of the Quraysh* (*Saqr Quraysh*) 2002, *Cordoba Spring* (*Rubiʾ Qurtuba*) 2003, *Petty Kingdoms* (*Muluk al-Tawaʾif*) 2005, and *The Fall of Granada* (*Suqut Gharnata*) 2007, join a host of other large-budget productions set in the distant past of Islamic Empire.[15] Dramas set in al-Andalus are seemingly designed to appeal to pan-Arab audiences and attract funding from conservative sponsors. Yet al-Andalus also offers an opportunity for subversive social and political commentary. It allows TV makers to reconfigure a cosmopolitan disposition within terms that are safely, Islamically authentic. As ʿAli puts it:

> I think we are on the brink of a true war of civilizations, one that is not limited to a battle of ideas, but is about to develop into a confrontation using traditional and probably not traditional weapons, in the future. In light of this, I began a project about the rise of the Andalusian state, which is probably a unique, exceptional experiment in the history of human kind, where you found, in one place on earth, Muslims of all ideologies, ideas, and aspirations, along with Christians—the original inhabitants of the land, and Jews. The presence of all of these in one place, in a democratic atmosphere, in a dialogue of civilizations, allowed for the establishment of one of the most important human civilizations, the Andalusian civilization, which was, I think, the gate through which Greek civilization entered what is today called Europe.[16]

Anzour adopts a similar strategy in *Ceiling of the World* (*Saqf al-ʿAlam*) 2007, contrasting the recent Danish cartoon controversy with a tale of tenth-century Muslim tolerance.

Folkloric dramas celebrate the customs and traditions of the bygone *hara*, the old city quarter. Director Bassam al-Malla employs this strategy to great success in *The Quarter Gate* (*Bab al-Hara*), Parts I–VII of 2006–2015. Al-Malla has been dramatizing Old Damascus since his 1993 *Damascene Days* (*Ayyam Shamiyya*), yet his more recent treatments feature lingering prayer scenes, depictions of pilgrimage, and exemplary sheikhs.[17] Audiences noted the series' religiosity. In an article posted on *islamonline*, Nabil Shabib, writing from Germany, argues that *The Neighborhood Gate*'s creators "were bound by neither a religious nor a secular position, but depicted the contradictions of both viewpoints at the same time."[18] Prominent Syrian cleric Salah al-Kuftaru "honored" the series and its creators for "returning us to morality, nobility, tradition and authenticity."[19] Kuftaru shared other critics' displeasure with *Bab al-Hara*'s passive, voiceless women characters, but also argued that the series did a "great service to Islam" by "confronting the aggressive Hollywood globalization that is commanding the attention of our young men and women."[20] Yet by associating Islamic references with a bygone era, al-Malla's work betrays a secularist agenda; making the *hajj* becomes, like wearing a fez or riding a donkey, an antiquated practice.

ISLAM AS ANTI-SALAFISM

Islam rarely features in Syria's most widely adopted dramatic form: contemporary social realism. Exceptions often garner considerable Arab and western media attention. In the controversial *al-Hur al-Ayn (The Beautiful Maidens)*, Najdat Anzour employs a strategy that secular cultural producers in the Middle East commonly adopt: contrasting a "good" Islam with an evil counterpart. Direct treatment of current events marks a departure for Anzour, who created the popular "fantasy" *(fantazya)* genre, fantastical adventure stories "with no time or place" *(la makan wa la zaman)*, in the late 1990s. The hype surrounding *The Beautiful Maidens*, in the Arab and western media and in conversations among television creators and critics, revolved around its terrorism subplot. While its condemnation of militant Islam echoes that of the Saudi state, the series also levies a powerful critique of Saudi society and its treatment of foreign Arabs, all of which are clearly linked to Salafi extremism. Anzour reveals a claustrophobic world of highly educated, upper-middle-class women who have left university study and successful careers in Jordan, Egypt, Syria, Lebanon, and Morocco to accompany their husbands to the Saudi kingdom, where restrictions on women in public life exceed those of any other Arab or Muslim majority nation. Most scenes take place in the luxurious yet sterile apartment complex to which the wives are largely confined. Pampered but bored, deprived of meaningful work and intellectual stimulation, torn from family support networks, they pester their husbands and betray each other. The hothouse environment renders wives vulnerable to their husbands' physical and emotional abuse. *The Beautiful Maidens* depicts terrorists perverting Islam, but also censures Saudi Arabia's religious custodianship.

Islamic references are infrequent and didactic. A few characters are shown praying, and all fast during Ramadan. An Egyptian professor's humanism provokes accusations of secularism and blasphemy but also attracts admirers and acolytes. Pondering the causes of terrorism over tea with a neighbor, the professor cites misunderstanding of Islam along with unemployment, poverty, and despair. Direct discussion of religion is largely confined to the minor subplot of a young man's religious radicalization. Fatherless and unemployed, the twenty-something Abdul-Rahim attends lessons with the gentle and aptly named Sheikh Abdul-Latif,[21] who emphasizes compassion, tolerance, and the common good, and denounces contemporary militants' understanding of jihad, a message too tame for Abdul-Rahim's explosive frustrations. A shadowy figure overhears the young man lamenting the plight of Palestinians, lures him from mosque to cave and then to a training camp. In the final episode, we see the young recruit driving an explosive-laden car through midday traffic in a Saudi city. Remembering the kind sheikh's words, he changes his mind and detonates the bomb in the desert. In the concluding shot, audiences learn—through voiceover and text—that a rehabilitated Abdul-Rahim has "returned to his society as a citizen, found work in a corporation, and attends lessons with Sheikh Abdul-Latif, in search of knowledge and the true path of Islam."

Other forms of Islamic revivalism are sometimes critiqued, and religious scholarship is used to censure revivalist practice. The growing women's piety movement in urban Syria features in director Hatim 'Ali's 2005 series, *Unable to Cry ('Asiy al-Dam'a)*. The serial refers to, but does not name, the Qubaysiyat, a network of home-based women's prayer groups. Here, secular critique of Islam is itself Islamized. The story, written by Ali's wife Dal'a Mamduh al-Rahbi, revolves around a promising young lawyer who files charges against a man who harasses her in the street. She draws on a wealth of textual knowledge to argue that abuse of women conflicts with correct interpretations of Islamic precepts. 'Ali himself plays her friend and would-be suitor, Samir, who cites both classical Islam—the acts and deeds of the Prophet Muhammad—and the early twentieth-century friendship between Christian writer May Ziadeh and Sheikh of Al-Azhar Mustafa 'Abd al-Raziq, to argue for a more progressive religiosity than that of his mother, leader of a piety group. The young judge advocates women's emancipation and debates the sharia's gender laws with his mother. Samir agonizes when forced to render decisions on custody cases that contradict his own belief—that Islamic law should evolve with changing circumstances—and sympathies, which lie with divorced mothers who lose their children upon remarriage. In the final episode, Samir resigns from the bench, unable to reconcile his own fluid religiosity with the rigidity of Syria's shariʿa-based personal status law. When a former colleague visits his newly opened clock repair shop and asks if he still enjoys fixing clocks, Samir ponders the metaphor:

> Sometime I watch people passing by, and I'm filled with despair. It's like our clock has stopped at the beginning of the last century—the same questions, and the same problems. Look around you, listen to a news broadcast, and judge for yourself. The modernization and reform projects, the search for identity, and I don't know what else, they all failed. Look at where we were, and where we are now: the ignorance, illiteracy, fanaticism, close mindedness (*inghilaq*), backwardness, and *takfir*.[22]

Like *Unable to Cry*'s hero Samir, drama creators operate in the space between the public they seek to reach and the state and nonstate forces that try to silence or exploit them. They also maintain notions of artistic integrity. Drama makers represent the state and speak through its institutions. Their works are broadcast in an increasingly Islamized public sphere. Yet many feel alienated from and disapprove of both secular Arab regimes and political Islam. The potential for co-optation, and the possibility of resistance, form an ongoing subject of debate among industry figures and audiences alike.

Anzour's own treatment of Islamic revivalism, 2010s *Ma Malakat Aymanukum*, is much more heavy-handed than Hatim Ali's. The title, literally, "what your right hand possesses," draws on a Qurʾanic reference to slavery. The serial follows the dilemmas of four young women, one of whom is a *munaqqiba*: a woman who wears a face veil. For some Muslims this practice reflects intense religious devotion; secular TV creators view it as retrograde extremism. The *munaqibba*'s brother, a fanatic, beats his sister over her romantic entanglement while conducting one of his own. Syria's officially sanctioned cleric Muhammad Ramadan al-Buti tried to get the series pulled, failed, but was compensated with his own TV station, which continued to air until his assassination in 2013.

ISLAM AS THE ABSURD

The serials discussed above, despite their renown, are exceptional among the works Syrians produce. Of the sixty episodes comprising the innovative *People in Love (Ahl al-Gharam)*, only two deal with religion. They offer no positive images to balance negative depictions of religious practice; instead they point to contradictions that impede intimate social relations. They were also the most discussed and acclaimed of the sixty stories. Aired on the Saudi-owned

MBC—the premier pan-Arab satellite entertainment network—*People in Love* departs from the usual continuous narrative of the conventional Arab TV drama; it consists of discrete, unhappily ending love stories. Leading Syrian writers scripted the individual stories that made up season one. For the second thirty-episode season, aired in Ramadan 2008, director Laith Hajjo and producer Adib Khair solicited viewer experiences, on the leading pan-Arab entertainment network. They received three thousand sad tales. Each story bears the title of a song by the legendary Lebanese singer Fairuz played periodically throughout and reflecting its theme.

Islamic law is the ideological target of Hajjo's *He's Still Cute (Ba'du Zharif)*, which recalls the Moroccan director Ibrahim Tazi's 1994 film, *Searching for My Wife's Husband*. This blackly comedic episode begins with a couple that have only just met awkwardly and unhappily signing a marriage contract, while a distraught man paces outside the courthouse. The circumstances behind this odd scenario are gradually revealed. Hisham, Nadia's frantic husband, had already divorced her twice in a fit of jealous rage, each time regretting his actions and renewing the marriage. When he flies into a tantrum at her choice of party outfit and divorces her a third time, Islamic law prevents him from remarrying her until she undertakes—and consummates—a marriage with another man. Nadia's uncle finds a willing groom, and the new couple has agreed to divorce the morning after the marriage contract is signed.

Nadia's husband for a night, the recently divorced Sharif, appears to suffer from obsessive-compulsive disorder. His awkwardness, what Uncle 'Adil refers to as "a lack of sociability," compounds the discomfort of the situation. He makes one well-meaning gaffe after another as he tries to welcome Nadia into his home. But the chill gradually warms as the pair exchanges their unlucky-in-love stories, and a mutual affection—even attraction—grows. A hysterical Hisham barges in to find the pair sharing what he called a "romantic dinner," and accuses them of breaking their agreement; the temporary coupling was meant to eschew intimacy. "What's this?!," he rages, "candles, tabbuleh, red roses?! Where are the glasses?! Why not pour a couple of drinks and really enjoy yourselves?!" Nadia pushes him out the door, while Sharif waits for her in the bedroom, caressing the nightgown she has laid out on the bed.

The next morning, Sharif wakes up to the sound of Fairuz singing, "He's Still Cute," and finds Nadia preparing coffee. She has lain awake all night; he has not slept so deeply in years. They sit down to breakfast, exchanging lovers' glances. Uncle 'Adil knocks, but Sharif hesitates, eyes welling, before he opens the door to sign the divorce papers that will return Nadia to Hisham. She pauses at the door, embraces her weeping soon-to-be ex-husband and comforts him with words "you're still cute."

The episode invokes a practice originally intended to prevent men from divorcing and remarrying their wives at whim to suggest the unsuitability of Islamic law to contemporary society. Its screenwriter, "The Silk Market" author Nihad Sirees, first titled the episode with the legal term, *khilwa*, for the requirement designed, he argues, "to punish the stupid husband" for his rash behavior. Sirees notes that modern day audiences took several scenes to understand the reason for the characters' ostensibly bizarre behavior. In conceiving the story, he sought to explore how "human beings find love in the strangest and most sensitive moments in their lives."[23] Sirees's lack of cultural specificity here is telling; small details point to a global modernity: Hisham's car is booted when parked illegally outside the courthouse, he relies on a mobile phone to interrupt the woman he still sees as his wife with another man. Sharif and Nadia lunch at a posh restaurant before retreating to Sharif's modern upscale apartment. The new couples' conversation about their failed marriages could take place almost anywhere: Sharif's wife never appreciated him and decided to emigrate, while Nadia would have left Hisham earlier had it not been for her children. The cosmopolitan setting and dialogue throws into relief what the episode's creators clearly see as the pre-modernity, even absurdity, of shari'a personal status laws.

The second episode focusing on religion broke new ground in openly condemning the social stigma of intersectarian marriage, and the limits and contradictions of Syria's religious tolerance. Leading screenwriter Najib Nusair's *Oh Virgin Mary* (*Ya Maryam al-Bakr*) depicts Muslim Fadi and Christian Lin as lifelong friends and neighbors. Their seemingly inseparable families dine together, celebrate each other's holidays, seek each other's advice, and encourage their children to disregard religious distinctions. As young adults, Fadi and Lin attend university together where, in a departure from the real, no women students wear the hijab (headscarf).[24] Yet when their friendship turns romantic, the pair fear discovery, anticipating their families' objections. When Fadi reveals the relationship to his parents, his father accuses him of selfishly trying to destroy the two families' thirty-year intimacy. "It's wrong (*haram*) to take this girl from her family and customs," argues Abu Fadi, "It's wrong to embarrass her family in front of their friends and relatives."[25] When Umm Fadi suggests that Lin's family might agree, her husband declares that he cannot ask his old friend for his daughter's hand because "I know my limits. Do you think we're living in Sweden?" "I wish," she replies, "she's like my own daughter." Lin's family also disapproves; she finds she cannot defy them. She decides to join her brother in Canada, and the last scene finds Fadi running after her airplane in a desperate but futile gesture.

The prominence of Christian cultural forms in *Oh Virgin Mary* reflects a secular orientation toward religious divisions. Lin sings in a church choir; key scenes feature haunting Arabic liturgical music and gilded icons. Cultural producers, like many other Syrians, value the presence of minorities as a mark of cosmopolitanism, and regard the relative sectarian harmony of pre-conflict Syria as a sign of national distinction. Drama creators generally stand against sectarian differences by aestheticizing religion. The notion of religious mosaic that western academics dismiss as essentialist is for them a source of national pride. On the small screen, Christianity becomes a metonym of Syria's religious diversity; foregrounding other minorities is more difficult. The ambiguous position of Syria's 'Alawi community — historically stigmatized, now controlling key al-Asad regime positions — renders a focus on 'Alawis particularly sensitive.[26] Drama creators sometimes refer to the departure of Syrian Jews as a national tragedy, yet the ongoing conflict with Israel precludes expression of this sentiment in their serials. "Oh Virgin Mary" complicates this self-perception of tolerance by juxtaposing a valorization of Christian aesthetics with a depiction of community endogamy that limits, indeed contradicts, this ethic. The serial's focus on Christianity enables critique of Islam in that it depicts sectarian marriage practices as social pathology.

CONCLUSION

Exploiting their limited autonomy, Syrian drama creators regularly test boundaries of public discourse on religion and society. They strive to meet the demands of state censors, al-Asad regime-linked producers, and Gulf-based buyers, while maintaining artistic integrity and social commitment. Television makers work through and around rigid state institutions. The forms of religiosity they condone seemingly reflect both Syrian and GCC state ideologies. However, given the range of viewpoints at play in the field of cultural politics, drama serials easily run afoul of powerful forces, including religious movements and authorities. As they find themselves compelled to address an Islamization of society and polity that they find alien, their answer has been an ambiguity open to subversive messages and readings. Strategies such as folklorizing Islam, aestheticizing religion, contrasting moderation with fanaticism, and exploring the contradictions of religious practice allow for subtle, yet powerful, forms of secular critique.

Syrian drama's language of critique has not been silenced by the violent conflict engulfing the nation since early 2011; the industry has managed to produce an average of twenty serials each year since the uprising began, roughly half of its production during the peak years of the drama outpouring. Many television creators now spend most of their time outside Syria, and some have found work in other Arab TV industries. Others return to film in Syria. Serials are shot in Damascus or neighboring Lebanon under arduous wartime conditions; they air despite Gulf boycotts. Beyond the reach of Syrian state-controlled production, Syrian drama's distinctively somber secular critique permeates the creative dissidence flourishing on the Internet and on oppositional television. Working from exile and through social media, a new generation of cultural producers inflects Syrian drama's dark, bitter aesthetic with revolutionary passion (Salamandra 2013).

NOTES

1. For more on the association of Ramadan with drama viewing, see Abu-Lughod 2005a; Armbrust 2002, 2005; and Salamandra 1998, 2004.

2. For a detailed analysis of Syrian drama's history, see Joubin 2013.

3. See, for instance, Abu-Lughod 1993, 1995, 1998, 2003, 2005a, 2005b; Armbrust 1996a, 1996b.

4. For a study focusing on the linkages between the Bashar al-Asad regime and television creators, see Della Ratta 2012.

5. An effort involving a public relations campaign that culminated in the infamously flattering *Vogue* magazine profile of First Lady Asma al-Asad, published weeks before the outbreak of protest and violent repression of March 2011.

6. http://www.al-bab.com/arab/countries/syria/basharooa.htm.

7. The Gulf Cooperation Council is composed of Saudi Arabia, the United Arab Emirates, Kuwait, Qatar, Oman, and Bahrain.

8. Salamandra, "Creative Compromise: Syrian Television Makers between Secularism and Islamism," *Contemporary Islam* 2, no. 3 (2008): 177–189; Salamandra, *A New Old Damascus: Authenticity and Distinction in Urban Syria* (Bloomington: Indiana University Press, 2004); Salamandra, "Television and the Ethnographic Endeavor: The Case of Syrian Drama." *Transnational Broadcasting Studies* 14 (Spring/Summer 2005), http://www.tbsjournal.com /Archives/Spring05/. abstractsalamandra.html, or http://www.arabmediasociety.com/topics /index.php?t_article=83; and Salamandra, "Moustache Hairs Lost: Ramadan Television Serials and the Construction of Identity in Damascus, Syria," *Visual Anthropology* 10, nos. 2–4 (1998): 227–246.

9. Author's interview with Rami Omran, Syrian advertising executive, 13 January 2007.

10. On the politics of pan-Arab satellite broadcasting, see Marwan Kraidy, *Reality Television and Arab Politics: Contention in Public Life* (Cambridge: Cambridge University Press, 2010).

11. Author's interview with Najib Nusair, 19 July 2006.

12. This is particularly true of Syrian intellectuals.

13. See *New York Times*, "Saudi Arabia: Clean TV Shows, or Else."

14. Salamandra, "Creative Compromise." For a discussion of Islamism in Egyptian media, see Lila Abu-Lughod, *Local Contexts of Islamism in Popular Media* (Amsterdam: Amsterdam University Press/ISIM Papers, 2006).

15. See Shoup 2005 for a detailed discussion of Andalusian series.

16. Author's interview with Hatim 'Ali, 7 January 2007.

17. For a discussion of *Damascene Days*, see Salamandra 1998 and 2004.

18. Nabil Shabib, "The Neighborhood Gate . . . and the Gates of Creativity" (bab al-hara. . . . wa abwab al-ibdaʿ), *islamonline.net*, 21 October 2007, http://www.islamonline.net/servlet/Satellite?c= ArticleA_C&pagename=Zone-Arabic-ArtCulture%2FACALayout&cid=1190886520200.

19. Hayyan Nayyuf, "Prominent Authority Criticizes the Depiction of Women: The Religious Trend in Syria Honors the Series 'Bab al-Hara'" (daʿiya bariz intiqada tariqat taswir al-nisa': al-tayyar al-dini fi suriya yukarrim musalsal bab al-hara), *alarabiya.net*, 11 October 2007.

20. Ibid.

21. Literally, "Worshipper of the Kind," one of the ninety-nine names of God.

22. *Takfir* is the practice of accusing fellow Muslims as heretics and threatening them with execution.

23. Author's interview with Nihad Sirees, 16 February 2014.

24. Armbrust 2012 discusses the erasure of the hijab from Egyptian cinema.

25. In this traditional form of Arabic nomenclature, parents are referred to as mother (*umm*) or father (*abu*) of their eldest son.

26. For more on sectarianism in Syria, see Salamandra 2004, 2012a, 2012b, 2013.

REFERENCES

Abu-Lughod, Lila. 1993. "Finding a Place for Islam: Egyptian Television Serials and the National Interest." *Public Culture* 5: 493–513.

———. 1995. "The Objects of Soap Opera." In *Worlds Apart: Anthropology through the Prism of the Local*, edited by Daniel Miller, 190–210. London: Routledge.

———. 1998. "The Marriage of Feminism and Islamism in Egypt: Selective Repudiation as a Dynamic of Postcolonial Cultural Politics." In *Remaking Women: Feminism and Modernity*, edited by Lila Abu-Lughod, 243–269. Princeton: Princeton University Press, 1998.

———. 2003. "Asserting the Local as the National in the Face of the Global: The Ambivalence of Authenticity in Egyptian Soap Opera." In *Localizing Knowledge in a Globalizing World: Recasting the Area Studies Debate*, edited by Ali Mirsepassi, Amitra Bassu, and Frederick Stirton Weaver, 101–127. Syracuse: Syracuse University Press.

———. 2005a. *Dramas of Nationhood: The Politics of Television in Egypt*. Chicago: University of Chicago Press.

———. 2005b. "On- and Off-Camera in Egyptian Soap Operas: Women, Television, and the Egyptian Sphere." In *On Shifting Ground: Muslim Women in the Global Era*, edited by Fereshteh Nouraie-Simone, 17–35. New York: The Feminist Press at City University of New York.

———. 2006. *Local Contexts of Islamism in Popular Media*. Amsterdam: Amsterdam University Press/ISIM Papers.

Al-Sayyid, Radwan. 1999. "Islamic Movements and Authenticity: Barriers to Development." In *Cosmopolitanism, Identity and Authenticity in the Middle East*, edited by Roel Meijer, 103–114. London: Curzon.

Armbrust, Walter. 1996a. *Mass Consumption and Modernism in Egypt*. Cambridge: Cambridge University Press.

———. 1996b. "The White Flag." *Mediterraneans* 8/9: 381–391.

————. 2012. "Dreaming of Counterrevolution: Rami al-I'tisami and the Pre-Negation of Protest." *Cinema Journal* 52, no. 1: 143–147.

Asad, Talal. 2003. *Formations of the Secular: Christianity, Islam, Modernity*. Palo Alto: Stanford University Press.

Bilal, Mazen, and Najib Nusair. 1999. *Syrian Historical Drama: The Dream of the End of an Era (al-Drama al-Tarikhiyya al-Suriyya*: Hilm Nihiyat al-'Asr). Damascus: Dar al-Sham.

Della Ratta, Donatella. 2012. "Dramas of the Authoritarian State." *MERIP* (February). http://www.merip.org/mero/interventions/dramas-authoritarian-state.

Dick, Marlin. 2007. "Syria under the Spotlight: Television Satire that is Revolutionary in Form, Reformist in Content." *Arab Media and Society* 3. http://www.arabmediasociety.com/countries/index.php?c_article=120.

Herzfeld, Michael. 1997. *Cultural Intimacy: Social Poetics in the Nation-State*. New York: Routledge.

Huntington, Samuel P. 1998. *The Clash of Civilizations and the Remaking of the World Order*. New York: Simon & Schuster.

Jubin, Rebecca. 2013. *The Politics of Love: Sexuality, Gender, and Marriage in Syrian Television Drama*. Lanham, MD: Lexington Books.

Kraidy, Marwan. 2010. *Reality Television and Arab Politics: Contention in Public Life*. Cambridge: Cambridge University Press.

————. 2013. "Saudi-Islamist Rhetorics about Visual Culture." In *Visual Culture in the Modern Middle East*, edited by Christiane Gruber and Sune Haugbolle, 275–292. Bloomington: Indiana University Press.

Kubba, Laith. 1999. "Towards an Objective, Relative and Rational Islamic Discourse." In *Cosmopolitanism, Identity and Authenticity in the Middle East*, edited by Roel Meijer, 129–144. London: Curzon.

League of Arab States. 2008. *Arab League Satellite Broadcasting Charter*. Unofficial English translation, March 2008. *Arab Media and Society*. http://www.arabmediasociety.com/?article=648.

Nayyuf, Hayyan. 2007. "Prominent Authority Criticizes the Depiction of Women: The Religious Trend in Syria Honors the Series 'Bab al-Hara'" (da'iya bariz intiqada tariqat taswir al-nisa': al-tayyar al-dini fi suriya yukarrim musalsal "bab al-hara"), 11 October, alarabiya .net.

New York Times. 2009. "World Briefing: Middle East. Saudi Arabia: Clean TV Shows, or Else," A8, September 13.

Salamandra, Christa. 1998. "Moustache Hairs Lost: Ramadan Television Serials and the Construction of Identity in Damascus, Syria," *Visual Anthropology* 10, nos. 2–4: 227–246.

————. 2000. "Consuming Damascus: Public Culture and the Construction of Social Identity." In *Mass Mediations: New Approaches to Popular Culture in the Middle East and Beyond* edited by Walter Armbrust, 182–202. Berkeley: University of California Press.

————. 2004. *A New Old Damascus: Authenticity and Distinction in Urban Syria*. Bloomington: Indiana University Press.

————. 2005. "Television and the Ethnographic Endeavor: The Case of Syrian Drama." *Transnational Broadcasting Studies* 14 (Spring/Summer). http://www.tbsjournal.com/Archives/Spring05/abstractsalamandra.html, or http://www.arabmediasociety.com/topics/index.php?t_article=83.

————. 2008. "Creative Compromise: Syrian Television Makers between Secularism and Islamism." *Contemporary Islam* 2, no. 3: 177–189.

————. 2012a. "Prelude to an Uprising: Syrian Fictional Television and Socio-Political Critique," Jadaliyya (May). http://www.jadaliyya.com/pages/index/5578/prelude-to-an-uprising_syrian-fictional-television.

————. 2012b. "Reflections on Sectarianism in Syria." Anthropology News (November). http://www.anthropology-news.org/index.php/2013/06/20/reflections-on-sectarianism-in-syria/.

————. 2013. "Sectarianism in Syria: Anthropological Reflections." Middle East Critique 22, no. 3 (2013): 303–306.

Shabib, Nabil. 2007. "The Neighborhood Gate . . . and the Gates of Creativity" (bab al-hara. . . . wa abwab al-ibda). islamonline.net, 21 October. http://www.islamonline.net/servlet/Satellite?c=ArticleA_C&pagename=Zone-Arabic-ArtCulture%2FACALayout&cid=1190886520200.

Shoup, John. 2005. "As It Was and Should Be Now: al-Andalus in Contemporary Arab Television Dramas." Transnational Broadcasting Studies 1, no. 2: 191–198.

Williams, Raymond. 1975. Television and Cultural Form. New York: Schocken Books.

CHAPTER 12

DISCOURSES OF RELIGIOSITY IN POST-1997 IRANIAN POPULAR MUSIC

LAUDAN NOOSHIN

THIS CHAPTER EXPLORES the problematic relationship between notions of religiosity and certain forms of popular music in Iran. The post-World War II period was marked by rapid processes of westernization and modernization, with which popular music became closely associated. Following the nationalist Revolution of 1979, popular music was targeted and banned by the new Islamic regime as representing both a form of western cultural imperialism and a potentially corrupting influence on young people due to its associated erotic dance movements, mixed-gender socializing, and so on. For almost twenty years popular music remained underground. And then, as part of the cultural thaw that followed the election of President Mohammad Khatami in May 1997, it started to enter the public domain once again, eventually leading to a renewed local popular music industry. As part of this, pop artists started to draw on overtly religious themes and present themselves in a manner compatible with Islam. One factor in this was the permit system operated by the Ministry of Culture and Islamic Guidance [Vezārat-e Farhang va Ershād-e Eslāmi] by which all music in public (performances and recordings) requires government approval.[1] Another was that artists sought to reach a demographic beyond the westernized middle and upper classes that had tended to be the main consumers of popular music in Iran. At the same time, since the dominant government discourses for the previous two decades had branded popular music as "un-Islamic," there remained an unresolved tension between the image of the pop singer and dominant discourses around religiosity. Some artists—such as Mohammad Esfahani, one of the first and most successful pop stars of the post-1997 period—managed this tension fairly unproblematically. Others used the opportunity to foreground alternative visions of Islam that did not necessarily accord with those promoted by the government. This subtle contestation was evident both in artists' presentation of self, as well as in their music and lyrics.

This chapter discusses some of the ambivalent discourses around religion within Iranian popular music since the late 1990s. I start with the historical context in order to understand the significance of the more recent changes, and then move on to discuss the work of musicians who have in different ways explored the tension between popular music and Islam.

THE HISTORICAL TRAJECTORY

One of the things that intoxicate the brains of our youth is music.
Music causes the human brain, after one listens to it for some time,
to become inactive and superficial and one loses seriousness . . .
Of course music is a matter that everyone naturally likes, but it
takes the human being out of the realm of seriousness and draws
him toward uselessness and futility. . . . A youth that spends most
of his time on music becomes negligent of life issues and serious
matters, and becomes addicted — just like someone who becomes
addicted to drugs. . . . There is no difference between music and
opium. Opium brings a sort of apathy and numbness, and so
does music. If you want your country to be independent, from
now on you must transform radio and television into educational
instruments — eliminate music.
AYATOLLAH KHOMEINI, FROM A SPEECH TO STATE RADIO EMPLOYEES,
JULY 1979. CITED IN SIAMDOUST 2013: 27[2]

On 1 April 1979, less than two months after the revolution that overthrew the monarchic rule of Reza Shah Pahlavi, Iran was declared an Islamic Republic. The culmination of several decades of social unrest and opposition to the Shah—widely regarded as a "puppet" of the West, particularly Britain and the United States—the revolution only became possible through a massive popular uprising that brought together a broad spectrum of political and religious groups. The Shah fled Iran on 16 January 1979, and on 1 February Ayatollah Khomeini—exiled since 1963 and to whom many religious revolutionaries looked for leadership—returned to Iran. In the power vacuum that followed the demise of the Shah's regime, Khomeini's timely return provided the revolution with a figurehead that, even many who were not in favor of religious rule felt had to be supported in order to defend the fledgling and still vulnerable revolution. So it was that in a referendum on 30 and 31 March, Iranians chose overwhelmingly to vote for the establishment of an Islamic Republic.[3] From the start, the new regime set about establishing the principles by which all aspects of social, legal, and cultural life would be governed according to Islamic sharia law, specifically in line with Shi'ah Islam as practiced

in Iran and the state religion since the seventeenth century. A new constitution
was adopted on 3 December 1979, replacing the constitution of 1906 that had
served to limit the powers of the monarchy for the first time in Iranian history.
As Papan-Matin observes:

> The new [1979] constitution was to guarantee that the monarchy was abol-
> ished and the Islamic system of government was enforced in its place. The
> constitution was to observe the Islamic and the nationalistic aims of the revo-
> lution with regard to the demands of a public that came from various social,
> religious, ethnic, and political backgrounds. (2014: 159)[4]

From the start, however, there was much debate over what an Islamic public
sphere might look like, particularly in an increasingly globalized world. By
1979, Iran was a modern, industrialized nation with a sizeable middle and
upper class who were cosmopolitan in outlook, increasingly secular in lifestyle, many educated in the West, and so on. However, there was also an immense economic and social gulf, brought about in large part by uneven economic development and distribution of oil wealth under Pahlavi rule, between
the westernized middle and upper classes and the more conspicuously religiously observant urban and rural poor; indeed, it was partly this gulf that
created the political tensions that led to the revolution and the hope of a more
egalitarian future.

One of the challenges of the revolution was to meet the aspirations of those
for whom it meant different things. The constitution refers to the "Islamic and
the nationalistic aims of the revolution." But was the revolution primarily a
movement for self-determination whereby Iran would reclaim control of its
own internal affairs? Was it a revolution of the oppressed that would lead to
greater social and economic equality? Or was it—as the emerging agenda of
the new regime increasingly became aligned with—a revolution whose aim
was to establish a state based on Islamic principles?

Certainly, there were tensions from the start between Khomeini's vision of
a pan-Islamic community beyond Iran's borders, and the strongly nationalistic
and anticolonial sentiments of the revolution. Issues of both national and religious identity have long been contested in Iran and, as I have discussed elsewhere (Nooshin 2005), music has often served as a forum for playing out and
"performing" such identities. There is a further dimension to this discussion:
the branch of Islam practiced in Iran—Shi'ism—emerged as the state religion
under Safavid rule in the early seventeenth century, at a time when the Safavids
were seeking to forge a national identity, if not necessarily in the modern form
of the nation-state. As such, Shi'ism has long had strong nationalist associa-

tions in Iran, having played an important role in unifying the nation during the Safavid period and distinguishing Iran from its Turkish and Arab neighbours. While practiced elsewhere, the particular brand of Shi'ism found in Iran is distinctive, evoking notions of nationhood.

As a cultural domain contested within Islamic orthodoxy for many centuries, music was particularly affected by the changes after 1979, and the earlier quotation from Ayatollah Khomeini gives a flavor of the kinds of discourses circulating at this time. And yet attitudes toward music were complex, as evidenced by the fact that the government (itself strongly divided on questions of cultural policy) used music for its own purposes. What the above quotation illustrates, however, is the kind of discourse that dominated the public sphere at the time of the revolution and has continued to do so, with varying degrees of severity.

Revolutionary anthems and such were regularly broadcast on the radio during the 1980s, and although live concert performances were rare in the early years of the revolution and life in general was not easy for musicians, certain kinds of music were tolerated to some extent. However, other types of music were prohibited altogether, specifically "western" — primarily European and North American — popular music and commercial mass-mediated Iranian popular music (see Nooshin 2005, 2009).[5] Euro-American popular music had arrived in Iran on the wave of modernization and westernization that followed World War II, and by the 1960s there was a growing local popular music industry, heavily influenced by western music, fashion, and image. For the regime of Reza Shah Pahlavi, seeking to develop Iran into a modern, secular, nation-state and a regional power, this music aligned well with official discourses that denigrated aspects of traditional culture, notably religion, and promoted the idea of tradition as regressive and incompatible with modernity. In this context, popular music came to symbolize the pro-western aspirations of the regime and was strongly promoted. As a result, and in reaction to this, popular music was banned after 1979, both because of its close association with the Shah's regime and because it was deemed to represent a form of western cultural invasion, and moreover potentially detrimental to young people with its "un-Islamic" lyrics and associated activities such as drinking and sensuous dancing. Many musicians left Iran, eventually settling in Europe or the United States. Los Angeles became the center of an expatriate music industry, which also served a thriving black market at home. In Iran, many continued to listen to popular music in the privacy of their homes and cars — both music from before 1979 and that purchased through the black market and later satellite channels and eventually the Internet (see also Hemmasi 2011). But this was not without risk.

So it was that for almost twenty years—until the cultural thaw of the late 1990s—popular music had no legal public presence in Iran, and there was no local popular music production.[6] While the central discussion of this chapter concerns the re-emergence of popular music into the public domain after 1997, examining the broad historical trajectory allows one to understand how popular music in Iran has been closely entwined with, and deeply affected by, sociopolitical change since its arrival in the 1950s. From the late 1990s, the emergence of a new kind of state-sanctioned popular music offered a public platform for musicians to open up discourses around Islam, and specifically for some to appear to go along with dominant discourses on religion while at the same time subtly contesting them. This aligns closely with the kinds of "hidden" transcripts discussed by James P. Scott (1990), which enable those in positions of relative weakness to make their voices heard in ways that fly under the radar of the state apparatus, and which stand in contrast to openly oppositional "public transcripts."

An important issue concerns the various contestations over questions of identity in Iran, whether between national and religious, between modernist and traditionalist, or between mainstream and more marginal Sufi-inflected interpretations of Shi'ism. Such binaries have been central to the ways in which identities have been negotiated and understood in Iran for more than a century.

It is instructive to compare the case of music with that of film, which like music was a contested art form at the time of the revolution, viewed as religiously unacceptable and branded as morally suspect and a form of western cultural imperialism (see also Nooshin 2005: 252–253). Several cinemas were subject to arson attacks, the most notorious being the burning of Cinema Rex in Abadan in August 1978 and the deaths of almost five hundred people. In the early 1980s, however, the government realized that it could mobilize this medium for its own purposes and began to support the training of film-makers with a view to building up a body of practitioners, particularly for the making of what came to be known as the "holy defense" films during the Iran–Iraq war (see Varzi 2006; Khosronejad 2012). Ironically, it was this support for the local film industry that led in the late 1980s to the emergence of a new generation of filmmakers who started to make their mark on the international stage in a way that the government could not have foreseen.

What is of interest here is the differential treatment of film on the one hand and popular music on the other. While the former was adopted and one might say domesticated on the government's terms—harnessed to serve a particular agenda—the latter was denigrated and banned; the former was within their control, the latter was not.

THE EMERGENCE OF AN ISLAMIC POP MUSIC IN IRAN

In late 1997, six months after the landslide election victory of reformist President Mohammad Khatami, Iranian popular music re-entered the public domain after almost twenty years of prohibition. The move was led by the national broadcasting organization, Seda o Sima, with a new brand of music that soon became known as *pop-e jadid*("new pop"). But very soon the cultural thaw of the late 1990s led to the re-emergence of an independent popular music industry and a mushrooming of popular music, both in the public domain (that is, with government permits) and—without permits—underground.

In the early years, Seda o Sima promoted a form of pop music that was Islamically acceptable. One perhaps cannot describe it as pious, but certainly it featured suitable lyrics as well as modest dress and demeanor—and when shown on television, minimal body movement was demanded of singers. Further, there emerged a new focus on religious themes and symbolism (see also Meftahi, this volume). While it is the case that some pop singers prior to 1979 made subtle references to religion, particularly following in the Persian mystical tradition whereby expressions of spiritual devotion often indirectly invoke more worldly pleasures, this was more often at a personal level, and explicit references to Islam were rare.

In this chapter, I present two case studies: Ali Reza Assar, one of the most successful "new pop" singers promoted by Seda o Sima in the late 1990s; and Arian, a grass-roots mixed-gender pop band whose first album, *Gol-e Aftab-gardoon* [The Sunflower, 2000], propelled them to national stardom. Both Assar and Arian began working in the early Khatami period and have functioned "above ground" with government permits in contrast to many other popular musicians who have chosen or been forced to work underground, without a permit. In each case I discuss how musicians negotiate the tricky terrain between popular culture and Islam.

ALI REZA ASSAR: "EVERY NIGHT I CALL 'YAHU'"

Among the initial crop of singers cultivated and promoted by Seda o Sima in the late 1990s was Ali Reza Assar (b. 1969). His music was widely disseminated on radio and television and he has remained one of the most popular singers of this generation. A central aspect of Assar's work is the prominence of Sufi symbolism, notably the setting of texts by medieval mystic poets such as Mowlana and Hafez.[7] As with many of the new pop singers, Assar sought to lend a certain gravitas to his music by using the kind of poetry traditionally associated with Iranian classical music. Certainly Assar's choice of poetry attracted an audience thirsty for a popular music with a stronger local flavor than the imported diaspora pop music, which was all that had been available for the previous two decades and which appeared increasingly disconnected from life in Iran (see Nooshin 2005; Siamdoust 2013: 136).

In this section I focus on one of Assar's songs—perhaps his most popular—in order to consider some of the issues arising from the discourses of religiosity, both in the music itself and in the persona presented by Assar. "Ghodsian-e Aseman" [Angels of the Sky] is the first track of Assar's 1999 debut album, *Kooch-e Asheghaneh* [Loving Migration] (see also Nooshin 2005: 251–252). The lyrics are by Mowlana with music by Assar's close collaborator: composer, arranger, and saxophonist Fouad Hejazi. There is a band with guitars, keyboards, drum kit, and so on, a large orchestral string section and backing choir, and a large section of *daff* frame drums. The piece starts with a strongly rhythmical instrumental introduction that has become so well known that in live performances, audiences usually only need hear the first three notes before recognizing the song and bursting into applause.[8] The lyrics, delivered in a declamatory style, reference the caravans of traders, pilgrims, and other travelers traversing the plains and deserts. The protagonist declares himself as—not a highway thief (man dozd-e shab ro nistam)—but a hero (man pahlevaan-e aalam-am); and every night I call God's name (yahu zanam).

The song received extensive radio and television airplay around the time of the Iranian New Year in March 1999, and with it—and the interviews, concerts, and so on that followed—Assar was projected to national consciousness. It remains his best-known song.

What is interesting about this song is that while it emerged in the context of a government-approved, religiously nuanced pop music of the late 1990s, it foregrounds elements of Islam, specifically references to Sufism, that are somewhat problematic in the context of the "mainstream" Shi'ah Islam sanctioned by the state. While Sufism has not been prohibited under the Islamic Republic, many Sufi practices are regarded with suspicion and sometimes-outright hostility, most obviously in relation to the use of music—and particularly instruments—and ecstatic practices. But the situation is complex, and some members of the religious establishment are sympathetic to Sufi philosophy even as they are ambivalent about some of the practices.

For those familiar with Iranian Sufism, the references in "Ghodsian-e Aseman" are immediately apparent: the setting of mystical Sufi poetry; the *daff* frame drums, an instrument closely associated with Sufi practice; the *zekr*-like chanting of the chorus, including invoking the name of God (yahu)—*zekr* being a form of chant used by Sufi groups to induce a state of ecstatic union with God; as well as Assar's self-presentation—the beard and long hair, the simple dress, the gestures including outstretched arms with palms turned upward, and the sombre demeanor (see Nooshin 2005).

Certain aspects of the music do align more closely with "mainstream" Islamic sonic practice. For instance, the original version of the song included a section performed by Mohammad Esfahani, already an established singer and perhaps the quintessential clean-cut "new pop" singer. Recordings of more recent concert performances of this song illustrate Esfahani's florid vocal melismas that reference both the classical tradition and also religious recitation, the original training ground for many classical singers.[9]

The process of gaining government permission to perform live or produce a commercial recording is a lengthy and convoluted one. In the late 1990s it was still difficult to gain permits for popular music, which had long been absent from the public domain and had to conform to certain principles of Islamic modesty and propriety, both in the music, the lyrics, and artist presentation. From the point of view of the Ministry of Culture and Islamic Guidance that issues permits, Assar's work was clearly considered to conform (enough) to those principles and to the "public transcript" of Shi'ah Islam. At the same time, through his references to Sufi practice and philosophy, Assar presents a subtle challenge to normative understandings of Islam as promoted by the state. After many centuries of one form of authoritarian rule after another, Iranian artists of all kinds, from poets to musicians to visual artists, have become adept at seeming to work within a system while challenging it from inside. As James P. Scott observes in his book *Domination and the Arts of Resistance: Hidden Transcripts*, "every subordinate group creates, out of its ordeal, a 'hidden transcript' that represents a critique of power spoken behind the back of the dominant" (1990: xii, cited in Siamoust 2013: 9–10). While the relationship between the "public" and the "hidden" is rarely aligned along a simple binary, in the absence of an open debate on the nature of Islam in Iran, the notion of "hidden transcripts" is useful for understanding how music and other arts offer a space for negotiating alternative visions of Islam. Thus, elements such as the mystical poetry, the *daff* frame drums, and Assar's self-presentation form part of a "hidden" transcript indexing Sufism, in contrast to the state-sanctioned "public transcript" of Shi'ah Islam.[10]

Assar's popularity can arguably be attributed in large part to his offering a form of religious musical experience that many listeners understand as a genuine and authentic expression of grass-roots faith, in contrast to the Islam of the state. By drawing on long-standing codes of devotion, Assar has invoked a "softer" presentation of Islam that in the late 1990s resonated well with the mood of a nation emerging from a long period of cultural austerity, and appealed particularly to a generation of young people increasingly interested in different forms of spirituality, including various new-age philosophies from outside Iran (see also Siamdoust 2013: 137).

I would suggest, therefore, that Assar's music came to serve as an icon of difference: on the one hand, it marked the difference between a more personal and spiritual Islam and the more political Islam of the state; and on the other a local musical expression that contrasted with the imported diaspora pop. In relation to the latter, for those who had shared the experience of living through two decades of war and associated austerity (1980s and 1990s), the new period of liberal reform drove the search for more local forms of expression in touch with life in Iran.

An interesting aspect of Assar's image is how it has been connected by some to one particular religious figure: Imam Ali, the son-in-law of the Prophet and according to Shi'ah Islam his rightful successor. Ali is the most revered figure in Shi'ah Islam after Mohammad and in Iran is the subject of great devotion, particularly as a symbolic defender of the oppressed. In nongovernmental public spaces such as shops and restaurants, one almost invariably sees a picture of Ali as well as the Prophet. Siamdoust explains how the popularity of "Ghodsian-e Aseman" was "aided by the fact that it was played frequently on national media at the time of *Eid-e Ghadir*, the holiday honoring the birth of Shi'ah Islam's Imam Ali, leading to the perception that the song commemorated him" (2013: 136). Further, a more specific iconic connection has been drawn with Ali, a connection that is partly validated through Assar's family heritage as someone who claims to be a "seyyed" (descendent of the Prophet) (see Siamdoust 2013: 90). An interesting example of this is a music video posted on YouTube by one Mostafa Allahyari in which images directly referencing Ali and his life, and the early history of Islam, alternate with pictures of Assar singing. The video is a curious pastiche of culturally dislocated images with no obvious connection to Iran and which it isn't possible to discuss further here; what is significant, however, is that at several points Assar is shown positioned within the same holy circle as that used for Ali and his distinctive two-bladed sword, Zolfaqar. In this way, Assar is presented as in some sense embodying a certain kind of religiosity and a direct connection with Ali.[11]

In the fifteen years since his debut album, Assar has maintained a fairly consistent persona, unlike some of his contemporaries who have moved toward a more upbeat and less conspicuously religious style. And yet, despite his popularity, Assar has deliberately avoided cultivating a high-profile public presence, particularly where that might suggest a close association with government organizations (see also Siamdoust 2013). Through his music, his choice of lyrics, his personal image, and strategic decisions about where and when to perform, Assar has managed to maintain a certain ambiguity about his position that has enabled him to appeal both to audiences who look for social comment in his songs as well as those who are attracted to the more spiritual side of his music (see also Siamdoust 2013: 199).

ARIAN BAND: "OUR BELOVED ALI"

The figure of Imam Ali provides a nice segue into another example of how musicians have negotiated the intersection of popular music and Islam in Iran. The Arian Band was formed in 1998 and was the first mixed-gender pop band to come to public prominence during the Khatami reform period. There is a core of nine band members, including three women: backing vocalists Sahar and Sanaz Kashmari and guitarist and composer Shahrareh Farnejad.[12] Arian's songs deal with a range of topical themes, with an emphasis on wholesomeness and family values (Nooshin 2009). For example, the song "Madar" (from their first album *Gol-e Aftabgardoon*, 2000) glorifies the self-sacrificing mother. "Mowla Ali Jan," from the same album, is dedicated to Imam Ali and was written by the band's lead singers, Ali Pahlavan and Payam Salehi. The (translated) lyrics to the first verse are as follows:

> *Ali, Ali . . .*
> *Our beloved Ali . . .*
> *Our spiritual master Ali . . .*
>
> Verse:
> *You are in the heavens*
> *Where are you from?*
> *You are from up above, from God*
> *You hear the pains of your friends*
> *Your color and fragrance are the best, from God*
> *Like the stars in the cosmos*
> *You are in every time and every place*
> *You are a brave comrade for the defenseless*
> *You are a relief for our spirit and peace for our body*
> *Oh, king of men, etc.*

And the song continues by describing Ali's sacrifice for his religion and as a helper for those in need. Originally available as a sound recording, Arian have since posted a rather kitsch music video of the song on YouTube.[13] The comments appended to this clip are very interesting, not least in demonstrating the strength of attachment to Ali and the level of emotion he evokes among Iranians. One Iranian respondent commented:

> [1370809013708090, 2009] This is song that Arian band made in 1997. For the first time in our history we have a happy song about a religious charactor [sic] which is great . . . I mean can you imagine how many people who are not religious love this song? I think they also chose the right person . . . We Iranians love Ali, he is kind of special for us and this song makes us even closer to him.

To which a non-Iranian listener responded:

> You shia's are very strange people . . . you make more songs about imam Ali and imam Hossein than you do about prophet Mohammad (PBUH).[14]

Indeed. In fact I would argue that both this song and "Ghodsian-e Aseman" engage a distinctly Iranian religious sensibility, whether in the deployment of Sufi codes or in the reverence for Ali as the central hero of Shi'ah Islam.

As with the earlier example, this meeting of popular music and Islam prizes open new spaces for contesting dominant discourses. I would like to focus on two points: the role of women in the band and discourses of modernity versus religious tradition. Arian was the first pop band in Iran in which women were foregrounded, particularly guitarist-composer Sharareh Farnejad. The opening image on the video is a close-up of Farnejad's hands playing the guitar, even before the viewer knows that the guitarist is a woman. The camera then pans up to her face as she lifts her head and looks straight at the viewer, directly contravening traditional ideas about female modesty in Iran that include averting the eyes. Farnejad is then transformed into a lantern-bearing figure searching for Imam Ali, and it is to her that he appears at the end of the video.

The central role of women in the song and the video—including a close-up of Farnejad singing and her positioning as guitarist at the center of the group—contrasts with official discourses around women and music in Islam generally, and in the case of Iran specific policies, which since 1979 have served to control the activities of female musicians (see Youssefzadeh 2004). This includes a prohibition on female solo singing in public, except to all-female audiences. Group singing is permitted but there are stipulations (that vary periodically) on the minimum number of voices required for a performance or recording permit. Partly as a result of this, there has been an extraordinary growth of female instrumental talent since 1979 and in general women are much more active musically than before the revolution. In the case of Arian, the prominence of women in a song with such obvious religious connotations is significant and might reasonably be read in a similar way as the use of Sufi symbols by Assar: as a subtle questioning of the normative position of Islam vis à vis women and music and a challenge to the antimusical rhetoric of so much official discourse in Iran. This has not been lost on audiences, seen for instance in the heated debate prompted by the YouTube posting concerning the permissibility of singing about Ali in a performance that also includes instruments and women performers.[15] Here are some examples of comments since 2008:

[javedabidi, 2009, in reply to KhomeiniFollower] salam u praise this video which contain haram musical instruments it is shame to take name of imam ali (a.s) by this way. your name is khomeinifollower do imam khomeini (r.a) allowed this way. please reply

[Askari, clearly not an Iranian listener from the greeting, 2012] Salamu aleikum :) Are this kind of music allowed i islam?

This prompted a more general discussion about whether music is *halal* (allowed) or *haram* within Islam. Javedabidi commented:

yes there is no problem with religious song BUT with haram musical instruments it will be HARAM. i know its a iranian band not a rock band BUT IT RESEMBLE LIKE WESTERN ROCK BAND

This leads nicely to the second point: this video doesn't just push at boundaries in relation to gender, but also challenges the tendency for official discourses in Iran to position religion and modernity in a mutually exclusive binary relationship. Here we see young men singing about Imam Ali dressed in leather jackets and sporting long hair of a rather different and more suggestive kind than Assar, particularly the violinist Siamak Khahani and the unidentified guest guitarist: a modernized and cosmopolitan youth, prompting comments such as the following:

[KavehAhangarirani, Iranian, 2008] The Guys seem to live in the 1970s hair style (Jason King and company); can you see anyone with that hair style anywhere in the world today? Let alone singing about the most charismatic person in Shia Islam? Ali would cut them into half with Zolfaghar if he was alive today. I spare the girls. Does Ali need them? Does anyone need them? Are they good for anyone? Signed; Little Black Fish.

In contrast, the following listener clearly picks up on and values the cosmopolitan cross-cultural connections:

[acerb45666555, 2008] cool!! its like Spanish-Persian fusion!

Unlike the men, the women in the video are modestly dressed, as though the singing and playing of instruments has sufficiently stretched the limits in relation to gender.

It is difficult to assess the extent to which songs such as "Mowla Ali Jan" are rooted in the musicians' personal convictions, and to what extent they are strategically aimed at helping to secure a permit, particularly since the song appeared on Arian's debut album (2000) before they became well known and at a time when securing a permit for popular music was still fairly difficult. It's clear from the video that, like Assar, Arian are seeking to convey an authentic expression of faith. While musicians are understandably unforthcoming on their motives, this embedding of religious discourse and symbolism in popular music serves partly as a validating mechanism and a way for musicians to present themselves as upholding traditional values, particularly given the earlier polarizing discourses that separated popular music and Islam.

This new confluence of what were previously presented as incompatible domains appears to be having an impact on audience demographics. The re-emergence of a local industry in the late 1990s afforded pop music a wider social acceptance, attracting listeners beyond the cosmopolitan, secular-oriented middle and upper classes who had previously, by and large, been the primary consumers of Iranian pop. A 2002 DVD of an Arian concert includes interviews with audience members in the foyer, and we see women enveloped in black chadors—and therefore from quite religious families—who would previously have been extremely unlikely to have attended such events.

CONCLUSION

What do the various discourses of religiosity discussed in this chapter tell us about the intersection of popular music and Islam in Iran since 1997? The reform period saw the meeting of two domains that had hitherto been kept firmly apart by the polarizing discourses of those in power, whether before 1979, or, for different reasons, after. None of the musicians discussed here use solely religious themes or define their work as a whole in religious terms; on one level, what I have described can perhaps be understood as serving to validate a problematic form of musical expression, and more pragmatically, as a means of oiling the wheels of the permit system. While Seda o Sima and the Ministry of Culture and Islamic Guidance sought to encourage Islamic sensibilities, musicians had to tread a fine line, expressing religious sentiment through an artistic medium (music) long contested by Islamic orthodoxy and a musical style (western popular music) presented in Iran as problematically un-Islamic.

This chapter has considered some of the strategies by which musicians have negotiated this tricky terrain. In general the use of music to invoke God unsettles its characterization as a morally suspect activity, and it is clear that the confluence of Islam and westernized popular music remains a conflicted domain, always potentially a site for ambiguous representations of and subtle contestation of dominant discourses on religion and a place to raise questions about Islam itself, whether in relation to its own margins (for example, Sufism), in relation to gender issues, or the place of religion in modernity.

While the old binaries that position western cultural forms as antithetical to Islamic religious expression remain potent, I suggest that the various discourses of religiosity considered here offer a means by which musicians can challenge and bridge the divide, taking popular music in Iran beyond some of the discourses of alterity in which it and its meanings have long been caught up.

NOTES

1. See Siamdoust (2013) and Yousefzadeh (2000) for further discussion of the permit system. Siamdoust provides the most comprehensive overview to date of the permit and regulation systems in relation to music in Iran.

2. Siamdoust's doctoral thesis, "Iran's Troubled Tunes: Music as Politics in the Islamic Republic," is a study of the intersection of popular music and politics in Iran in the post-1979 period. Chapter 3 provides the most detailed discussion to date of Ali Reza Assar's early career and some of the factors that led to his emergence as one of the most popular singers of this period (2013: 129–137, 184–207). Encountering Siamdoust's work after the primary research for this chapter had been undertaken, I found that many of her ideas on Assar aligned with my own findings, with the addition of further contextual information.

3. The choice on the ballot paper simply being "yes" or "no" for an Islamic Republic. Further discussion of the broader context and events leading up to the Iranian Revolution lie beyond the scope of this chapter. For more detailed information, readers are referred to: Keddie (1981), Parsa (1989), Chehabi (1990), Farhi (1990), and Martin (2000), among others.

4. Papan-Matin (2014) is a translation of the 1989 edition of the Constitution of the Islamic Republic of Iran, indicating the changes made from the original 1979 version.

5. There are many kinds of traditional popular music in Iran, but for the purposes of this chapter "popular music" refers broadly to commercial mass-mediated music. I use the terms westernized or western-style popular music to distinguish this from more traditional forms of popular music.

6. See Nooshin (2005).

7. Jalāl ad-Dīn Muhammad Balkhī (1207–1273)—generally known in Iran as Mowlana and outside Iran as Rumi—is one of Iran's most beloved poets. His poetry has become

popular in translation in many parts of the world in recent years due to a growing interest in Sufism and mysticism more generally. According to some reports he is one of the most widely read poets in the United States.

8. This can be heard in the following performance from a concert held in Tehran in 2001, http://www.youtube.com/watch?v=pRN7o_T2Nks. For Assar's official site, see http://www.alirezaassar2.com/. For his fan site: http://assarfans.com/Newspage.aspx?nid=1129.

9. See http://www.youtube.com/watch?v=j-xfc6bXLfs.

10. This point is also discussed in Siamdoust 2013.

11. See https://www.youtube.com/watch?v=5AyRkbK6oHo. The comments section on YouTube includes some quite offensive and xenophobic (anti-Arab) comments by Iranians that it is not possible to discuss further here. For a detailed discussion of Shi'ism in Iran, see Dabashi 2011.

12. For further information on the band, see http://www.arianmusic.com/.

13. http://www.youtube.com/watch?v=R9DHWr5nROg.

14. http://www.youtube.com/watch?v=ATYllRF_Aj8.

15. Some of the specific comments on women and music have been removed since I undertook the initial research for this chapter in 2012, http://www.youtube.com/all _comments?v=R9DHWr5nROg.

REFERENCES

Chehabi, Houchang E. 1990. *Iranian Politics and Religious Modernism: The Liberation Movement of Iran under the Shah and Khomeini.* Ithaca: Cornell University Press.

Dabashi, Hamid. 2011. *Shi'ism: A Religion of Protest.* Cambridge, MA: Harvard University Press.

Farhi, Farideh. 1990. *States and Urban-based Revolutions: Iran and Nicaragua.* Urbana: University of Illinois Press.

Hemmasi, Farzaneh. 2011. "Iranian Popular Music in Los Angeles: A Transnational Public beyond the Islamic State." In *Muslim Rap, Halal Soaps, and Revolutionary Theater,* edited by K. van Nieuwkerk. Austin: University of Texas Press.

Keddie, Nikki. 1981. *Roots of Revolution: An Interpretive History of Modern Iran.* New Haven: Yale University Press.

Khosronejad, Pedram. 2012. *Iranian Sacred Defence Cinema: Religion, Martyrdom and National Identity.* Herefordshire: Sean Kingston.

Martin, Vanessa. 2000. *Creating an Islamic State: Khomeini and the Making of a New Iran.* London: IB Tauris.

Nooshin, Laudan. 2005. "Subversion and Counter-subversion: Power, Control and Meaning in the New Iranian Pop Music." In *Music, Power and Politics,* edited by Annie J. Randall, 231–272. London: Routledge.

———. 2009. "'Tomorrow Is Ours': Re-imagining Nation, Performing Youth in the New Iranian Pop Music." In *Music and the Play of Power in the Middle East, North Africa and Central Asia,* edited by Laudan Nooshin, 245–268. Farnham, Surrey: Ashgate.

Papan-Matin, Firoozeh. 2014. "The Constitution of the Islamic Republic of Iran." 1989 Edition, English translation. *Iranian Studies* 47, no. 1: 159–200.

Parsa, Misagh. 1989. *Social Origins of the Iranian Revolution.* New Brunswick, NJ: Rutgers University Press.

Scott, James C. 1990. *Domination and the Arts of Resistance: Hidden Transcripts*. New Haven: Yale University Press.

Siamdoust (Seyedsayamdost), Nahid. 2013. "Iran's Troubled Tunes: Music as Politics in the Islamic Republic." PhD thesis, University of Oxford.

Varzi, Roxanne. 2006. *Warring Souls: Youth, Media, and Martyrdom in Post-Revolution Iran*. Durham, NC: Duke University Press.

Youssefzadeh, Ameneh. 2009. "The Situation of Music in Iran since the Revolution: The Role of Official Organizations." *British Journal of Ethnomusicology* 9, no. 2: 35–61.

———. 2004. "Singing in a Theocracy: Female Musicians in Iran." In *Shoot the Singer! Music Censorship Today*, edited by Marie Korpe, 129–134. London: Zed Books.

CHAPTER 13

SACRED OR DISSIDENT: ISLAM, EMBODIMENT, AND SUBJECTIVITY ON POST-REVOLUTIONARY IRANIAN THEATRICAL STAGE

IDA MEFTAHI

WHILE THE ABSENCE OF public female performers in Iran prior to the twentieth century has often been linked to Islam and its restrictions on women, cross-dressing for the enactment of female roles—even for religious purposes—also has had its own antagonists, namely Islamic clergies and secular nationalists of the early twentieth century. The intrusion of female sexuality into the public space and onto the theater stage (especially) after the unveiling of 1937 raised new moral issues in Iran, resulting in the association of female performing bodies with immorality, corruption, "eroticism" (*shahvat*), "prostitution" (*fahsha*), and "degeneration" (*ibtizal*). Informing the revolutionary discourse, these responses were largely instigated by the "enticing" image of the dancing subject of the popular entertainment scene of cabaret during the Pahlavi era (1926–1979). The postrevolutionary genre of "rhythmic movements" (*harikat-i mawzun*), however, introduced a new public dancing body, one whose corporeal characteristics are sublime enough to enact the narratives of Islam and the revolution.

This chapter sheds light on the historical processes of the formation and the aesthetic configuration of silent performing bodies on the postrevolutionary theatrical stage. It first situates the emergence of the genre in the immediate postrevolutionary cultural context and it's the discourse of "committed" arts; further, the chapter explores its transformation into a vehicle for visualizing holy figures and "eternalizing" the revolutionary narratives. Ultimately, the chapter examines the genre as a confluence of multiple (and often conflicting) prerevolutionary performative and ideological constituents that have shaped the form and its chaste dancing bodies.

13.1. Shams-i Paranadah (the Flying Shams, 2000); Directed by Pari Saberi; Choreographer Nadir Rajabpur; Photographer Farshid Saffari.

THE RE-EMERGENCE OF DANCE IN THE POSTREVOLUTIONARY COMMITTED THEATRICAL SCENE

With the advent of the Islamic revolution of 1979, there was an immediate disruption of the performing art forms and venues that were deemed to be improper, or that signified "prostitution," "eroticism," and "degeneration"— most of which involved women's bodies. These included the cabaret scene; popular theater, and music featuring dance and women's solo voice; as well as all forms of public dancing. Consequently, the former state-sponsored National Ballet Company and National Dance Company (Iran National Folklore Organization) were also dissolved, and their members were dismissed or offered work within the Ministry of Culture as actors or office employees (see Citron 1989: 20; Shirvani 1979: 1–2).

The purging of the theater stage was a longer process. Nonetheless, in the politically active theatrical milieu of the immediate postrevolution era, themes reflecting the sociopolitics of the day, including the revolution, anti-imperialism, and Islam, as well as the Iran–Iraq war, became inspirations for artistic endeavors (see figures 13.2 and 13.3).[1] With the settling of the new Islamic state and the purging of the art sphere in the process of "cultural revolution" (inqilab-i farhangi), the question of the ways the arts could serve the revolution—meaning the new state—came to the foreground of the new government's cultural planning. Arts and culture were identified as the means for

13.2. In Fasl Ra Ba Man Bikhan (Read with me this chapter!, 2009); Directed by Hussein Parsa'i; Choreographer Nadir Rajabpur; Photographer Farshid Saffari.

"eternalizing" the revolution—which later materialized as the state (Khatami 1987: 523; Mazlumi 1996: 80). The prerevolutionary concept of committed art was also integrated into the state's discourse. While a range of terms, including "religious art" (*hunar-i dini*), "Islamic art" (*hunar-i islami*), and "doctrinaire art" (*hunar-i maktabi*), were used in this discourse, the new notion of "committed art" (*hunar-i muti'ahhid*) was positioned to merge and depict Islam as both a religious and political ideology (for instance, see Mazlumi 1996: 83). Such a fusion of Islam, politics, and the arts was, however, a prerevolutionary phenomenon that had entered into the religious cultural realm of Iran, especially through the teachings of Ali Shari'ati (1933–1977)—the Islamic-Marxist ideologue of the revolution (Qadiri 1990). The postrevolutionary committed art promoted by the state, however, had to embody and promote the state's ideology, instead of subverting the power (Burji 1996: 283; Hujjat 1982: 354). In this historical context, the notion of "art for art's sake," and indeed all other performing-art forms of the prerevolutionary era, were distrusted as degenerate (Hujjat 1982: 355).

In this discourse, theater was especially found to be an appropriate and effective medium for visualizing and eternalizing the narratives of the revolution, and the Iran–Iraq war (1980–1988), as well as a means for exporting the revolution and for "awakening the impoverished nations of the world" (Hashimi-Rafsanjani 1987: 547). The ritualistic roots of theater were used to justify its religious functions, while *ta'ziyah*—the Iranian/Shi'i religious performative drama—further vindicated the theater's capacities for fostering the state ideology, revolution, and the war, all of which discursively deployed Shi'i metaphors and motifs (Mukhtabad 1996: 383).

Adopting revolutionary values was regarded as a means for "popularizing" theater and for making peace between traditional and religious sectors of the society and actors—who were presumed to have held a social stigma prior to the revolution (Khatami 1987: 527). Women's recruitment to the stage in this discourse was to "create awareness" and showcase "healthy" arts instead of depicting corruption and "lewdness"—a term used to refer to the representation of women in the prerevolutionary era (Burji 1996: 311). Women's presence onstage was linked to their participation in the revolutionary scene and the postrevolutionary society; thus, as articulated by the Mahdi Hujjat, a state authority in arts, the "cabaret dancers" (*raqqas*) could not be shown onstage as no *raqqas* existed in the society anymore (Hujjat 1983: 58).

Within a few years religious and the Holy Defense (referring to the Iran-Iraq war) performances became established genres with festivals, expertise, and publications. In the meantime, tasked as a committed art, rhythmic movements (*harikat-i mawzun*)—a renamed and reshaped notion of dance—permeated these scenes.[2] Gradually, this new movement-based genre became a common means to stage stories of the holy figures of Shi'i Islam (such as Ali, Fatimah, Husayn, and Zaynab), their highly regarded followers (including Muslim Ibn-i 'Aqil and Hurr), and in particular, stories of the 'Ashura (the day the third Shi'i Imam and seventy-two of his companions were martyred in 680 CE in Karbala).[3] Produced in varying lengths, these performances have also been commissioned for different purposes by governmental organizations.

In the meantime, as sequences within the plays, *harikat-i mawzun* gradually found more dominance, especially in mystical plays, those of which provided the groundwork for a combination of Iranian mystical music, poetry, and dance. In the absence of a distinct dance scene, such combination had a popular reception.

With the state's support, and after years of attempts at staging religious narratives, theorization of these themes and characters became a new venture for committed scholars and practitioners. One of the main issues was to adapt traditional and community-based performances to the contemporary stage setting for an audience more attuned to contemporary technology.

The topics and questions prevalent in this discourse include: (1) What is religious theater? (Furutan 2006: 87),[4] (2) What topics and historical periods can it cover? (3) What is the purpose of it? Is it to commemorate the heroes? Or does it presume to create heightened emotion and thus purification in the audience? (Abbasi 2006: 17), (4) How can Qur'anic narratives be translated to the stage? (Salari 2008), (5) What are the dramatic capacities of the stage for presenting unearthly characters?, and (6) How might one make these themes accessible and attract younger audiences through the use of contemporary theatrics (Furutan 2006: 91)?

Among such theoretically inclined writers, Hasan Bayanlu viewed the element of "wonder" (*shigifti*) as a commonality between religious narratives and the theater stage (Bayanlu 2006). He argued that the stage could enhance time and space between the other, invisible world and the material world, both of which are embedded in religious narratives (ibid.: 41). He attested that the stage can be used to present religious plots, superhumans including the mystics and prophets, and invisible beings, such as angels and Satan; the "forcible" (*qahir*) manifestation of God on earth; and those hyper-real (*fara-vaqi'yat*) and mystery elements of religious narratives (ibid.: 142, 63). To him, the holy figures embodied wonder and drama: they seldom made mistakes, they were aware of the invisible and unknown and communicated with angels, and they suppressed their "evil-inciting sel[ves]" (*nafs-i 'ammarah*). Their prayers, mortification, and self-disciplining exceeded those of regular people (Furutan 2006: 72, 114, 82, 89, 86).

Other writers discussed the ways stage design can enhance presenting the metaphysical and spiritual aspects of religion and improve audience responses by triggering their potential sensitivity toward religious performative forms and symbols (Furutan 2006: 86). For instance, Sirus Kahurinejad, a stage designer who worked in this genre, asserted that the design for these performances should include both a physical image onstage and a mental image in the audience members' minds, especially when depicting a metaphysical character such as the Prophet, whose face may not be illustrated (quoted in Furutan 2006: 116).

It is within this discourse that the rhythmic movements genre has become an essential element of contemporary religious theatrical stagings. Being deployed as a mobile set, rhythmic movement has been enhancing the scenic affects of the plays. In the meantime, acting as a chorus, it has been contributing to mood creation and intensification of the emotional response in the audience, especially in scenes that require "mystical" or "heroic" ambience.[5] Moreover, it has improved the presentation and sensory appeal of holy figures and otherworldly beings, such as Satan and angels in religious narratives, as well as the scenes pertaining to the (Iran–Iraq) war and the Revolution (see "Intiqad az" 2013). Meanwhile, in the absence of a distinct dance scene, the rhythmic movements genre has been presenting dancing bodies onstage, thereby attracting audiences (Sadiqi 2008: 71).

PREREVOLUTIONARY ELEMENTS OF
RELIGIOUS RHYTHMIC MOVEMENTS

The postrevolutionary genre of rhythmic movements is arguably a construct largely informed by the prerevolutionary performative modes and mediums as well as the lived experience and ideas of visible dancing bodies in public. Among the key pre-twentieth-century inspirational sources for rhythmic movements are the vernacular theatrical genre of *ta'ziyah*, and the Muharram mourning processions for the deaths of the Third Shi'i Imam Husayn.

As a religious dramatic form, *ta'ziyah* had its own highs and lows prior to and throughout the twentieth century. Genealogically, it has often been traced back to the mourning ritual processions that began in the tenth century, but it was during the Safavid dynasty (1501–1722), which established Shi'i Islam as the state religion in Iran, that the Muharram rite received royal encouragement. The Qajar era (1794–1925) has been regarded as the "golden age" of *ta'ziyah* as when it was professionalized as a theatrical form (Shahriari 2008: 33). While *ta'ziyah* is a religious performative form, the occasional entrance of Qajar kings into the religious narratives, as well as the implementation of comedic elements into the performances in that era, prompted a negative response from the clergy of the time (Sarsangi 2010: 310). A particular clerical issue with *ta'ziyah*, as one can speculate from contemporary clergies' responses to the form, has been the cross-dressing of men in order to portray women (Husayni *Ahkam-i Nigah* 2010: 111–115; Burji 1996: 287–305; Shahriari 2008: 34).

Likewise, the early twentieth-century nationalist-modernists were also against the cross-dressing of male actors, known as *zanpush*, in the traditional Iranian vernacular forms of *ta'ziyah*, as they were perceived to be embodying an ambiguous sexuality that was not perceived as conforming to the ideals of modern Iran (Meftahi 2014). Furthermore, the intelligentsia held *ta'ziyah* as a ceremony that caused and exhibited Iran's backwardness. This secularist-nationalist ethos was then echoed by Reza Shah Pahlavi who, in 1928, banned the form (Gaffary 1984: 317). *Ta'ziyah* was then marginalized to being performed in remote rural areas (Sarsangi 2010: 312). This situation drastically changed in the 1960s and 1970s due to a nativist movement known as "return to the self," as well as the international overtures toward *ta'ziyah* bringing the genre to the locus of the attention of scholars, artists, and the state as a national theatrical expression. *Ta'ziyah*'s fortune continued after the revolution as the religious theater became a constituent of the government's cultural programming, and the genre's metaphors began to be deployed in day-to-day politics, including during the Iran–Iraq war.

Another performative element of rhythmic movements, as explored else-where (Stellar 2011), has been national dance. The transmission of ideas and aesthetics of national dance in rhythmic movements was made possible by the national dancers of the prerevolutionary era who stayed in the theatrical milieu and struggled to shape their dance forms to fit the criteria of the new milieu. Borrowing from literature, historical imaginations, folk culture, and ancient symbols, national dance was an invented tradition that was constructed to meet the demand for a national high art form and to visualize narratives of the nation onstage. Replacing the cross-dressing male dancers of previous eras, the female national dancer distantiated herself from the transgressive sexuality of the *raqqas* of the popular cabaret stage (Meftahi 2014).

Sharing continuity with national dance, and adapting to the postrevolu-tionary theatrical situation, the performer of rhythmic movements appropri-ates selected elements from the religious and vernacular performances while presenting a chaste body. She also distantiates herself from the dancing sub-ject of the popular entertainment scene of cabaret who signified the corporeal characteristics of eroticism and degeneration, those of which were merged into the revolutionary discourse and have remained in the sociocultural imagi-nation of the society.

The notion of *ibtizal* arguably materialized in the Marxist art discourse of prerevolutionary Iran to denote art forms that were not committed to edu-cate the audience and serve the class struggle but instead distracted audiences with comedic affect and recreation (see Sultanpur 1960: 33; Guran 1981: 187). *Shahvat*, on the other hand, was a nodal point in the moralizing politically con-scious Islamic discourse of prerevolutionary Iran since 1930. While this notion was also used in the nationalist debates on art and society, it was mainly the Islamic discourse that associated a cluster of practices, spaces, and media with "eroticism." This was especially in response to the expansion of new sites of sociability, the permeation of new communication media, the transformation of the public spheres, the unveiling of women in 1937, and the mingling of un-veiled women in public. Such an intrusion of female sexuality and the erotic into the public sphere was perceived to lead to unbridled sex and thus lead to social corruption and prostitution (Khuldi 1948: 2; "Islam va banuvan" 1944: 5).

Furthermore, dance, music, cinema, and theater were all seen as mediums of sexual desire, enticing the society into corruption and prostitution (Yaraqchi, "Azadi-i zanan, 3" 1948a: 2; Yaraqchi, "Sukhani dar piramun-i hijab" 1948b: 2; Faqihi-Shirazi 1947: 1–2; Karbasi 1945: 2, 4). The body of a female café dancer was purported to be inciting evil when captivating the souls and hearts of the youth, who would lose themselves in watching dance and "coquetry" (*qammazi*) ("Raqs va shahvat" 1962: 43). The café and cabaret dancers were accused of making the youth hate marriage and thus causing the extinction of the human race (Karbasi 1947: 2).

Initially emerging as an anticolonial discourse that linked the Pahlavi cultural programming and the expansion of erotic spheres to foreign governments who sought to destruct the Iranian soul and Islam, in the 1970s the anti-obscenity discourse became a constituent of the larger anti-imperialist Islamic revolutionary discourse ('Imadzadah 1952: 1–2; Nik-khu 1948: 19). An example of this attitude is evident in an article that recognized sex, dance, alcohol, and drugs as weapons of US imperialism through which the "disinherited" countries were held back and weakened (Bihishti 1980: 25). It is within this context that with the Revolution of 1979, the purging of the environment from public presentations of *shahvat* became a part of the postrevolutionary agenda.[6] What's more, veiling became the utmost solution for preventing women's exhibitionism and the performance of "femininity" or "coquettishness" (*'ishvahgari*) (Hasani 1980: 107). This also included the banning of dance (*raqs*).

Therefore, the return of dance to the stage not only needed a defamiliarization of the term but also the eradication of *shavat* and *ibtizal* from the dancing body, as well as its veiling. Coming to replace *raqs* on the postrevolutionary stage, the term *harikat-i mawzan* had been in use in reference to movements in theatrical and sportive contexts from the early twentieth century. Unlike the term *raqs*, which could also imply negative meanings in the collective imagination of society, *harikat-i mawzun* have had only positive connotations even prior to the revolution.

Similarly, the postrevolutionary return of the term was meant to ascribe a different meaning to the movement-based performances that were happening on the theater stage. Starting in 1983, early rhythmic movements were often segments of plays with diverse themes, ranging from international plays to those written by Iranian playwrights on vernacular literary, mystical, and religious and revolutionary themes (see Shuja'i and Pakravan 1989, 337–452). Most choreographers in these plays were former dancers with the major dance companies prior to the revolution.[7]

RHYTHMIC MOVEMENTS AND STAGING RELIGIOUS AND REVOLUTIONARY THEMES

The recurrence in contemporary stagings of religious and revolutionary themes includes the *ta'ziyah*, Shi'i Islamic history, and the Iran–Iraq war. Two of the main inspirational and performative sources for these contemporary performances have been *taʿziyah* and Muharram funeral rituals, to the extent that in narrating the Iran–Iraq war, sometimes the Battle of Karbala on the Day of ʿAshura has been merged into a stage scene (Furutan 2006: 101).[8]

In these productions, a variety of contemporary techniques and mediums, including video projection, lighting, stage machinery, as well as music and sound effects, are also deployed. As in *taʿziyah*, the use of props and stage sets in these contemporary productions has been symbolic. Imaginary sceneries of seventh-century Arabia have often been created by the use of elements assumed to have existed in the everyday life of the early Islamic era.[9] These include palm trees and items such as swords, flags, daggers, and tents. Candles and lanterns are often used to imply waiting, especially in regard to the twelfth Imam, Mahdi. The Shiʿi symbolic colors black, green, and red have also been enhanced to distinguish between the protagonists' roles of Husayn supporters (who are represented with green) and Husayn enemies, the antagonists signified by red. The depiction of Iran–Iraq war scenes is achieved through weapons, military clothing, as well as video projection of images of the war and the martyrs.

Sound signifiers have also contributed to the narration of the story. For instance, in enacting historic religious narratives, horse-riding sounds and military-like music have often signaled the arriving of an army, and romantic choral music has accompanied the protagonists. In *Dar Qab-i Mah* (In the Moon's Frame, 2007–2008), the rhythmic Arabic music—often used for belly dance—accompanied the antagonists. Narration in the form of poetry broadcast from a house speaker has been used to represent and accompany movements of an actor onstage or to explain the story behind the movements of the performers.

The female performers in religious *harikat-i mawzun* have often been cast as angels, an archetype present in the Qurʾanic narratives as well as in *taʿziyah* performances (Bayanlu 2006: 63). Acting as the mediators between the God and earth, the white-dressed angels appear in a variety of themes including the contemporary stagings of *taʿziyah* and revolutionary themes (see figure 13.1).[10] This archetype also is genealogically related to the dancing bodies developed in the early twentieth-century nationalist-modernist theater scene in Iran and its by-product, the Iranian national dance genre. Similar to the early twentieth-century situation, the casting of women as desexualized angels on the postrevolutionary stage has been a legitimate means for the staging of female bodies, a realm in which engaging female performers has been proven very difficult.

Additionally, other key roles at work have included sacred figures such as Fatima and Zaynab, as well as ordinary women engaged in praying, mourning, or escaping the war. The predominant male actions, with the exception of the sacred figures, have involved participating in war, praying, or moving in celebratory scenes or in simple scenes of daily life. While traditionally the depiction of the key protagonists in *ta'ziyah* required certain corporeal specifications in appearance and actions, the representation of the sacred figures on the contemporary stage has been greatly enhanced by the combination of stage technology and rhythmic movements. If appearing onstage, their faces are covered, as most interpretations of Islam prohibit the depiction of holy figures.[11] Their costumes fully cover their bodies and include long robes and loose pants, as well as headscarves. On top of these articles of clothing, women wear additional swaths of long fabric that provides more coverage of their bodies.

The actors playing the holy figures have often been positioned upstage behind the cyclorama curtain, where the audience only sees their silhouettes.[12] When appearing on stage, a spotlight follows them to create a mystical aura usually associated with holy figures. Their voices have often been heard from the house speakers, separating the voice from the performing body, as if an otherworldly message is being transmitted via the medium of the performing body.[13] These actors' holy figure presence onstage has also been signified by the way they move, often at a much slower pace than the other performers. Their signature movement has been to open their arms, with face and palms facing upward, to resemble prayer. Such codification in movements has also been drawn from *ta'ziyah* conventions (Nassirbakht 2007: 77).

By using technology and rhythmic movements, the personification of religious characters has reached a new level of distantiating the actor's body from that of the (holy) character. This perhaps has answered some of the original clerical issues with the impersonation of holy figures by earthly human bodies in the traditional *ta'ziyah* performances (see, for instance, "Nazar-i maraji'" 2010; Shahriari 2008: 34). Moreover, the recruitment of women in these contemporary productions has also resolved the clerical issues with the cross-dressing in the original *ta'ziyah* performances where male actors performed the female roles (Husayni, *Ahkam-i Nigah* 2010: 111–115; Burji 1996: 287–305).

Another major difference between the prerevolutionary secular national dance and "religious" rhythmic movements lies in the intention behind the performance. Presumably the recent religious productions—just like the "traditional" religious performances, including the *ta'ziyah*—have aimed to create a uniform emotional response in the audience by purifying their souls when they mourn for the martyrs. Some scholars view the message behind the religious performances as rather universal, standing for the ongoing battle between purity and impurity, virtue and vice, and for human resistance against tyranny (Sarsangi 2010: 203; Shahriari 2008: 18). A similar notion has also been expressed by the dancers enacting such performances: the aim was not the exact religious ideology that the government has been dictating, but the spiritual message behind those narratives.[14]

While these performers have often been trained as national dancers in secular settings, they have been transforming into new spiritual performing selves when on the religious stage. As they themselves report, this transformation has not been just a regulatory process. Several characteristics of performance have been providing the foundation for epiphanic and otherworldly experiences for performers: the situation of high emotionality embedded in the narrative, the witnessing of the audience members' responses (which often include bursting into tears), and the enacting of sacred characters by moving slowly with a covered face while possessing a technologically produced aura.[15] While these onstage "dancer-believers" could be identified as having a "contented self" (*nafs-i mutma'innah*)—as opposed to the "evil-inciting self"(*nafs-i 'ammarah*) associated with the common notion of *raqs*—state scrutiny has nevertheless been fully exerted against these stagings of movement-based works, in a similar (or even more formidable) manner as that against all other theatrical performances.

A condition for staging performances of rhythmic movements has been their acceptance in a preview process held by an inspection and evaluation committee. Responsible for deciding whether a work is suitable for public staging, the committee has to ensure that no component of a performance, including its theme and performers' appearances and actions, is against Islam and the government's policies. One main responsibility of this committee is to verify that the performers' appearance and actions onstage do not provoke sexual desires in the audience. Due to sensitivities toward (female) dancing bodies, the preview and permission process for the movement-based works, especially the full-length rhythmic movements productions, have been more challenging compared to regular plays.

The committee has often expressed over-sensitivity toward women's bodies and their affects—including instances when the profile of their figure became visible under multiple layers of fabric due to lighting. Similarly, the committee's hypersensitivity toward female performers' incidental breast movement has forced the female performers to use wide elastic garments to flatten their breasts.[16] Movements that are not considered expressions of a proper Muslim, and/or resemble lightness, carefree-ness, or spontaneity, have also raised red flags for the committee. These have included manners of walking or small gestures that could be read as flirtatious. Another requirement, as articulated by an interviewee, has been the elimination of movements that involve rotations of the wrist, hip, and/or chest, as these are thought to signify *raqs* for the public.[17] The sensitivity of the inspection committee members toward *raq*s conceivably relates to their exposure to the common discourses that associated the dancing body with *shahvat* and the behavior of the unconstrained body of a prerevolutionary cabaret dancer.

Arguably, a main function of the preview process has been to eradicate "eroticism" from female performers' bodies. Another "aesthetics" outcome of this process has been tasking staged female bodies with immediate functions, including carrying various props. This has been done to represent the female performing bodies and their movements as purposeful and thus "committed," rather than merely exhibitionist and entertaining for the gaze of the spectators and to differentiate them from the prerevolutionary cabaret dancers who were associated with "degeneration."

DANCE, BODY, SPACE, AND SUBJECTIVITY
ON POSTREVOLUTIONARY STAGE

This section examines the ways the performer of rhythmic movements has been constructed onstage through choice of movement, costume, music, sensory appeal, appearance, behavior, and gender performativity and relations.[18] This phenomenological analysis investigates the theatrical process through which the dancing self of the postrevolutionary stage corresponds with a respectable "contented self" (*nafs-i mutma'innah*); this correspondence conformed the performer to the postrevolutionary theatrical stage, and in doing so contrasted her with the prerevolutionary cabaret dancer who was associated with enticing *shahvat* and the "evil-inciting self" (*nafs-i 'ammarah*). While focusing on semiotic and sensory examinations of the performing body on stage, this analysis relies on the socio-historical study of dance in Iran, Islamic law (*ahkam*), and contemporary clerical responses to the veil, Muslim behavior, gazing, dance, music, and performance. I also make reference to the Islamic anti-obscenity discourses of prerevolutionary Iran, which have largely informed the social imagination as well as the knowledge of art practitioners, audiences, and regulators of theatrical space in the postrevolutionary period.

The transition from the prerevolutionary national dance to the rhythmic movements genre was made possible by the conversion of the theatrical space, and by obliging four elements of performance—theme, message, structure, and the performer—to follow Islamic regulations and values (Burji 1996: 284). While the theme, message, and structure of rhythmic movements have appeared to be easily adaptable and to even reflect the ideology of the state, creating a chaste (de-eroticized) dancer appears to be an impossible task. As Laurence Senelick indicates, the stage, and the staged body as a "com-

modity for strangers' gaze," are both essentially imbued with eroticism (Senelick 1992: xii). Not only do most contemporary clerics identify dance with
shahvat—only allowing a woman to dance for her husband—but a close ex-
amination of the prerevolutionary discourse of the Islamic press indicates that
the public dancing body was associated with *shahvat*, exhibitionism, *fahsha*,
and evoking *nafs-i ʿammarah* then too (for contemporary clerics' response see,
Husayni *Ahkam-i Musiqi* 2010: 80–85).

Moreover, while those texts largely reflected details of the corporeal characteristics of unveiled "modernized" (*mutajaddid*) women, ideal Muslim women
were identified as embodying chastity and veiling and were described as following their wisdom, obeying their husbands, and raising healthy children.
The actual corporeal characteristics and behavior of these women, however,
were largely invisible in society for the Islamic writers, and thus in their texts.
Additionally, as the recent compilation and interpretations of Islamic jurisprudence on women's behavior indicates, women have been encouraged to practice the "veiling of behavior" (*hijab-i raftar*) through chaste and "wise" movements and have been prohibited from exhibitionism and flirtatious movements
that lead to sexual arousal in men. These sources, however, do not provide
further details on specifically what movements are considered chaste and wise
(Rukni-Lamuki 2007: 86).

This dichotomy of eroticism associated with the dancing body and the invisibility of (the corporeal characteristics of) a chaste Muslim female body
have posed a challenge in the construction of a theatrical chaste dancing body,
as dancing after all is a corporeal performance.

To overcome the difficult task of sublimating the dancing subject into a
chaste performer, a range of techniques and stage elements have been deployed.

The costumes used in performances of rhythmic movements have been
mostly black, white, or other muted tones, and loosely fitted so as to obscure
the shape of the body. This multilayered costuming has not only been working
to cover female bodies, but also to de-eroticize them: by covering the feminine curve and flattening the breasts, the costumes have been used as a strategy
of distantiating the dancer's body from a woman's body (For example, see
figure 13.1). Sometimes, in mixed performances, both men and women have
similar costuming, which occasionally also covers the face, thereby practicing
a strategy of de-gendering to reduce the sensitivity toward the public female
dancing body.[19] Arguably, this absence of gendered female bodies on stage correlates with the invisibility of the bodies of the ideal veiled women described
in the Islamic sources.

Music has also been used to de-eroticize the performer of rhythmic move-

13.3. In Fasl Ra Ba Man Bikhan (Read with me this chapter!, 2009); Directed by Hussein Parsa'i; Choreographer Nadir Rajabpur; Photographer Farshid Saffari.

ments: to keep these performances from becoming "celebratory," romantic choral music with slow rhythms has been deployed. This has also been to de-eroticize the performance, as, according to my interviewee Guli, an upbeat environment is considered to be imbued with eroticism in the postrevolutionary context.[20]

Although appropriated to fit the biopolitics of the time, movement is still the most obvious element shared by the (docile) dancing bodies of prerevolutionary national dance and postrevolutionary rhythmic movements. The choreographed genre of *harikat-i mawzun* is predictable and can be previewed and controlled. Contrasting with the "unrestrained" *raqqa*s, this predictability of the performer of rhythmic movements creates an image of a chaste subject who submits to her wisdom that is considered a prerequisite for chastity.

A major distinction between the prerevolutionary and postrevolutionary genres is the absence of movements that signify the solo improvised dance, as these movements would connote *raq*s for the public. Instead, the vernacular movements with religious and mystic associations are often highlighted in rhythmic movements. Especially to distantiate women's movements of *harikat-i mawzun* from *raqs*, the free-flowing rotation of the wrists, triplet steps, and delicate shoulder movements borrowed from the solo improvised Iranian dance are either less emphasized or completely nonexistent. Instead, in *harikat-i mawzun*, women mostly move their arms for a defined purpose in a way that resembles prayer, or for carrying props such as books, candleholders, flowers, and fabrics. The use of props implies that female bodies are not exhibitionist but are performing a task.

Similar to national dance, rhythmic movements rely on ballet aesthetics: this has emphasized a straight spine and thus given a verticality to performers in both genres, with restrictions in the horizontal movements of the hips and chest. Using Andrée Grau's explanation of the correlation between ballet and spirituality, I argue that this verticality in rhythmic movement has helped the ascending image of the performer who, in communication with heaven, danced upward (Grau 2012: 10). This verticality in rhythmic movements also matches Mohamad Tavakoli-Targhi's observation of ascendance ('uruj)—a vertical movement toward heaven and God—in Iran–Iraq war paintings that aimed to promote "martyrdom" as a result of participation in war (Tavakoli-Targhi 2002: 13, 38).

The dominant characteristic of the female performer of *harikat-i mawzun* has been her embodiment and performance of the expressions of heaviness, modesty, chastity, and austerity. To remove the connotations of unrestrained gazing, the *harikat-i mawzun* performer has had to control her gaze and smile when facing an audience, especially in celebratory occasions. Her behavior contrasts that of the *raqqa*s who enacted a confident performance of sexuality, gazing directly at the audience, and enacted gestures with sexual undertones (such as blinking) with which she invited customers to offstage interactions. Such unrestrained gazing on the part of women was associated with *shahvat* and evoking *nafs-i 'ammarah* in the prerevolutionary anti-obscenity discourse and was discouraged by Islamic law (Husayni *Ahkam-i Nigah* 2010: 111–115; Burji 1996: 283–326).

With the exception of some performances and key roles, including Zaynab, who not only is a holy character but is also a religious symbol of agency and resistance, the construction of dancing women on stage has been mostly passive and obedient, contrasting to men's more active and strong roles, especially in terms of expressing sexuality. The recurring appearance of women angels is an example of such characterizations. Furthermore, the female performer in rhythmic movements often cautiously crosses the stage, making separate lines upstage and keeping a gap with her male colleagues. Her positioning onstage is meant to consciously emphasize a distance between men and women's bodily zones.

The postrevolutionary societal restrictions on gender relations have manifested in a rather exaggerated way onstage, especially when the script requires a female character to be in a romantic or sexual relationship with her male counterpart. Since these "mute" performers of the postrevolutionary stage have not been allowed to touch each other, expressions of sexuality have been mediated through other methods, including pauses between movements to express doubt or affection, the exchange of props, the use of fabric, and gestural hints of lovemaking while the bodies of the performers are apart from each other.[21] Arguably, not only has the eroticism of female bodies been eliminated by the mediation of gender through other means, but also the depiction and sensory experience of *shahvat* has been reconfigured to be transmitted through other mediums, leading to the establishment of a new aesthetics regime for gender representation on the postrevolutionary stage.

With all these attempts toward de-eroticizing the performing body, and regardless of its use in staging sacred figures, the postrevolutionary forms have their own opponents within the system. For instance, the carrying of the Qur'an in an official ceremony by a woman with a rhythmic walk who was also accompanied by a dozen female drum players was a serious predicament for the organizing institution in 2008, as her walking was read as dance (Blair 2008).[22]

CONCLUSION

The term rhythmic movements legitimized dance to return to the postrevolutionary stage, introducing a dancing body that defamiliarized the corporeal characteristics of the "eroticism" and "degeneration" associated with the cabaret dancer. This resurgence was the product of the negotiations between the dance artists who remained in the theatrical milieu, as well as the postrevolutionary quest for new forms of committed performances. Similar to its predecessor, national dance, the postrevolutionary genre of rhythmic movements distantiated itself from the signifiers associated with the dancing subject of the popular scene, *raqqa*s. A hybrid dance form, the rhythmic movements genre has also been borrowing heavily from performative elements of Iranian culture, but with a greater emphasis on the religious rituals and performances.

Desexualized and controlled, the performer of this genre embodies the virtues of an Iranian Muslim, conveying a message often related to God and revolutionary values. Through connecting to God and overcoming the evil-inciting self, the performing subject in rhythmic movements correlates with the "contented self" (*nafs-i mutma'innah*). Reinforcing the image of a "proper" Muslim through embodying the expressions of heaviness, chastity, purity, and spirituality, the "purified body" of this subject continues to enact the bio-ideology of the government. Contributing to the reception of religious performances, the genre has also resolved some of the contested issues related to the presentation of the body within the traditional religious performances.

Similar to popular performative forms of Islam, including *taʿziyah*, as well as secular performances, the new stagings have provoked negative responses from the more conformist interpreters of Islam. Nevertheless, with all contestations—and similar to the Pahlavi state—the Islamic government of Iran has used dance as part of its ideological state apparatus, particularly useful for promoting its domestic and foreign policies. The theatrical movement-based productions on themes of the Iranian Revolution, the Iran–Iraq war, and the holy figures of Islam are only a few of the productions commissioned by the government. Yet, the issue of mute female performing bodies still remains the most challenging problem of the theatrical stage in Iran.

NOTES

1. For a list of these productions, see Shujaʿi and Pakravan 1989: 337–452.
2. These include *Pargar-i Mihr* (Compass of Love, 1998), *Hamassahʾi ʿIshq* (The Saga of Love, 1999), *Bahar-i Surkh* (The Red Spring, 2000), and *In Fasl ra ba Man Bikhan* (Read with Me This Chapter!, 2009).
3. Examples of movement-based performances enacting the narratives related to the Iran–Iraq war include *Hamsaraʾi-i Mukhtar* (Mukhtar's Choir, 1993), and *Hurr* (2000), by Mahmud ʿAzizi; *Ghazal-i Kufr* (The Poem for Blasphemy, 2006) by Husayn Musafir-Astanah. *Mir-i ʿIshq* (The Prince of Love, 2001), about Imam Ali, by Hadi Marzban are some of the theatrical works narrated by religious stories.
4. As Furutan describes, the notion of religious theater has been interpreted in two ways: some believed that most theaters are religious as they deal with human elements and thus godly roots; and some interpreted religious theater as that dealing with religious concepts and values, e.g., the lives of imams and the Prophet, as well as religious narratives. But, it is the second interpretation that has commonly been used in the postrevolutionary era (2006: 87).
5. This resembles Erin Hurley's description of the function of the chorus in tragedies (see Hurley 2010: 40–42).
6. Islamic Consultative Assembly, Majlis 1, 19 Bahman 1362/8 February 1984, Official Gazette, no. 10, 824, retrieved from the DVD *Parliamentary Proceedings* (Mashruh-i Muzakirat-i Majlis) published by Kitabkhanah, Muzah va Markaz-i Asnad-i Majlis-i Shawra-yi Islami (The Library, Museum, and Document Center of Iran's Parliament).
7. Some of the most active choreographers included Nadir Rajabpur, Farzanah Kabuli, and Asghar Faridi Masulah.
8. It is important to note that like the Iran–Iraq war, along with the religious aspect of the form, *taʿziyah* has had great (secular) nationalist appeal. (For instance, see Nassirbakht 2007: 1, 12–13.)
9. This is observable in *Ghazal-i Kufr*, *Dar Qab-i Mah*, and *Hamsaraʾi-i Mukhtar*.
10. For instance in the ʿAshura scene in *Dar Qab-i Mah*, the angels carried Ali-Asghar, the infant son of the third Shiʿi Imam, to his aunt Zaynab and father Husayn.
11. Examples of this include *Zaynab* and *Ghazal-i Kufr*.
12. *Tavallud ta Tavallud* (Birth by Birth, 1996) directed by Nadir Rajabpur is an instance in which Prophet Muhammad and other holy figures are only shown behind the cyclorama.

13. Instances of this include *Sirisht-i Sugnak-i Zindagi* and *Tavallud ta Tavallud*.

14. Ali, interview with the author, Tehran, 23 June 2010.

15. Ali, interview.

16. Maryam, interview with the author, Tehran, 5 August 2010.

17. Guli, interview with the author, Tehran, 10 July 2010.

18. For this section, I have consulted available videos of national dance as well as recordings of postrevolutionary theatrical productions. For cabaret dancing, I have relied on the reconstructions of these dances and their audiences in *filmfarsi* commercial cinema of prerevolutionary Iran. In this analysis, to provide a broader perspective, in addition to rhythmic movements, instances of other theatrical performances have been used.

19. This is especially evident in *Raz-i Sarzamin-i Man* (The Secret of My Land, 2004) by Nadir Rajabpur and *Rastakhiz-i 'Ishq* (The Resurrection of Love, 2006) directed by Husayn Musafir-Astaneh.

20. Guli, interview with the author, Tehran, 10 July 2010.

21. For instance, in *Othello* (2011), directed by 'Atifah Tihrani, two columns were used as mediators in a sex scene: Desdemona was standing behind a column with her back to the audience; standing behind the next column while facing the audience, Cassio was pretending to be having sex.

22. The organizing institution was Iran's Cultural Heritage, Handcrafts, and Tourism Organization (Sazaman-i Miras-i Farhangi, Sanayi'-i Dasti va Gardishgari).

REFERENCES

Abbasi, R. (1385/2006). "Jilvah-hay-i imam riza dar namayish-ha-yi dini-i iran" (The Manifestations of Imam Riza in Iranian Religious Performances). In *Namayish dar Harim-i Hashtum*. F. Payam et al., edited by F. Payam et al., 17. Tehran: Intisharat-i Namayish.

Ali. 2010. Interview with the author. Tehran, 23 June 2010.

Anon. 1962. "Raqs Va Shahvat, Rah-i Jadid-i Tabligh-i Masihiyat" (Dance and Eroticism: The Newest Form of Preaching Christianity). In *Maktab-i Islam* 4, no. 11 (Azar 1341/ November–December 1962): 43–44.

———. 14 Tir 1389/5 July 2010. "Nazar-i maraji' nisbat bah nishan dadan-i chihrah'i hazrat-i 'abbas" (Religious Authorities' Opinion on Showing the Face of Hazrat-i Abbas), honaremotaali.org/NewsDetail.aspx?itemid=201.

———. 18 Farvardin 1392/7 April 2013. "Intiqad az bitavajjuhi-i mas'ulan bah harikat-i mawzun" (A Critique of the Responsible Parties' Neglect of the Rhythmic Movements Genre). *Tasnim New Agency*, www.tasnimnews.com/Home/Single/38777.

———. 31 Shahrivar 1323/ 22 September 1944. "Islam va Banuvan-i Imruz" (Islam and the Women of Today). A'in-i Islam: 5.

Bayanlu, H. 1385/2006. *Vadi-i Hayrat: Namayish-i Dini va 'Unsur-i shigifti" (Territory of Wonder: Religious Dramas and Wonder Element: A Collection of Researches on Religious Theater)*. Tehran: Intisharat-i Namayish.

Bihishti, A. 1980. "Mustaz'f Kist?" (Who Is the Disinherited?). *Maktab-i Islam* 20, no. 2 (Urdibisht 1359/April–May 1980): 22–28.

Blair, E. 2008. "Iran Vice-President under Fire over Koran 'Dance.'" 16 November. www.reuters.com/article/2008/11/16/us-iran-politics-ahmadinejad-idUSTRE4AF1E620081116.

Burji, Y. 1996. "Chishmandaz-i Fiqh Bar Namayish" (The Perspective of Religion on Performance). *Fiqh*, nos. 4–5 (Tabistan va Pa'iz 1374/Summer and Fall 1996): 283–326.

Citron, P. 1989. "Ali Pourfarrokh Remembers Iran." *Dance Magazine* 63, no. 9 (September 1989): 20.

Faqihi-Shirazi. 1947. "Ghugha-yi Raqs" (The Uproar of Dance). *Parcham-i Islam* (3 Urdibi-hisht 1326/24 April 1947): 1–2.

Furutan, P. 1385/2006. "Barrasi-i sahanah-pardazi dar namayish-i mazhabi" (An Exploration of Scenery Design in Religious Performances). In *Namayish dar Harim-i Hashtum (Theater in the Eighth Sanctuary)*, edited by P. Furutan et al. Tehran: Intisharat-i Namayish.

Gaffary, F. 1984. "Evolution of Rituals and Theater in Iran." *Iranian Studies* 17, no. 4 (Autumn 1984): 361–389.

Grau, A. 2012. "Dancing Bodies, Spaces/Places: A Cross-Cultural Investigation." *Journal of Dance and Somatic Practices* 3, nos. 1–2 (April 2012): 5–24.

Guran, H. 1360/1981. *Kushish-ha-yi Nafarjam: Sayri dar Sad Sal Ti'atr-i Iran* (Futile Efforts: A Journey in One Hundred Years of Theater in Iran). Tehran: Intisharat-i Agah.

Hasani, A. 1980. "Nazari Bah Qavanin-i Jaza'i-i Islami" (A Brief Look at the Laws of Islamic Punishment). *Maktab-i Islam* 20, no. 2 (Urdibisht 1359/April–May 1980): 106–110.

Hashimi-Rafsanjani, A. 1987. "Hunar-i Ti'atr Dar Rasta-yi Bidari-i Millat-ha-yi Mahrum-i Jahan" (Theater in the Service of Awakening the Impoverished Nations of the World). *Faslnamah'i Hunar*, no. 13 (Zimistan 1365 and Pa'iz 1366/Winter and Spring 1987): 520–547.

Hujjat, M. 1982. "Jahanbini-i Islami Va Hunar" (Religious Worldview and Art). *Faslnamah'i Hunar*, no. 1 (Pa'iz 1360/Fall 1982): 352–355.

———. 1983. "Vaqi'iyat-i Rishah Afarinish-i Asar-i Hunari [The Truth about the Roots of Artistic Creation]." *Faslnamah'i Hunar*, no. 3 (Bahar 1362/Spring 1983): 42–61.

Hurley, E. 2010. *Theatre and Feeling*. London: Palgrave Macmillan.

Husayni, S. M. 1389/2010a. *Ahkam-i Nigah va Pushish, Mutabiq ba Nazar-i Dah Tan az Marajai'i 'Uzam* (The Laws of Gaze and Clothing According to Ten Religious Authorities). Qom, Iran: Daftar-i Nashr-i Ma'arif.

———. 1389/2010b. *Ahkam-i Musiqi bah Zamimah'i Raqs va Qumar, Mutabiq ba Nazar-i Dah Tan az Maraji' (The Laws of Music, Dance, and Gambling According to Ten Religious Authorities)*. Qom, Iran: Nahad-i Namayandigi-i Maqam-i Mu'azzam-i Rahbari Dar Danishgah-ha.

'Imadzadah. 1952. "Dalai'l-i Zindah Dar Ist'mari Budan-i Barnamah'i Farhang (The Real Reasons for the Colonialist Nature of Cultural Programming)." *Nida-yi Haq* (9 Mihr 1331/1 October 1952): 1–2.

Karbasi, H. 1945. "Salun-i Raqs, Kilass-i Dars" (Dance Room, the Classroom). *Parcham-i Islam* (2 Urdibihisht 1324/22 April 1945): 2, 4.

———. 1947. "Tihran Dar Atash-i Fisad Misuzad" (Tehran Is Burning in the Fire of Immorality). *Parcham-i Islam* (2 Azar 1326/4 December 1947): 1–2.

Khatami, M. 1987. "Natijah'i Jashnavarah-ha-yi Mantaqah'i Mardumi Kardan-i Hunar Ast" (The Result of Local Festivals Is the Popularization of Art). *Faslnamah'i Hunar*, no. 13 (Zimistan 1365/Winter 1987 and Bahar 1366/Spring 1987): 522–531.

Khuldi. 1948. "Az Bara-yi 'ffat Va Pakdamani Zanan Luzum-i Hijab Yik Amr-i Musallam Va Tabi' Ast" (The Enforcement of Veiling Is Necessary and Natural for the Safekeeping of Women's Chastity and Morality). *Dunya-yi Islam* (11 Urdibihisht 1327/1 May 1948): 1–2.

Maryam. 2010. Interview with Author. Tehran, 5 August 2010.

Mazlumi, R. 1996. "Nigahi Bah Mazamin-i Hunari Dini" (A Survey of Religious Art's Topics). *Faslnamah'i Hunar*, no. 28 (Bahar 1374/Spring 1996): 79–92.

Meftahi, I. 2016. "Dancing Angels and Princesses: The Invention of an Ideal Female National Dancer in 20th-Century Iran." In *Oxford Handbook on Dance and Ethnicity*, edited by A. Shay and B. Sellers-Young. Oxford: Oxford University Press.

Mukhtabad, M. 1996. "Diram-i 'badi" (Drama for Servitude). *Faslnamah'i Hunar*, no. 29 (Tabistan va Pa'iz 1374/Summer and Fall 1996): 373–384.

Nassirbakht, M. H. 1386/2007. *Naqshpushi dar shabihkhani (Wearing the Character in Shahbihkhani)*. Tehran: Intisharat-i Namayish.

Nik-khu, H. 1327/1948. "Aksariyat-i Mardum Dar in Kishvar Vazifah'i Khud Ra Anjam Nimidahand" (Most People in This Country Run Away from Their Responsibilities). *A'in-i Islam*, no. 21 (3 Day 1327/24 December 1948): 19.

Qadiri, Na. 1990. "Raz Naguftah1i Va Surud Nakhandahi'" (You Haven't Told a Secret and Haven't Sung a Hymn). *Namayish* (Khurdad 1369/June 1990): 8–9, 49–50.

Rukni-Lamuki, M.-T. 1386/2007. *Ahkam-i Arastigi-i Zahiri (The Commandments on Adornment of the Appearance)*. Qom, Iran: Zamzam-i Hidayat.

Sadiqi, Q. 2008. "Furmalism-i Jahan, Iran-i Diruz, Imruz" (World's Formalism, Iran of the Past, Iran of Today), Transcribed Lecture. *Namayish*, nos. 109–110 (Mihr and Aban 1387/ October and November 2008): 66–72.

Salari, M. (1387/2009). *Darun Mayah-ha va Dast-Mayah-ha-yi Namayishi dar Quran (Dramatic Themes and Situations in the Qur'an)*. Tehran: Intisharat-i Surah'i Mihr.

Sarsangi, M. 1389/2010. *Muhit-i T'iatri va Rabitah'i Bazigar va Tamashagar va Namayish-i Dini (The Theatrical Space and the Relationship between Performer and the Audience in Religious Theater)*. Tehran: Intisharat-i Afraz.

Senelick, L. 1992. *Gender in Performance: The Presentation of Difference in the Performing Arts*. Hanover, NH: University Press of New England.

Shahriari, K. 2008. *A Different Approach to a Unique Theater: Taziyeh in Iran*. Kista, Stockholm: Kitab-i Arzan.

Shirvani, H. 1979. "Anchah Ra Ma Az Dast Midahim" (What We Are Losing). *Khurus-i Jangi* (12 Khurdad 1358/2 June 1979): 1–2.

Shuja'i, M., and S. Pakravan. 1989. "Kitabshinasi-i Sahnah'i Namayish (Bibliography of Performance/Theater). *Faslnamah'i Ti'atr*, no. 6–8 (Tabistan, Pa'iz, Zimistan 1368/Summer, Fall, Winter 1989): 337–452.

Stellar, Z. 2011. "From 'Evil-Inciting' Dance to Chaste 'Rhythmic Movements': A Genealogy of Modern Islamic Dance-Theatre in Iran." In *Muslim Rap, Halal Soaps, and Revolutionary Theater: Artistic Developments in the Muslim Cultural Sphere*, edited by K. van Nieuwkerk, 231–256. Austin: University of Texas Press.

Sultanpur, S. 1349/1960. *Nu'i Az Hunar, Nu'i Az* Andishah (A Kind of Art, a Kind of Thought). Tehran.

Tavakoli-Targhi, M. 2002. "Frontline Mysticism and Eastern Spirituality." *ISIM Newsletter* 9, no. 1: 13, 38.

Yaraqchi, M. 1948a. "Azadi-i Zanan, 3 [Women's Emancipation, 3]." *Dunya-yi Islam* (1 Isfand 1326/21 February 1948): 1–2.

———. 1948b. "Sukhani Dar Piramun-i Hijab" (Some Words on Veiling). *Dunya-yi Islam* (12 Farvardin 1327/1 April 1948): 1–2.

CHAPTER 14

PUBLIC PLEASURES: NEGOTIATING GENDER AND MORALITY THROUGH SYRIAN POPULAR DANCE

SHAYNA SILVERSTEIN

"SUWAR-NI! SUWAR-NI!" (Record me!) implored the youngest daughter of the family I was visiting in Jubata El Khashab, a rural village in the Quneitra province of Syria. She was enthusiastically participating in the traditional Syrian line dance known as *dabke* with her extended family and myself inside their home. We had been celebrating their cousin's wedding and were taking a break from the intense summer heat and nuptials to refresh ourselves with air conditioning and cold juice. An aunt put on *dabke* hits by Ali al-Dik and Fares Karam, popular singers who dominated satellite and mass media in Syria and Lebanon. We did not resist the infectious *dabke* rhythms. Led by uncles and male cousins in the lead positions of the dance circle, we repeated the cross-stepping pattern of *dabke*, distinguished by a foot stomp with the left foot. A few skilled participants embellished their *dabke* steps with skips, double-time step patterns, and shoulder raises. An uncle picked up my video camera to capture his niece in this lighthearted, intimate moment.

Our casual *dabke* circle attests to the ubiquity of this popular performance tradition in everyday life in Syria. A social dance practiced in private and public spaces, friends and family often *dabke* during gatherings at home, in restaurants and nightclubs, and other spaces of leisure. However, this *dabke* session surprised me because my hosts explicitly informed me that *dabke* would not be taking place during this particular visit. They had invited me to attend an "Islamic" wedding. This categorical marker communicated that the family chose certain wedding traditions that aligned with their personal interpretation of Islamic doctrine, including a performance by an *anasheed* ensemble (Islamic vocal music) and gender-segregation at the religious ceremony. Observant of how the performance of instrumental music and popular dance transgresses their Islamic morals, they chose not to host a *sha'bi*-style dance party with *mawwal* (improvised song) and *dabke* (social dance) traditions that typifies Syrian weddings.

While marriage practices generally reflect the diversity, flexibility, and fluidity of norms and practices, these choices enabled my host family to fulfill their aspirations for Sunni Islamic revivalism. As with many others participating in piety movements in Syria at this time, they drew on gendered norms of public space, such as the separation of men and women during Qur'anic recitation and the taboo placed on women's dancing in public, as a means to enact their understandings of Islamic morality. Their wedding became a site for the Islamization of public space that emerged through the performance of gendered codes of conduct. These norms depended on and reinforced Islamic discourses of female modesty.

Yet the particular set of constraints placed on female participation in the public nuptials starkly contrasted with the performance of dabke in private as described above—together, unscripted, and among family. The young woman who excitedly asked to be recorded on video embraced *dabke* as a means to express her sense of self. Moreover, she cultivated these techniques of the self within the domestic space of her family's home, a space of privacy and intimacy that she wanted to capture on camera. The contrast between placing constraints on feminine movement in public and embracing feminine movement within the home reinforce what some scholars have recognized as a dichotomy between public and private domains in which the former is equated with men and the latter with women. Other scholars contest that concepts of publicness and privacy are not necessarily stable. They argue that such emerge in relation to structures of gender, class, and religion, and shift in relation to who defines such distinctions (Ghannam 2014). Individuals, both male and female, draw on normative understandings of public and private domains as a means to establish a moral framework in which to situate their actions, gestures, and movements.

Research for this chapter is based on fieldwork conducted throughout Syria in 2007–2008. This was a complex moment that seemed to convey economic and cultural openness but in fact concealed underlying forces of tension and polarization, many of which have been linked to the March 2011 uprising against the Assad regime that quickly escalated into a full-scale conflict (Gelvin 2012). In the context of war, the overwhelming number of male casualties and detentions, and the Syrian refugee crisis, women's roles at home and in the public sector have shifted in response to the need to provide for their households. As well, women's networks have mobilized in ways that cut across class, religious, and sectarian lines (Yazbek 2012) and, as in Egypt (Winegar 2012), transformed domestic spaces into sites of political dissent and witness.

In light of the shifting dynamics of public and private spaces, this chapter illustrates how Syrian women situated themselves in public discourses on the body, gender, and Islamic morality, and negotiated the increasing Islamization of public space in a predominately secular society before the 2011 uprisings. Their choices assert a sense of agency that may be understood "not as locus of representations, but as engaged in practices, as a being who acts in and on a world" (Taylor 1993: 49, quoted in Elyachar 2011: 89). In turn, my focus on embodiment draws on longstanding debates on social class in the Islamic world that consider how individuals are predisposed to act in ways consistent with their social milieu, or habitus (Bourdieu 1977, Starrett 1995). Social groups become distinguishable through the gestures, movements, dancing, and other "dynamically embodied practices" (Farnell 2000) that shape the bodily disposition of their members (Bourdieu 1977). This chapter thus approaches the body as both an object and an agent of social life in ways that contribute to understandings of how femininity becomes embodied in the Muslim world (Abu Lughod 1986, Ahmed 1992, Mahmood 2005). In so doing, it goes beyond dichotomies that position female corporeality in opposition to male rationality or as embodied resistance to hegemonic masculinity.[1]

Exploring the fluidity of public and private spaces, I argue that these domains emerge in dialogic relation to each other. Given how "Islam is one powerful factor among several in the construction of gender distinctions and the making of public and private spaces" (Ghannam 2014), I am interested in how young Muslim women in contemporary Syria express their religious aspirations by conforming to or resisting gendered norms in relation to contemporary understandings of public and private spaces. In particular, I focus on the female body in popular dance practices as a site for agency and power. Whether onstage or at family gatherings, weddings, and nightclubs, shifting attitudes toward dance reflect the fluid subjectivity of the female body in broader configurations of class, gender, and religion. This chapter argues that young women draw on the heuristics of public and private domains in order to strategically position themselves in the contested moral arena of popular dance.

THE ISLAMIZATION OF PUBLIC SPACE
IN THE BASHAR AL-ASSAD ERA

The Bashar al-Assad era (2000–present) has been characterized by economic reform launched in 2005 as a "social market economy" model (Abboud and Arslanian 2009). Around this time, the eastern regions of Syria were afflicted by extreme drought, which prompted labor migration out of the area due to reduced agricultural yield (Ababsa 2009). While urban areas absorbed these workers, cities were impacted by high rates of unemployment, particularly among college graduates, as well as increasing economic disparity that severely affected those on the urban periphery. Though political and economic power was further consolidated among clientalist networks of the business and political elite (Haddad 2011), and though a speculative economy emerged in banking and real estate sectors that benefited the upper middle class and Syrian bourgeoisie, the state could not sustain the same levels of social welfare that it maintained prior to economic reform. Public social services shifted toward religious or civil associations and development efforts became increasingly privatized in most domains, including the cultural sector (Donati 2013). Despite, or perhaps because of, these bleak horizons in the public sector, many middle-class Syrians whom I met during my fieldwork in 2007–2008 increasingly depended on communal and faith-based networks.

Personal forms of piety became increasingly popular in the Bashar al-Assad era, particularly Sufism (Pinto 2006), Salafism, and Sunni Islamism (Pierret 2009). Relatedly, the regime began to desecularize state institutions in its efforts to contain religious radicalization, maintain state authoritarianism, and enable new ideals for secularism that sought to integrate religious difference and identity (Khatib 2012).[2] Religious clergy became more influential and attracted a broader popular base of support as relations between Islamic clerics and the regime became less antagonistic and more permissible (Pierret 2009). Many of these activities centered on the mosque as a space for prayer, learning, socializing, and debating. Naqshbandi-based Sufi movements incorporated "organizational models based on spiritual bonds, informal circles (halaqat) and daily lessons in the mosque" (Pierret 2009: 3). Local sheikhs expanded these efforts to increase religious liberties and visibility in the fields of education, charitable activities, and the mass media. They aimed to attract lay people, particularly educated middle-class youth, and inspire them toward pious lifestyles.

The rise in popular Islam and personal forms of piety during this period was further characterized by the legitimation of Islamic female authority, particularly in Damascus. The Qubaysi movement, a Sunni Muslim revivalist and piety movement pioneered by Munira al-Qubaysi in the 1980s and 1990s, was officially recognized by the government as a legal religious entity in 2006 and Qubaisiyyat (female religious leaders) were allowed to preach in public spaces including Damascene mosques. Considered the most visibly influential religious movement in Damascus (Islam 2011), Qubaisiyyat authority is based on the formal study of Islamic doctrine, production of teaching texts, and personal piety practices. Its popularity is driven by members' commitment to socioeconomic mobility for women. By emphasizing individual worship and refraining from religious activism, Qubaisiyyat have avoided being perceived as a political threat and have not been subjected to the state repression experienced by the Muslim Brotherhood and Salafi movement. Though not as visibly powerful in the public sphere, other movements have also aspired to construct female, pious, and ethical senses of self. In the female *halaqat* (religious circles) of the Kufsariyya Sufi order, a Damascus-based branch of the Naqshbandiyya, female religious authorities inculcate spiritual teachings and manage religious life through their work in the mosque, particularly Abu Nour in Damascus (Chagas 2013). By encouraging recruitment and self-initiative among disciples, the work of female Sufi leaders over the last few decades has enabled the growth of female piety in mosques and in private homes. As well, mainstream Sunni Islam has incorporated space for female teachers to exert religious authority and enter the religious sphere over the last twenty years without threatening the existing religious order (Kalmbach 2008).

Public participation in Islamic revivalist and piety movements has presented particular challenges for pious Muslim women who do not necessarily seek to challenge gendered and religious constraints in Syrian society but aspire for more inclusive forms of Islamic participation and authority. They have struggled to uphold conservative religious and ethical values within their private lives while living in an authoritarian state that privileges secularism, egalitarianism, and feminism. Scholars have pointed out that life in Baathist Syria has generally increased women's economic burdens, imposed a double standard of obligations for women in both the public sector and family life, and challenged them to navigate between political rhetoric that accords "equal status" to women and personal status laws based on shari'a that limit their autonomy outside of the family household (Rabo 1996).

As the increasing popularity of pious lifestyles, from Salafism to Sufism, permeated everyday life for all Syrians, secular-oriented intellectuals expressed anxiety over losing the benefits and privileges of a secular state that held no mandated ties to religion. Female religious modesty became an object of public discourse as more women began to veil, and as the hijab became increasingly visible in metropolitan areas. In 2010, the government banned the full headscarf (*niqab*) in order to constrain pious identity markers to private domains and maintain the secularization of public spaces. The ban reflected the interests of the state in applying regulatory forces and punitive measures that ultimately reinforced distinctions between public and private domains. Assad reversed the *niqab* ban in April 2011 in response to popular protests.

Debates over the Islamization of public space affected Muslim women, for whom the hijab simultaneously challenged and reified stereotypes. Some young women narrated to me their decision to "take on" the hijab as a coming-of-age story, which typically occurred around twelve years old. In these stories, the hijab stood as a marker of agency, self-expression, and empowerment by which these young adults situated themselves morally among their peers. Becoming *muhajaba* (veiled) was arguably less a statement of "conscious piety" but rather indicative of a certain generation raised to take certain pious practices for granted (Deeb and Harb 2013). As Mona Harb and Lara Deeb suggest, scholarly focus on Islamic piety distracts from the role of morality, which is not necessarily rooted in religion, and may be related to other social and political ideas. Their ethnography of leisure practices in south Beirut examines occasions in which pious Shiʿa Muslim youth "have to navigate complex moral terrain in order to have fun while feeling good about themselves" (Deeb and Harb 2013: 136). They demonstrate how these youth balance religious rules and social obligations, that is, how they employ moral flexibility in their discourse and practices of leisure.

The next section explores these debates on morality, piety, and gender in relation to casual dance practices among Muslim youth in Syria. I focus on how one young Muslim woman navigated morality during a leisurely occasion among friends and family that took place in a private space. When perceived as an overtly sexualized form of behavior, her moving body threatened those apprehensive of "fun," or an ad hoc moment in which an individual breaks free of the disciplined constraints of daily life, norms, and obligations (Bayat 2007).[3] In the context of the Islamization of the public sphere in the Bashar al-Assad era and the emergence of popular female religious authority, this and other leisure practices expose broader social and religious tensions that circulate in the public sphere.

DANCING FOR HERSELF

Situated in the intersections of morality and bodily hexis, Syrian popular dance is embedded in complex politics of class, taste, and embodiment. Social distinctions emerge through the practice of specific forms of Syrian popular dance within particular contexts of leisure and entertainment. Whereas solo belly-dancing (*raqs sharqiyya*) tends to be denigrated by middle-class Syrians as an over-sexualized and licentious practice that occurs in Arab nightclubs (as distinct from western-oriented nightclubs that offer electronic dance music as well as Arab pop music for upwardly mobile young Syrians), many of the middle class enjoy dancing social forms of belly-dancing (*raqs ʿarabiyya*) and line dancing (*dabke*) at banquet halls and other venues for respectable social gatherings, as well as at home. The collective line dance of *dabke* is generally embraced as a popular (*shaʿbi*) custom and celebrated in the public sphere as a national and secular performance tradition (Silverstein 2012). However, *dabke* also signifies popular aesthetics in ways that often register as lower class and less civilized, also referred to as *sha'bi*. Muslim women are generally discouraged from pursuing careers in the performing arts, especially dance. While speaking with members of professional dance ensembles based in Damascus, I found that many performers, particularly women, felt conflicted about their career aspirations. Though they remained committed to the arts and artistic expression, they shared stories of others who negotiated conflicts and pressures related to family and religious values—many either deceived their families to pursue dance or left a successful performance career for modesty's sake. These situations occurred much more often among female dancers than male dancers. While most young Syrian women do not aspire to dance professionally, they must also navigate the complicated double standard of how to pursue professional aims and uphold family values. They are encouraged to limit dance to private spaces in which women tend to have more agency through gestures, movement, and mobility. Even as they have been encouraged to pursue higher education and professional careers in education, health care, and administration, young Syrian women are disciplined and regulated by patriarchal systems of kinship and paternalistic codes of morality. The paradox lies in the juxtaposition of, on the one hand, public perceptions of modesty among career women and immodesty among professional dancers, and on the other hand, the private obligations and expectations of a mother, daughter, and sister.

Movements like the Qubaisiyat have empowered women to tackle this double standard of success in their professional lives and at home. They actively discuss these tensions in meetings and encourage socioeconomic mobility by bringing together elite and nonelite social strata through teachings, practices, and social networks (Islam 2011). However, many young Muslim women may not wish to consciously pursue a pious disposition with such intentionality but rather fold their religious and moral expectations, norms, and standards into their everyday life. The narrative below recalls a leisurely afternoon of grilling, swimming, dancing, and lounging that I spent with a group of pious Muslim youth outside Aleppo in July 2008. Fridays are typically welcomed as occasions for getaways—to mountainside resorts, shopping malls, or new luxury developments constructed in outlying areas of metropolitan regions. This particular occasion reveals how interactions among peers construct gendered subjectivities and, in particular, how feminine movement mediates young Muslim identity in spaces of leisure.

On a Friday morning in July 2008, I joined a group of twenty-something Muslim professionals and entrepreneurs to head for a private complex outside Aleppo. We looked forward to grilling and refreshing ourselves at the outdoor pool that provided respite from the intense August heat. Friends invited others that they met through university studies, professional networks, as well as younger siblings and parents. I was invited by a young male friend with an interest in the literary arts that I had met on a visit to Aleppo several months before. These young professionals and entrepreneurs were more or less committed to social welfare and development in ways that positioned them to debate future directions of their city as members of the modernizing middle class. One young Kurdish man staffed the Aga Khan Development Network's initiative for urban revitalization and community development in Aleppo. Others were employed as graphic designers and software engineers. One entrepreneur would go on to establish a cultural center and exchange program for students of Arabic and English. Romances came and went in the group, such as that between a young medical student from Jordan and a female law student from Aleppo who both pursued studies at the University of Aleppo. The Friday gathering was a regular happening that fulfilled recreational needs and expanded social contacts among religious and secular Muslim youth in middle-class Aleppo.

After lunch, the boys got antsy and began to indulge in poolside antics. Some girls had changed into swimwear, which ranged from swimsuits to modest swimwear that extended to wrists and ankles. The girls did not remove their hijabs. The boys playfully abducted friends, both girls and boys, and threw them into the pool. If a girl was still wearing her sunglasses, they politely waited for her to remove her valuables then tossed her in. Most of the snatched giggled and screamed. The pool activities slowly morphed into song and dance entertainment with a microphone and amplifier. A poet recited classical and modern literary works and a singer performed a talented interpretation of 'Abd al-Halim Hafiz's "Lahn al-Wafa'" (Song of Faithfulness). A young man picked up a *darbukka* (single-headed goblet drum) to accompany the singer and a couple of girls started to sway their hips and dance softly. Depending on the tune, tempo, and mood of the dancers, dance sessions flowed between different styles, from *raqs 'arabiyya* to *dabke*. Individuals stepped into the center of the circle to highlight distinct moves, including a breakdance session by a talented DJ from Latakia.

Anisa, a young female lawyer, returned from a walk with a young male medical student, Khaled, with a tense look on her face.[4] After a pause, she began to *raqs 'arabiyya*. All of our gazes turned toward her as she elevated the energy in the dance circle through her skillful movements. Several minutes later, Khaled walked through the gate and dove immediately into the pool. He swam vigorous laps with a crawl stroke. We continued to dance but furtive looks were passed from one friend to another as we tried to assess the tense scenario. Khaled continued to swim laps with an aggressiveness that transformed a sense of disquiet among us into outright concern. A friend yelled at him to stop but he ignored the command. He began to seizure after hoisting himself out of the pool. Male friends carried him into a back room, where he regained breath control but was barely conscious. Eventually a car came for him and he was driven to a local hospital for diagnosis and recovery. On the bus ride back home, word spread that the young couple had fought during their walk outside the complex. He accused Anisa of bringing shame upon herself through her provocative dancing earlier that day. He claimed that her dancing, which had been collectively admired, roused his male friends' desire for her. Anisa argued back, claiming that she was among friends and kin and that he had no right to control her body. She accused him of jealousy and called off their relationship. She then returned to the complex and joined our dance circle.

This scenario suggests how one young woman resisted one young man's expectations of how to modify her conduct and manage her body among their peers. In this instance, Anisa's dancing was perceived as overtly sexual and threatened Khaled's masculinity. In response to her boyfriend's desire to control her body, Anisa rejoined our group to dance. By choosing to continue dancing, she asserted her agency and resisted her boyfriend's morality, thereby reclaiming relations of object, power, and sexuality embedded in feminine movement. Through Anisa's ability to respond to shifting social expectations and challenges, her femininity became linked to not only embodied norms of female modesty but also her assertive sense of individuality.

It is not insignificant that this play of desire, sexuality, and power was manifested through female movement. Anisa did not forsake her modesty by choosing to dance among family and friends and rejecting the social expectations of her boyfriend. Her dancing was a performative statement that articulated her desire to have "fun" with her body without being controlled by Khaled's understanding of gendered norms. Anisa and Khaled discovered that their ability to employ moral flexibility during times of leisure was incompatible with their different understandings of masculine and feminine norms. Their embodied interactions played out an unstable and competing set of masculine and feminine dynamics that demonstrate how gendered identities are produced and elaborated through interactions rather than the separation or opposition of masculine and feminine norms (Ghannam 2014). As Farha Ghannam articulates in her ethnography of embodied masculinity in urban Egypt, "it is not a unidirectional flow of power [in which men dominate women] but a complex web of signification and multiple flows of power that structure how gender is embodied, reproduced, and transformed" (Ghannam 2013: 104–105).

Unlike the pious selfhood cultivated by women in Syrian mosque movements, whether Sufi, Qubaysi, or mainstream Sunni Islam, Anisa's sense of self was not informed by authoritative sources and foundational texts. In the young professional Muslim Aleppene universe that shaped the interactions between Anisa and Khaled, her friends judged, legitimized, and recognized her and Khaled's interactions. Leisure sites and practices are arguably alternatives to religious authority and piety movements that provide spaces in which Muslim youth express themselves and reinforce moral norms. They are a means by which pious youth move away from those family, religious, and political authorities that dominate the public sphere and cultivate their own moral frameworks in more intimate domains.

Weddings are also a site in which popular dance mediates gender dynamics and morality. Approaching weddings as occasions that affirm social distinctions based on class, religion, and region, the next section explores lower-class *sha'bi* weddings held in a rural village that were attended by local residents and extended family. By examining the intimate dynamics and interactions that took place at a *sha'bi* Islamic wedding in the Quneitra governate of southwestern Syria, I illustrate how my interlocutors' moral and religious aspirations to host an Islamic wedding depended on gendered norms, embodied practices, and the discourse of female modesty.

CONSTRUCTING PIETY AT AN ISLAMIC WEDDING

This section demonstrates how different formations of public space are constituted by social, moral, and religious distinctions. As weddings often blur boundaries between public and private domains, here I focus on who defines these boundaries and how morally ambiguous practices, whether music or *dabke*, mediate the formation of publics. Throughout the Muslim world, *sha'bi* weddings are an occasion during which many activities, from drinking to mixed-gender festivities, may be deemed impermissible. In Lebanon in the 1980s and 1990s, *dabke* at weddings came under scrutiny (Deeb and Harb 2013). When speaking with pious Shi'a in south Beirut, Deeb noted that the appropriate moral choice was not always clear to wedding guests. People struggled to identify different strategies that would both respect their social obligations and their moral sensibilities—one groom tactfully left his wedding before dancing began. Religious guidance from the Lebanese cleric Fadlallah has not clarified this social conundrum as he issued a fatwa that permitted mixed gender *dabke* at weddings yet also insisted that women not dance in front of men. Comparatively, the recent development of popular Islamic weddings in Egypt (Van Nieuwkerk 2012) and *nasheed* bands in Morocco (Ter Laan, this volume) offer "clean" alternatives to the "vulgar" or immoral *sha'bi* wedding.

While performing *dabke* at a rural wedding in the Houran valley, an agricultural zone bordering the Golan Heights and Mount Hermon in southwestern Syria, I was befriended by a family who wanted to help me better understand local popular traditions. Like Shi'a Lebanese in south Beirut, they navigated complex moral terrain between *sha'bi* and pious practices by drawing on normative understandings of gender roles in private and public domains. Like Islamic wedding ensembles in Egypt, they ascribed to highly prescriptive conditions for pious nuptials. The following ethnographic vignette illustrates how the intersection of the body, morality, piety, and gendered conventions at weddings structures the social spaces accessible to men and women.

The family invited me to return to Jubata El Khashab, a village in the Quneitra province, for their Islamic wedding (*'ars al-Islamiyya*). With a majority Sunni population of approximately 2,000 to 5,000, Jubata El Khashab's primary industry is agricultural. This family maintained two substantial parcels of land that harvested olives and fruit for domestic markets. Most residents of the village were invited to attend the wedding, along with family and friends who lived in Damascus (about an hour's drive north). Though it was not clear to me what an Islamic wedding entailed, given the diversity of Islamic marriage practices, I was interested in finding out how they distinguished their event from the non-Islamic *sha'bi* wedding at which we had met. The public events of the wedding consisted of a religious ceremony with *anasheed*, a wedding processional, and the ritual slaughter of a sheep. The *anasheed* genre is a male Islamic vocal practice that, in strict accordance with Islamic guidelines against musical instruments and women's voices, permits only the single-headed frame drum (*daf*) as an accompaniment to men's musico-poetic recitation of Sufi, Islamic, and popular Arabic lyrics. This particular performance ensemble (*firqa*) was composed of a local sheikh and eight men who recited praises of the Prophet Muhammad with rhythmic accompaniment on *daf*. The religious ceremony was held under a white tent and segregated by gender—men participated from inside the tent while women observed quietly from the periphery. Though as a woman I could not step inside the tent, my host offered to record and document the *anasheed* for my research. After the performance concluded, we walked to the house of the bride's family to present the groom with his formal wedding attire. The groom changed in the salon while men performed sung poetry in a call-and-response pattern and danced in a style known as *dabke 'al-naba* (stepping backward and forward in a two-step rhythmic pattern while clasping hands tightly to form a line). From outside, women accompanied the songs with *darbukka* (goblet drum) and *zaghareet* (vocal ululations). Once the groom assumed his wedding attire, we passed into the street for the wedding processional (*raddat al-zaff*) as the older women offered candy and threw grains of rice.

During the processional, women performed folk songs accompanied by *darbukka* and *zaghareet*. Rather than arriving to a public square or other outdoors space to begin the music and *dabke* segment, as typical of *sha'bi* nuptials, we processed to the tent for another set of *anasheed* and the signing of the *nikah*, or legal marriage contract. The ceremony concluded with the ritual slaughter of a sheep in front of the tent. Later, the bride's family would prepare the ritual dish of *munsaf*, a pilaf of spiced rice and mutton, and distribute portions to neighbors as gestures of generosity, hospitality, and communality that mark a wedding. After the formal proceedings, the guests dispersed and the bride and groom drove around the entire village in a borrowed car, merrily announcing their newlywed status with the car horn. They returned to his family home where they exchanged gold rings in front of several family members.

Their choice of wedding traditions aligned with specific Islamic principles in ways that distinguished this event from typical village weddings. Their interpretation of an Islamic wedding was flexible insofar as it included religious (Islamic) and non-religious (*sha'bi*) practices, from Qur'anic recitation to a wedding processional and ritual slaughter. But they placed greater emphasis on those practices that made the wedding distinctly Islamic, including abstinence from music and *dabke*, the separation of men and women at the religious ceremony, and a performance of *anasheed* by an Islamic vocal ensemble. The choice to Islamicize their nuptials by displacing popular performance traditions with the religious performance of *anasheed* arguably aligned with their aspirations to exemplify Islamic moral standards within the community of Jubata El Khashab. As I would find out through subsequent visits, the family tended to structure and principle their everyday decisions as Islamic ethics grounded in Sunni doctrine. They made clear to me that these decisions differentiated their lifestyle from others by cultivating a body disciplined by Islamic morality. By replacing music and *dabke* with *anasheed* at a public event, the wedding hosts asserted their commitment to a pious lifestyle.

"I DON'T KNOW HOW?" PERFORMING FEMALE MODESTY

Dabke practices were not fully prohibited from the nuptial events of the wedding described above. Rather, they were displaced to domestic spaces in ways that speak to the complex interplay between public and private spheres. I now turn to a women's-only dance party that took place among kin and close friends the evening before the wedding. Hosted by the bride's family, the *hafla al-ʿarusa* (bride's party) was attended exclusively by female kin, with the exception of the bride's brother and a couple of young boys related to the family. I was invited to participate in this event as female next-of-kin and because the family recognized that it would be the only occasion for me to observe and participate in dancing during the wedding. At approximately 9 p.m. that evening, my hosts and I began dressing for the festivities—skirts, jeans, and matching *chador* (head covering). With the exception of one sister still in high school and another too tomboyish for cosmetics, we applied tinted foundation and black kohl to our festive faces. The seven of us walked two houses over to the bride's brother's house and were among the first to arrive. After a few technological blips and scratched CDs, we launched the boom box, clasped hands, and began to dance the *dabke* together.

The dancing was generally not distinct from other dance parties that I had attended. Styles alternated between regional variants of *dabke* in a group formation and *raqs ʿarabiyya* in pairs—this time in pairs of girls, women, and the occasional young boy instead of heterosexual couples. Three women in their thirties commanded the dance floor for some time with their competent display of *raqs ʿarabiyya* and regional variants of *dabke* such as Iraqi, Hourani, and Jazira. Two girls, a high schooler and a married twenty-one year old, alternated taking the lead role in the *dabke* line. The married woman performed with rhythmic precision by accenting certain movements, shifting her hips, and kicking her legs. The high schooler, an exceptionally lanky young girl, moved her feet quickly with double-time steps and performed several embellishing figures. Personalities began to emerge: there were those least willing to participate, those who demonstrated stamina and endurance, and those who performed *dabke* with zestful competence, nimble agility, and individual style.

Later that evening, the hostess put on a track of "western-style music" and invited me to dance in the center of the circle. I obliged with some generic pop dance moves yet insisted against dancing by myself. I felt oddly exposed and wanted to transform this moment into interaction rather than exoticization. One or two women joined me briefly, but my hosts resisted my pleas. They replied: "*ma b-ʿarif*" (I don't know how), and remained as they were. Their refusal to try a new form of movement surprised me, especially given their openness to introducing me to local dance practices and their enthusiasm for *dabke*. I was curious about why they denied themselves the privilege to acquire new forms of embodied knowledge when they encountered the unfamiliar and unknown, not only with regard to western popular dance but also Iraqi styles of *dabke*.

Phenomenological approaches to the study of modesty in Muslim societies insist that modesty is experienced, learned, or cultivated by women themselves (Abu Lughod 2014). In the comparative context of Greek dance, Jane Cowan (1990) persuasively argues that feelings of pleasure through dancing are contingent on how a woman conducts herself through movement. Though sexual expression is a feminine ideal, women cannot control how others may interpret their acts. This lack of agency makes women vulnerable to shame should movements be judged as hypersexualized, aggressive, or too timid. Dance problematically evokes what Cowan terms "ambivalent pleasure" (Cowan 1990: 188–202). Even though the *hafla al-ʿarusa* in Jubata El Khashab was attended almost entirely by female kin, modesty norms and ambivalent pleasure circumscribed conditions of participation to the extent that few felt comfortable taking risks with their bodies.

At this party, my hosts were likely ambivalent about trying out a nonlocal dance style because they could not control how others might interpret their movements. The act of denial, *"ma b-ʿarif,"* was arguably a performative statement by which each young woman situated herself socially and morally within her community. Their preferences for how to enjoy themselves and have fun at this particular occasion were structured by the broader moral terrain occupied by feminine movement, popular dance, and socioreligious norms. This female public space became defined as much by the protection of female honor and modesty as by participation in leisurely activities.

Throughout my visit, I noticed that the young women managed their bodies in different ways depending on the particular setting. Some were conservative about their bodily conduct in public settings such as the *hafla al-ʿarusa*, but were less cautious and took more risks when lounging among family at home. How each woman chose to shape her own identity through her relationship with her body was in part cultivated by her relationship to *dabke*. After the *hafla al-ʿarusa* wrapped up, I asked my hosts how often they perform *dabke* and whether they follow other dance styles. One replied that it had been three years since the last wedding in their household and that they had rarely danced so vigorously as this night. Another sister laughed at this and insisted that she dances *dabke* as often as she walks—she could never tire of performing *dabke*, and often plays a wedding CD in order to practice at home. This young woman was the same woman mentioned in the introduction to this chapter who had insisted that her uncle record her—*"Suwarni, suwarni!"*—when we broke out into an impromptu *dabke* session in their home. Yet despite her enthusiasm to dance at home, she also held back from participating on the dance floor at the *hafla al-ʿarusa*. These young women negotiated their participation in social dance based not on the setting of domestic space but rather on the presence of others, whether close family or extended social networks. Despite the segregation of men and women that occurs in public spaces, women enhanced their family status and honor when they visited and networked in this private space (Meneley 1996) through embodied *sha'bi* practices, modesty discourse, and gendered norms. These interactions suggest that distinctions between public and private spaces emerge from how social actors evaluate and use these categories rather than on the physical settings of domestic space and public life.

The ways in which women chose to discipline their bodies throughout these Islamic nuptials in Jubata El Khashab also suggest how gendered and moral norms are mediated by *dabke* practices. Whether through the exclusion, regulation, or pleasure associated with this *sha'bi* performance practice, *dabke* is a means by which individuals signify their relationship to Islamic morality. As this wedding suggests, women were not permitted to dance in front of men and women also chose not to dance particular styles in front of each other. Female movement is central to the production of moral, modest, and pious identities. However, these identities emerge not through unidirectional flows of power in which men control women's movement, but rather through the legitimation and recognition of men and women by and upon each other.

CONCLUSION

Contemporary piety movements are reshaping relations between movement, gender, and Islamic subjectivity while also creating new spaces for female religious authority. This chapter has explored how young Syrian Muslim women negotiate these shifts in public life within their own intimate spheres of family and friends. As they navigate the complex morality of the female body through popular dance, they construct "definite and distinctive life styles of new religious taste and preferences" that are linked to piety practices of contemporary Islam (Turner 2008, quoted in Van Nieuwkerk 2008: 172). Performance traditions produce religious meaning in ways that enable us to consider Islamic popular culture as more than patterns of consumption and taste that indicate emerging markets and reinforce socioeconomic stratification. Rather, we may better understand the role of religion as contemporary sense-making and as living culture by analyzing how young Muslim women negotiate public discourses on the body, gender, and Islamic morality in a predominately secular yet increasingly Islamic society.

Embodied practices in spaces of leisure are critical junctures in which young Muslim women refrain or assert a sense of self through performative statements. One young Aleppene woman mediated incompatible moral differences with her boyfriend by shunning him and dancing with her peers. Her actions declared her newfound romantic independence and intimated a new social status among her peers while also reestablishing her own moral boundaries. In contrast, the *hafla al-ʿarusa* in Jubata El Khashab was an occasion in which young women resisted using their bodies to gain new social skills. Rather, they declined to participate in unfamiliar dance practices in order to maintain their sense of honor and status among women in their family. These scenarios suggest how feminine movement mediates relations of female modesty, honor, and status.

This brief ethnography demonstrates the complex interplay between public and private domains. Rather than a strict dichotomy that maps gender roles onto and as modes of embodiment, I have argued here that these social actors embrace techniques of the body and employ these techniques to distinguish between the heuristics of public and private, pious and secular, male and female. From the emergence of a female public at the *hafla al-ʿarusa* to the construction of a pious public at the Islamic wedding, concepts of publicness and privateness shift in relation to structures of gender and religion. These distinctions are defined not by religious authorities but rather by the choices individuals make in their everyday lives as they draw on normative understandings to establish moral frameworks in spaces of leisure.

NOTES

1. Farha Ghannam (2013) points out that these studies do not account for the embodiment of masculinity and the contestations through which hegemonic masculinity emerges.

2. Policies of desecularization of state institutions included: the lifting of a long-standing ban on religious practices in military barracks (2005); clerical participation in cadet lectures in military schools (2007); expansion of the number of Islamic institutions in Syria and recognition of the rising demand for Islamic theology and law by endorsing a *sharʿia* faculty at the University of Aleppo and continuing its support for *sharʿia* faculty at Damascus University (2007) (Khatib 2012).

3. Asef Bayat has questioned why radical Islamic clerics target "fun" as detrimental to Islamic morality through religious edicts and censorship. He attributes this morality agenda to the "fear of exit from the paradigm that God and Islam frame and uphold mastery of certain types of moral and political authorities, be they individuals, political movements, or states" (Bayat 2007: 155).

4. All names are pseudonyms.

REFERENCES

Ababsa, Myriam. 2009. *Raqq: Territoires et Pratiques Sociales d'une Ville Syrienne.* Beirut: IFPO.

Abboud, Samer, and Ferdinand Arslanian. 2009. *Syria's Economy and the Transition Paradigm.* University of St. Andrews Centre for Syrian Studies. Boulder, CO: Lynne Rienner.

Abu-Lughod, Lila. 1986. *Veiled Sentiments: Honor and Poetry in a Bedouin Society.* Berkeley, CA: University of California Press.

———. 2014. "Modesty Discourses: Overview." *Encyclopedia of Women and Islamic Cultures,* edited by Suad Joseph. Leiden: Brill.

Ahmed, Leila. 1992. *Women and Gender in Islam: Historical Roots of a Modern Debate.* New Haven: Yale University Press.

Bayat, Asef. 2007. *Making Islam Democratic: Social Movements and the Post-Islamist Turn.* Palo Alto: Stanford University Press.

Berlant, Lauren. 2000. *Intimacy.* Chicago: University of Chicago Press.

Bourdieu, Pierre. 1977. *Outline of a Theory of Practice.* Cambridge: Cambridge University Press.

Browning, Barbara. 2010. "Rethinking Technique and the Body 'Proper.'" *Dance Research Journal* 42, no. 1: 81–83.

Chagas, Gisele Fonseca. 2013. "Female Sufis in Syria: Charismatic Authority and Bureaucratic Structure." In *The Anthropology of Religious Charisma: Ecstasies and Institutions,* edited by Charles Lindholm, 81–100. New York: Palgrave Macmillan.

Cowan, Jane K. 1990. *Dance and the Body Politic in Northern Greece.* Princeton: Princeton University Press.

Deeb, Lara, and Mona Harb. 2013. *Leisurely Islam: Negotiating Geography and Morality in Shi'ite South Beirut.* Princeton: Princeton University Press.

Donati, Caroline. 2013. "The Economics of Authoritarian Upgrading in Syria: Liberalization and the Reconfiguration of Economic Networks." In *Middle East Authoritarianisms: Governance, Contestation, and Regime Resilience in Syria and Iran,* edited by Steven Heydemann and Reinoud Leenders, 35–60. Palo Alto: Stanford University Press.

Elyachar, Julia. 2011. "The Political Economy of Movement and Gesture in Cairo." *Journal of the Royal Anthropological Institute* 17, no. 1: 82–99.

Farnell, Brenda. 2000. "Getting Out of the Habitus: An Alternative Model of Dynamically Embodied Social Action." *Journal of the Royal Anthropological Institute* 6, no. 3: 397–418.

Gelvin, James L. 2012. *The Arab Uprisings: What Everyone Needs to Know.* New York: Oxford University Press.

Ghannam, Farha. 2013. *Live and Die Like a Man: Gender Dynamics in Urban Egypt.* Palo Alto: Stanford University Press.

———. 2014. "Public/Private Dichotomy: Overview." In *Encyclopedia of Women and Islamic Cultures,* edited by Suad Joseph. Leiden: Brill.

Haddad, Bassam. 2011. *Business Networks in Syria: The Political Economy of Authoritarian Resilience.* Palo Alto: Stanford University Press.

Islam, Sarah. 2011. "The Qubaysiyyat: The Growth of an International Muslim Women's Revivalist Movement from Syria (1960–2008)." In *Women, Leadership, and Mosques: Changes in Contemporary Islamic Authority,* edited by Masooda Bano and Hilary Kalmbach, 161–184. Leiden: Brill.

Kalmbach, Hilary. 2008. "Social and Religious Change in Damascus: One Case of Female Islamic Religious Authority." *British Journal of Middle Eastern Studies* 35: 37–57.

Khatib, Line. 2012. *Islamic Revivalism in Syria: The Rise and Fall of Ba'thist Secularism.* London: Routledge.

Mahmood, Saba. 2005. *Politics of Piety: The Islamic Revival and the Feminist Subject.* Princeton: Princeton University Press.

Mauss, Marcel. 1936. "Techniques of the Body." *Economy and Society* 2, no. 1: 70–88.

McDonald, David A. 2010. "Geographies of the Body: Music, Violence and Manhood in Palestine." *Ethnomusicology Forum* 19, no. 2: 191.

Meneley, Anne. 1996. *Tournaments of Value: Sociability and Hierarchy in a Yemeni Town.* Toronto: University of Toronto Press.

Nelson, Cynthia. 1974. "Public and Private Politics: Women in the Middle Eastern World." *American Ethnologist* 1, no. 3: 551–563.

Pierret, Thomas. 2009. "City Clergy Politics in the Cities of Ba'thist Syria." In *Demystifying Syria*, edited by Fred Lawson, 70–84. London: Saqi Books.

Pinto, Paulo G. 2006. "Sufism, Moral Performance and the Public Sphere in Syria." In *Revue des mondes musulmans et de la Méditerranée*, edited by Sylvia Chiffoleau, 115–116.

Rabo, Annika. 1996. "Gender, State and Civil Society in Jordan and Syria." In *Civil Society: Challenging Western Models*, edited by C. M. Hann and Elizabeth Dunn, 153–174. London: Psychology Press.

Silverstein, Shayna. 2012. "Mobilizing Bodies in Syria: Dabke, Popular Culture, and the Politics of Belonging." PhD diss., University of Chicago.

Starrett, Gregory. 1995. "The Hexis of Interpretation: Islam and the Body in the Egyptian Popular School." *American Ethnologist* 22, no. 4: 953–969.

Van Nieuwkerk, Karin. 2008. "Creating an Islamic Cultural Sphere: Contested Notions of Art, Leisure and Entertainment: An Introduction." *Contemporary Islam* 2, no. 3 (December): 169–176.

———. 2012. "Popularizing Islam or Islamizing Popular Music: New Developments in Egypt's Wedding Scene." *Contemporary Islam* 6, no. 3: 235–254.

Winegar, Jessica. 2012. "The Privilege of Revolution: Gender, Class, Space, and Affect in Egypt." *American Ethnologist* 39 no. 1: 67–70.

Yazbek, Samar. 2012. *A Woman in the Crossfire: Diaries of the Syrian Revolution.* Translated by Max Weiss. London: Haus Publishers.

PART V

GLOBAL FLOWS OF POPULAR CULTURE
IN THE MUSLIM WORLD

IN THIS SECTION the transnational and global flows of popular culture as well as its local appropriations—also caught by the term "glocalization"—are analyzed, thus highlighting important aspects of global connectivity and local identity. This section fleshes out the cosmopolitan character of popular culture and the privileged vantage point of popular culture to study multiple forms of belonging.

Anne Rasmussen's chapter introduces Islamic ritual and recreational performance in Indonesia, the country with the largest Muslim population in the world. Informed by the circulation of music, language, material goods, and cultural capital around the Indian Ocean for the last half millennium, the expression of religion as popular culture is a crucial aspect of the Islamization of Indonesia. The chapter outlines a continuum of Islamic musical arts and popular culture from Qur'anic recitation and collective Islamic singing on one end of the spectrum, to music videos and fetishized Internet commodities on the other. Situating Indonesia comparatively alongside regions in the Arab world that have informed the archipelago's Muslim culture for centuries helps us to think about how musical practices convey piety and how musical messages of any kind take on meaning in new cultural contexts. In Indonesia, Islam was consistently identified as civic duty and national citizenship. In the Sultanate of Oman, located on the opposite shores of the Indian Ocean in the Arabian Peninsula, a very different picture emerged: styles of Islamic music are largely absent while a large and vigorous development plan for the performing arts was launched encouraging secularist musical initiatives. Despite the different roles of religion, arts have been a tool for nation building in both regions.

Michael Frishkopf's chapter develops a multi-sited perspective on global differences in Muslim tolerance of ritual difference by comparing Ghana and Egypt. Religious tolerance is generally far higher in Ghana than in Egypt.

Yet contemporary Ghanaian Muslim "reform" and missionary organizations, linked to Salafi-Wahhabis of the Arab world and the West, are far *less* ritually tolerant than their conservative Egyptian Muslim counterparts. It is precisely interreligious tolerance — promoted by Ghana's secular, pluralistic, and democratic political culture — and the corresponding free religious market, that promotes conflict and even violence at the intra-Islamic level, by enabling the formation of distinctive, bounded Muslim movements competing for members. Music offers a powerful social technology for self-definition and invigorates social solidarity, thus making it into a key field of contestation for group membership. Ghanaian Salafis apparently feel more threatened by musical practices than do their counterparts in Egypt, whose criticism of analogous musical festivals (*mawalid*) is almost never accompanied by action. This chapter accounts for these differences in ritual tolerance in terms of demographic, cultural, historical, and political differences between Egypt and Ghana, as well as connections situating both locales within complexly connected transnational networks.

Thomas Hodgson's chapter looks at migration and multiculturalism in Britain, exploring how traditional music festivals have travelled from Pakistan to England and the role of the state in their subsequent development. Urban life is increasingly taking center stage in thinking about identity and global connectivity, that is, people understand connections in terms of cities rather than nation-states. Pakistanis, the vast majority of whom originate from the Mirpur area, are plugged into a transnational imaginary that connects Bradford with Mirpur. Music and the arts, especially the Bradford Mela, have been promoted as a rare symbol and success of multiculturalism. In a time of immense public spending cuts, ironically, some of the defining characteristics of the Mirpuri Muslim community — practices that are often labeled as self-segregating and isolationist — has meant that they have escaped relatively unharmed from the kind of funding cuts experienced by broader South Asian arts organizations. Mirpuris organize their own local (music) events. This chapter analyzes these examples as competing *kinds* of cosmopolitanism: forms that are controlled along multicultural lines by the Bradford Council, such as the Bradford Mela, and other forms such as the Mirpuri "grassroots" transnationalism that is about regions and cities rather than the national level.

Kendra Salois's chapter also analyzes the local as the site of global positioning and interconnectedness by focusing on the legendary Casablancan band Nass el-Ghiwane. The band combined local expressions of Muslim piety with regional expressive traditions, creating the first homegrown popular music with genuine national reach. Grounded in the local and global Black Atlantic forms of the Moroccan Gnawa and of 1970s rock, their music nonetheless reaffirmed a widely held narrative linking Moroccan identity and Muslim faith. Today, young Moroccan hip-hop musicians, especially those born and raised in Casablanca, proudly claim descent from this creative lineage. Moroccan hip-hop artists follow their predecessors in 1970s popular music when they draw from multiple transnational currents to create their contemporary hip-hop, showing that "glocalization," or the process of adapting globally circulating media to local needs and practices, occurred then and continues today.

This section thus not only highlights the transnational links and global "routes" of influence but also the key role of popular culture—or music in the case studies in this section—on issues of "roots." Popular culture is a key field to study identity-making processes, covering the demarcation of group identities as well as the creation of overlapping local, urban, national, or cosmopolitan identities.

CHAPTER 15

PERFORMING ISLAM AROUND THE INDIAN OCEAN BASIN: MUSICAL RITUAL AND RECREATION IN INDONESIA AND THE SULTANATE OF OMAN

ANNE K. RASMUSSEN

SITUATING INDONESIA

ALTHOUGH INDONESIA is the country with the largest Muslim population in the world, its Islamic traditions are rarely seen as representative of Islam as a world religion.[1] Rather, Indonesian Islam with its syncretic rituals and kitschy pop culture has been viewed as a variation, a derivation, an imperfect imitation, or a naïve distortion of the authentic practices of the Arab Muslim world and its geographically close, but culturally and linguistically distinct, cousins in the Turkic and Persianate Muslim world communities of the Middle East and Central Asia. For centuries, however, Indonesia has been connected to the Middle East and Arab world and particularly to the southern Arabian Peninsula, through the trade routes of a maritime "silk road" around the Indian Ocean. The Indonesian archipelago is not only a part of the Indian Ocean world, the archipelago, in fact, defines the waterways that link the Indian Ocean with the Pacific Ocean, the route that facilitates connections among Africa, Arabia, Mesopotamia and the Persian Gulf, the Indian Subcontinent, and East Asia since maritime travel and trade began. Cultural exchange of all kinds between those at sea and those on the shore was and still is an obvious by-product of these maritime flows (Ho 2006, Kaplan 2010).

In this chapter I establish the routes of performance practices that migrate among divergent ports of call based on my work in Indonesia and some preliminary observations that I have made in Yemen and Oman (2009–2015).[2] Situating Indonesia comparatively alongside regions in the Arab world that have informed the archipelago's Muslim culture for centuries helps us to think about how musical practices convey piety and how musical messages of any kind take on meaning in new cultural contexts. My comparative ethnography also reveals two very different stances regarding the development of pious arts

15.1. The renowned reciter, teacher, college administrator, and religious expert Maria Ulfah stands in front of a banner (*spanduk*) for an "Exposition of Islamic Arts" (*Pageleran Seni Islami*), organized in honor of the author in January 2010. Held at the small religious boarding school (*Pondok Pesantren Bayt il-Qorro'*) owned and operated by Maria Ulfah and her husband Dr. Mukhtar Ikhsan, the event involved the students from that *pesantren* along with the college students from the *Institut Ilmu al-Qur'an*, a college for women who pursue Qur'anic studies. Photo by author.

in the public sphere. In the Indonesian context performing Islam through a variety of media: music, drama, literature, journalism, the visual arts, and even cuisine, is in line with civic duty and Indonesian national citizenship. Various kinds of *Seni bernafaskan Islam*, or art that "breathes," were consistently identified to me by my consultants, most of them who, themselves were involved in what I call "the business of religion."

In the Sultanate of Oman on the shores of the Arabian Peninsula a very different picture was painted for me. When in the capital city of Muscat, I was, in fact, discouraged from looking for styles of Islamic music and was assured that although I might have discovered such things in Indonesia, there was "none of that" in Oman. What I found in Oman, rather, is a development plan for the performing arts, the scale and vigor of which seem disproportionately large for a country of less than three million people. Since the founding of the modern nation in 1970, its sovereign leader, Sultan Qaboos, has launched one secularist musical initiative after another, almost all of them in the spirit of creating an identity and profile befitting of a modern country fit for participation on the stage of nation-states.[3]

MUSICAL PERFORMANCE IN ISLAMIC INDONESIA

My work describes Islam in Indonesia as it is created and experienced through recitation, song, and the Islamic music that was introduced to me through ethnographic fieldwork with women and men in this part of the circum-Indian Ocean Islamic world (see Rasmussen 2001, 2005, 2010, and Harnish and Rasmussen 2011). Key to Indonesian Islamic arts, I argue, are the aesthetics of Arabic language and music, which emanate from the recited Qur'an, and from a range of ritual and recreational performance practices. Qur'anic "performance" constitutes a global aesthetic system that Indonesian artists both reference and resist depending on their cultural background and political orientation. When we move from recitation, to song, to music we can hear many sonic markers of the Middle Eastern Muslim world. Musical instruments, such as the 'ud (lute), the mizmar (oboe), the qanun (zither), or the large string section typical of the Arab orchestra might be realized on a keyboard synthesizer. Instrumental and vocal genres and styles, song texts, or other building blocks of musical organization, such as rhythmic patterns, melodic modes and phrases, nontempered intonation, and aspects of the social act of music making, reception, and interaction that is typical of Arab music are other features that help make music look, sound, and feel Islamic. From the mosque to the recording studio the contexts for and contents of Islamic music in Indonesia constitute a vibrant stream of Indonesian culture as well as an aspect of global Islam that is authentic, historic, and dynamic (see Rasmussen 2010 and 2005).

THREE GENRES OF INDONESIAN ISLAMIC SONG: THE *TAWASHIH* TRADITION, *QASIDA REBANA*, AND *HAJIR MARAWIS*

A continuum of pious popular arts exemplifies the complementary and ongoing processes of the Islamization of Indonesia and the Indonesianization of Islam. Many styles of Arabic-language song emanate from Egypt and the eastern Mediterranean region (Palestine, Jordan, Lebanon, Syria) from where a powerful Turko-Arab tradition has radiated for centuries; let's call this the *tawashih* tradition. *Hajir marawis*, another popular Islamic music takes its cue from the southern shores of the Arabian Peninsula, the present-day nations of Yemen and Oman. Between these two Arab-Indonesian musics, the unique genre, *qasida rebana*, reflects the Arab music that has come to Indonesia and which has taken root in performance practices considered by many to be quintessentially Indonesian.

THE *TAWASHIH* TRADITION: MUSIC FROM THE OVERLAND SILK ROAD AND EASTERN MEDITERRANEAN

The *tawashih* tradition consists of a family of Arabic-language song genres from the overland Silk Road cities of Aleppo, Istanbul, Baghdad, and especially Cairo, Egypt. Its performers, both men and women, cultivate vocal virtuosity and artistry through their practice of Qur'anic recitation. To recite the text of the holy Qur'an they use a musical system of Arab melodic modes called *maqamat*. They learn this system through singing *tawashih* in Arabic with Arab *maqamat*. At this point we have to ask: How could a completely foreign musical system take root in Indonesia and become naturalized through religious practice? Here is part of the answer to that question.

Although many kinds of Arab culture must have been introduced to the coastal areas of Indonesia through trade and Islamization, the Arab melodic system was institutionalized only after independence in 1945 when the new nation-state began to interact politically, economically, and culturally with other nations. A landmark of the new era of independence was the Asia-Africa conference of 1955. Held in Bandung, West Java, the conference convened a group of about thirty nations, most of them newly independent and all of them searching for ways to distance themselves from their colonial histories and realities. While religious exchange was not an explicit goal of the conference, it is fair to say that forming what I call "identity partnerships" among the nations of Asia and Africa that had majority Muslim populations went hand-in-hand with forging postcolonial identities and agendas.[4] It is within this context that Egyptian reciters came to independent Indonesia.

The world famous reciters of Egypt were already well known at the time of Indonesian independence in 1945; their voices along with all kinds of Egyptian musical performance were heard in the archipelago through a "media-scape" that involved the technologies of short-wave radio, films, and recordings.[5] Indonesia's relationship with Egypt and respect for its Islamic traditions dates well before the advent of mass media, however, due to the influence of Cairo's Al-Azhar University, where generations of *'ulama'*, or learned religious men, received their training from at least the mid-sixteenth century onward.[6] As Qur'anic studies are central to such training, there is no question that some of the early *'ulama'*, who studied and lived in Egypt, must also have been fine reciters. But the real florescence of Egyptian-style recitation came with the Egyptian reciters themselves when they visited Indonesia, to teach the country's best male and female reciters, who in turn institutionalized the classic *mujawwad* style of virtuosic melodic recitation in Jakarta. This variety of recitation, also referred to as *tilawa*, follows the system of *tajwid* for matters of pronunciation and the sectioning and timing of the inimitable text of the Qur'an. Reciters also practice the musical discourse of the Arab, Egyptian-style *maqamat*, through learning *tawashih*, a repertoire of Arab song that uses the modal system of Arab music. This is a music that is practiced by singers and instrumentalists in a much celebrated and rich culture of repertoires, institutions, and artists of Egypt and the Levant. This music culture, sometimes referred to as Turko-Arab or Ottoman-Arab music, is one that traces its roots to the music cultures of ninth-century Mesopotamia.

During the zenith of the Islamic cultural productions that flourished during the end of the Suharto era and at the beginning of the *Reformasi* (essentially the decade of the 1990s, when I lived in Indonesia), the ubiquity of the Egyptian style of recitation that permeated the soundscape, both live and mediated, made it so that the highly ornamented modal melodies, strident vocal timbres, and nonmetric rhythms of recitation, along with the predictable progressions of modal performance with its periodic cadences (Arabic, *qaflat*) were experienced by everyone, whether they were a practicing Muslim or not. The result, I suggest is that although an imported tradition, Indonesians of all walks of life became able to recognize, appreciate, and to ascribe meaning, however abstract, to the Egyptian-Arab aesthetics of melody and language through what Shannon writing about Sufi ritual in Syria calls "techniques of the body" (Shannon 2006: 119–120, following Mauss 1979 [1936]). Furthermore, because the strains of Qur'anic recitation, the ubiquitous call-to-prayer, and a variety of para-liturgical and recreational religious song genres are constantly present in the soundscape of the public sphere, when heard in other contexts, for example, in various Islamic musics or even popular styles, such as *dangdut*, these sounds—namely, the strident vocal production, unique scales and approach to melodic phrasing, and highly ornamented virtuosity—index religion and spirituality.[7] That this completely imported musical system, one that Arabs themselves often represent as being accessible only to culture bearers, found fertile ground in island Southeast Asia is a world music phenomenon that exemplifies the processes of globalization and cosmopolitanism facilitated by the Maritime Silk Road.

"The Association of Male and Female Reciters and Male and Female Memorizers of the Qur'an" or IPQAH (*Ikaten Persaudaraan Qari dan Qaria, Hafiz dan Hafiza*) is the professional association of the archipelago's finest reciters and the exemplar of Indonesia's *tawashih* tradition. In July 2004, during the week-long, Twentieth National Competition in Qur'anic Recitation in Kalimantan, the members of IPQAH and I prepared for a performance that was televised nationally during one of the festival evenings. As we practiced the repertoire and rehearsed the arrangements that they had in mind, I was able to experience the way in which these professional reciters conceptualize and talk about song through their demonstration and performance of melody, rhythm, form, and details of arrangement. One of our arrangements began with my improvisation (*taqasim*) on the *'ud* (Arab lute) in the musical mode of the piece, *maqam Naha-wand*. The group's lead singer, Gamal Abdul Nasser Lubis, followed my intro-ductory improvisation with a nonmetric solo called *mawwal*, and I echoed his phrases approximately using a technique called *tarjama* in Arabic, literally, "translation." In the choral sections, male and female voices sang in alterna-tion while Gamal and his brother Zaini played the rhythmic pattern or *iqa'*, a simple pattern in triple meter with some embellishment. Calls of elation and encouragement, "Allah, Allah, Allah," complemented the solos by voice and *'ud*, cueing the participants' reception and response and constituting *tarab*, a term that refers to the repertoire and contextual dynamics for Arab traditional music of the eastern Mediterranean Arab world (see Racy 2003).

One of the pieces we prepared for our program was "*Nur al-Huda*," a *tawashih* that is a variant of the classic Arab *muwashshah*, "*Lamma Bada Yata-thena*," a song that is known throughout the Arab world in part because of its legendary connections to Arab Spain or Andalusia.[8]

A: Nur al-huda wa faana	Bi husnihi akhyana *(x2)*
The light of huda *guided;*	*With his grace he revived us*
B: Wa b'il liiqaa' hiyyana	Salla alayhi mawlaanaa *(x2)*
And with the meeting he greeted us;	*Greetings upon him our Master*

IPQAH is at the apex of *Arab* Islamic music making in Indonesia. The singers are champion reciters, capable of reading, writing, and singing in Arabic. Their powerful voices, their phenomenal breath control, and their sensibili-ties regarding the treatment of melody and phrasing, are all functions of their training as reciters. Through their performances and recordings, and those by their students, and their interest in Arab music, they confirm an unapologetic connection between recitation and music, a factor that propels Islamic music into the public sphere as pious production, performance art, and popular cul-ture. While the Arabic singing and the authentically Arab repertoire and per-formance practice they cultivate are both by-products of and catalysts for the

Nur al-Huda

IPQAH
Gamal Abdul Naser Lubis and Ensemble

15.2. Transcription—*Nur Al Huda*

continuous Islamization of Indonesia, the involvement of women in this performance culture as well as its prominent placement in the public sphere are notable indicators of the way this Arab tradition has been locally indigenized.

QASIDA REBANA: THE INTERSECTION OF RELIGIOSITY AND RECREATION

Learning to sing religious songs (*quasida*) and to play *rebana* (frame drums) in organized groups is a common activity in both rural and urban Indonesian settings, for women, men, and teenagers, alike. *Rebana* groups typically commission a set of instruments, decorate them with their own logo, and rehearse or get together to play for fun, and then perform at social and religious gatherings, at civic events, or in competitions. In performance, groups of girls, teenagers, or women usually add matching costumes and coordinated choreography to the mix (see figure 15.4). In the 1990s, when I first began my research, women's *qasida rebana* and *qasida modern*, which include melody instruments such as flute, keyboard, and guitar, were the Islamic musics I most commonly witnessed, in live performance and in the mass media (see Rasmussen 2010, chapter 5, and Capwell 1995).[9]

During the course of my research, I visited nine *pondok pesantren* or Islamic boarding schools; each of them had one or more *rebana* ensembles that performed either for my benefit or for the events that were already scheduled. I also witnessed numerous rehearsals, competitions, and performances of such groups in other contexts. The frame drum, *rebana*, also called *terbang*, is seen as an index of spirituality throughout the Islamic world, and the performance of *qasida rebana*, as all public Islamic activity, has the explicit goal of *dakwa* (from the Arabic, *da'wa*), the mission of strengthening or celebrating faith or bringing in new believers. Even when pop songs or love ballads are performed, the fact that they are in Arabic and sung with the accompaniment of *rebana* confers upon them a quality of spirituality and, when performed in particular contexts, of missionary zeal. Nevertheless *qasida rebana* performances are entertaining and fun. Arrangements are dynamic, usually up-tempo, and because of the choreography and the physicality required to play the instruments, can be purposefully athletic. Playing *rebana* involves collectively produced, interlocking percussion techniques, another factor that contributes to the social aesthetics of the music. Several players or groups of players are required to produce a complete rhythmic groove, over which a strophic song, with solo verse and chorus, is sung. Such interlocking rhythmic patterns are not at all characteristic of the Turko-Arab music of the *tawashih* tradition just described. Rather, the interlocking rhythms of *rebana* mimic the performance practice of Indonesian gong-chime ensembles, called gamelan.[10]

Let me describe a rehearsal and performance of the *rebana* group from the *pondok pesantren* Bayt al-Qorro'. The participants were kids, both boys and girls, who lived at the school, and most of them, like the school's directors, Maria Ulfah and her husband, are from East Java, the region of the country that is the heartland of traditional Indonesian Islam. The *santri* (as the student residents of Islamic boarding schools are called) sang and played in an ensemble that included two *rebana*, named *kendung* and *kendong*, hanging on gong stands (the names are onomatopoetic syllables for the higher and lower sounds they make when struck with a mallet), hand-held *rebana* with jingles (*kechrek* and *rotet*), *rebana* drums, large frame drums held in the lap (these were named *ketak*, *kenting*, and *kentung*), and a frame drum with a metal frame (with no skin) called *malkis*.

The following skeletal transcription illustrates two contrasting patterns, one played for the chorus and the second for the verse of a song, which are

Qasida Rebana "Demak"

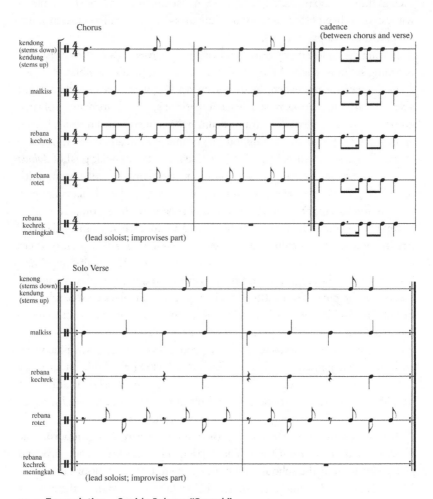

15.3. Transcription—*Qasida Rebana "Demak"*

usually linked by a transitional cadence. Of interest are the names given for the instruments, which in each case describe the pitches (high, medium, low) that they make and thus their role in the collective, layered, interlocking, whole ensemble texture (see figure 15.3).

In Indonesian gamelan ensembles, the gong-chime orchestras that are associated with the archipelago's court musics, assigning to instruments the onomatopoetic names that imitate the instruments' sounds, is also a distinctive organizing principle of the music. For example various kettle gongs in the Javanese gamelan are named *ketuk, kenong, kempul, kempyang,* and so on. When musicians pronounce the rhythmic and melodic patterns that these instruments are assigned, they typically speak or sing the instrument's name over and over as a kind of solfége or note-naming system. That this practice has been adapted for a percussion ensemble that accompanies Islamic songs with religious texts (in Arabic and local languages) is just one example of the ways in which Islamic praxis has become localized in Indonesia. The function of pitched gamelan instruments, which are essentially tuned idiophones, most of them hanging gongs, kettle gongs, and metallophones, was transferred to an ensemble of percussion instruments for two important reasons. First, *rebana* frame drums and their variants are cheaper than the costly bronze instruments of the gamelan, which are usually only owned by elite rulers and associated with social and spiritual power. Second, *rebana,* because they are just drums and not capable of producing melodies, are considered more appropriate for the accompaniment of Islamic song.

Qasida rebana exemplifies the unique qualities of Indonesian Islam in several ways. While the music is associated with Islam, it is also recreational *dakwa;* costumes, logos, choreography, arrangements are encouraged. Even more than the other two styles I describe, *qasida rebana* is women's music, and the public activity of girls and women in Islamic work and Islamic performance is, again, something that is pervasive in Indonesia, compared with other places in the Muslim world. Finally, beyond Southeast Asia, there is nothing like *qasida rebana* anywhere else in the Arab or Muslim world.

HAJIR MARAWIS: NEW MUSICAL INFLUENCES FROM THE ORIGINAL LANDS OF ISLAM

A third example of Islamic popular music in Jakarta is *hajir marawis,* a genre that travelled along the routes of cultural transmission between Island Southeast Asia and the Arabian Peninsula. While Indonesians established contact with Egypt through the technologies of the modern age, steamship, air travel, and modern mass media, relationships of exchange with the Arabian Peninsula were part and parcel of the circum-Indian Ocean maritime culture that connected these two regions as far back as the fourteenth century. Hadrami seafarers, that is, people from the Hadramaut region of what is now Yemen, were the most active in the exchange of goods and information. As this exchange of materials and ideas took root, Indonesians, now adherents of the new religion of Islam, also began to travel to the Arabian Peninsula for pilgrimage, education, marriage, and business.

Musical manifestations of the Arabian Peninsula in Indonesia are remark-

15.4. Women's *hajir marawis* group from the *Institut Ilmu al-Qur'an*, Jakarta, in performance 2010. Note the coordinated costumes, also typical of the women's *qasidah rebana* groups just described. Photo by author.

able because they are both historically antiquated, now only a musical memory of those with a connection to performers of the past, and because of their visceral contemporary connection to Arabia through continuous trade, travel, religious pilgrimage, and the dominant mass media and economic patronage of powerful nations, particularly Saudi Arabia. For example, although the Meccan melodic modes (*lagu Makkawi*), so called because they were adapted for recitation and song by travelers to and from Mecca, were largely eclipsed in the last half-century by the widely disseminated practices of Egyptian reciters, recitation styles from Saudi Arabia, including that used for the call-to-prayer, have made an audible comeback in Indonesia. The influence of Saudi styles is due to the continuous broadcast of religious ritual from Mecca, during Ramadan, itself, in part a by-product of the powerful influence of Wahabi funding in Indonesia. These sociopolitical and economic developments have fascinating and significant musical repercussions and speak to the continuity and change or the wax and wane of musical praxis; moreover, the return of Saudi styles, born on the airwaves of the contemporary global "technoscape," is testament to the soft-power of the Arabian Gulf states and the sometimes-cyclic nature of musical processes.

An even more distinctive marker of the return of Arabian influence is the emergence of *hajir marawis*. The instrumentation of such groups varies but generally includes only singers and percussionists who all play the small double-headed laced *mirwas* drum complemented by three performers who play: (1) the goblet-shaped Arab *dumbek* (also *tabla*), (2) cymbals and/or frame drum (*markiss*), and (3) the double-headed *hajir* drum, essentially a larger version of the *rahmani*, *kaser*, or *mahjar* drums found in costal Oman and Yemen (see figure 15.5).

While I saw only a handful of groups in the course of my initial fieldwork in Indonesia (1996 and 1999), this type of ensemble consistently gained momentum during the first decade of the twentieth century, particularly among teenage boys and girls. In my subsequent visits to Indonesia between 2000 and 2014, *hajir marawis* was flourishing. When I prepared this chapter, there were dozens and dozens of video clips of Indonesian *hajir marawis* posted to YouTube.[11]

Although the texts of *hajir marawis* are often sung with *maqam*-based modality in the Egyptian/Near-Eastern Mediterranean style, the social formation

15.5. Instruments of the *Hajir Marawis* ensemble. Photo by author.

of this ensemble, the playing techniques employed, and the resulting musical texture are strikingly different from the Arab musical aesthetics of the *mashriq*. The Group *Hajir Marawis "Bait al-Qurro'"* demonstrated the rhythmic groove *sharh*, for me, which, along with the dance rhythms *zapin* and *zahife*, is widely recognized as being performed both in the coastal Arabian Peninsula and in insular Southeast Asia, particularly among communities of descendants from the Hadramaut, for at least a century (see Berg 2011, Capwell 1995, and Van den Berg 1886). These music-dance genres are also the staple of *gambus* music, an Arab-derived Islamic music ensemble and musical style that features the *gambus* lute (now the modern *'ud*) as well as violin, *qanun*, bamboo flute (the side-blown *suling* tuned to accommodate Arab temperament), and keyboard synthesizer. During the first decade of my research, *gambus* music, which was played by communities of ethnic Arabs in Indonesia, seemed to be in decline, while *hajir marawis* was certainly on the rise. I speculate that reasons for the ebb and flow of these performance styles are multiple. For example, the recreational athleticism of *hajir marawis*, which requires only a variety of drums, is great fun and does not require finding and learning more demanding and expensive melodic instruments like the *'ud*, violin, or keyboard. Second, a connection to the ethnic Arab communities who play *gambus* is not a prerequisite for affiliation with the *hajir marawis* scene. A third possible reason for its rise in popularity is that without melody instruments, *hajir marawis* is unobjectionable as a form of Islamic music.

The musical texture of a *hajir marawis* group performing the *sharah* groove results from the combination of layered isorhythms, or small repeated rhythmic patterns, produced by each player or group of players, who locks into their own ostinato pattern within an overarching group of six or twelve beats, depending on how you count it.[12] The polyrhythm created by the instruments playing simultaneously in a ⁶/₈ feel and a ³/₄ feel is quite unlike the approach to rhythm that is characteristic of the Arab *mashriq* of Egypt and the eastern Mediterranean, where rhythmic patterns are linear rather than cyclic and poly-metric. As with *qasida rebana* performance, different patterns are used for solo verses and choral refrains and dramatic cadences are employed for introductions and endings. When the repertoire of songs from the Arabian Gulf are performed, such as the genre *dana dana*, a continuity in circum-Indian Ocean connections is confirmed. The connection between these two Indian Ocean axes is further solidified by the instrument types and names (*hajar* or *mahjar* and *mirwas*, pl. *marawis*) and the dance style, *zapin*, which involves pairs of men who, dancing side by side, independently but in synchrony, gracefully process toward the musicians and back again, usually within in the perimeter of a rectangular area. Called *bar'a* in Oman and *jambia* in Yemen (the

Hajir Marawis

sharah (syara) rhythm

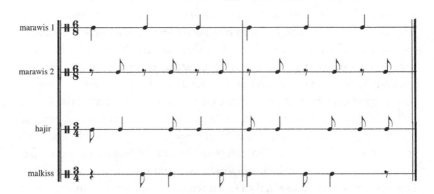

15.6. Transcription — The *sharah* (*syara/sharh*) rhythm.

name for the dagger that is held overhead), this dance exists in Indonesia as recreation, ritual, and "performative Sufism" (Nor 2013).

THE INDIAN OCEAN CONNECTION: FIELDWORK IN PROGRESS

My description of three pervasive styles of Islamic music in Indonesia samples the rich sonic tapestry of pious arts in the world's most populous Muslim nation. The *tawashih* tradition, *qasida rebana*, and *hajir marawis*, are complemented by a variety of other genres, from the cool pop sounds of *a cappella* (also *nasyid*), to the blaring of amateur marching bands. The active realization of Islam through the media of theater, literature, painting, dance, film, or music, while perhaps controversial for the country's conservative communities, is a process that originates with the praxis of conversion to and intensification of religious faith, something that is repeated over and over again through the institution of *dakwah*. In Indonesia, learning, knowing, and worshiping through hearing and being heard in musical ways has been viewed (and heard) positively at the intersection of religion, art, and popular culture. This coexistence of Islam and performance may be a characteristic unique to Indonesian culture as will be demonstrated by my preliminary comparative fieldwork.

My quest for the roots of some of the practices described in the first part of this chapter, on the northwest shores of the Indian Ocean, in Yemen and the Sultanate of Oman, yielded some remarkable surprises. It is actually the Hadramaut region of southwestern Yemen that has been so interconnected with Indonesia for centuries. This region borders Oman, and while the politics and economics of these two modern nations have diverged from one another, shared traditions of music, dance, and poetry are continuous in the region, perhaps since antiquity. In fact, Omanis assert that their traditions of poetry and song, that indeed all of their culture originally came from Yemen. After one visit to Yemen in 2009, research opportunities in that country ended for me while simultaneously opening in Oman, a country that I was able to visit several times between 2010 and 2015. I knew that there was common ground between Yemen and Oman and in their relationships to Indonesia. I hoped, furthermore, that an awareness of the connections between southern Arabia and Southeast Asia might be alive in the popular imagination of Omanis and also a part of Oman's national narrative, a story that highlights the country's multicontinental diplomacy through centuries of maritime trade. Several factors, both broad and detailed, supported my hypothesis. For example, many families, particularly those in the Dhofar region of southern Oman and its city Salalah, trace their origins to Yemen. In specific musical terms, at least two drum types (the *mirwas* and *hajar*), and performance practices such as the song type *dana dana*, the dance styles, *barʿa* and *zapin*, and rhythmic grooves such as *sharah* are common to all three countries: Yemen, Oman, and Indonesia.[13]

In Indonesia, musical and cultural resonance with Oman is found not only in the instrumental ensembles and their musical organization described above, but also in the seated dance, *mueseukat*, described by Kartomi (2011), which likely derives its name from the city of Muscat. Indonesian families who trace their roots to Oman are also called *Muscati*, a reference to Oman's capital city.[14] Finally, the Jewel of Muscat, a reconstruction of a ninth-century ship (an Omani *dhow*) that sailed successfully from Muscat to Singapore in 2010 using traditional methods of astral navigation, was modelled after the shipwreck found off the coast of the island of Bilitung to the east of Lampung, Sumatra, and just north of West Java, Indonesia, in 1998. Yet, in spite of the contemporary evidence for the long-term relationship between southern Arabia and Southeast Asia, a circum-Indian Ocean connection to Indonesia does not seem to "ring a bell" among many of the Omanis I have queried, nor does the penetration of the music of southern Arabia to places as far away as Southeast Asia seem to be part of the official story of the nation, a narrative that, like all national narratives, can be interpreted as strategically xenophobic.

PERFORMING ISLAM AROUND THE INDIAN OCEAN BASIN

So far, my discoveries of similarities in musical instruments, styles, and approaches to musical organization around the Indian Ocean have been a productive way to confirm a musical connection between regions that are known to have cultural connections that date back half a millennium. What I did not expect was the very different place I found for the performing arts in this part of the Muslim world. The Omani reaction to my interest in Islamic music and performance revealed to me a stance diametrically opposed to that to which I had become accustomed in Indonesia, or even that of the Arab world scholarship on music, where the interrelationship between music and Islam is acknowledged, vigorously debated, and even celebrated.

Whereas Indonesia has numerous categories of Islamic musical and popular culture that are recognized in a wide variety of discursive circles, when I inquired about where to find the cultural expressions of religion in Oman I was told by officials in Muscat: "there is none of that here." "No songs for the holidays of the Muslim calendar?" I questioned. "No special traditions for Eid, the end of Ramadan?" "No" was the answer to my questions. These responses were exaggerations, if not falsehoods, but the fact that the officials I met dismissed even the possibility of Islamic performance in the cultural sphere of modern Oman may be indicative of several trends.[15]

First, in an effort, beginning only in the late 1970s, to define and preserve a national culture, many genres of music and dance once considered "spiritual" or "religious" have been recast and elevated by various efforts of the Oman Center for Traditional Music (est. 1983) to the status of *Funun Taqlidiyah* or Traditional Arts. Omani ethnomusicologist Majid Al Harthy challenges the official assertion that traditional arts are now only performed for entertainment, however, when staged in a festival context and then televised, such performances do seem to be largely secularized.[16] Second, conservative minorities voice objection to musical activities in the public sphere, which they consider to be *haram* (forbidden). The tribes of Oman, adherents of Ibadhi Islam, historically eschewed musical activities among their own communities, tolerating it only among their slaves, the majority of whom were from East and Central Africa. Of particular concern today is the ROHM, the Royal Opera House Muscat, which opened its opulent doors for business in November 2011. Considered a symbol of cosmopolitan decadence, the expense of the opera house along with, occasionally, certain programs, has been decried by conservative religious groups. As a result, programming "appropriate" productions (concerts, dance, and opera) is top priority among Opera House staff. I have found that a hypersensitivity to the possible public objection to music at the Opera House also leads to self-censorship in other institutions, for example, universities and schools that might otherwise produce public musical events. My sense is that, in the case of Oman, these kinds objections to music, whether situated in the past or voiced in the present, encourage self-censorship and preclude the association of music with religion.

15.7. Musicians and dancers perform at the Salalah Tourism Festival (Dhofar province, Oman) in 2010. Note the male and female dancers, the bagpipe and keyboard instruments, and the variety of drums in the ensemble. The female backup singers are out of range of the frame. Photo by author.

In an age when the media is saturated with music and dance from around the world, objections to music in the public sphere may seem ludicrous. In the aftermath of the Arab Spring of 2011, however, allowing the conservative voices in Oman some public resonance may be a politically expedient way to allow parts of the society to let off steam. It is understandable that conservative voices, particularly those from the more religiously zealous interior of the country, might find all kinds of music objectionable, even some kinds of Arabic music. Traditional, "endogenetic" Omani music, namely the music of Arab tribal elite, is largely bereft of instrumental traditions, and even drumming, when performed to accompany songs or chant, is done not by Omani Arabs but by their servants or formerly by their slaves (Shawqi 1994). Omani tribal or Bedouin music focuses on responsorial song, with the majority of more complex and celebrative singing, drumming and dancing, and now instrumental ensembles, developing among Afro-Omani populations.

It is not surprising that the two regions that were consistently identified to me as "rich in music," were the eastern Sharkiyah region and the southern region of Dhofar, where Afro-Omani peoples and practices are dominant.

While Afro-Omani musicians appear in Muscat during cultural festivals, I was able to more fully experience their exciting performances during a short trip to Sur in the Sharkiyah region and then during two longer research trips I made to the Dhofar region in 2011 and 2012 for the summer festival that occurs during the monsoon season there known as the *Mahrajan al-Khareef* or the *Salalah Tourism Festival*. The Afro-Omani musics that are special to the Dhofar region, such as *bar'a*, *rabouba*, and *sharh*, involve multiple drums and idiophones and percussive aerophones (like the conch shell) as well as *'ud* (lute), keyboard, *nay* (flute), and even bagpipes and the single-reed, double-piped folk clarinet, called *mizmar*. Adjacent to Yemen and not so far from its culturally rich regions of Hadramaut and Maha, musicians and dancers I met in Salalah (both Omani and Yemeni) perform music and dance and with some of the instruments and rhythms that were first made known to me in Indonesia as *Seni Musik Islam* (Indonesian Islamic Musical Arts). How these genres are shared between continents that are thousands of miles apart is intriguing. Were these instruments and styles borne on the monsoon winds of centuries passed? Were they introduced recently, following 350 years of colonial rule, in the mid-twentieth century? Have Gulf or *Khaliji* styles seeped into the micro-musical subcultures of Indonesia through the cassette and compact disc trafficking that accompanies religious pilgrimage? And, are they renewed by the exchange of YouTube clips and file sharing today? By simply posing these questions I affirm them as probable scenarios, ones that will be substantiated by more research.

Theories of diffusionism advance the idea that "cultural traits diffuse or move from one place to another over time" (Stone 2008: 27). Such theories also recognize significant variations in the origins, histories, reception, ideas, and use of similar things in different places. Associated with the work of anthropologist Franz Boas and comparative musicologists Eric von Hornbostel and Jaap Kunst, for example, theories of diffusionism may be considered passé. Current research in ethnomusicology and cultural studies seems to focus on local communities and specific actors as they relate to larger entities like the nation-state or the globalized mediascape. Such is not the case among historians such as Sugata Bose, whose work on the historiography of the Indian Ocean, while acknowledging the importance of "micro-approaches," suggests that too much attention to "local communities and the nation" have eclipsed "broader comparisons" (2006: 7). Bose suggests we "render permeable and then creatively trespass across rather rigidly drawn external boundaries (of the Indian Ocean)," an "interregional arena of human interaction." Amidst a chorus of political strategists and public intellectuals such as, for example, Robert Kaplan, who argue for renewed attention to the Indian Ocean as a strategic zone of trade and security, Bose's academic voice makes the case for culture. Bose encourages "the exploration of the Indian Ocean as a cultural milieu" and asserts: "The overemphasis on trade has tended to obscure much else that went along with it, especially the flow of ideas and culture"(2006: 11).

Among the preliminary conclusions that may be drawn from my comparative work are, first, that one country's religious expression is another country's national heritage. Second, while scholars of Southeast Asian music acknowledge, sometimes reluctantly, the influences of the Muslim Middle East, connections between this region and African practices are rare. My analysis of the rhythmic grooves, the instruments, and the nomenclature that are found in both Indonesia and coastal Afro-Omani communities of the Arabian Peninsula suggests that there may be just a bit more Africa in the Indian Ocean trade winds that reached Indonesia than originally documented by scholars of Southeast Asian music.

As a symbol of class and distinction, the arts build cultural capital (Bourdieu 1986), and they have been a tool for nation building and diplomacy worldwide. I hope that this chapter demonstrates that such cultural capital is composed not just of western or colonial productions but also of cultural capital from the Arab world and Middle East, as the examples from Indonesia and the Arabian Gulf clearly demonstrate, albeit in significantly different ways. As scholars and students celebrate the myriad styles of Islamic popular culture in this volume, and observe the ways in which ritual and folk performances are staged for audiences with modern, media-driven production values, we may also lament the loss of some kinds of performance due to religious conservatism, secularist multicultural nationalism, or the march of globalization. This study points to the ways that sonic discourse, whether or not it is framed as spiritual, is being imported and localized in the Islamicate world. Taken collectively, the music of Indonesian Islam, considered key to the Islamization of the region since the onset of Indian Ocean trade relations, constitutes a singular repertoire of music and a Muslim music culture that has remained largely invisible to the Arab world and Middle East. My initial foray into the Arabian Peninsula not only confirms this assertion but also reveals a different approach to and raison d'être for the proactive development of arts, largely devoid of any association with religion.

Even more than Qur'anic recitation, a phenomenon whose status is perceived as uncontested and stable, music is a barometer of the complementary and dynamic processes of ongoing Islamization in Indonesia and of the continuous indigenization of Islam. Whether the performance of *tawashih* in styles originating in the Turko-Arab *maqam* tradition, the Afro-Arab rhythms and instruments of *hajir-marawis*, or the uniquely indigenous *qasida-rebana*, Islamic music in Indonesia should be considered a vanguard of popular culture in the Muslim world. Geographically vast and culturally diverse, Indonesia is just one place in the Muslim world where globally circulating systems of musical praxis and aesthetics—whether they originate in the lands of Arab authenticity, in colonial hybrids and international airwaves, or in regional roots and re-imaginations of tradition—are continuously sampled and recycled in imaginative ways.

NOTES

1. The sources for this claim are myriad and diverse. Descriptions of Indonesian Islam as a "special case" stem from the landmark ethnography by Clifford Geertz, *Religion in Java*. Among many other works that address representations of and assumptions about Indonesian Islamic practice, see, for example, Woodward 1996, Rasmussen 1996, 2001, 2005, 2010, Bowen 1996, Madjid 1996, and Harnish and Rasmussen 2011.

2. In 2010–2011 I was the Sultan Qaboos Cultural Center research fellow. I have made only one exploratory trip to Yemen in June 2009, when I got a sense of musical life in Sanaʿ. Thanks to Jean Lambert and Philip Schuyler for putting me in touch with some of the musicians in Sanaʿ. In Oman I acknowledge Majid Al Harthy, Nasser Al Taee, Fathi Mohsin Al Balushi, Issam El Mallah, and Faisal Al Busaidi. I am also grateful to Michael Frishkopf and Salwa El Shawan Castello-Branco for their support.

3. Oman, with less than three million inhabitants, boasts a military band program with numerous performing regiments, national symphony orchestras and Arabic Oriental orchestras, and the Oman Center for Traditional Music; and numerous publications on music have been commissioned by the Sultanate (see El Mallah 1985, 1998; Shawqi 1994; Christensen 2002, 2008; and Christensen and El Shawan Castelo-Branco 2009). National festivals feature musical pageantry on a monumental scale. The Sultan Qaboos University has established a department of music and musicology and the Royal Oman Opera House opened November 2011. See Al Harthy and Rasmussen 2012 and Rasmussen 2012.

4. A prototype for the national competitions in Qurʾanic recitation that I document (Rasmussen 2010) was held at the Asia Africa Conference.

5. The terms "technoscape" and "mediascape" derive from Appadurai's view of a global cultural economy composed of five scapes (1990). These "scapes" were first applied to ethnomusicology by Mark Slobin (1992). The efficacy of the technoscape and mediascape in facilitating global flows of recitation technique and style was made evident to me in my fieldwork in Indonesia. See also Rasmussen 2010, 78.

6. Kinoshita in her study of the influence of Al-Azharite alumni and the establishment of Islamic education in Indonesia, particularly the National Islamic University System (I. A. N., *Institut Agama Negri*), acknowledges that ʿulamaʾ from the Malay-Indonesian world had departed to the Middle East for the sake of pursuing Islamic knowledge at least from the mid-sixteenth century onward (Kinoshita 2009: 1), al-Azhar University in Cairo, the institution of Islamic learning since the tenth century, being a primary destination.

7. As Andrew Wientraub remarks about *dangdut*, Indonesia's most popular and durable urban music, "Although not a form of Islamic music *per se*, the *dangdut* vocal style cannot be separated from its roots in Islamic-related music and religious chant" (2011: 323). Ironically, while the major singers of *dangdut* point to the influence of Qurʾanic recitation on their vocal style, the music often comes under fire by critics for its promotion of risqué eroticism.

8. The performance discussed here can be heard on the website for my book posted by the University of California Press. http://www.ucpress.edu/book. php?isbn=9780520255494. Scroll down to the tab "Audio/Video." Nur al-Huda by IPQAH is track 16. I am grateful for the assistance of Bridget Robbins, who refined the transcriptions for this article. The lyrics of *Nur al-Huda*, like those of many *sholawat*, praise the Prophet Muhammad.

9. In Arabic, *qasida* denotes a poem in literary Arabic or, more specifically, the Arabic classical ode that is distinct in line structure and rhyme scheme. In the Indonesian language, however, the word *qasida* has been adapted as a collective noun for songs with religious or moral overtones.

10. A quick search on YouTube produces hundreds of videos. Search Qasidah Rebana Klasik or Qadisah Rebana Modern or Lomba Qasidah Rebana to get started. Such an approach to musical performance is also characteristic of the gong-chime ensembles of Southeast Asia and more specifically the gamelan ensembles of Indonesia.

11. I am grateful to the group *Ar-Rahman* and its lead singer Joendy, in East Jakarta (July 2004) for an invitation to their rehearsal and to two *hajir marawis* groups (one all male, one all female) associated with the *Institut Ilmu al-Qur'an* that performed at an exhibition of Islamic Arts organized in my honor in January 2010 (see figure 15.1).

12. As Capwell describes it, when heard in the context of the *gambus* ensemble, the *sharah* rhythmic complex "is in triple rhythm—to be more precise, it is in an ambiguous compound duple that confuses duple and triple rhythms in a constant hemiola" (1995, 85).

13. Video excerpts from my fieldwork of the instruments and performances mentioned may be made available by the author.

14. Personal communication, Ismail Fajrie Alatas, January 2011 (see Alatas 2011).

15. My official hosts were from the Royal Court (the Diwan), from the Center for Islamic Culture, and from the Ministry of Heritage and Culture. For programmers of the Muscat Festival (February 2011), Islam or religion did not seem to be organizing categories in the way that they would have in Indonesia where Muslim fashion, calligraphy, music, technology, pageantry, etc. might be categories in any civic celebration, festival, or exhibition. Nevertheless the Qur'an school is required for the display of Omani regional traditions, and the mosque is an important architectural feature of the reconstructed traditional village in Omani cultural festivals. Shi'a and Sunni Muslim minority populations do have Muslim musical traditions, for example, Malid. See my blog at: http://blogs.wm.edu/2011/02/10/akr-in-oman-part-2-1-the-muscat-festival-2011/. See also Christensen and El Shawan Castelo-Branco (2009) for numerous references to *malid* and other performance genres related to religious rituals and festivals.

16. Al Harthy asserts that non-Islamic and African origins of certain musical practices such as *tambura* and *leiwa* might be seen as controversial if taken as anything but entertainment by cultural officials. He also questions the notion, put forward by researchers in Oman in the 1980s, that distinct ethnic identities, either among people or as heard in music, have been lost (2010, 12).

REFERENCES

Alatas, Ismail Fajrie. 2011. "Becoming Indonesians: The Ba'Alawi in the Interstices of the Nation." *Die Welt des Islams* 51: 45–74.
Appadurai, Arjun. 1990. "Disjuncture and Difference in the Global Cultural Economy." *Public Culture* 2, no. 2: 1–24.

Berg, Birgit A. 2011. "'Authentic' Islamic Sound': *Orkes Gambus* Music, the Arab Idiom, and Sonic Symbols in Indonesian Islamic Musical Arts." In *Divine Inspirations: Music and Islam in Indonesia*, edited by David D. Harnish and Anne K. Rasmussen, 207–240. Oxford and New York: Oxford University Press.

Bose, Sugata. 2006. *A Hundred Horizons: The Indian Ocean in the Age of Global Empire.* Cambridge, MA and London, England: Harvard University Press.

Bourdieu, Pierre. 1986. "The Forms of Capital." In *Handbook of the Theory of Research for the Sociology of Education*, translated by Richard Nice, edited by J. E. Richardson, 241–258. New York: Greenwood Press.

Bowen, John R., ed. 1996. *Islam in an Era of Nation-State: Politics and Religious Renewal in Muslim Southeast Asia.* Honolulu: University of Hawai'i Press.

Capwell, Charles. 1995. "Contemporary Manifestations of Yemeni-Derived Song and Dance in Indonesia." *Yearbook for Traditional Music* 27: 76–89.

Christensen, Dieter. 2002. "Musical Life in Sohar, Oman." In *The Garland Encyclopedia of World Music*. Vol. 6, *The Middle East*, edited by Virginia Danielson, Scott Marcus, and Dwight Reynolds, 671–684. New York and London: Routledge.

———. 2008. "Oman." In *The New Grove Dictionary of Music and Musicians*. Oxford Music Online. http://www.oxfordmusiconline.com.

Christensen, Dieter, and Salwa El Shawan Castelo-Branco. 2009. *Traditional Arts in Southern Arabia Music and Society in Sohar, Sultanate of Oman.* Wilhelmshaven: Intercultural Music Studies, Florian Noetzel Verlag.

Geertz, Clifford. *The Religion of Java.* Chicago: University of Chicago Press.

Harnish, David D., and Anne K. Rasmussen, eds. 2011. *Divine Inspirations: Music and Islam in Indonesia.* Oxford and New York: Oxford University Press.

Al Harthy, Majid Hamdoon. 2010. "Performing History, Creating Tradition: The Making of Afro-Omani Musics in Umm Ligrumten, Sur Li'fyyah." PhD diss., Indiana University.

———. 2012. "African Identities, Afro-Omani Music, and the Official Constructions of a Musical Past." *The World of Music (New Series)* 1, no. 2: 97–130.

Al Harthy, Majid, and Anne K. Rasmussen. 2012. "Music in Oman: An Overture." *The World of Music (New Series)* 1, no. 2: 9–42.

Ho, Engseng. 2006. *The Graves of Tarim: Genealogy and Mobility across the Indian Ocean.* Berkeley: University of California Press.

Kaplan, Robert D. 2010. *Monsoon: The Indian Ocean and the Future of American Power.* New York: Random House.

Kartomi, Margaret. 2011. "'Art with a Muslim Theme' and 'Art with a Muslim Flavor' among Women of West Aceh," in *Divine Inspirations: Music and Islam in Indonesia*, edited by David D. Harnish and Anne K. Rasmussen, 269–296. Oxford and New York: Oxford University Press.

Kinoshita, Hiroko. 2009. "Islamic Higher Education in Contemporary Indonesia: Through the Islamic Intellectuals of al-Azharite Alumni." Kyoto Working Papers on Area Studies, no. 79 (G-COE Series 81).

Madjid, Nurcholish. 1996. "In Search of Islamic Roots for Modern Pluralism: The Indonesian Experience." In *Toward a New Paradigm: Recent Developments in Indonesian Islamic Thought*, edited by Mark R. Woodward, 89–116. Tempe: Arizona State University Program for Southeast Asian Studies.

El Mallah, Issam. 1998. *Oman Traditional Music Parts 1 and 2.* Muscat, Oman: Publications of the Oman Center for Traditional Music and Hans Schneider Verlag.

El Mallah, Issam, ed. 1985. *The Complete Documents of International Symposium on the Traditional Music of Oman*. Wilhelmshaven: Florian Noetzel Verlag.

"Mapping the Global Muslim Population." 2009. *The Pew Forum on Religion and Public Life*. Analysis, 7 October 2009. http://pewforum.org/Muslim/Mapping-the-Global-Muslim -Population(3).aspx.

Mauss, Marcel. 1979 [1936]. "Body Techniques." In *Sociology and Psychology: Essays*, edited and translated by B. Brewster. London: Routledge and Kegan Paul.

Nor, Mohd Anis bin Md. 2013. "Ritual of the *Qalb*: Performative Sufism in *Zapin*." Paper presented at the 42nd World Conference of the International Council for Traditional Music, Shanghai, China. 11–17 July 2013.

Racy, Ali Jihad. 2003. *Music Making in the Arab World: The Culture and Artistry of Tarab*. Cambridge: Cambridge University Press.

Rasmussen, Anne K. 1996. "Theory and Practice at the 'Arabic Org': Digital Technology in Contemporary Arab Music Performance." *Popular Music* (Special issue edited by Martin Stokes and Ruth Davis) 15, no. 3: 345–365.

———. 2001. "The Qur'an in Daily Life: The Public Project of Musical Oratory." *Ethnomusicology* 45, no. 1: 30–57.

———. 2005. "The Arabic Aesthetic in Indonesian Islam." *The World of Music* 47, no. 1: 65–90.

———. 2010. *Women, the Recited Qur'an, and Islamic Music in Indonesia*. Berkeley, Los Angeles, London: University of California Press.

———. 2012. "The Musical Design of National Space and Time in Oman." *The World of Music (New Series)* 1, no. 2: 63–96.

Shannon, Jonathan H. 2006. *Among the Jasmine Trees: Music and Modernity in Contemporary Syria*. Middletown, CT: Wesleyan University Press.

Shawqi, Yusuf. 1994. *Dictionary of Traditional Music in Oman*. English edition revised and expanded by Dieter Christensen. Wilhelmshaven: Intercultural Music Studies, Florian Noetzel Verlag.

Slobin, Mark. 1992. "Micromusics of the West: A Comparative Approach." *Ethnomusicology* 36, no. 1: 1–82.

Stone, Ruth M. 2008. *Theory for Ethnomusicology*. Upper Saddle River, NJ: Prentice Hall.

Van den Berg, L. W. C. 1886. *Le Hadhramout et les Colonies Arabes dans L'Archipel Indien*. Batavia: Impreimerie du Gouvernment.

Weintraub, Andrew N. 2011. "Morality and Its (Dis)contents: *Dangdut* and Islam in Indonesia." In *Divine Inspirations: Music and Islam in Indonesia*, edited by David D. Harnish and Anne K. Rasmussen, 297–317. Oxford and New York: Oxford University Press.

Woodward, Mark R. 1996. "Talking across Paradigms: Indonesia, Islam, and Orientalism." In *Toward a New Paradigm: Recent Developments in Indonesian Islamic Thought*, edited by Mark R. Woodward, 1–46. Tempe: Arizona State University Program for Southeast Asian Studies.

CHAPTER 16

MUSLIMS, MUSIC, AND RELIGIOUS TOLERANCE IN EGYPT AND GHANA: A COMPARATIVE PERSPECTIVE ON DIFFERENCE

MICHAEL FRISHKOPF

MY FIRST ETHNOMUSICOLOGICAL research took place in 1988, when I traveled to Ghana to study traditional song composition among Ewe-speaking people hailing from the Volta Region. My studies centered on traditional Ewe composers, such as Norvor (aka Emannuel Afornorfe). Traditional Ewe music accompanies African Traditional Religion, but there was also traditional music in Christianity, and Christianity in traditional music. Most Ewes are nominal if not always practicing Christians; nearly all receive Christian names, but many continue to practice elements of African Traditional Religion.

Generally, Ghanaians classify themselves in three main religious groups: Christian, Muslim, and Traditionalist.[1] But minority religious communities in Ghana include the Baha'i faith, Buddhism, Judaism, Hinduism, Shintoism, and Rastafarianism. Divisions are not clear-cut, because many Ghanaians affiliate (in word, deed, or both) to more than one religious tradition, and may occasionally change their affiliations.

Religion in Ghana is diverse and complex due to interreligious tolerance. Government surveys misrepresent Ghana's religious reality, explicitly through single-response multiple-choice questions; implicitly via authority favoring high-status answers. So eager was I to experience "traditional Ghana" that I hardly noticed this complex diversity—except to observe that the spread of Christianity appeared to threaten traditional performance.

During my research on an Ewe singing-drumming-dancing style called *Kinka*, I was thus surprised to discover that my composer friend Norvor had composed a song explaining why Christians should accept traditional drumming ensembles, even including in its lyrics the Lord's Prayer (see Frishkopf 1989: 180). Later, I found that African Independent Churches such as the Ewe Apostles' Revelation Society (founded around 1940) are especially hospitable to traditional African music and culture, incorporating neo-traditional styles such as *Borborbor* or even traditional *Agbadza*, but so are mainline churches such as Anglican or Catholic.

Ghana's Muslims were still largely invisible for me, though I had met some Buddhists. But for my doctoral degree, I shifted gears and focused on Islam in Egypt. I lived in Cairo from 1992 to 1998 while conducting dissertation research centered on the sounds of Islam, including performances by professional Sufi singers, such as Egypt's star *munshid* Shaykh Yasin al-Tuhami, and musical liturgies of Sufi orders, or *turuq*. Along with Egyptian Sufis, I found this music profoundly moving, especially when performed at a saint festival (*mawlid*). Progressive elites, however, criticized Sufi music as mere "folklore," while for an expanding class of modernist fundamentalists and Islamists—Salafis and Muslim Brothers—such music, along with its associated dance, saint veneration, and ecstatic behavior—was *bid'a* ("innovation," i.e., heresy).

Throughout these years, I observed the broader religious intolerance of Egyptian society, both legally and practically. Egyptians enjoyed limited religious freedom, and Christians (around 10 percent of the population) were unequal to their Muslim compatriots. Religion was almost entirely hereditary. Conversion was condemned. Non-Abrahamic faiths[2] were forbidden. Christians were informally banned from certain specializations. Sectarian violence, mainly inflicted upon Christians, was deplorably common.

Yet, though the 1990s were a period of tremendous militant Muslim activism, during which terrorist atrocities were committed with disturbing regularity, large public performances of Sufi music continued to be performed undisturbed. Salafi discourse might rail against them, but there was no physical violence.

A wide array of Sufi orders displayed diverse liturgies, or *hadras*, including religious chant (*inshad*); two modern orders founded in the twentieth century were typically contrastive: the ecstatically musical Jazuliyya and the more restrained Ja'fariyya (Frishkopf 2000, Frishkopf 1999). Foremost among professional Sufi singers was Shaykh Yasin al-Tuhami (Frishkopf 2002), drawing crowds of ten thousand or more when performing for large saint festivals (*mawalid*) or memorials (see figure 16.1).

Most Muslims exhibited considerable tolerance of multiple Muslim groups—not just Sufi orders but Salafi groups as well—so long as they remained peaceful, posed no political threat, and remained grounded in a shared, coherent substrate of normative Sunni Islam. The integrity of this substrate was expressed and maintained from below, through common practices, including broadly accepted vocal genres, such as *ibtihalat* (solo supplications*)*, *murattal* Qur'anic recitation, and popular *anashid* (religious hymns) (Frishkopf 2000, 2001, 2008), as well as from above, by government institutions

16.1A AND B. Shaykh Yasin al-Tuhami performing two public *hadras* for *mulids* (saint festivals) in Cairo, mid-1990s: (left) accompanied by percussion and *kawala* (reed flute) for Sufi scholar-saint Imam al-Laythi; (right) accompanied by *kamanja* (violin; not shown), for mystical poet-saint Sidi 'Umar ibn al-Farid). Poetry evokes the mystical relation between Muslim and God, using ecstatic symbols of love, intoxication, and song. Audio and video recordings of his performances are sold all across Egypt. Photos by author.

(mainly al-Azhar University, the Ministry of Religious Endowments, and state radio and television broadcasts). The long-standing global authority of Egyptian Islam also limited the possibility of external influences that might otherwise divide this substrate.

But if there was intra-Islamic tolerance, there was little real choice. Egyptian Muslim identity was additive—one was a Sunni Muslim first and then layered voluntary associations on top of that. Aside from rare (and, all too frequently, persecuted) exceptions, one didn't "convert" to a new religious group in Egypt. The shared substrate could not be openly questioned. There were, virtually, no "sects."

I reconnected with Ghanaian music and culture after accepting a position at the University of Alberta in 1999, where I continue to teach ethnomusicology today. There I founded the University of Alberta West African Music Ensemble, befriended members of the local Ghanaian community, and rediscovered my personal and research connections to West Africa.

When I finally returned to Ghana in 2006 in order to establish a study abroad program centered at the University of Ghana, I found my Egyptian experience had opened my eyes to new trajectories for inquiry. I had become intensely curious about Islam and Muslims in Ghana, especially their musical practices. And I wanted to understand what I now observed—in retrospect—to be a remarkable degree of religious tolerance there.

From my casual readings in Ghanaian history, I'd come to associate Muslims with the various peoples—Dagomba, Mamprusi, Gonja—of the northern regions, where Juula and, later, Hausa traders had carried the religion starting around the fifteenth century. But now my Egypt-trained eyes saw mosques and Muslims everywhere. Most larger Ghanaian cities contain a *zongo* (Hausa for "stranger"), a district originally settled by nonnative Muslims, primarily Hausas—often traders, or soldiers transferred during colonial times by the British from Nigeria (Pellow 1991). With substantial conversion to Islam among some ethnic groups—especially the Ga and Fante along the coast and the Akan near Kumasi—combined with urbanization, Muslim populations have become more heterogeneous today, in ethnicity, class, profession, and residence, diffusing throughout Ghana. In fact, there are many mosques even in towns of the predominantly Christian Volta Region. Most serve "immigrants," but I also met a few Ewe Muslims.

In 2008 I had the opportunity to travel north, and began to conduct fieldwork in the Muslim-majority vicinity of Tamale, capital of Ghana's Northern Region. It was during this period that a question began to take shape in my mind about the nature of religious tolerance in both countries, its relation to the structure and history of religious groups, and the role of music in connecting or dividing them.

INTERRELIGIOUS TOLERANCE

Compared to Egypt, Ghanaian religious tolerance and diversity seemed positively utopian, with mosques and churches of multiple denominations commingled in nearly every town. Religion appeared to constitute a real and personal choice. I even encountered single families with Christian, Muslim, and Traditionalist members. Religious identity was fluid—affiliation was often dynamic and multiple, especially when combining African Traditional Religion with Islam or Christianity. Today, Muslim as well as Christian holidays are officially recognized as national holidays in Ghana, even though according to the 2000 census Ghana is roughly 71 percent Christian and only about 18 percent Muslim (Ghana Statistical Service 2012: 6). By contrast, in Egypt, only Christmas is nationally recognized among Christian holy days, and only since 2002.

Differences in tolerances in social practice both reflect and support differences in legal systems. Intolerance is embedded in Egyptian law and imposed by an authoritarian political system fearful of free religious affiliations. Egypt's laws effectively prohibit real religious freedom, and these prohibitions are socially reinforced.

Chapter 1, article 2 of Egypt's 1971 constitution (reaffirmed in both the 2012 constitution and in the draft 2013 constitution) states that "Islam is the Religion of the State, Arabic is its official language, and Islamic Jurisprudence (Sharia) is the principal source[3] of legislation" ("Constitution of Egypt," 2013).[4]

Although chapter 3, article 40 states, "All citizens are equal before the law. They have equal public rights and duties without discrimination due to sex, ethnic origin, language, religion or creed," Egypt's laws prohibit:

- a Muslim from converting to any other religion
- a Muslim woman from marrying a non-Muslim man
- repairing a church without the Governor's permission
- building a church without the President's permission (the Hamayouni law of 1856)
- official recognition of religions other than Islam, Christianity, and Judaism

In Egypt, everyone necessarily has one—and only one—religion. One's religion is considered—by the law and by the vast majority—to be a deeply embodied element of one's identity—second, perhaps, only to one's gender, and, under ordinary circumstances at least, not subject to change. This static, permanent affiliation is nearly always born out in practice. Indeed, religion is predictable, being almost entirely hereditary, through the patriline. Conversion is condemned: legally in one direction (Islam to other), socially in the other.[5] Mixed religion families are rare: intermarriage is legally forbidden (Muslim woman to non-Muslim man) or strongly discouraged (the reverse); in the latter case, children are unequivocally Muslim. One's religion is, therefore, stamped on one's official identity card or passport as indelibly as one's birthdate.

Further, only the "Abrahamic" faiths are accepted: Islam (in practice, only its Sunni variety), Christianity, and Judaism, the latter today nearly vanished (and subject to suspicion). The common Egyptian legal code leaves "personal status law" (concerning such matters as marriage, divorce, and inheritance) entirely to the jurisdiction of one's religion ('aqida), rendering otherworldly faith an important reference for this-worldly legal rights and obligations. Christians' religious and even civil rights are unequal to those of their Muslim compatriots. Churches cannot be constructed or even repaired without government approval. Discrimination extends into secular life, as certain professions (e.g., Arabic teacher) and high political or military office are nearly impossible for Christians to attain. Sectarian violence between Muslims and Christians is deplorably common in practice, despite a national ideology of unity. Additionally, the Mubarak dictatorship was keen to nip in the bud any religious movement threatening the Sunni substrate, especially one with political potential. In this way they moved to ban the popular but esoteric Burhaniyya Sufi order (Hoffman 1995), and have typically reacted quickly against Shi'ite preaching (El-Gundy 2014).

In contrast to Egypt, Ghana is a secular state, its citizens enjoying legal guarantees for religious freedom and equality. And unlike Egypt these lofty principles seemed to be realized in the practical diversity and fluidity of Ghanaian religious life. Religious freedom, equality, and harmony appeared to prevail, just as I'd observed nearly twenty years earlier. It appeared that Ghana's citizens enjoyed a remarkable freedom to select and change religious affiliations without prejudice. The idea of Ghana as religiously tolerant reappeared again and again in both scholarly and popular discourse (e.g., Owusu-Ansah 2013; "President Commends Ghanaians for Religious Tolerance" 2013).

Practical and legal tolerance appeared to be linked. In contrast to the religious intolerance embedded in Egyptian law, Ghana's constitution establishes a secular state, guaranteeing freedom and equality in matters of religious choice. Chapter 5 (Fundamental Human Rights and Freedoms) of Ghana's 1992 constitution states:

> Every person in Ghana, whatever his race, place of origin, political opinion, colour, religion, creed or gender shall be entitled to the fundamental human rights and freedoms of the individual . . . A person shall not be discriminated against on grounds of gender, race, colour, ethnic origin, religion, creed or social or economic status. All persons shall have the right to freedom of speech and expression . . . freedom to practice any religion and to manifest such practice; Every person is entitled to enjoy, practice, profess, maintain and promote any culture, language, tradition or religion subject to the provisions of this Constitution. (*The Constitution of the Republic of Ghana* 2013)

And unlike Egypt, where practical oppression tends to undermine religious freedom even as practiced within legal boundaries, these lofty principles seemed to be realized in the everyday diversity and fluidity of Ghanaian religious life.

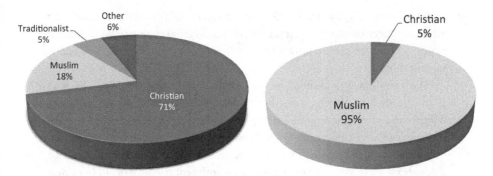

16.2A AND B. Religious diversity in Ghana (left) and Egypt (right). Ghana displays diversity, fluidity, and interfaith tolerance, as compared to Egypt. Single-affiliation survey statistics misrepresent Ghana's complex multiaffiliative religious reality, and the "other" category conceals representation of every major world faith, including religions of East and South Asia. In Egypt, by contrast, religion is (literally) stamped on one's identity (card) or inscribed on one's body (Copts frequently tattoo crosses; many Muslim men cultivate the *zabiba*, a mark on the forehead indicating frequent prostration), and there are only three Abrahamic choices. (Sources: Ghana Statistical Service 2012; "The World Factbook: Egypt" 2014)

ISLAMIC TOLERANCE

Yet my utopian vision of Ghanaian religious tolerance was shaken following a fieldwork journey to Ghana's Northern Region, in summer 2009. Based in Tamale, I made an excursion to the town of Diare, about 50 km north, for a *mawlidi*, a celebration of the Prophet's birthday. My trip revealed that while interreligious tolerance may prevail in Ghana, Muslim communities are divided and frequently intolerant of one another—sometimes violently so.

Tamale and environs is the traditional home of the Dagomba people, though other ethnic-linguistic groups also abound. Here the majority is Muslim. Some retain the local syncretic Islam rooted in chieftaincy, but during the twentieth century many others joined reformist groups seeking an Islam validated by connections to global Muslim authorities. There are four such groups: the Tijaniyya (a Sufi order), the Ahmadiyya (a Muslim movement), the Ahlussunna wal-Jama'a (a Salafi or "fundamentalist" organization), and a small Shi'a community.

Each group professes to reform traditional, localized, syncretic Islam, claiming authority via socio-spiritual linkages to authorities located outside Ghana. Each group is exclusivist, its social boundaries well maintained, providing a total religious identity; in joining one effectively "converts." Each group presides over a particular mosque in Tamale, which is empowered—

spiritually, socially, and financially—by transnational connections, appearing all the stronger because Ghana (in contrast to Muslim-majority West African states, and in complete contrast to Egypt) is relatively lacking in indigenous Islamic authority.

The Tijaniyya was founded by Sidi Ahmad al-Tijani (1737–1815). He was born and died in North Africa but traveled widely, studying in Cairo and Mecca, and joining several Sufi *turuq* (Abun-Nasr 1965). He claimed to have experienced a waking vision of the Prophet, who authorized him to found a Sufi order. This order, already prominent in Cairo and North Africa, spread throughout West Africa following the nineteenth century jihad of al-Hajj Umar Tal (1797–1864) of Futa Toro (present-day northern Senegal and southern Mauritania), who likewise traveled to Mecca and Cairo, and became the regional Tijaniyya leader or *khalifa*. Despite its Sufi orientation, the Tijaniyya actually emerged as a reformist movement in West Africa—advocating shari'a over syncretism, while adding mystical beliefs and practices. These converge most spectacularly in the *mawlidi* (from the Arabic *mawlid*): music and dance-filled celebrations for the Prophet and Tijani saints.

The Tijaniyya appears to have entered the boundaries of present-day Ghana in the nineteenth century, via Hausa and Juula traders. The Ghanaian Tijaniyya is strongly linked to Senegal, via the celebrated Tijani Shaykh Ibrahim Niasse (1900–1975) from Kaolack, Senegal. More than a Sufi shaykh, Niasse was a world Muslim leader (for instance, vice president of the Saudi-based Muslim World League). He first visited Ghana in the 1950s, attracting thronged attention from religious and political luminaries of the day. One of Niasse's spiritual disciples, Shaykh (Mallam) Abdullah (Abdulai) Ahmed Maikano (1923–2005) of Prang, Ghana, became the de facto leader of Tijanis in Ghana (and imam of the Ghana Armed Forces) until his death in 2005, when the mantle fell to his son, Shaykh Abd al-Fayir Khalifa Maikano. In Tamale, the Tijaniyya occupy—quite literally—a central position. Tamale's Central Mosque is overwhelmingly Tijani. But they are strongly criticized by the Ahmadiyya and the Ahlussunna for deviating from "true" Islam.

The Ahmadiyya movement was founded in 1889 in Qadian, India (Punjab) by Mirza Ghulam Ahmad (1835–1908). For followers, he was the awaited *mahdi*, the messiah, even (for some) a prophet. Coastal Fante Muslims invited the Ahmadiyya to Ghana in 1921, as Muslim missionaries who could support education as their Christian counterparts did. Today they are widespread throughout Ghana; Tamale contains a large, ornate Ahmadi mosque. While this chapter centers on conflict with the Tijanis, the Ahmadis also receive much criticism for deviance, primarily due to their veneration of Ghulam Ahmad, but also for other practices such as the Ahmadi choir, a musical tool for social bonding, drawing on Fante music and church choir organization. Some of these songs praise the Ahmadiyya movement itself.

Objecting to these musical accretions is a third group, Ahlussunna wal-Jamaʿa ("people of the tradition of Muhammad and the community"), representing the modernist wave of transnational, revivalist, fundamentalist Islam. Many of its leaders visited Mecca via the *hajj* or ʿumra, while others received scholarships from Egypt or Saudi Arabia to study in those countries. They returned bearing a Salafi Islam centered squarely on Qurʾan and Sunna; some established schools and mosques to propagate it further. The Ahlussunna reject key Ahmadi and Tijani beliefs and practices, including performance of music, as "*bidʿa*." The ranks of the Ahlussunna wal-Jamaʿa have rapidly expanded since the oil-empowerment of Saudi Arabia after 1973. There are also a smaller number of Shiʿa in Tamale, due to Iranian funding of mosques and provision of scholarships.

While association with one of these Muslim reformist groups—Tijani, Ahmadi, Ahlussunna, or Shiʿa—is voluntary and dynamic, the groups themselves are mutually exclusive and well-bounded, unlike Egyptian Muslim groups, which often overlap. Also unlike Egypt, Ghanaian reformist groups do not build upon a common substrate. Rather, each Ghanaian Muslim group offers a total self-contained, distinctive religious ideology, identity, and socio-ritual life. They are, essentially, Muslim "sects," as different from each other as Ghana's Catholic church is from the Apostles' Revelation Society. Hence they are inherently incompatible, unlike the space between Traditionalism and Christianity or Islam, which can be more fluid and syncretic. As they exist in a country relatively lacking in indigenous Islamic authority, and as they are empowered instead by authoritative sources outside Ghana, they are far more predisposed to conflict than Egypt's Muslim groups, despite—or, as I argue, because of—Ghana's prevailing interreligious tolerance.

MAWLIDI

While visiting Tamale in July 2009, my Tijani friend Muhammad (half Hausa, half Dagomba) invited me to a *mawlidi* in celebration of the Prophet's birthday, including praise singing, drumming, dancing, and speeches, to take place in Diare, a Dagomba village some 50 km to the north.

In Ghana, Tijani *mawlidi* music and dance is called *kwashi-rawa* (a Hausa phrase, interpreted in Ghana as "let's dance"), and it draws heavily on Hausa musical and poetic traditions originating in Nigeria (Ibrahim 2011: 176). Spiritually, the Ghanaian *mawlidi* is closely linked with Shaykh Ibrahim Niasse of Senegal.

16.3A AND B. Contrasting two pressure drums, in morphology, technique, and sound: the Hausa-derived *kalaku* (left; photo by David Ewenson, 2014) and the Dagomba *lunga* (right; photo by author, 2014). The distinctive musical meanings of each are highlighted when juxtaposed.

I had attended numerous Tijaniyya rituals in Cairo; their practices were firmly grounded in normative Egyptian Sunni Islam, and—aside from distinctive Tijani prayers (e.g., Salat al-Fatih) and the prominence of Ahmad al-Tijani himself—had little in common with the Ghanaian *mawlidi*. But such localization is common in Sufism.

We rode north from Tamale for about one hour on Muhammad's scooter, reaching Diare by mid-afternoon. My severe anxiety at traveling helmetless on the back of a tiny scooter, amidst enormous grinding trucks speeding toward the northern border with Burkina Faso was, to some degree at least, offset by the stunning beauty of Tamale's countryside.

There I immediately met a small group of Tijani musicians by the roadside, Muhammad's friends. Some were drumming, while another replaced the head on his *kalaku* pressure drum in preparation for the evening's festivities. The operation required the drum to be completely disassembled. Deconstructed in this way the *kalaku*'s contrast to a similar Dagomba drum, the *lunga*, became apparent from the inside out. The Dagomba are famous for their drumming ensembles, including a pressure drum, *lunga*, and bass drum, *gung-gong*, that feature in Dagomba Islamic festivals, such as *Damba*, a local celebration of the Prophet's birthday (Locke 1990). Despite resemblances in the details of construction—materials, size, lacing—as well as playing technique (faster), and sound (higher)—all of which I had the opportunity to observe very closely that afternoon and evening—the Tijani pressure drum is definitively not Dagomba, and projects a non-Dagomba identity in performance.

Rather, the *kalaku* and indeed the entire complex of *kwashi-rawa*, including drumming, singing, poetry, and dancing, along with the larger ritual complex of *mawlidi* (including sermons delivered in Hausa and translated into Dagomba for the sake of local attendees) strongly indexes the northern Nigerian Hausa culture from which it is said to derive, a culture closely associated with the Tijaniyya in Nigeria. Musically linked to the Hausa, spiritually to Shaykh Niasse of Senegal, the Tijaniyya carries a transnational Muslim authority in Ghana, ensounded and embodied in music and dance.

Besides *kalaku*, other Tijani drums include *kurkutu*, *tuni*, and the so-called "side-by-side," all contrasting sharply with local Dagomba musical culture. Indeed, the contrast is only intensified by commonalities in playing technique and morphology, making differences all the more conspicuous.

All afternoon, visitors were streaming into Diare by microbus, thronging

16.4. *Kalaku, tuni, kurkutu,* and *kalaku* (left to right). Photo by author, 2009.

the town. *Kwashi-rawa* drumming was performed for these guests as they arrived. Throughout, the *mawlidi* drumming accompanied dignitaries processing toward the main performance site, and similar music accompanied gender-segregated dancing throughout the night.

In addition to drumming and dancing, the *mawlidi* featured singing. The *madaha* (the word is derived from Arabic "*madh*," praise) performs *zikiri* (again from Arabic, "*dhikr*," remembrance), sung praise poetry, which can be directed toward God, the Prophet, shaykhs, chiefs, or other dignitaries. A well-known young *madaha* named Iddi, with several published recordings to his credit, performed for me in a beautiful penetrating nasal voice (contrasting sharply with traditional Dagomba singing), accompanied by the *kwashi-rawa* ensemble.

Shaykh Abd al-Fayir Khalifa Maikano, one of contemporary Ghana's primary Tijani leaders, attends each village *mawlidi*. This becomes nearly a full-time occupation during the season of the Prophet's birthday. My new friends—knowing my fluency in Arabic—proudly informed me that he spoke Arabic too, and that I should meet him. I found him to be gentle and kindly, speaking Arabic impressively. In fact he had studied in Cairo, and we knew the same Tijani shaykhs there.

Afterward we crowded into the open space before the town mosque. An enormous crowd accumulated, comprising villagers and hundreds of visitors, thronging the area. Special seats were reserved for the shaykhs. Proceedings started around 9:30 p.m., and continued until the following day: drumming, dancing, *zikiri*, sermons, and life stories of the Prophet and shaykhs. Translations into Dagbani helped to recruit villagers to the Tijani way. We headed home after *fajr* (dawn) prayer, but the *mawlidi* continued on to morning.

For the Tijaniyya, these all-night events constitute a form of religious worship. But they are also crucial for sustaining solidarity and attracting new members away from competing movements. Many, many *mawlidi*s are held each year throughout Ghana—not just for the Prophet but for Tijani shaykhs as well. Each draws on broad overlapping catchment areas, so that co-participation at multiple *mawlidi*s is common. This fact, together with the intensity of the *mawlidi* experience, wrapped in *kwashi-rawa*, induces a tight solidarity among Tijanis, while drawing converts.

In other words, it is not only the emotional intensity of the *mawlidi* itself but the ramifications of participatory overlap that appear crucial for Tijani solidarity.

For their distinctive practices, most visibly the *mawlidi*, the Tijaniyya are not only denounced but also physically opposed by the Ahlussunna. Muhammad told me that these "Sunnis" had recently failed to stop a *mawlidi* performance,

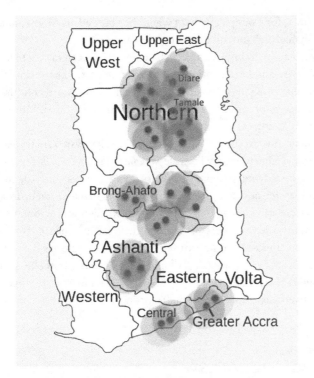

16.5. Hypothetical *mawlidi* overlaps. *Mawlidis* are celebrated annually, but not simultaneously, enabling participants to attend multiple events. Most attendees come from a geographical catchment area, but these areas overlap. Others, especially Tijani leaders, travel widely to attend *mawlidi*s throughout Ghana. Map based on "Regions of Ghana" 2004 Thfc. Downloaded from Wikipedia and reprinted here under a CC BY-SA 3.0 license.

despite violence leading to several deaths. Since the Tijanis had to fight back, the police weren't sure who was responsible, so the next *mawlidi* was performed under police supervision. The police, he said, loved the event, even dancing along. Thus it was clear, to him at least, that it had been the Sunnis who were creating the problems. He told me they view their anti-*mawlidi* behavior as a form of jihad, purifying Islam.

The Tijanis counter by citing a common Sufi expression, "that which is not explicitly forbidden is accepted," and pointing to music as a key factor making people happy and drawing them to Islam. Sometimes they also counter with violence of their own, for example, in 1997 when they burned an Ahlussunna mosque in Wa, Ghana (N. Samwini 2006: 142–143 n. 401).

Similar clashes, leading to injuries and even deaths, have been taking place for forty years or more and have continued into 2012 at least. I heard similar stories from Muslims in Kumasi, where the two communities are continually at loggerheads, with occasional flares of violence (Ibrahim 2003, Iddrisu 2009, N. I. Samwini 2003).

Despite denunciations from the Ahlussunna, the Tijaniyya remain exceedingly popular, perhaps precisely because *mawlidi* music—*kwashi-rawa*—induces powerfully satisfying social and religious experiences. Indeed, the Ahlussunna-Tijaniyya tension is reproduced within the *mawlidi* itself, in a self-defining discourse of tolerance. Sermons and *zikiri* denounce "Sunnis" as intolerant, unable to leave others to practice their faith in peace, praise Tijani tolerance, and oppose Islamic extremism worldwide, clearly capitalizing on post-9/11 discourses. In Tamale, I obtained the Hausa text of one such song, actually a *zikiri* about singing *zikiri*, by Shaykh Maikano's praise singer, Waddud, who answers his critics in a poem, retorting:

> *You've worried us,*
> *That you will thrash us,*
> *Thrash! (After that they hid behind a door*
> *That they should treat Waddud the way he was treated*
> *What has Waddud done to them?*
> *That he is the vociferous one?)*
> *I let everyone enjoy, because I like joy*
> *But after taking joy,*
> *You go and hide behind a door*
> "DEFENDING WADDUD," A HAUSA SONG BY THE *MADAHA*, CRITICIZING
> HIS CRITICS (WITH THANKS TO DR. ABDULAI IDDRISU FOR PROVIDING
> AN ENGLISH TRANSLATION)

Thus, while Ghanaian religious tolerance appears to be relatively high at the interreligious level—between Christianity, Islam, and Traditionalism—within Islam intrareligious tensions between multiple, well-bounded, reformist sects run high and sometimes erupt into violence. By contrast, Egypt's Muslim population is relatively undivided—integrated by a shared Islamic substrate, despite additive identities defining individuals as Salafis, Sufis, or other. Intrareligious conflict between Muslim groups is exceedingly rare. During the 1990s, Egyptian fundamentalists may have criticized Sufi practices, but reserved most of their vitriol and all of their action for the dictatorial government. Meanwhile Christian/Muslim violence is relatively frequent in Egypt but uncommon in Ghana. I began to wonder how I might understand these differences.

COMPARISON

The process of Islamization has been quite different in each region. Populous Egypt was forcefully conquered by Muslim Arab armies in 639 CE, and Islam thereafter spread, top-down, under the constant pressure of religious discrimination, particularly the *jizya*, a head tax levied on non-Muslims. Egypt soon became a primary religious center for the Muslim world, particularly after construction in 970 CE of the prestigious al-Azhar University. Thus Egypt has always enjoyed tremendous Islamic authority.

By contrast, Islam entered Ghana more gently and gradually, and far later—starting around the fifteenth century—via Juula Muslims, who lived initially in enclaves at the periphery of the Muslim world. These traders brought both economic and symbolic capital—wealth, and the prestige of Arabic writing. Consequently, local chiefs of various ethnic groups cultivated their friendship, and sometimes converted, together with their families (Levtzion 1987, Robinson 2004, N. Samwini 2006). But the political power of these chiefs depended on maintaining traditional religion, deeply implicated as it was in social life, and so it was in the interest of neither Juula nor chiefs to challenge such tradition. Islamization thus followed "Suwarian" accommodationist Islam (after the Malian Hajj Salim al-Suwari, who advised Muslims living as minorities in West Africa to practice tolerance) (Wilks 1989). This meant that traditional Islam in Ghana was syncretic, localized to harmonize with each ethnic group. Such harmony came at the price of broader uniformity and authority. Traditional Islam was highly variable and quite different from Islam of dominant urban centers such as Cairo or Mecca. Localized Islamic traditions of West Africa lacked global authority and were vulnerable to charges of *bid'a*.

Into this authority vacuum flourished reform movements, including, successively, the Tijaniyya, the Ahmadiyya, and the Ahlussunna. Despite their contrastive ideological characters and resultant clashes, these movements shared certain characteristics, namely:

- drawing on nonelites, against traditional, syncretic local Muslim authority as vested in chieftaincy
- emphasizing empowerment of transethnic, transnational unity
- reforming local practice by reference to broader Islamic norms
- demonstrating linkages to powerful global centers of Islamic authority

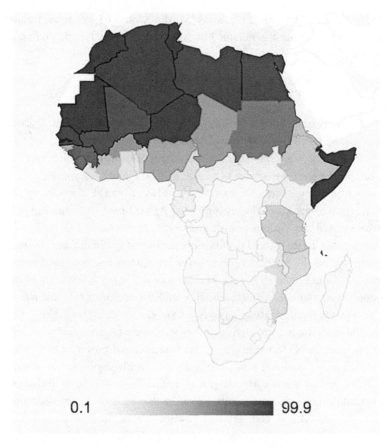

0.1 ▭▬ 99.9

16.6. Distribution of Muslim population in Africa. Darker shading indicates a higher percentage of Muslims. Reproduced with kind permission of http://www.americansecurityproject.org/ (based on data provided by Pew Research).

The various reform movements naturally maintained sharp boundaries, because they did not grow out of a common matrix of local religious culture, but rather represent foreign intrusions, fueled by powerful, yet contrastive, transnational Islamic currents. The older syncretic Islam, which they opposed, clearly was not positioned to provide a common Islamic substrate in Ghana. Precisely the reverse situation obtains in Egypt.

But why do they clash? I develop a speculative explanation by applying concepts from social network theory, and from economics.

Each movement seeking to reform traditional Ghanaian ethnic Islam deployed individuals privileged by linkages to transnational Islamic authorities:

places or people conferring high social capital. Such linkages may be direct, or indirect, mediated through genealogical lineages, the Sufi *"silsila"* (initiatory chain), the scholarly *"isnad"* (chain of hadith authorities), a line of teacher-shaykhs, or the like.

I suggest that this empowerment has been amplified by a social network phenomenon first observed by Mark Granovetter (1973) as "the strength of weak ties," and developed further by Ron Burt (1992) as a theory of "structural holes." What these social scientists have observed is the power of brokers—individuals connecting otherwise disconnected social networks—despite the weakness of their ties on either side. The broker's prestige—his or her high social capital—stems not from intrinsic abilities, but rather results from a unique social structural position, that of connection.

What I would like to argue, in a religious context, is that when actors linked to a distant, high-prestige place, institution, or person (whether Mecca, al-Azhar University in Cairo, Shaykh Ibrahim Niasse of Kaolack, or Sidi Ahmad al-Tijani in Fez), each of them carries great prestige. This explains the initial appeal of those Muslims appearing in Ghana who could write or speak

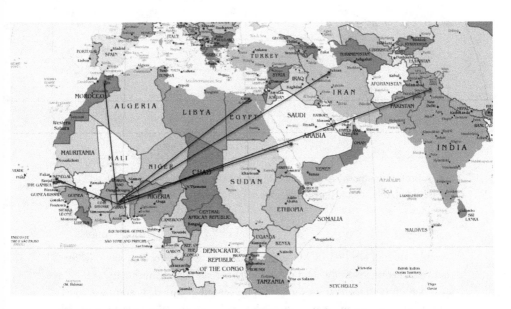

16.7. Global Muslim authorities bear upon Tamale from Senegal, Nigeria, and Morocco (Tijani), Egypt and Saudi Arabia (Ahlussunna), South Asia (Ahmadi), and Iran (Shi'a) catalyzing formation of distinctive Muslim communities empowered from without. Map courtesy of the University of Texas Libraries, the University of Texas at Austin.

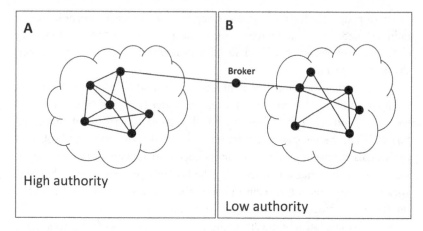

16.8. Broker, occupying a structural hole, thereby acquiring authority from A in B.

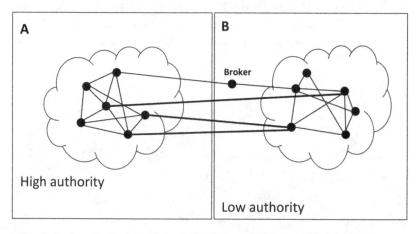

16.9. Broker's authority is weakened when structural holes are filled. With additional links added, this actor loses prestige. Weak ties strengthening brokers tend to be singular.

Arabic, or had studied in Mecca or Cairo, or with a foreign shaykh. Such actors collectively established weak ties to global Islamic authority.

Each of the reformist movements represented in Tamale is empowered as a separable sectarian movement through such linkages to transnationally recognized authorities and places: Mecca, Cairo, Kaolack, Fez, Tehran. Each sect's local representatives thus bridge structural holes, focusing all the power of a worldwide religious movement on a relatively small community, resulting in a kind of metaphoric contest of opposing torques, forces amplified through the long levers of the social network. No wonder the danger of clash is always imminent.

But as these powers are symbolic, they are incommensurate, and thus clashes are irreconcilable—no one will ever be able to determine, for instance, whether the Tijaniyya or the Sunnis present a "more correct" version of Islam, since they are equally global in scope and authority. Egypt, by contrast, has always appeared as a global center of Islamic authority in itself. With its authoritative local substrate and a profusion of links, individual prestige is diminished; it is well-nigh impossible for any individual to become a broker, claiming greater Islamic legitimacy by recourse to external authority.

This picture is intensified by two additional external factors, resulting from differences in colonial history. First, unlike Egypt, Christian and Muslim conversion in Ghana occurred roughly in historical parallel. The latter (Muslim conversion) was strongly conditioned by the former (Christian conversion), which has normalized the model of the bounded church-sect for Muslim groups as well. Mosques thus frequently become exclusivist, a phenomenon virtually unknown in Egypt. Indeed the Ahmadis have even established choirs, apparently modeled on those of Ghana's churches.

Second, Ghana represents the common African case of an arbitrary post-colonial country, one whose borders have been drawn by colonial powers to enclose an ethnically, linguistically, and religiously heterogeneous population. Egypt is quite the opposite; its territorial integrity exhibits a long history, and its people are relatively homogeneous in culture, language, and religion. As a political necessity, Ghana thus became a secular state, maintaining English as a lingua franca. Since 1992 this ideal has been realized in Ghana's remarkably well-functioning democracy and free market system. Egypt, by contrast, became the scene for an Arab-Islamic religious nationalism, developing into an unrelenting, undemocratic dictatorship.

Ghana, unlike Egypt, thus provides a kind of religious free market as well, in which multiple sects compete for adherents, unconstrained by the legal system, as a means of accumulating social capital (ultimately exchangeable for political or economic capital). Muslims are in the minority, and thus represent a scarce resource. Each Muslim reformist group, amplified by broker authorities enjoying high transnational Islamic status, provides a complete, exclusive, and contrastive religious identity. Further empowered by the relative vacuum of weak local Islamic authority, these groups compete, head to head, over a limited supply of followers. In short, Ghana's secular society and official religious tolerance enables free competition, while a limited supply of potential converts intensifies it.

Basic economics states that an inverse relation exists between competi-

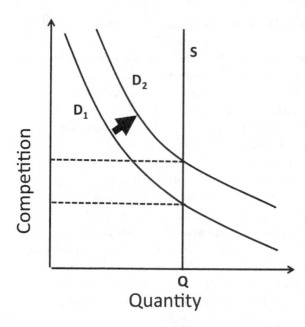

16.10. The Law of Supply and Demand: Competition over a limited, inelastic supply of Muslims. As demand increases (D_1 to D_2), competition increases.

tion and supply, given a fixed level of demand. Given an inelastic supply, as demand increases, so does competition. As new transnational Islamic movements entered Ghana during the twentieth century, demand increased, producing greater competition over an inelastic supply of Muslims, and leading to sectarian strife.

In Muslim majority Egypt, by contrast, external authority is comparatively weak. Muslim groups, sharing a common Sunni substrate unified by common ritual and vocal practices, provide additive rather than exclusive identities, while limited religious freedom precludes a free market in which competition and conflict could develop. Within Egyptian Sunni Islam there is considerable tolerance, but no real choice. Ironically, interreligious intolerance, combined with Egypt's global Islamic authority, has forged a relatively high degree of Islamic unity: there are no "sects." Rather, conflict emerges between Muslims and Christians, though not due to competition for members, since conversions are virtually prohibited.

In Ghana, the situation is nearly reversed: interreligious tolerance prevails, while distinctive Muslim groups are intolerant of one another and of local syncretism. Meanwhile, European mainline churches have become more, not less, tolerant of traditional religious practice, and so tolerance prevails in Christianity, where supplies are, in any case, high.

What is the place of music in these conflicts? Is music merely a pretext for

Table 16.1. Religious Conflict, Compared

Egypt: Inter-religious Conflict

	Muslims	Christians
Muslims	no	**yes**
Christians	**yes**	no

Ghana: Muslim Intrareligious Conflict

	Muslims	Christians
Muslims	**yes**	no
Christians	no	no

sectarian arguments, or does it touch on deeper issues? Ideological opposition to music is a well-known and long-standing discursive thread in Islam, wending its way throughout Islamic history, legitimated by particular interpretations of Qur'an and hadith, and taken up most recently by today's Salafis.

Globally, music serves religion not only spiritually but also socially — invigorating social solidarity and expanding membership. In Ghana, intolerance centered on rejection of music and dance signifies far more than the Salafi's reflexively negative ideological response to such expression; rather, this rejection constitutes a practical, urgent defense against music's power.

For in the hands of Tijanis and Ahmadis, music offers a powerful social technology for self-definition. At Diare I witnessed this technology galvanize an entire village for twelve hours, providing a wallop of Durkheimian "effervescence," attracting scores of new members and binding them to each other. The series of annual *mawlidis* celebrated by Tijanis each year—not just for the Prophet but for Shaykhs Ibrahim Niasse, Maikano, and others as well—infused by music and dance—effectively serves to renew connections among Ghana's extensive Tijani community through affiliation networks linking members through co-participation. The strong social appeal of such unity, combined with the spiritual beauty of musical performance itself, presents a powerful incentive to convert to the Tijani way.

According to this interpretation, the Ahlussunna oppose musical ritual not simply because they believe Islam forbids it as *bid'a*; rather, they oppose musical ritual as the critical social technology underlying the expansion and solidarity of their principal competitor in the religious marketplace.

The irony is that it is precisely interreligious tolerance—promoted by Ghana's secular, pluralistic, and democratic political culture—and the concomitant free religious market, that promotes conflict and even violence at the intra-Islamic level, by enabling the formation of distinctive, bounded Muslim movements competing for members. But music is a technology to which the Sunnis—for all their ideological reasons—do not have access. In the religious free market, it's no wonder they oppose such a technology with all their might.

NOTES

1. So-called African Traditional Religion (ATR) is a catchall term designating myriad indigenous beliefs and practices not differentiated as "religion" before contact with Muslims and Christians. The category of ATR has lately been formalized by its presence in the national census and conceptualized—in juxtaposition to and imitation of Islam and Christianity—as a legitimate, coherent religious system, e.g., in the Afrikania Mission. Syncretic forms, along with participation in multiple practices, are common. See Witte 2008: 9, 215.

2. Judaism, Christianity, and Islam are considered the three Abrahamic religions, as they trace their spiritual traditions to the biblical prophet Abraham.

3. According to a 1980 constitutional amendment, Islamic law (*shariʿa*), formerly "a principal source" became *the* principal source of legislation.

4. The 1971 constitution remained in force until the revolution of 2011, when it was replaced by a provisional constitution. In December 2012 a new constitution was approved by general plebiscite and signed into law by President Mursi, reflecting priorities of his Islamist party, *Hizb al-Hurriyya wa al-ʿAdala* (Freedom and Justice Party). While article 2 remained unchanged, the reference to shariʿa, previously vague and hence capacious, was narrowed and concretized in article 219: "The principles of Sharia include general evidence and foundations, rules and jurisprudence as well as sources accepted by doctrines of Sunni Islam and the majority of Muslim scholars." In this way, Shiʿa interpretations were explicitly excluded. Reference to personal status law was now enshrined in the constitution: "The principles of the legislations for Christian and Jewish Egyptians are the main source of legislation that organizes their civil status and religious affairs." The new constitution also explicitly affirmed Islam as a defining character of the nation: "The Egyptian People form part of both the Arab and the Islamic community" (part 1, chapter 1, article 1) (Saleh 2013). Following President Muhammad Morsi's ouster on 3 July 2013, a new, more liberal constitution was drafted and submitted to President Adli Mansour on 3 December 2013, subject to a public referendum to be held 14–15 January 2014. (El-Dabh 2014; Carlsstrom 2014).

5. The consequences for religious freedom of the 2013 draft constitution are unclear. Article 2, affirming shariʿa as the primary legislative source, is retained, but the contentious article 219 has been removed, and political parties based on religion are banned. Article 64 promises "Freedom of Belief: Freedom of belief is absolute. The freedom of practicing religious rituals and establishing places of worship for the followers of revealed religions is a right organized by law." Should this constitution be ratified, the implications of article 64, in apparent partial conflict with article 2, and whose legal formulation is yet to be worked out, remain to be seen (indeed article 43 of the 2012 constitution contained similar language). While some Egyptians are sanguine, global opinion is more reserved (El Sharnoubi and Rizk 2014; Al-Ali 2014; Essam El-Din 2014; Cole 2014).

REFERENCES

Abun-Nasr, Jamil M. 1965. *The Tijaniyya, a Sufi Order in the Modern World*. New York: Oxford University Press.

"AfricaMap." 2014. http://worldmap.harvard.edu/africamap/. Accessed 16 September 2014.

Al-Ali, Zaid. 2014. "Egypt's Third Constitution in Three Years: A Critical Analysis; West Asia and North Africa International IDEA." http://www.idea.int/wana/egypts-third -constitution-in-three-years-a-critical-analysis.cfm. Accessed 6 January 2014.

A.R.S. Church. 2011. http://www.youtube.com/watch?v=C8c1e42SJpQ&feature=youtube _gdata_player.

Burt, Ronald S. 1992. *Structural Holes: The Social Structure of Competition*. Cambridge, MA: Harvard University Press.

Carlsstrom, Gregg. 2014. "Egypt President Sets Date for Referendum—Middle East-Al Jazeera English." http://www.aljazeera.com/news/middleeast/2013/12/egypt-president -sets-date-referendum-20131212141146564381.html. Accessed 6 January 2014.

Cole, Juan. 2014. "Egyptian Constitution: Army Strengthened, Religious Parties Banned, Freedom of Belief, Speech Enshrined, Informed Comment." http://www.juancole.com /2013/12/constitution-strengthened-religious.html. Accessed 6 January 2014.

"Constitution of Egypt." 2013. *Wikisource, the Free Online Library*. http://en.wikisource.org /wiki/Constitution_of_Egypt. Accessed 11 February 2013.

El-Dabh, Basil. 2014. "Mansour Receives Amended Constitution—Daily News Egypt." http://www.dailynewsegypt.com/2013/12/03/mansour-receives-amended-constitution/. Accessed 6 January 2014.

Essam El-Din, Gamal. 2014. "Egypt's New Constitution to Guarantee Absolute Religious Freedom: Salmawy-Politics-Egypt-Ahram Online." http://english.ahram.org.eg/News /84992.aspx. Accessed 6 January, 2014.

Fahim, Karim. 2014. "Egypt, Dealing a Blow to the Muslim Brotherhood, Deems It a Terrorist Group." http://www.nytimes.com/2013/12/26/world/middleeast/egypt-calls -muslim-brotherhood-a-terrorist-group.html?_r=0. Accessed 6 January 2014.

Frishkopf, Michael. 1989. "The Character of Eve Performance." MA thesis, Tufts University.

———. 1999. "Sufism, Ritual, and Modernity in Egypt: Language Performance as an Adaptive Strategy." PhD diss., University of California, Los Angeles.

———. 2000. "Inshad Dini and Aghani Diniyya in Twentieth-Century Egypt: A Review of Styles, Genres, and Available Recordings." *Middle East Studies Association Bulletin* 34, no. 2: 167–183.

———. 2002. "Shaykh Yasin Al-Tuhami: A Typical Layla Performance." In *The Garland Encyclopedia of World Music* Volume 6. Edited by Virginia Danielson, Scott Marcus, and Dwight Reynolds. New York: Garland.

———. 2008. "Music." In *The Islamic World*, edited by Andrew Rippin, 510–526. London, New York: Routledge.

———. 2009. "Mediated Qur'anic Recitation and the Contestation of Islam in Contemporary Egypt." In *Music and the Play of Power in the Middle East, North Africa and Central Asia*, edited by Laudan Nooshin. Burlington: Ashgate.

Ghana Statistical Service. 2012. *2010 Population and Housing Census: Summary Report of Final Results*. Accra: Ghana Statistical Service. http://www.statsghana.gov.gh/docfiles /2010phc/Census2010_Summary_report_of_final_results.pdf.

Granovetter, Mark S. 1973. "The Strength of Weak Ties." *American Journal of Sociology* 78, no. 6 (May 1): 1360–1380.

El-Gundy, Zeinab. 2014. "The Shias: Egypt's Forgotten Muslim Minority-Features-Egypt-Ahram Online." http://english.ahram.org.eg/News/67170.aspx. Accessed 6 January 2014.

Hoffman, Valerie J. 1995. *Sufism, Mystics, and Saints in Modern Egypt*. Columbia, SC: University of South Carolina Press.

Ibrahim, Mohammad Saani. 2003. "The Tijaniyya Order in Tamale, Ghana: Its Foundation, Organization and Role." MA thesis, McGill University (Canada).

———. 2011. "The Decline of Sufism in West Africa: Some Factors Contributing to the Political and Social Ascendancy of Wahhabist Islam in Northern Ghana." PhD diss., McGill University (Canada).

Iddrisu, Abdulai. 2009. "Contesting Islam: 'Homegrown Wahhabism,' Education and Muslim Identity in Northern Ghana, 1920–2005." PhD diss., University of Illinois at Urbana-Champaign.

Levtzion, Nehemia. 1987. "The Eighteenth Century: Background to the Islamic Revolutions in West Africa." In *Eighteenth-Century Renewal and Reform in Islam*, edited by John Obert Voll. Syracuse: Syracuse University Press.

Locke, David. 1990. *Drum Damba: Talking Drum Lessons*. Crown Point, IN: White Cliffs Media.

Owusu-Ansah, David. 2013. "Ghana." http://lcweb2.loc.gov/frd/cs/ghtoc.html. Accessed 16 February 2013.

Pellow, Deborah. 1991. "The Power of Space in the Evolution of an Accra Zongo." *Ethnohistory* 38, no. 4 (1 October): 414–450.

"President Commends Ghanaians For Religious Tolerance." 2013. http://www.ghana.gov.gh/index.php/news/general-news/17227-president-commends-ghanaians-for-religious-tolerance-. Accessed 22 February 2013.

Robinson, David. 2004. *Muslim Societies in African History*. New York: Cambridge University Press.

Saleh, Nivien, trans. 2013. "The 2012 Constitution of Egypt." http://niviensaleh.info/constitution-egypt-2012-translation/. Accessed 11 February 2013.

Samwini, Nathan. 2006. *The Muslim Resurgence in Ghana since 1950: Its Effects upon Muslims and Muslim-Christian Relations*. PhD diss., Berlin: Lit Verlag.

Samwini, Nathan Iddrisu. 2003. *The Muslim Resurgence in Ghana since 1950 and Its Effects upon Muslims and Muslim-Christian Relations*. Birmingham: University of Birmingham Press.

El Sharnoubi, Osman, and Mariam Rizk. 2014. "Egypt's Constitution 2013 vs. 2012: A Comparison-Politics—Egypt-Ahram Online." http://english.ahram.org.eg/News/88644.aspx. Accessed 6 January 2014.

The Constitution of the Republic of Ghana. 2013. http://www.judicial.gov.gh/constitution/chapter/chap_5.htm. Accessed 22 February 2013.

"The World Factbook: Egypt." 2014. https://www.cia.gov/library/publications/the-world-factbook/geos/eg.html. Accessed 16 September 2014.

Wilks, Ivor. 1989. *Wa and the Wala: Islam and Polity in Northwestern Ghana*. New York: Cambridge University Press.

Witte, Marleen de. 2008. "Spirit Media: Charismatics, Traditionalists, and Mediation Practices in Ghana." PhD diss., Proefschrift Universiteit van Amsterdam.

CHAPTER 17

MUSIC FESTIVALS IN PAKISTAN AND ENGLAND

THOMAS HODGSON

THIS CHAPTER LOOKS AT migration and multiculturalism in the UK, exploring, in particular, how traditional music festivals travel with migrant groups and the role of the state in their subsequent development—in this case, from Pakistan to England. UK Pakistanis, the vast majority of whom originate from the Mirpur area of southern Kashmir, have been a prominent part of the UK's cultural and religious landscape for over sixty years. Their influence in the UK is felt on many levels, from politics, health, and education, to cuisine, sport, and music. Pakistanis, needless to say, are heterogeneous in their ethnicity, religiosity, and piety. And yet, three generations since the first Mirpuri migrants came to Britain, they are still frequently understood on one level: Muslim.[1] This narrow definition has since crystallized, with ideas of segregated communities, parallel lives, and terrorism all informing public epistemologies of Islam. Moreover, Muslims in Britain are also often thought of as being moored to particular geographic areas, whereby the religious marker is coupled with locality and visa-versa.[2] According to many media and political reports, these characterizations are all symptomatic of a failed multicultural state (Vertovec and Wessendorf 2010). Nowhere is this more apparent than in discourses surrounding Muslims in the northern city of Bradford.

Perhaps unsurprisingly (given that cities are common migration destinations), urban life is increasingly taking center stage in thinking about identity and global connectivity; people understand connections in terms of cities rather than nation-states. Within a migratory framework this makes a certain amount of sense, both in a vertical (i.e., municipal/civic) way—cities are frequently "twinned" with urban centres elsewhere—but also horizontally through more mundane, intimate transnational ties, established through migration and perpetuated through, among other things, travel, festivals, marriage, and mass media. Both these migratory theoretical axes seem to transgress, or at least supplement, the nation-state: physically, through the penetration of a nation's borders by people, and ideologically in terms of scale. From this perspective, the local becomes the site of global positioning and interconnectedness, rather than the national.

Mirpuris are deeply plugged into a transnational imaginary that connects Bradford with Mirpur. An understanding of the Mirpuri diaspora cannot therefore be reduced to traditional nation-state–bound ways of thinking about multiculturalism (i.e., one that posits that Muslims are not integrating into British society). It must surely also be able to take into account a more cosmopolitan dimension—one that incorporates the many diverse and diffuse activities that constitute people's lives.

Ethnomusicologists have been able to demonstrate, through music, the limits of theories that reify cultures and nationalities as fixed, and, instead, have shown that people—like music—define cross-cultural "boundaries" and landscapes in complex ways. As sites of musical and cultural interaction, festivals such as the Bradford Mela or, say, the Notting Hill Carnival, present a rich seam of enquiry (see Cohen 1993; Cantwell 1993; Dundes and Falsassi 1975; Ronström, 2001; Cooley 1999).[3] An annual multicultural music and arts festival established in 1988, the Bradford Mela is a musical world in which multiple kinds of cosmopolitanism compete and, at times, overlap. While there has been a good deal of attention paid to music and migration (Lomax 1959; Allen 1971; Gross 1996; Baily 1990, 2006; Turino 1999; Schade-Poulsen 1999; Toynbee and Dueck 2011) and music and cosmopolitanism (Turino 2000; Stokes 1994, 2004, 2007; Werbner 2008), there has been little consideration afforded to how festivals migrate and develop in diasporic settings. Recent studies of migrant musics (Toynbee and Dueck 2011) have looked to music as a way of teasing out the tension between movement, on the one hand, and locality, on the other. How do people and music travel across the globe? By what means? On what levels do people interact through music? These are important questions, particularly in places such as the UK, with rapidly increasing ethnic diversity—to the extent that the term "super-diversity" has now been coined to describe its cities (Vertovec 2007).[4] This chapter situates these questions in the context of South Asian festivals, or "*mela*-s." In particular, how do official projections of multiculturalism "from above" articulate with the different kinds of migrant and postmigrant experience at the festival?

MULTICULTURAL BRADFORD

Bradford expanded greatly during the Industrial Revolution as a center of the textile and worsted industry. By the mid-nineteenth century, the city's industry had boomed, transforming both the physical and cultural landscape. New mills filled the town center, their towering chimneys exclaiming Bradford's economic rise and newfound wealth. This new wealth attracted people to the city by the thousands, not just from surrounding areas, but from farther afield as well. The first wave of international migration to Bradford came mostly in the form of Irish workers and German Jewish merchants. These merchants built their own warehouses and factories in the eastern quarter of the city center, in what came to be known as Little Germany. Opulent municipal buildings soon followed, including the construction of Bradford's first concert hall.

As the city expanded, mills and workers' houses, built with yellow Yorkshire sandstone, sprawled across the valley and up the dales in a steep rise of rapid urbanization. On the edges of the city, terraced houses gave way to fields separated by dry-stone walls, and, in many places, this remains the case to this day. As well as building model villages to house their workers, industrial philanthropists, such as Sir Titus Salt (1803–1876) and Sir Samuel Cunliffe Lister (1815–1906), built large municipal parks on land they subsequently donated to the city—a feature that came to play an important role in the development of festivals in Bradford a century later.

Substantially higher rates of migration occurred after World War II. The UK had sustained heavy losses of life during the war that left large employment gaps in the textile and manufacturing industries. This particularly affected northern industrial towns such as Bradford, Birmingham, Burnley, and Oldham. Invitations in the form of work visas and permits were offered to people from countries in the new Commonwealth. With a history of recruitment to the merchant navy, men from areas of Pakistan such as Mirpur took up the invitation in substantial numbers.[5] Early pioneer migrants played an important role in the continuation of migration over the following decades. Letters and photographs would be sent back to family in Pakistan displaying their newfound wealth.[6] Once encouraged to relocate to England, established migrants would help with housing and finance until paid work was found. The mills, houses, and parks of the nineteenth century all played an important role in bringing Mirpuris to the city, and these neighborhoods remain areas where large numbers of Mirpuris live today. Most recently, Poles, Latvians, and Romanians have migrated to the area, making Bradford one of the most ethnically diverse places in the UK outside London.[7] By the time of the 2011 census Bradford had the highest proportion of Pakistanis of any city in the UK (20.4 percent, compared with 2.6 percent who described themselves as Indian or British Indian, and 1.9 percent as Bangladeshi or British Bangladeshi). In a city of 522,452 people, nearly a quarter of the population (24.7 percent) identify themselves as Muslim.[8]

BRADFORD, TWINNED WITH MIRPUR

Mirpur, meanwhile, lies over 6,000 kilometres away, on the edge of the Mangla Dam, in the southernmost tip of Pakistani-controlled Kashmir. Despite the vast distance separating Bradford and Mirpur, the two cities are intimately connected. The reason for this intimacy lies not simply in a sustained period of migration from Mirpur to Bradford, but through the continual reinforcement of transnational ties between the two cities via return travel, marriages, and cultural practices. The two cities are "twinned," both officially and unofficially, with Bradford commonly referred to in Britain as "Bradistan," while Mirpur carries the local nickname, in Kashmir, of "Little Britain."[9] "It's like one community, just in two places," explained one radio DJ, who broadcasts simultaneously from Mirpur and Bradford.[10]

It is easy to see why. Walking down Oak Lane in the Manningham area of Bradford, one will encounter the smells of spices and coriander emanating from the street's curry houses and greengrocers; bright colors in tailors' shop windows display the latest Kashmiri fashions; jewellers jostle for space, attracting prospective Mirpuri buyers from around the country. The majority of these shops have signage in both Urdu and English script.

The picture is not too dissimilar in Mirpur. Within the city, grocery stores cater for expatriate British Pakistanis, selling such quintessentially British staples as Weetabix and Marmite.[11] On a recent fieldwork trip to Kashmir, I experienced a steady stream of people enquiring as to where I was from. Upon hearing the word "Bradford," most would exclaim, "Ah! Bradford! I have many family there. Where do you live, BD7? BD8?" For Mirpuris, the two cities are personally connected. But these examples also suggest a deeper connection that extends beyond the Mirpuri community itself. Most obviously, this can be seen through cuisine. "Indian" food is a staple of the British diet. Mirpuri music has had less attention paid to it, but South Asian festivals—*mela*-s—more broadly, have become a symbol of multicultural harmony. In the context of Mirpuris' transnational connections with Bradford and Mirpur, the following two sections provide an ethnographic account of the kind of *mela*-s held in Pakistan and Britain.

THE ARRAH *MELA*, KASHMIR

During the summer of 2010, I attended a mela in Arrah, approximately thirty kilometres east of Mirpur. During most of the year, the town of Arrah was relatively quiet and consisted of a small variety of shops—including butchers,

17.1. The mosque of local Sufi saint and poet Mian Muhammad Bakhsh at the center of the mela in Arrah, Azad Kashmir. Photo by author.

barbers, grocers, and tailors—lining the sides of the main roads, which formed a T-junction. At this junction one sees enclaves of houses and the large mosque of a local Sufi saint and poet much venerated by Mirpuris, Mian Muhammad Bakhsh. As I approached the town on the evening of the *mela*, hundreds of cars, scooters, and motorbikes, flanked by thousands of people, clogged the T-junction—all on their way to the mela. The mela itself took place just outside the town, with the mosque at its center (see figure 17.1).

Surrounding the mosque were dozens of temporary market stalls. The stalls sold a wide range of goods, including clothes, pictures, crockery, ornaments, rugs, and cooking ingredients. In addition to this, the air was permeated by the smell of freshly fried samosas, *pakora*-s, and hot Kashmiri tea.[12] As I walked toward the end of a line of stalls, the frenetic sounds of people and trade began to be replaced by the percussive rhythms and piercing melodies and rhythms of the *shehnai* (double-reed oboe) and *dhol* (a large double-headed drum found across South Asia). Here were pockets of people surrounding one or several men dancing, accompanied by a group of musicians. The musicians usually consisted of two or more *dhol* players, either one or several *shehnai* players, and sometimes bagpipes. These melas are important times for musicians, both as means of generating income and as a way of advertising their ability so that they can gain employment at weddings and events throughout the year.

The musicians would begin by playing popular *raag*-s (modes) in order to attract an audience. Once a crowd had assembled, one member of the troupe would liaise with the audience and take requests. During the performance, members of the audience would spontaneously jump up and dance. While this was going on, members of the troupe would collect donations of money from the crowd and also solicit requests. At the end of the performance, the crowd would slowly peter out and the musicians move onto a different patch where they would begin the ritual again.

The music at the mela in Azad Kashmir was informal and yet regulated by space. The mela itself did not have any fixed boundaries. These were, rather, determined by the number of people there and the amount of different activities taking place. Despite this openness and spatial ambiguity, there were, nevertheless, certain zones that broadly marked out different activities. These were the central mosque area, car parks that utilized adjoining fields, market and food stalls, open spaces for performance, and fringe areas of minor commerce and music. The performance of music mainly took place in these latter two peripheral areas and away from the mosque. For the performers themselves there was no set program, and the musicians would travel between different locations. This informality of programming was an important aspect of the mela for musicians, who had traveled from far and wide, as it allowed them to maximize their exposure to audiences and so increase their income. In Pakistan, then, melas serve as important moments in time and space when people from surrounding villages come together in celebration and also to exchange goods (be it clothes, food, or less tangible services such as music). Melas thus serve multiple purposes: they are economic hubs while also being rare areas of the public sphere within which aspects of religious and cultural identities are rehearsed and performed.

MIGRATING THE MELA

Despite the intimate ties between Mirpur and Bradford described above, this description of a mela in Pakistan contrasts sharply with those found in Britain today.[13] In the late 1980s, debates about multiculturalism in Britain began to jostle for space in national newspapers and political circles. The Rushdie affair had recently brought the dynamic between liberalism and cultural assimilation into sharp focus, and questions about immigration were raging.[14] Vivid images of Muslims burning books in postindustrial northern cities fueled the arguments against multiculturalism, which claimed that the multicultural experiment was over.[15] While these debates gathered momentum, South Asian communities in Bradford responded by holding a festival that celebrated those aspects of multiculturalism that were less commonly seen or heard about in the press: music and the arts. The Bradford Mela emerged in 1988 as a small festival above the university's playing fields. It was a resounding success. An estimated 10,000 people attended that first festival, but by 1998 it had moved to Peel Park and was attracting 150,000 people to the event from the UK and abroad. Bradford Council, recognizing the Mela's political and social role in community cohesion, began to pour in the money. Middle-class (and predominantly non-Muslim) South Asian communities quickly capitalized on the newly available capital, setting up South Asian music and arts organizations, such as Kala Sangam and Oriental Arts, to program Indian classical music concerts, exhibitions, dance, and educational workshops. These organizations channeled Bradford Council and Arts Council funding into the Bradford Mela, promoting it as the counter-symbol of success to multiculturalism's supposed failure.[16]

From its beginning as a South Asian music festival, then, the Bradford Mela—the largest in the UK—has since developed to include a wide variety of music programming, including bhangra, Chinese ribbon dancing, British punk, Indian brass bands, and Komodo drumming, inter alia. Routes between stages are fixed, channeling people through retail and food spaces that include fish and chips alongside Kashmiri curry, and Christian Aid and Islamic Relief charity tents working together for donations. The 2001 Mela was described by its organizers as "The World in a City" and by 2010, over thirty-two hours of music were being programmed over two days in Peel Park. Throughout this period, local arts organizations played an integral part in programming the Mela. The carefully selected mix of different genres responded to Bradford Council and the Arts Council's push to engage more communities in the arts.[17]

More recent years have seen further transformations of the Mela. Following the worldwide recession sparked by the 2008 financial crisis, arts organizations in Bradford, and elsewhere in the UK, have suffered massive funding cuts. Traditional sponsors and programmers of the festival, such as Kala Sangam and Oriental Arts, have not only endured cuts to their funding, but have also been squeezed out of the festival's organization. Bradford Council faced spending cuts to their overall budget of £67 million over two years, and this had an immediate impact on the Mela. In 2011 the Council assumed full control, reducing the festival to a single day rather than its traditional full weekend. To make matters worse, following a torrential downpour of rain, the plug was pulled on the 2012 Mela the day before it was due to begin.

17.2. Taiko drumming at the Bradford Mela. Photo by author.

The financial losses sustained through this late cancellation provoked the local council to rethink its cultural strategy.

During this period (2011–2012), the city center's Centenary Square—an area directly in front of the grand Victorian Town Hall—underwent a £24 million transformation and became rebranded as City Park. Gemma Wilkinson, Bradford Council's Major Events organizer, explained that while central Government funding cuts had fallen in other departments and areas, the Major Events budget in Bradford had remained stable. Despite this apparent stability in funding, the previous two years' trouble with rain and the newly redeveloped City Park meant that centralizing the festival (both organizationally and geographically) became a priority. In 2013, the Bradford Mela thus moved farther away from its South Asian roots and was restricted to a single day in City Park, preceded now by the newly reintroduced Bradford Festival—a move that took the festival away from its traditional home in Peel Park (which is located in a predominantly Pakistani neighborhood). In other words, there has been a political and geographical centralization of the festival. The impact of this centralization has rippled down through the arts' organizations and is felt at grass-roots level. As Wilkinson explained to me in an interview:

Our [new] Festival is a mishmash. We've retained a music element, so there's a stage and music. Street Theater is a big element. We've gone for the street theater and music, foods on offer, and potentially an arts market as well. And other activities, fringe activities . . . Just to give you an example, we had Demon Barbers. They recently won the BBC 2 Folk Awards. We had Edward Niebla who's a flamenco guitarist. We had a calypso band. A real mix that kept people down there for the afternoon. On the Sunday, on the Mela day, we had a "World" kind of feel, so we had the Taiko drummers. We did have the Bollywood Brass, but we had the Taiko drummers, and a whole mix of things. (Interview with the author, July 2013)

This dilution of South Asian culture, not only in the new Bradford Festival but the Mela as well, has left the local arts organizations reeling; a feeling acknowledged by Wilkinson: "There's a sense of, with some of those organizations, of 'why is the council running the festival and why aren't we running the festival?' And there's a whole history there. The Council is the major funder, at the end of the day."[18]

Large, publicly funded South Asian arts organizations, like Kala Sangam and Oriental Arts, who interact between the state and communities in Bradford, have dominated the South Asian musical landscape in the UK's cities over the last two decades. These organizations—set up by South Asian communities that, in Bradford, have often distanced themselves from Muslims and are, generally, considered better "integrated"—have enjoyed substantial funding through the Arts Council and Bradford Council. The examples above provide a brief insight into the role of local government as it attempts—successfully or otherwise—to create multicultural spaces in Bradford. Entwined within these discussions are competing narratives of money, centers and peripheries, agency and affect, and undertones of a general distrust of power. This is not a unique position for arts organizations in the UK, and it is certainly not the first time the arts sector in general has experienced funding cuts.[19]

What the discussion above brings into focus are some of the nonfinancial implications of funding cuts for tertiary (i.e., nongovernment and noncouncil) arts organizations, which have previously played a key role in state-led community cohesion initiatives. Public funding in the form of government subsidies has allowed the Mela to expand and attract internationally renowned artists while, importantly, retaining a policy of free entry for the public. The rise and success of the Mela has also coincided with the Mirpuri community becoming more firmly established and culturally confident in Bradford's social landscape. Music and the arts were identified by Bradford Council as the force driving this cultural confidence. Yet, it has also brought with it a sense of disempowerment and disenfranchisement for those at grass roots level, particularly Mirpuris, as musical programming and organizational autonomy is taken out of their hands by those holding the purse strings.[20] And so the issue of public funding is full of ambiguities and seen differently by many Mirpuris. Public spending cuts have focused attention on Mela, and contributed to a discussion and argument about what the event is for—an advantageous moment for an ethnomusicologist, of course, to observe some of the mechanisms and processes at play in multicultural events such as this. And also to ask what the waxing and waning fortunes of the Bradford Mela in recent years have meant for Mirpuri musicians, and how they situate themselves, to which I shall now turn.

MIRPURI COSMOPOLITANISMS

Ironically, some of the defining characteristics of the Mirpuri Muslim community in Britain—practices that often see them labeled as self-segregating, isolationist, and generally not integrating into society—has meant that they have escaped relatively unscathed from the kind of funding cuts experienced by broader South Asian arts organizations such as Kala Sangam and Oriental Arts. Moving through Bradford today, Mirpuri musicality is both audible and visible: the city's curry houses have the constant hum of Bollywood music in the background; a mixture of Imran Khan and the late Nusrat Fateh Ali Khan will, more often than not, accompany a late night taxi ride;[21] barbershops in Manningham form a nexus in which musicians coalesce to organize Patwari poetry evenings; on street corners, rap music is used to mark out territories from rival gangs; in schools, despite a growing anxiety among teachers about music's permissibility in Islam, young Mirpuris are utilizing recording studios to create their own musical theater in the form of "hip-hoperas"; and, in youth centers, rap workshops are organized by social workers to discuss crime, education, racism, and religion.

The latter of these examples—rap workshops—are complex spaces of music making because, as with the Mela, they also involve mediated interactions between young Mirpuris and the state. The workshops, which take place in schools and youth centers, are funded by a combination of Arts Council funding and grants from the city council. During a workshop, young Mirpuris are encouraged to talk about the issues they face—crime, drugs, racism, inter alia—on a day-to-day basis. These discussions are then written down by the youth worker and turned into raps. Backing tracks are chosen and the teenagers perform their newly created rhymes in front of their peers, which are recorded onto a CD for them to take away.

Like the Mela, these rap workshops are carefully designed spaces, and are seen by the city council, and Local Education Authority, as a way to engage with problem youths. Rap music in this context, then, is not just about subaltern resistance (as is often thought to be the case) but is a civic project. The council utilizes rap music as a social force to "connect" young Mirpuris with other young people across the city, with an agenda of countering the kind of racial segregation highlighted in anti-multiculturalism discourses.[22]

Lacking any particular representation among local arts organizations, elder Mirpuris have long organized their own concerts outside of official channels—arts organizations and NGOs—such as those described in the example of the Bradford Mela. Patwari poetry gatherings are funded with Mirpuris' own structures of finance, support, marketing, and venues. Incidentally, financial self-sufficiency, volunteerism, and community-led organization are all virtuous hallmarks of the kind of big society/small-state cosmopolitics of the UK's current coalition government. From the perspective of elder Mirpuris, patronizing performances of Patwari sung poetry (*sher khavani*) is important because it establishes and reaffirms ties and senses of belonging with Mirpur.[23] For musicians who are visiting from Pakistan, many of whom will have performed and been recruited at the kind of Kashmiri mela described above, the degree to which they are looked after and patronized means that they will return to Kashmir and the Punjab with stories of their host's generosity. These stories circulate widely, affecting the host's standing in both Pakistan and England.

And yet this patronage is not primarily about economics, but about cosmopolitan moments of cultural intimacy. During an all-male Patwari performance, status is continuously negotiated through the patrons showering the musicians with bank notes for all to see. The showering of money, followed by the reading out of patrons' names and the emotional cries of approval (*Wah! Wah!*) are all part of asserting levels of cultural connoisseurship, under the constant scrutiny of those who are there. Patwari concerts (*mehfil*-s)[24] are thus intimate, cosmopolitan spaces of Mirpuri male subjectivity, in which levels of status are won and lost; the ramifications of which are felt across the city and beyond.

Yet, despite these diverse examples, ignorance of Mirpuri cultural practice runs deep elsewhere in the city in a political climate dominated by anxieties surrounding Muslims. Even though Mirpuris possess strong senses of community, fiscal responsibility, give money to charity as a matter of course (*zakat*), and look after their elderly at home, they are Muslim and are thus defined in public discourse by the negative, stereotyped connotations that that label brings. They are consequently deemed to be particularly in need of the kind of connections and articulations with the outside world that the Mela supposedly brings, and with it civility, integration, and cultural status. We have already seen how selective and partial such multicultural civility is, and how exposed to the vagaries of funding (and its sudden withdrawal). Mirpuris may have good reasons to keep their distance from the Mela, or not to participate particularly energetically. And this distance may not simply be about a desire to remain isolated and "traditional." In fact music, along with sport and dance, suggests quite the opposite: that Mirpuris live highly cosmopolitan lives. But this is a cosmopolitism that is not always easy to see, at least to eyes conditioned by the conventional multiculturalism model.

The way in which Mirpuris derive, embed, and sustain meanings from their local surroundings—both in the UK and in Mirpur—is articulated to a large degree by transnational flows, cultural and financial, between Bradford and Mirpur and beyond. Back in Pakistan, the diasporic experience returns not just through new and old musical styles but also through social and economic remittances. These reverse transnational flows, in turn, reshape and redefine local musical culture and sociopolitical hierarchies in Mirpur. This perspective, which emphasizes first and foremost the importance of "the local," is also a site of enquiry that is alive to transnational flows of culture and meaning.[25] Such transnational connections represent a kind of cosmopolitanism that is, ultimately, about local regions and cities, not ethnically defined nationalities or religiously defined polities.

At stake in these examples, then, are competing *kinds* of cosmopolitanism, which can be defined by type, style, and social locality: one controlled along multicultural lines by Bradford Council, such as the Bradford Mela; another, as with the rap workshops, that is in the hands of arts organizations and NGOs; and a Mirpuri "grassroots" transnationalism, organized through events like the Patwari *sher*, that is about regions and cities.

CONCLUSION

Philip Lewis has recently argued for the importance of paying attention to Mirpuris' lives because "the public profile of Islam and Muslim communities in Britain is likely to be shaped less by sophisticated Muslim professional groups in London or Manchester than by what happens in those cities with young, growing Muslim communities, such as Birmingham, Bradford, and Burnley, where Islam has a largely Pakistani face" (2007: 29). By the start of the second decade of the twenty-first century a number of events occurred that had the potential to make history repeat itself. In early 2010, the English Defence League (EDL)—a group with a history of Islamophobic sentiment and violence—threatened to march through the city in much the same way that the British National Party (BNP) had done a decade earlier, while in the summer of 2011, London saw what has been described as the "worst rioting in a generation."[26] The London riots swept through other UK cities, particularly those with poor, working class postmigrant populations. Against all expectations, Bradford remained peaceful. In both cases (the EDL march and the London riots), mosques across Bradford played a crucial but largely unrecognized role in intervening with young Mirpuris, who were growing more and more agitated, and, contrary to the BNP's march a decade earlier, successfully encouraged them to stay away from the protests and from rioting.

Such marked difference, from one decade to the next, I would argue, lies not in a sudden ascension of social mobility, or as a result of top-down government policy, but from a deeper sense among Mirpuris that they are at home simultaneously in Bradford and Mirpur, a sense deepened and made meaningful by the kinds of musical practices I described in the previous section. Their embeddedness in Bradford's physical and cultural landscape, as well as its history, provokes new reflections on segregation discourses, national identity(ies), and Britishness, as emerging generations are more confidently and progressively asserting their identity and sense of belonging in Bradford, moving beyond the anxieties of first generation migrants.[27] That is not to say that this emerging "cultural confidence" is without its tensions. Mirpuris today face a range of challenges and issues that continue to marginalize them in profound and particular ways. At a time when government-led policies like the "Big Society"[28] are couched in terms of "integration" and "common values," how can we talk about diversity in such dichotomous "us" and "them" terms? Who "they" are is usually pretty clear, but who "we" are and what "our" values might or should be is much less so. This has strong implications not just for how we imagine multiculturalism in Britain but how cosmopolitanism is understood in an increasingly globalized world.

NOTES

1. Such characterization has not only occurred in politics and the media, but in sociological literature too. See Modood 1990; Lewis 1994, 2007; Abbas 2009; Emerson 2011.

2. In the early 2000s there was a proliferation of literature and UK government reports that blamed the failure of multiculturalism on self-segregating Muslim communities. See Cantle 2001; West 2005; Phillips 2005.

3. For Abner Cohen 1993, the Notting Hill Carnival represents a creative expression of

dynamic power relations, embodying the tension between subculture (black communities) and dominant culture (hegemonic white society).

4. Increasing levels of migration and technological communication in Europe, and elsewhere in the world, has led to a growth in anthropological enquires as to how states regulate and respond to diversity. See Goldberg 1994; Bennett 1998; Baumann 1996, 1999; Modood 2000; Kosnick 2007; Vertovec and Wessendorf 2010.

5. The primary reason for emigrating from Mirpur to the UK was economic, with "wages for labouring jobs in Britain in the 1960s . . . over 30 times those offered for similar jobs in Pakistan" (Shaw 1988: 9). The money earned in England would be used to buy land in Pakistan on which to build new houses and so increase their social status. A further reason that a significant number of people migrated from the Mirpur district was the construction of the Mangla Dam. Built in the 1960s, the dam is located on the border of Azad Kashmir and the Punjab where the foothills begin to rise out of the plain. The construction of the dam displaced over 100,000 people and completely flooded the old town of Mirpur and the surrounding area. Many of those displaced received compensation from the Pakistani government. Some used it to buy land in new Mirpur, on the edge of the dam, while many others used the money to join relatives in England. See also Allen 1971: 32.

6. Within the city there was a photographic studio where new migrants could go and hire western-style suits and money, with which they would be photographed. These photos would then be sent back to kin in Pakistan as a display of their new-found wealth.

7. The others being Leicester and Tower Hamlets. See http://www.ons.gov.uk/ons /guide-method/census/census-2001/index.html. Accessed 17 February 2011.

8. For more census data, see http://www.ons.gov.uk/census.

9. This moniker resembles many suburban neighborhoods around the world in which migrant communities are concentrated (for example, Little Italy in New York City, China Town in London, and Little Germany in Bradford).

10. Aisha Chourdry, Presenter, Rose FM. See http://www.bbc.co.uk/news/magazine -17156238.

11. A good example, perhaps, of outward as well as inward migration, comparable to the kind of shops found in southern Spain and other Mediterranean destinations favored by sun-seeking Britons.

12. Samosa (fried pastry with a spiced savory filling) and *pakora* (a kind of fritter made with potato and onion, or other vegetables) are a staple of South Asian cuisine, found across the subcontinent.

13. Melas are commonly found in cities across the UK, particularly those with South Asian communities. To a large degree, the character of these melas has been determined by the largest of the South Asian communities in that area. The Leicester Mela, for example, has traditionally had a Punjabi feel due to the number of Indian Gujaratis who migrated to the city following their expulsion from Uganda and Kenya in 1972.

14. For more on the Rushdie affair, see: Parekh 1990 and 2000 and Ruthven 1991. For discussions of the affair in relation to music, see Sharma, Hutnyk, and Sharma, eds. 1996; Hyder 2004.

15. Fay Weldon, quoted in Lewis 1994: 2. These debates have been rehearsed again since, particularly following the Bradford Riots (7 July 2001), 11 September 2001, and the riots that occurred in several English cities in August 2011.

16. In 2008, Bradford Council bid (unsuccessfully) for the title of European Capital of Culture. Paul Brookes, who led the bid, explained, "The Mela was most certainly seen

as a demonstration of something that brought together communities in a celebratory way. 'Europe's biggest and best Mela' is how we described it. The multiculturalism that the Mela represents, the way the Mela was a symbol of some of that multiculturalism, was absolutely at the centre of the bid." (Paul Brookes in Quershi 2010: 18).

17. In 2008 the Arts Council England launched an initiative of "National Indicator 11" targets, which committed local authorities to improve the representation of communities in culture and sports (Arts Council 2008. Oriental Arts would often discuss the ways in which their musical programming met these NI11 targets.

18. Ibid.

19. In 2010 the UK government cut their entire University teaching grant for the Humanities (the Sciences were protected as a government priority).

20. See also Hodgson (forthcoming in 2016), "The Multicultural Mela: Music and Space at the Festival," *Les Cahiers d'Ethnomusicologie*, Issue 27. There are also significant and relevant parallels to be drawn here with how the Notting Hill Carnival developed in London. For more on this see Abner Cohen 1993.

21. Nusrat Fateh Ali Khan (1948–1997) was a popular and influential *qawwali* singer from Faisalabad, Pakistan. Imran Khan is a Dutch Pakistani rap singer/songwriter and producer.

22. For more on these workshops and other examples of young Mirpuri music in Bradford, see Hodgson 2013.

23. Patwari *sher* is a type of poetry that originates from the Pothohar plateau in northeastern Pakistan. Its performance is now common across the UK in places where Mirpuri communities have formed.

24. A *mehfil* is a gathering historically found in Mughal courts. Traditionally poets, musicians, and dancers performed in *mehfils* for their Muslim patrons.

25. Through an emphasis on the "global hierarchies of value" (Herzfeld 2004: 2–3), Richard Wolf (2009) argues that the significance and importance of local level music practice for people or groups is often lost. "From some perspectives," Wolf argues, "music that transcends locality is more interesting and lucrative than so-called traditional music of a particular place" (2009: 5).

26. *The Guardian*, 5 December 2011.

27. These anxieties have been well documented by Khan 1977 and Anwar 1977.

28. To summarize, in David Cameron's vision for the future of Britain, Big Society will foster: localism and devolution of power away from central government; volunteerism within local communities; and the support of entrepreneurism, charities, and co-operatives. And at the heart of the £200m Big Society is a return to what Mr. Cameron calls "family values": "Family is where people learn to be good citizens, to take responsibility, to live in harmony with others. Families are the building blocks of a strong, cohesive society." See http://www.number10.gov.uk/news/speech-on-the-big-society/. Accessed 18 July 2011.

REFERENCES

Abbas, T. 2009. "Multiculturalism, Islamaphobia and the City." In *Pakistani Diasporas: Culture, Conflict, Change*, edited by V. S. Kalra, 285–299. Karachi: Oxford University Press.
Allen, S. 1971. *New Minorities, Old Conflicts, Asian and West Indian Immigrants in Britain*. New York: Random House.
Anwar, M. 1979. *The Myth of Return: Pakistanis in Britain*. London: Heinemann Educational.

Baily, J. 1990. *The Making of Lessons from Gulam: Asian Music in Bradford; A Study Guide to the Film*. London: Royal Anthropological Institute.

———. 2006. "'Music Is in Our Blood': Gujarati Muslim Musicians in the UK." *Journal of Ethnic and Migration Studies* 32: 2.

Baumann, G. 1996. *Contesting Culture: Discourses of Identity in Multi-Ethnic London*. Cambridge: Cambridge University Press.

———. 1999. *The Multicultural Riddle: Rethinking National, Ethnic and Religious Identities*. London: Routledge.

Bennett, D., ed. 1998. *Multicultural States: Rethinking Difference and Identity*. London: Routledge.

Cantle, T. 2001. *Community Cohesion: A Report of the Independent Review Team*. Great Britain: Home Office Community Cohesion Review Team.

Cantwell, R. 1993. *Ethnomimesis: Folklife and the Representation of Culture*. Chapel Hill: University of North Carolina Press.

Cohen, A. 1993. *Masquerade Politics: Explorations in the Structure of Urban Cultural Movements*. Oxford: Berg.

Cooley, T. 1999. "Folk Festival As Modern Ritual in the Polish Tatra Mountains." *The World of Music* 41, no. 3: 31–55.

Dundes, H., and A. Falassi. 1975. *La Terra in Piazza: An Interpretation of the Palio of Siena*. Berkeley: University of California Press.

Ellits, D. 2008. "National Indicator 11: Baseline for Local Authorities." London: Arts Council England.

Emerson, M. 2011. *Interculturalism: Europe and Its Muslims in Search of Sound Societal Models*. Brussels: Centre for European Policy Studies.

Goldberg, D., ed. 1994. *Multiculturalism: A Critical Reader*. Oxford: Blackwell.

Gross, J., D. McMurray, and T. Swedenburg. 1996. "Arab Noise and Ramadan Nights: *Rai*, Rap, and Franco-Maghrebi Identities." In *Displacement, Diaspora, and Geographies of Identities*, edited by L. Smadar and T. Swedenburg. Durham, NC: Duke University Press.

Herzfeld, M. 2004. *The Body Impolitic: Artisans and Artifice in the Global Hierarchy of Value*. Chicago: University of Chicago Press.

Hodgson, T. 2013. "'Do What the Qur'an Says and Stay Away from Crack': Mirpuri Muslims, Rap Music and the City." In *Rescripting Religion in the City: Migration and Religious Identity in the Modern Metropolis*, edited by Jane Garnett and Alana Harris. Farnham, Surrey: Ashgate.

Hodgson, T. Forthcoming. "The Multicultural Mela: Music and Space at the Festival." *Les Cahiers d'Ethnomusicologie*, Issue 27.

Hyder, R. 2004. *Brimful of Asia*. Burlington, VT: Ashgate.

Khan, V. S. 1977. "The Pakistanis: Mirpuri Villagers at Home and in Bradford." In *Between Two Cultures: Migrants and Minorities in Britain*, edited by J. Watson. Oxford: Blackwell.

Kosnick, K. 2007. *Migrant Media: Turkish Broadcasting and Multicultural Politics in Berlin*. Bloomington: Indiana University Press.

Lewis, P. 1994. *Islamic Britain*. London: IB Tauris.

———. 2007. *Young, British and Muslim*. London: Continuum.

Lomax, A. 1959. "Folk Song Style." *American Anthropologist* 61, no. 6: 927–954.

Modood, T. 1990. *Muslims, Race and Equality in Britain: Some Post-Rushdie Affair Questions*. Birmingham: Centre for the Study of Islam and Christian-Muslim Relations.

———. 2000. *Multiculturalism*. Cambridge: Polity.

Parekh, B. 1990. *The Rushdie Affair and the British Press: Some Salutary Lessons*. London: Commission for Racial Equality.

———. 2000. *The Future of Multi-Ethnic Britain*. London: Profile Books.

Phillips, T. 2005. "After 7/7: Sleepwalking to Segregation." Website of Commission of Racial Equality. http://www.equalityhumanrights.com/publications/. Accessed 15 November 2010.

Qureshi, I. 2010. *Coming of Age: Celebrating 21 Years of Mela in the UK*. Bradford: City of Bradford.

Ronström, O. 1991. "Concerts and Festivals: Public Performances of Folk Music in Sweden." *The World of Music* 43, nos. 2–3.

Ruthvan, M. 1991. *A Satanic Affair: Salman Rushdie and the Wrath of Islam*. London: Chatto and Windus.

Schade-Poulsen, M. 1999. *Men and Popular Music in Algeria: The Social Significance of Rai*. Austin: University of Texas Press.

Sharma, S., J. Hutnyk, and A. Sharma, eds. 1996. *Dis-Orienting Rhythms: The Politics of the New Asian Dance Music*. London: Zed Books.

Shaw, Prakash. 1988. *Law and Ethnic Plurality: Socio-legal Perspectives*. Boston: Martinus Nijhoff.

Stokes, M. 1994. *Ethnicity, Identity and Music*. Oxford: Berg.

———. 2004. "Music and the Global Order," *Annual Review of Anthropology* 33: 47–72.

———. 2007. "On Musical Cosmopolitanism." Institute for Global Citizenship: Macalester International Roundtable.

Toynbee, T., and J. Dueck, eds. 2011. *Migrating Musics*. Nashville: Abingdon Press.

Turino, T. 1999. *Moving Away from Silence: Music of the Peruvian Altiplano and the Experience of Migration*. Chicago: University of Chicago Press.

———. 2000. *Nationalists, Cosmopolitans, and Popular Music in Zimbabwe*. Chicago: University of Chicago Press.

Vertovec, S. 2007. "Super-diversity and Its Implications." *Ethnic and Racial Studies* 30, no. 6: 1024–1055.

Vertovec, S., and S. Wessendorf, eds. 2010. *The Multiculturalism Backlash: European Discourses, Policies and Practices*. Abingdon: Routledge.

Werbner, P. 2008. *Anthropology and the New Cosmopolitanism*. Oxford: Berg.

West, P. 2005. *The Poverty of Multiculturalism*. London: Civitas.

Wolf, R. 2009. *Theorizing the Local: Music, Practice, and Experience in South Asia and Beyond*. Oxford: Oxford University Press.

CHAPTER 18

FLEAS IN THE SHEEPSKIN: GLOCALIZATION AND COSMOPOLITANISM IN MOROCCAN HIP-HOP

KENDRA SALOIS

IN JUNE 2011, I watched Morocco's most beloved "fusion" band, Nass el-Ghiwane, perform their 1979 song "Lebtana" (The Sheepskin) in front of over a thousand fans. On a stage in Place Boujeloud, a square just outside the oldest part of Fez, the band was joined by professional Gnawa percussionists dressed in long, satiny robes and cowrie-decorated beanies. Midway through the set, the band let a few moments of silence hang in the air. Then, from his seated position center stage, his *bendir* (frame drum) balanced on his knee, vocalist and founding band member 'Omar Es-Sayed leaned toward his microphone and spoke the words everyone was expecting to hear.

"Slaves of enslaving money, you hearts of stone," he intoned. A roar of recognition went up from the audience, and then just as quickly hushed, as Es-Sayed continued to recite the famous poem that begins "Lebtana." As he reached the lines that give the song its title, many chanted along, overrunning Es-Sayed's measured pace as they gathered momentum.

"This is the twentieth century
We're living the life of the flea in the sheepskin
There's the great difference between the apple and the pomegranate
What's the difference between you"—crowds of young men behind me yelled
along, syllable by syllable—
"and you"—the chanting was deafening now—
"and you and me?"

The *guimbri* (three-string rectangular bass lute) player launched into a familiar melodic phrase, dense layers of percussion clicked into place, and the audience cheered, whistled, and clapped their approval.

The music of Nass el-Ghiwane represents an earlier generation's adaptations of both local and international musical trends. Grounded in the Black

18.1. Nass el-Ghiwane in performance at the Fes Festival de la Ville, June 2011. Photo by author.

Atlantic forms of the Moroccan Gnawa and rock from the United States and Britain (Gilroy 1993), they and similar bands of the 1960s and 1970s were like nothing Moroccan audiences had ever heard. Nonetheless, their music simultaneously evoked nostalgia for the recent past and reaffirmed the discursive bond between Moroccan identity and Muslim faith. Today, young Moroccan hip-hop musicians proudly claim descent from this creative lineage.

Since the early 1990s, urban Moroccan youth have eagerly adopted and adapted the music, dance, art, and fashions of hip-hop culture. Like Nass el-Ghiwane, Moroccan hip-hop musicians also draw on Afro-diasporic traditions from home and abroad to refigure Moroccanness for the present day. But today, hip-hop musicians also use Nass el-Ghiwane itself to call up visions of the past and to comment on the present. Armed with hip-hop's aesthetic and critical approaches, musicians legitimate themselves to defenders and detractors alike by quoting cherished lyrics, imitating the band's arrangement practices, and invoking their narratives of loss in contemporary critiques of socioeconomic change.

In this chapter, I compare two generations of musicians' adoptions and adaptions of western popular musics through the lens of the song "Lebtana."

18.2. Nass el-Ghiwane in performance at the Fes Festival de la Ville, June 2011. Photo by author.

I explore both generations' exchanges across geopolitical and cultural boundaries as two-way streets conditioned by each generation's encounter with related, yet distinct, forms of globalization. Such exchanges between the "global" and the "local" change the shape of both.

GLOCALIZATION AND NEOLIBERALIZATION

Under globalization, people, things, and ideas travel to more places than before and reach more of those places simultaneously. Technological developments as varied as just-in-time manufacturing, cellular phone networks, and the Internet have massively reduced the time needed to make such links, making previously foundational categories of the "local," the "national," and the "international" appear nearly irrelevant (e.g., Giddens 1991: 21). Glocalization, a combination of "globalization" and "localization," first entered Anglophone business lexicons in the 1980s from Japanese corporate culture (Robertson 1995: 28). The word captures the cyclical dynamic imagined between large-scale forces introducing the same cultural forms in different places simultaneously, and smaller-scale forces—including ordinary individuals—transforming those cultural forms in ways appropriate to local needs and politics. In turn, those inflected "local" forms can and do circulate anew, setting up an ongoing process that Ian Condry refers to as the "mutual construction" of global and local (2006: 17).

Since the end of World War II, a reorganization known as neoliberalism has enabled the global market economy that underpins glocalization's patterns of circulation and exchange. As a political ideology, neoliberalism frames the free market as the solution to most social and economic inequalities and argues for a reduced role for the state (e.g., Harvey 2005; Brown 2003). Globalizing the free market economy requires a legal and political framework supported by nation-states and international institutions, including the World Bank and the International Monetary Fund, which were established in 1944 to provide centralized loans, aid, and support to developing countries and those recovering from World War II. Entities that regulate or recommend economic activity between nations, such as the World Trade Organization and the Organization for Economic Co-operation and Development, promote an ideology of free trade. Through these institutions, wealthy countries mostly in the "global North" fund and lead organizations that make or influence policy for both themselves and less wealthy countries of the "global South."

Morocco began to neoliberalize when it adopted an International Monetary Fund structural adjustment program in the early 1980s. Like several other postcolonial states, Morocco was asked to shed public sector jobs, cut domestic subsidies, privatize state-owned industries, open capital and consumer markets, increase foreign direct investment, deregulate, lower taxes on enterprise, and undertake other tasks in exchange for loans and expertise (Cohen and Jaidi 2006; Maghraoui 2001; Pfeifer 1999).

Neoliberalization had profound socioeconomic consequences. In the 1990s and 2000s, urban inequality was exacerbated by the uneven development characteristic of Moroccan neoliberal policies. The state intervened to support markets for both new high-end and low-end housing, well separated from each other in newly established prefectures (Barthel and Planel 2010; Bogaert 2012: 715). At the same time, both upwardly mobile and impoverished urban youth encountered many more Europeans and North Americans through the nation's expanded cultural tourism industry (see Kingdom of Morocco 2001: 4–7). Today, hip-hop practitioners connect to other Maghrebi fans through shared cultural and musical affinities. But they also reach fans of different nations, religions, languages, and racial and ethnic backgrounds.

The interactions hip-hop fanship enables are central to practitioners' cosmopolitan practices.

Moroccan hip-hop practitioners come from all parts of the socioeconomic spectrum, but even the most affluent feel their positions are precarious compared to their fellow artists in Europe and North America. In this mostly informal musical economy, few have access to professional-quality studios, and very few are contracted to a label. Performance opportunities, which come predominantly from state-sponsored festivals and concerts, could vanish at any time. Even nationally popular musicians are dependent on relationships with just one or two people for opportunities in transnational markets. The precariousness of most Moroccan youths' lives under neoliberalizing policies, and of all musicians' efforts to earn a livelihood, leads practitioners to consume and connect transnationally—to become cosmopolitan consumers of hip-hop and other media—out of a struggle for economic and social mobility as well as for aesthetic interest.

The generation that came of age in the 1960s and 1970s experienced its own forms of globalization and cosmopolitanism, just as the generation of the 1990s and 2000s did. Historicizing the forms prevalent in each generation, and tracing connections from one to the next, allows scholars to avoid depicting residents of developing countries as either passively accepting or blindly rejecting globalization (see Stokes 2004: 51), while also stressing the fragility and contingency of the transnational and translocal connections Moroccans have made and can make today. In the examples below, two generations localize "global" musical forms not only to claim membership in a self-consciously cosmopolitan youth culture, but also to make persuasive arguments against local economic and political inequality.

NASS EL-GHIWANE

The original members of Nass el-Ghiwane included Larbi Batma (tbola, sing. tbila, a pair of single-headed goblet ceramic drums played with hands or sticks, and lyrics), Omar Es-Sayed (bendir, frame drum with one skin head and a gut snare), Boujem'a Hagour (ta'rija, a small clay goblet drum, and lyrics), Allal Yaala ('ud, a lute played throughout the Middle East, and banjo), and Abd al-Aziz Tahiri (guimbri, the bass lute played by the Gnawa). Tahiri was replaced in the early 1970s by Abdelrahmane "Paco" Kirouch. As first- or second-generation migrants to Casablanca, Nass el-Ghiwane's members combined a variety of expressive traditions, creating what is recognized as the first national popular music.

The original members of the band grew up in a low-income neighborhood known as Hay Mohammedi. Their mix of instruments, rhythms, and influences was made possible by the waves of urbanization that brought people from all over the country to Casablanca's working-class neighborhoods between the 1930s and 1950s. Hay Mohammedi housed some of the city's poorest citizens and most recent immigrants. It encompassed the municipal slaughterhouse, a swath of French-owned factories on what was then the northern edge of the city, and the informal housing that factory workers built for themselves and their families known as *bidonvilles* ("tin towns").

Each member of Nass el-Ghiwane came from a different region of the country and brought knowledge of different musical traditions to their ensemble.[1] Allal Yaala was the only band member with formal musical training; he taught 'ud and classical Arab music theory at the state-run youth house in the neighborhood. "Paco" Kirouch was a practicing Gnawa from Essaouira, a traditional Gnawi center (Schuyler 1993). Larbi Batma's musical family and roots in the Chaouia, the plains of central Morocco, lent him familiarity with 'aita. This genre of song is known for female vocalists (*sheikhat*), whose profession placed them outside both the restrictions and the approval of Muslim society (see Ciucci 2012). 'Omar Es-Sayed sang in the contemporary Egyptian style, and played the *bendir*, a frame drum used in 'aita and many other genres. In addition, they heard traditional music and storytelling in outdoor live performances that took place daily in Hay Mohammedi (Caubet 2004: 196).

Nass el-Ghiwane's lyrics are widely considered a form of resistance to the corruption and violence of the Moroccan state during the period that came to be known as the "years of lead" (Fr. *les années de plomb*; Ar. *zaman al-rusas*). In this period, roughly between 1960 and 1990, political repression resulting in the forced disappearance, jail, or torture of opponents of the government was not uncommon; freedom of the press was minimal; and overt expressions of opposition were prohibited (see Slyomovics 2005: 50–51; Gilson-Miller 2013: chapter 6).

Nass el-Ghiwane's lyrics were—and are—usually interpreted as an alternative to state-controlled media of that era (Dernouny and Zoulef 1980: 14). These texts were full of allusions to traditional poetry, song, and proverbs (Es-Sayed in Caubet 2004: 196).[2] The lyrics' obscurity promoted speculation about their political meanings, even as the traditional material allowed the band to avoid censorship or punishment. Yet the band's choice to invoke the music of socially marginal groups to create its "national" sound, while equally important to its reception, has been comparatively less discussed by both scholars and fans.

"Lebtana" ("The Sheepskin") is considered one of the band's most openly oppositional songs because of its famous opening text. However, its oppositional and countercultural significance is grounded in its thoroughly Gnawa-influenced music. The Gnawa trace their ancestry to sub-Saharan Africans brought to southern Morocco as slaves between the sixteenth and nineteenth centuries. Their ethnic background, religious rituals, and social class marked them as one of the most marginalized groups in Moroccan society during the 1960s and 1970s (Kapchan 2007: 17–23).

In the original 1979 recording, Kirouch recites the famous opening text in free rhythm.[3]

> *Slave of enslaving money, oh you hearts of stone*
> *Thoughtless hearts full of treachery*
> *You chained up the graves . . . here is truth, and there is falsehood*
> *The mosses on the rock from the ocean complained*
> *And the strong wind left the lightning and thunder*
> *Between the frozen rocks and the blazing fire*
> *To calmness [went] the hot wind.*
> *This one is spurred to action, this one contains himself*
> *There is no drug that can cure you*
> *I added ten and ten, I knew how much it added up to*
> *This is the twentieth century*
> *We're living the life of the flea in the sheepskin*
> *You know there's a great difference between the apple and the pomegranate*
> *What's the difference between you and you and me?*

As soon as he concludes his spoken verse, Kirouch launches into a new tempo on the *guimbri* and is eventually joined by the banjo and percussion. Eight minutes into the performance, the band transitions into a new meter, and the banjo and *guimbri* introduce a melody that the group will use to perform its version of a Gnawa invocation and the following call-and-response. The invocation begins with unison singing on the phrase "*Ah, ya marhaba, wallah ya sidi marhaba*" ("Welcome, by Allah, oh sir, welcome"). Next, the band trades new call-and-response lyrics using "welcome" as the response. Though the call-and-response is an original text, the invocation is melodically, texturally, and textually similar to typical invocations sung in parts of the Gnawa ritual ceremony. Throughout this section, the *ta'rija* and *tbola* play the rhythm normally performed by the *qraqeb* (metal clappers) used by the Gnawa. Finally, the recording concludes with unison choral singing (Fuson 2009: 172). The entire progression of the fifteen-minute piece displays some of the characteristics of a connected subsuite of Gnawa songs, including a steady acceleration from beginning to end and an increase in the pace of call-and-response (Fuson 2009: 160).

The opening verse of "Lebtana" clearly seems to indict someone as greedy and perhaps worse. However, to 'Omar Es-Sayed, listeners miss the point when they characterize "Lebtana" as the band's "most political song."

> They thought we were saying that the flea was sick of living in the sheep's hide . . . But that wasn't it. After all, a sheep's hide is the natural home for a flea, right? . . . However, that is where it is supposed to live when the sheep is *alive*, not dead. . . . We—Moroccans, our generation—were living within the remains of something that no longer exists. (Muhanna 2003: 146; italics in original)

For Es-Sayed, "Lebtana" allegorizes the passage of an older socioeconomic order. It is an intensely personal lament, speaking to the band members' and many urban dwellers' separation from their rural and ethnic roots, traditional sources of social and personal identity. Es-Sayed does not acknowledge the political import of these reflections, claiming instead that the band is scrupulously apolitical. Yet in characterizing the 1970s in terms of deprivation, dislocation, and death, the band was heard by many as criticizing King Hassan II's regime for its inability to maintain Moroccans' standard of living and cultural continuity.

Thus the Gnawa signifiers in "Lebtana" remain open to interpretation. On the one hand, the marginalized position of the Gnawa underscores the powerlessness central to the conventionally oppositional reading of the lyrics. On the other hand, the story of the Gnawa's forced dislocation and migrancy from sub-Saharan Africa resonates with a reading in which Nass el-Ghiwane was instead mourning its own dislocation from the band members' ancestral regions and lifeways.

By mixing together sounds from multiple Moroccan traditions, Nass el-Ghiwane produced a nonsacred music with a profoundly Moroccan Muslim orientation. The sacred music that influenced the band was drawn primarily from the Gnawa and two Sufi brotherhoods, the 'Aissawa and the Hamadsha (Dernouny and Zoulef 1980: 15). Although traditionally, Sufism has been central to the ways Islam is practiced in Morocco, each of these groups' devotional practices fall outside Morocco's state-sponsored form of Sunni Islam.

By incorporating sounds from the *fraja*, or "entertainment," section of the Gnawa ritual into their own compositions, Nass el-Ghiwane began a process of recuperating the Gnawa into mainstream approval that continues today.

Within Nass el-Ghiwane's music, Gnawi indices—especially in the figure of Paco, the authentic Gnawi and *guimbri* player—signified "the coded voice of the subaltern" (Fuson 2009: 13). By integrating Gnawa music into what was heard as a deliberately national mix, the band simultaneously appropriated and neutralized the Gnawa's outsider status, reframing the "coded voice" as a site of critique.

In addition, the ʿAissawa and Hamadsha were historically subject to recurrent episodes of repression at the hands of state religious authorities, who considered the actions of trancing practitioners during ceremonies excessive or primitive (Crapanzano 1973: 17–18; Spadola 2008). As a result, their sacred performances became associated with resistance to state control and, implicitly, a critique of the monarch's dual function as head of the state and of the state religion. By using musical influences from all three of these groups, Nass el-Ghiwane evoked their moral and religious authority and their associations with resistance, provoking audiences to perceive the band as opposing the government in an era in which open critique was prohibited.

Nass el-Ghiwane also innovated by engaging with trans-Atlantic youth culture during the 1960s and 1970s. As Es-Sayed recalled, "The hippie revolution arrived in Morocco by way of Casablanca. We were listening to Western music, the Beatles, Jimi [Hendrix], the Stones" (Muhanna 2003: 140). The band members would have heard the widespread influence of the 1960s folk revival on UK and US bands. Philip Schuyler points out Nass el-Ghiwane's debts to trans-Atlantic rock bands, including the use of a group name for the band, instead of a star vocalist's name; a rock-band format in which each performer spread out in a line on stage, rather than forming a tight circle of musicians; the replacement of the ʿud or *rebab*, stringed instruments found in Andalusian music, with the louder and more timbrally distinct banjo (known in Moroccan Arabic as *snitra*); and the adaptation of the *guimbri* from Gnawa music and traditional percussion from a variety of sources to the interdependent roles of electric bass and drum kit (1993: 289–290). The band may have been influenced by Julian Beck's Living Theatre Group and other countercultural youth that visited the resort towns of Essaouira, Diabet, and Agadir in 1969 as part of a wave of musicians and artists interested in the Gnawa.[4]

Nass el-Ghiwane produced a "national" popular music for the first generation of postcolonial Moroccans by mixing sounds from what were seen as local, authentically Moroccan ways of being Muslim unsanctioned by the government and its Islamic authorities. Simultaneously, it assimilated them all into a contemporary musical and performance setting inspired by trans-Atlantic rock. Whatever its political intentions, the band's use of sonic expressions from Moroccan Muslim traditions emphasized the moral dimensions of its lyrical nostalgia, and made their songs an excellent vehicle through which fans could question the state's ethics and powers.

HIP-HOP IN MOROCCO

In the context of Morocco's sweeping socioeconomic changes and increased economic insecurity since the 1980s, the hip-hop arts have become another terrain on which defenders and detractors alike debate how best to be Moroccan, Muslim, and "modern." In the mid-1970s, in New York City's South Bronx, teenagers with ties to Puerto Rican, Caribbean, and African American music and culture developed the "four elements" of hip-hop—the interdependent arts of rapping, deejaying, dancing (b-boying and b-girling), and writing (graffiti art). The musical arts of the emcee and deejay quickly spread in all directions, sparking interest from youth in the rest of the United States, Britain, and France in the early 1980s (Cross 1993; Gilroy 1993; Quinn 2005; Prévos 1998).

The relatively small number of hip-hop practitioners in Morocco spans traditional social boundaries. The first wave is based in major urban areas, and today range from their mid-twenties to mid-thirties. A second wave includes teens and youth in small cities and towns across the country. Though the most celebratory version of the rhetoric around the transnational hip-hop tradition locates authenticity and purpose in impoverished practitioners, Moroccan practitioners and their fans range from disenfranchised urban poor to children of the political and economic elite.

Moroccan musicians form part of a generation of hip-hop music making around the world who encountered the hip-hop arts through their internationally mass-mediated forms, rather than through face-to-face meetings, starting in the early 1990s (Daoudi 2000: 34; Jones 2011: 181; Dennis 2012: 21; Bennett 1999: 81). Most of the earliest adopters in Morocco first encountered the music as teenagers when their friends and family returned from abroad with records and cassettes. Between 1996, when the first full album of Moroccan hip-hop was released, and 2003, networks of hip-hop musicians and fans in cities such as Casablanca, Salé, Meknes, Fez, and Marrakesh grew in relative isolation from one another. The rest of the nation, and the wider hip-hop world, started to become more aware of Moroccan hip-hop in the early 2000s, in part because media privatization and increasing access to the Internet enabled broader circulation.[5]

The seemingly sudden wave of homegrown hip-hop on Moroccan radio, TV, and festival stages has sparked lively debate. For some Moroccans, hip-hop practitioners' dedication to a genre associated with "the extreme even within the West" brings to life their worst fears of corrupting influences from secularist western culture (Abkari, quoted in Cestor 2008, my translation). For others, mushrooming networks of contemporary music making, including hip-hop, rock, metal, electronic dance music, and fusions of all kinds, signal a welcome cultural "uprising" (*nayda*) easily conflated with a political "renaissance" (*nahda*).[6]

Nass el-Ghiwane's potent brand of nostalgia, produced during the political, economic, and cultural instability of the 1970s, provides sonic and ethical inspiration for youth struggling to define themselves under the equally profound instability wrought by neoliberalization since the 1990s. By sampling lyrical, musical, and conceptual resources from Nass el-Ghiwane, hip-hop musicians authenticate themselves within the nation and within transnational hip-hop practice by representing their particular urban heritage.

Several of the most prominent artists in the first wave have cited Nass el-Ghiwane lyrics or adopted the band's practices of musical selection and arrangement.[7] In 2006, Casablancan emcee Don Bigg (a.k.a. MC Bigg or *al-Khasser*, the loser) released his first solo album *Magharba Tel Mout* (Moroccans Until Death). Bigg caused a sensation by skewering those benefiting from the contemporary socioeconomic order, those traditionally close to the Makhzen (the royal government and its circle), and ordinary Moroccans unwilling to challenge the status quo. The song "Bladi Blad" (My country is the country of)[8] features Rabat emcee Kolonel, whose verse alludes to "Lebtana" in multiple ways.[9]

> *My country is a country [where] your money is well hidden*
> *You pass your time calmly even though you're destined for the sheepskin*
> *And we are in the era of our mistakes*
> *And our bribes drive us to poverty*
> *Like the Ghiwane said, the flea lives in the sheepskin*
> *Dear mother, our talk's about the children of the country and we're changing*
> *Hip-hop culture is our escape, that's what we're doing*
> *They shook up the country until it died*
> *Here are today's youth*
> *Moroccans until death.*

By building up allusions throughout his verse, Kolonel treats "Lebtana" as Nass el-Ghiwane treated its own textual inspirations. At the same time, in the best hip-hop tradition, Kolonel pays respect to his source through creative reuse. In the first line, he indicates that the "you" to whom the verse is directed, the country personified, has "well hidden," possibly illicit, wealth.

This person or people live "calmly, even though you're destined for the sheep-skin." As in the popular interpretation of this lyric, the sheepskin is not any-one's "natural home," as Es-Sayed put it. Here, it is instead the punishment at the end of an immoral life.

Following the shift from "you" to "us," Kolonel again references "Leb-tana's" central metaphor. In context, this line suggests that the flea in the sheepskin is a greedy elite, not impoverished Moroccans. By dropping the human subjects from the phrase, situating it in an eternal present tense, and citing Nass el-Ghiwane as his source, he effectively refashions the line in the form of a traditional proverb (e.g., Westermarck 1931: 15). Kolonel thus legiti-mizes his use of the image by drawing upon the band's prestige. Next, Kolo-nel's "us" moves from referring to the entire nonelite population to referring to his own generation. Finally, the last image of the verse is of a country shaken "until it died." Here, Kolonel recalls "Lebtana" more subtly by comparing "today's youth" to the fleas living in the "dead" country. The changing socio-economic order has not led to more mobility or freedom from poverty for most. Instead, the youth of the twenty-first century are stuck, Moroccans not for life, but "until death."

After the final chorus, "Bladi Blad" closes with a sample of "Lebtana." The sample begins with Kirouch, Nass al-Ghiwane's Gnawa vocalist, intoning the first line of the opening poem, then skips to the final four lines. As Kirouch continues, the reverb applied to the vocal sample intensifies, approximating a live performance in a large arena. The steady pulse of the backing track falls apart; the synthesized organ chords stop, and the refrain melody wheezes to a halt. As the sample of the verse finishes, echoes of the *tbola* played by Batma, Nass al-Ghiwane's percussionist, sound under the last two lines; only the at-tacks are audible, as if the beatmaker could not fully separate the vocal sample from the mixed recording, or as if the sound of the drums bled through onto the wrong side of a sampled cassette tape.

The echoing percussion reinforces a connection between the late, iconic members of Nass el-Ghiwane and Don Bigg and Kolonel, and hints at the elec-tric atmosphere surrounding the live performance of this song up to the present day. Yet at the same time, since they are only a ghost of the drums' original sound, the echoes suggest the song and its moral force belong to a fading past. In effect, Bigg's choice to end "Bladi Blad" with a sample from "Lebtana" re-produces the dramatized nostalgia pioneered by Nass el-Ghiwane. In 2006, "Lebtana" held some of the same significance for Bigg's generation as the then-marginalized Gnawa did for 1970s youth, in that Nass el-Ghiwane's work rep-resented a musical heritage uncorrupted by the failings of the present.

CONCLUSION

The notion of a youth-oriented version of Moroccan music making that could resonate with and unify an entire nation was introduced in spectacular fashion in the early 1970s by Nass el-Ghiwane and the bands that followed it. It was into this field, in which musical choices were held to represent the nation at the same time that they provided space for counternarratives against the state, that hip-hop and other "western" popular musics would emerge under neo-liberalization in the early 1990s. When Kolonel alluded to "Lebtana" as if it were one of el-Mejdoub's quatrains, and when Bigg concluded "Bladi Blad" with a dramatically reworked sample of the original, each followed poetic and musical techniques pioneered by Nass el-Ghiwane to imagine the nation and legitimate their own addresses to it.

In the 1970s and today, as we have seen, these genres' foreignness enables commentary on both Morocco's past and its future. Both take the national as the frame of discussion, and both use their cosmopolitan practices to develop musical interventions that bring new insights to that discussion. As Philip Schuyler has pointed out, second-generation Casablancans were able to develop a "national" identity precisely because they were distanced from traditional forms that privileged the local and regional (1993: 288). Nass el-Ghiwane's music and lyrics valorized the ongoing retrenchment of the rural in the heart of the urban, and helped enable a positive vision of Casablancan identity.

Hip-hop practitioners build upon this and more recent neoliberal celebrations of urban identity to claim their cosmopolitan stance, lyrical authority, and hip-hop authenticity. As in the transnational hip-hop tradition, Moroccan emcees, deejays, and beatmakers express their allegiance to their street, neighborhood, and city in a nuanced politics of place. Here, that politics of place resonates not only within hip-hop's practices of self-representation (Forman 2002), but also within Moroccan discourses that bind identity to lineage and lineage to land. Seen from within the heritage of 1970s popular music-making, Moroccan hip-hop musicians' allegiances are also celebrations of urban and sometimes working-class creativity and citizenship.

Both Nass el-Ghiwane and its hip-hop inheritors respond to processes of globalization by thoroughly adapting mass-mediated Afro-diasporic genres. Nass el-Ghiwane and its contemporaries dealt with the disorientation of post-Independence urban life by attempting to re-integrate Moroccan expressive and spiritual sensibilities into music that spoke to—but not always in the voice of—international trends in the 1970s. In contrast, the generation that pioneered hip-hop musicking in Morocco, that came of age in the first decade of the twenty-first century, adopts and invests with meaning a genre that puts them in a position to attempt translocal connections in the wider world they can access via their country's continuing neoliberalization. Despite their many economic and social differences, Moroccan hip-hop practitioners share a particular cosmopolitan practice, constantly reaching out to other musicians and fans between cities and beyond the nation in order to make musical, professional, and personal contacts.

Today, North African hip-hop reaches centers of media production and distribution in Europe through networks of fans and Maghrebi migrants, bypassing both hip-hop's original sites in the United States and multinational recording companies. Both musicians and fans use their love of hip-hop as cultural capital in their national and transnational networks. They strive to generate opportunities for social, economic, and physical mobility through their shared aesthetic preferences and attraction to the narratives of freedom, opposition, and difference historically associated with hip-hop and other Afrodiasporic musics (see Perry 2008: 640; Shipley 2009). At the same time, national pride and national signifiers both differentiate Moroccan hip-hop in its circulation abroad and link practitioners to other postcolonial hip-hop. Moroccan musicians are intricately embedded within the transnational hip-hop tradition, both as translocally linked practitioners sharing aesthetics across national borders, and as consumers of its commercially circulated form as a product of multinational corporate capital.

Simultaneously evoking narratives of resistance and fears of cultural invasion, first rock and now hip-hop have traveled a circuitous trans-Atlantic route to Moroccan youths' ears. Hip-hop artists, the current "westernizers," replicate the logic of their predecessors. Though the political and economic policies of neoliberalization have raised the stakes for Moroccan youth, patterns of circulation and ways of responding to that circulation bear the traces of both colonial history and contemporary intervention. Inspired in part by Nass el-Ghiwane, hip-hop musicians justify their critical speech and their adoption of a form coded as both "western" and "urban" by authenticating themselves as appropriately Moroccan and Muslim. While Moroccan hip-hop cannot be analyzed without reference to local traditions, those traditions themselves are never without connections to transnational currents.

NOTES

This research was funded by the International Institute for Education and the Al-Falah Program of the UC Berkeley Center for Middle Eastern Studies. I thank the reviewers and editors for their insightful comments.

1. According to Jeffrey Callen, Boujemâa H'gour's family is of Saharan origin; 'Omar Es-

Sayed's are Tashelheit Imagzighen from southern Morocco; Larbi Batma's family are Arabs from the nearby Chaouia region; Yalal Allal's mother's family are Arabs from the Houari tribe who relocated to Casablanca from southern Morocco (2006: 91 n. 10). No citations are given for this note, but some of this information can be found elsewhere.

2. The band members' knowledge of oral tradition was enhanced by their early work with producer and playwright Taieb Saddiki. His experimental theater, known in Derija as "*bsat*," brought poetry and song from the *halqa* to the proscenium stage (Amine 2001). Saddiki used poetry from the sixteenth-century Moroccan Sufi, Sidi ʿAbd el-Rahman el-Mejdoub, as song texts and adopted *melhun* texts and melodies created by the eighteenth-century Sufi Sidi Qaddur el-Alami (Schuyler 1993: 288).

3. This translation is much indebted to Davis and Najmi (2008); I have referred to the original Arabic in Es-Sayed (2010).

4. It is possible, though not documented, that Kirouch interacted with Beck and other artists, as Schuyler claims that he moved to Casablanca in late 1969 or 1970 (Schuyler 1993: 292 n. 4).

5. Starting in the mid-2000s, the Moroccan state also supported hip-hop by sponsoring performances and by other means. In February 2003, fourteen members of Moroccan heavy-metal bands in Casablanca were arrested, accused of Satanism and actions that undermined the Islamic faith, found guilty in a heavily publicized trial, and sent to jail (Belghazi 2009). In an unrelated event, on 16 May 2003, twelve to fifteen young men from informal housing in Sidi Moumen, on the outskirts of Casablanca, staged a coordinated suicide bombing in Casablanca. Public outrage, and the state's crackdown on Islamists in response to the bombings, gained international media attention. See "Terror Blasts Rock Casablanca," BBC News, 17 May 2003. http://news.bbc.co.uk/2/hi/africa/3035803.stm. Accessed 21 April 2007. After these events, the Moroccan state invested in "youth culture" as a means of combating violent extremism. Hip-hop programming in Morocco's summer music festivals, supported wholly or in part by state funds, grew strongly through the end of the 2000s.

6. See Caubet 2010 and Zekri 2010. Zekri suggests that *nayda* and *nahda* have the same root in Arabic, the former being a Moroccan corruption of the latter, and thus share core semantic values.

7. The late beatmaker of the Marrakesh group Fnaire, Hicham Belkas, brought Nass el-Ghiwane's folklorization and recombination of disparate musical elements into the digital era with his production for *Yed al-Henna* (Hand of Henna 2007), a practice the Fez group Rwapa Crew continues today. The Meknes quartet H-Kayne cites Nass el-Ghiwane in much the way I describe Kolonel doing below in "Fi al-Houma" ("In the Neighborhood") (Bentahar 2010: 46). In an interview, pioneering Casablancan emcee Amine Snoop told me that as a teenager in the mid-1990s, he practiced his flow (the placement of syllables in relation to the beat) by reciting the opening text of "Lebtana" (Casablanca, 2 August 2010).

8. Aomar Boum (2012) translates this song title as "My country is the country of." Within the song, most of Bigg's verses are structured as a litany, that is, with repetitive naming of things, people, and actions, so that every two-measure phrase begins with "*bladi blad*." Kolonel's verse does not follow this pattern.

9. My translation from Derija. The original, transliterated:

Bladi blad fik al-flous ʿandk ḥassana
duwwuz waqtik hani wakha ttiḥ lebtana
U hena zaman tkhatana

U l faqir zid rashana
Kif ma galou al-ghiwane, ʿaich al-debbana fil btana
mwima, hdarna rah oulad al-blad u anghirou
hip-hop thqafa sllouna ash ndirou
nifdou al-blad bi al-mout
hnaya shbab al-youm
u magharba tel mout

REFERENCES

Amine, K. 2001. "Crossing Borders: Al-Ḥalqa Performance in Morocco from the Open Space to the Theatre Building." *Drama Review* 45, no. 2: 55–69.

Barthel, P.-A., and S. Planel. 2010. "Tanger-Med and Casa-Marina, Prestige Projects in Morocco: New Capitalist Frameworks and Local Context." *Built Environment* 36, no. 2: 176–191.

Belghazi, T. 2009. "The Enemy Within: Perceptions of Moroccan Hard Rock Musicians." *Langues et Litteratures: Publications de la Faculte des Lettres et des Sciences Humaines-Rabat* 19: 143–162.

Bennett, A. 1999. "Hip Hop am Main: The Localization of Rap Music and Hip Hop Culture." *Media, Culture and Society* 21: 77–91.

Bentahar, Z. 2010. "The Visibility of African Identity in Moroccan Music." *Wasafiri* 25, no. 1: 41–48.

Bogaert, K. 2012. "The Problem of Slums: Shifting Methods of Neoliberal Urban Government in Morocco." *Development and Change* 42, no. 3: 709–731.

Boum, A. 2012. "Youth, Political Activism and the Festivalization of Hip-Hop Music in Morocco." In *Contemporary Morocco: State, Politics and Society under Mohammed VI*, edited by Bruce Maddy-Weitzman and Daniel Zisenwine. London: Routledge.

Brown, W. 2003. "Neoliberalism and the End of Liberal Democracy." *Theory and Event* 7, no. 1.

Callen, J. 2006. "French Fries in the Tagine: Re-Imagining Moroccan Popular Music." PhD diss., University of California, Los Angeles.

Caubet, D. 2004. *Les mots du bled: création contemporaine en langues maternelles.* Paris: L'Harmattan.

———. 2010. "La Nayda par ses textes." *MLM: Le Magazine Littéraire du Maroc* 3–4: 99–115.

Cestor, E. 2008. "L'irruption du rap au Maroc: entretien d'Élisabeth Cestor avec Hicham Abkari." *Africultures.* http://www.africultures.com/php/index.php?nav=article&no=8120. Accessed 28 July 2010.

Ciucci, A. 2012. "'The Text Must Remain the Same': History, Collective Memory, and Sung Poetry in Morocco." *Ethnomusicology* 56, no. 3: 476–504.

Cohen, S., and L. Jaidi. 2006. *Morocco: Globalization and Its Consequences.* London: Routledge.

Condry, I. 2006. *Hip-Hop Japan: Rap and the Paths of Cultural Globalization.* Durham, NC: Duke University Press.

Crapanzano, V. 1973. *Tuhami: Portrait of a Moroccan.* Chicago: University of Chicago Press.

Cross, B. 1993. *It's Not About a Salary: Rap, Race and Resistance in Los Angeles.* London and New York: Verso.

Daoudi, B. 2000. "Le cri des jeunes Algériens contre la guerre." *The UNESCO Courier* 53, no. 7: 34–36.

Davis, D., and M. Najmi. 2008. "Nass El Ghiwane: The Sheepskin (1st stanza)." http:// d2ssd.com/ cybermaroc/ghiwane_lebtana_english.htm. Accessed 27 September 2010.

Dennis, C. 2012. *Afro-Colombian Hip-Hop: Globalization, Transcultural Music, and Ethnic Identities*. Littlefield, MD: Scarecrow Press.

Dernouny, M., and B. Zoulef. 1980. "Naissance d'un chant protestataire: le groupe Marocaine Nass el Ghiwane." *Peuples Mediterranéens* 12: 3–31.

Forman, M. 2002. *The 'Hood Comes First: Race, Space, and Place in Rap and Hip-Hop*. Middletown, CT: Wesleyan University Press.

Fuson, T. 2009. "Musicking Moves and Ritual Grooves Across the Moroccan Gnawa Night." PhD diss., University of California, Berkeley.

Giddens, A. 1991. Modernity and Self-Identity: Self and Society in the Late Modern Age. Palo Alto: Stanford University Press.

Gilroy, P. 1993. *The Black Atlantic: Modernity and Double Consciousness*. Cambridge, MA: Harvard University Press.

Gilson-Miller, S. 2013. *A History of Modern Morocco*. Cambridge and New York: Cambridge University Press.

Harvey, D. 2005. *A Brief History of Neoliberalism*. Oxford: Oxford University Press.

Jones, C. M. 2011. "Hip-Hop Quebec: Self and Synthesis." In *Popular Music and Society* 34, no. 2: 177–202.

Kapchan, D. 2007. *Traveling Spirit Masters: Moroccan Gnawa Trance and Music in the Global Marketplace*. Middletown, CT: Wesleyan University Press.

Kingdom of Morocco. 2001. *Vision 2010: Accord Cadre*. Agadir, Morocco.

Maghraoui, A. 2001. "Monarchy and Political Reform in Morocco." *Journal of Democracy* 12, no. 1: 73–86.

Muhanna, E. 2003. "Folk the Casbah: A Conversation with Omar Sayyed, Leader of Nass el-Ghiwane." *Transition* 94: 132–149.

Perry, M. D. 2008. "Global Black Self-Fashionings: Hip-hop As Diasporic Space." *Identities* 15, no. 6: 635–664.

Pfeifer, K. 1999. "How Tunisia, Morocco, Jordan and even Egypt Became IMF 'Success Stories' in the 1990s." *Middle East Report* 210: 23–27.

Prévos, A. J. M. 1998. "Hip-Hop, Rap, and Repression in France and in the United States." *Popular Music and Society* 22, no. 2: 67–84.

Quinn, E. 2005. *Nuthin' but a "G" Thang: The Culture and Commerce of Gangsta Rap*. New York: Columbia University Press.

Robertson, R. 1995. "Glocalization: Time-Space and Homogeneity-Heterogeneity." In *Global Modernities*, edited by M. Featherstone, S. Lash, and R. Robertson, 25–44. London: Sage Publications.

Es-Sayed, 'O. 2010. *Klam el-Ghiwane [Words of Ghiwane]. Casablanca: Matb'a al-Njaḥ al-Jadid [New Success Press]*.

Schuyler, P. 1993. "A Folk Revival in Morocco." *Everyday Life in the Muslim Middle East*, edited by D. L. Bowen and E. Early, 287–293. Bloomington: Indiana University Press.

Shipley, J. 2009. "Aesthetic of the Entrepreneur: Afro-Cosmopolitan Rap and Moral Circulation in Accra, Ghana." *Anthropological Quarterly* 82, no. 3: 631–668.

Slyomovics, S. 2005. *The Performance of Human Rights in Morocco*. Philadelphia: University of Pennsylvania Press.

Spadola, E. 2008. "The Scandal of Ecstasy: Communication, Sufi Rites, and Social Reform in 1930s Morocco." *Contemporary Islam* 1, no. 2: 119–138.

Stokes, M. 2004. "Music and the Global Order." *Annual Review of Anthropology* 33: 47–72.

Westermarck, E., and S. el-Baqqali. 1931. *Wit and Wisdom in Morocco: A Study of Native Proverbs*. New York: Liveright.

Zekri, K. 2010. "De la Nahda à la Nayda: où en est le renouveau de la littérature dans le monde arabe et au Maroc?" MLM: *Le Magazine Littéraire du Maroc* 3–4: 88.

Joseph Alagha, visiting professor of political science at Haigazian University, Beirut, Lebanon, is a prolific writer on Islamic movements and the democratization and liberalization processes in the Middle East and North Africa. He is the author of four peer-reviewed university press books: *Hizbullah's DNA and the Arab Spring* (2013), *Hizbullah's Identity Construction* (2011), *Hizbullah's Documents* (2011), and *The Shifts in Hizbullah's Ideology* (2006), the last three published by Amsterdam University Press. His current research deals with political mobilization and performing arts in the Middle East.

Cynthia Becker is associate professor in the History of Art and Architecture Department at Boston University. She specializes in the history of visual culture from northwestern Africa. She has served as a consultant for numerous museum exhibitions and published articles on the visual and performing arts of the Imazighen as well as the Afro-Islamic aesthetics of the Gnawa. Her book, *Amazigh Arts in Morocco: Women Shaping Berber Identity* was published in 2006.

Michael Frishkopf is an ethnomusicologist, professor of music, and director of the Canadian Centre for Ethnomusicology at the University of Alberta, Canada. His research focuses on the music and sounds of Islam, the Arab world, and West Africa. He published an edited collection, *Music and Media in the Arab World* (bit.ly/musmedaw) and produced two CDs: *Kinka: Traditional Songs from Avenorpedo* (kinkadrum.org) and *Giving Voice to Hope: Music of Liberian Refugees* (http://bit.ly/buducd), as well as numerous book chapters and articles. His current research foci are music and architecture in the Muslim world, and music and global human development (m4ghd.org), in Liberia, Ghana, Egypt, and Ethiopia.

Thomas Hodgson is an ethnomusicologist and British Academy Postdoctoral Fellow at King's College London. His interests include ethnomusicological approaches to Islam, migration, and globalization, particularly in relation to Pakistanis in Britain and South Asia.

Deborah Kapchan is associate professor of performance studies at New York University. A Guggenheim fellow, she is the author of *Gender on the Market: Moroccan Women and the Revoicing of Tradition* (University of Pennsylvania Press 1996), *Traveling Spirit Masters: Moroccan Music and Trance in the Global Marketplace* (Wesleyan University Press 2007), *Cultural Heritage in Transit: Cultural Rights as Human Rights* (edited volume 2014, University of Pennsylvania Press), as well as numerous articles on sound, narrative, and poetics. She is translating and editing a volume entitled *Poetic Justice: An Anthology of Moroccan Contemporary Poetry* and is also completing an edited volume entitled *Theorizing Sound Writing*.

Mark LeVine is a professor of modern Middle Eastern history at the University of California, Irvine, and distinguished visiting professor at the Center for Middle Eastern Studies at Lund University. His publications include *Religion, Social Practice and Contested Hegemonies: Reconstructing the Public Sphere in Muslim Majority Societies* (co-editor with Armando Salvatore, New York: Palgrave Macmillan, 2005), *Heavy Metal Islam: Rock, Resistance, and the*

Struggle for the Soul of Islam (New York: Random House, 2008), and *Struggle and Survival in Palestine/Israel* (Berkeley: University of California Press, 2012), and the *Five Year Old Who Toppled a Pharaoh* (University of California Press, forthcoming). He is a senior columnist at *al-Jazeera English* and an advisor to the musical artists' human rights organization Freemuse.

Ida Meftahi is a visiting assistant professor in contemporary Iranian culture and society at the Roshan Institute for Persian Studies, University of Maryland, in the academic year 2014–2015. She completed her doctoral studies at the University of Toronto's Near and Middle East Civilizations program in August 2013 and was a 2013–2014 postdoctoral fellow at the Institute for the Arts and Humanities at Pennsylvania State University. Her first book, *Gender and Dance in Modern Iran: Biopolitics on Stage*, will be published in 2016 by Routledge. Offering a novel approach to corporeality in twentieth-century Iran, Meftahi's historical research transcends the studies of gender, dance, theater, cinema, and political economy of public entertainment. She has presented and published in fields ranging from Iranian and Middle Eastern studies to dance studies.

Laudan Nooshin is senior lecturer in ethnomusicology at City University London. She has research interests in contemporary developments in Iranian traditional and popular music, music and gender, globalization, music and cultural identity, and music in Iranian cinema. Her publications include *Music and the Play of Power in the Middle East, North Africa and Central Asia* (ed., Ashgate, 2009), *The Ethnomusicology of Western Art Music* (ed., Routledge, 2012) and *Iranian Classical Music: The Discourses and Practice of Creativity* (Ashgate, 2015). Between 2007 and 2011, Laudan Nooshin was co-editor of *Ethnomusicology Forum* (Routledge).

Jonas Otterbeck is professor of Islamic Studies at Lund University. His research on music and Islam includes articles in *Contemporary Islam*, an edited special issue of the journal (vol. 6, no. 3), and a chapter in the book *Shoot the Singer! Music Censorship Today* (2004), ed. M. Korpe. Otterbeck has also written on Islamophobia, Muslim migration, Islam in Sweden, Islamic comic books, and Muslim youth in Sweden.

Anne K. Rasmussen is a professor of music and ethnomusicology and the Bickers Professor of Middle Eastern Studies at the College of William and Mary, where she directs the Middle Eastern Music Ensemble. Rasmussen's research interests include music of the Arab and Islamicate world, music and multiculturalism in the United States, music patronage and politics, issues of orientalism, nationalism, and gender in music, fieldwork, music performance, and the ethnographic method. She is author of *Women, the Recited Qur'an and Islamic Music in Indonesia* (2010); co-editor with David Harnish of *Divine Inspirations: Music and Islam in Indonesia* (2011), co-editor with Kip Lornell of *The Music of Multicultural America* (1997, 2015), and editor of a special issue of *The World of Music*, "The Music of Oman" (2012).

Bryan Reynolds is Chancellor's Professor of Drama at the University of California, Irvine. He is the artistic director of the Amsterdam-based Transversal Theater Company, a director of theater, a performer, and a playwright, whose plays have been produced in the United States, Europe, and Asia. His academic books include *Transversal Subjects: From Montaigne to Deleuze after Derrida; Transversal Enterprises in the Drama of Shakespeare and his Con-*

temporaries: Fugitive Explorations; Performing Transversally: Reimagining Shakespeare and the Critical Future; and *Becoming Criminal: Transversal Performance and Cultural Dissidence in Early Modern England.* He is editor of *Performance Studies: Key Words, Concepts, and Theories;* and co-editor of *The Return of Theory in Early Modern English Studies: Tarrying with the Subjunctive, Volumes I and II; Critical Responses to Kiran Desai; Rematerializing Shakespeare: Authority and Representation on the Early Modern English Stage;* and *Shakespeare without Class: Misappropriations of Cultural Capital.* He is also co-general editor of a book series, *Performance Interventions,* from Palgrave Macmillan. He is currently writing a book with Mark LeVine on performance activism in the Middle East and Africa.

Christa Salamandra is an associate professor of anthropology at Lehman College and the Graduate Center, City University of New York. She is the author of *A New Old Damascus: Authenticity and Distinction in Urban Syria* (Indiana University Press, 2004) and numerous articles on Arab culture and media. Her forthcoming ethnography is entitled *Waiting for Light: Syrian Television Creators in the Satellite Era.*

Kendra Salois is an ethnomusicologist (University of California, Berkeley, 2013) and visiting assistant professor in the Department of Performing Arts at American University in Washington, DC. Her dissertation explored the relationship between Moroccan hip-hop aesthetics, practitioners' ethics, and changing discourses of citizenship in the context of thirty years of economic neoliberalization. Her work appears in *Anthropological Quarterly*, the *Journal of Popular Music Studies, Sociology of Islam,* and the edited volume *Music and Diplomacy from the Early Modern Era to the Present* (2014).

Samuli Schielke is an anthropologist and a research fellow at the Zentrum Moderner Orient in Berlin. His ongoing ethnographic research in Egypt touches on topics of aspiration and frustration, migration and imagination, revolutionary experience, and literary lives. He is author or editor of the books "Hatit'khar 'ala al-Thawra" / "You'll Be Late for the Revolution" (in Arabic, 2011), *The Perils of Joy* (2012), *Ordinary Lives and Grand Schemes* (with Liza Debevec, 2012), and *The Global Horizon* (with Knut Graw, 2012), *In Search of Europe?* (with Daniela Swarowsky and Andrea Heister, 2013), and *Egypt in the Future Tense* (2015).

Shayna Silverstein is an assistant professor of performance studies at Northwestern University. She is currently working on a book that examines body, performance, and popular culture in contemporary Syria with a focus on *dabke* dance music. She has contributed to several edited volumes including *The Arab Avant-Garde: Music, Politics, and Modernity; Syria: From Reform to Revolt;* and the *Sublime Frequencies Companion.* She is also working on a translation of a manuscript on Syrian folk dance by Adnan Ibn Dhurayl. Previously a Mellon Postdoctoral Fellow in the Penn Humanities Forum, Shayna received her PhD in ethnomusicology from the University of Chicago.

Martin Stokes is King Edward Professor of Music at King's College, London. He is author of *The Arabesk Debate: Music and Musicians in Modern Turkey* (2nd ed., 2014), *The Republic of Love: Cultural Intimacy in Turkish Popular Music* (2010), and editor of *Ethnicity, Identity and Music: The Musical Construction of Place* (Berg, 1994). He is currently writing up his Bloch lectures, which he gave at the University of California, Berkeley in 2014. He is a Fellow of the British Academy.

Nina ter Laan is a cultural anthropologist with a special interest and expertise in Morocco, art, music, and popular culture. She is a PhD candidate in the department of religious studies at the Radboud University Nijmegen and works as a lecturer at the Institute for Cultural Anthropology at Leiden University in the Netherlands. Her dissertation focuses on dynamics of Sufi and Islamist musical practices in Morocco and their political deployment within the contexts of state-supported musical activities and, by contrast, Islamist movements.

Karin van Nieuwkerk is an anthropologist and professor of contemporary Islam in Europe and the Middle East at the Radboud University Nijmegen in the Netherlands. She is the author of *"A Trade Like Any Other": Female Singers and Dancers in Egypt* (1995) and *Performing Piety: Singers and Actors in Egypt's Islamic Revival* (2013). She is also editor of *Women Embracing Islam: Gender and Conversion in the West* (2006) and of *Muslim Rap, Halal Soaps, and Revolutionary Theatre: Artistic Developments in the Muslim World* (2011).

Jessica Winegar is an associate professor of anthropology at Northwestern University. She is the author of numerous articles on arts, culture, and revolution in the Middle East. Her book *Creative Reckonings: The Politics of Art and Culture in Contemporary Egypt* (Stanford, 2006) won the Hourani prize for best book in Middle East studies.